ECONOMIC ACCOUNTING
AND DEVELOPMENT PLANNING

REVISED AMERICAN EDITION

Economic Accounting and Development Planning

An Introduction to General Principles of
Accounting, Input-Output Analysis, and
National Income Accounts and Their Application
to Planning Economic Development.

REVISED AMERICAN EDITION

BRIAN VAN ARKADIE
MINISTRY OF ECONOMIC AFFAIRS, DAR ES SALAAM

CHARLES R. FRANK, Jr.
PRINCETON UNIVERSITY

NEW YORK

OXFORD UNIVERSITY PRESS

LONDON   1969   TORONTO

This is the American edition of *Economic Accounting and Development Planning,* published by Oxford University Press in Nairobi in 1966. The original work is part of the Series of Undergraduate Teaching Works in Economics being developed at Makerere College, University of East Africa, with the assistance of the Rockefeller Foundation.

Printed in the United States of America

PREFACE TO REVISED EDITION

This revised edition of *Economic Accounting and Development Planning* was motivated by a desire to adapt the first edition to a different class of readers. The first edition, which was written with African university students in mind, has been modified to include additional applications of economic accounting techniques and applications over a wider range of geographical areas. This increase in scope has been accompanied by more emphasis on comparative analysis of different regions and different types of economies. For example, a discussion of the United States system of national accounts and methods of estimation has been added. United States methods, then, are compared with techniques in less-developed countries. The addition of a discussion on India permits the contrast of a large less-developed economy with the much smaller economies of East Africa. Latin American economies, at a more-advanced stage of development, are compared with African and Asian economies at a less-advanced stage. The inclusion of a section on deflation of national accounts in Brazil points out the difficulties of estimation and differences in technique required for a highly inflationary economy.

The revisions in the text are largely confined to Parts II and III. Parts I and IV, which include few applications, deal more with theoretical constructs and have undergone only minor alteration.

In Chapter V an input-output table for the industrial sectors of Colombia has been included along with a discussion of this table. The appendix to Chapter VI, on the use of input-output tables, now includes a brief discussion of the inverse input-output matrix.

Applications of national accounts (Chapter XII) in this revised edition include the United States, India, and the East African countries, Uganda, Kenya, and Tanzania. The discussion of the Nigerian accounts, which appeared in the first edition, has been dropped. In Chapter XIII, on deflation of national accounts, Brazilian accounts replace those of the Federation of Rhodesia and Nyasaland. A discussion of the deflation of the accounts of the U.A.R. has been retained. Capital stock estimates for Ghana have been added to Chapter XV.

Where possible, data have been brought up to date throughout the book, and slight revisions to numerical examples have been made.

The revisions to the first edition were written by the author of this Preface with the able assistance of Mr. Vernon Dixon. Mr. Dixon's efforts were considerable and very much appreciated. Mrs. Dorothy Rieger typed the revisions in her usual efficient and amicable style. Mrs. Carol Allen and Mrs. Diane Sliney read the galley proofs with extreme perception, catching a number of errors which an author always misses in the fourth or fifth reading of his own work. I apologize for any remaining errors and invoke the usual assumption of sole responsibility for the revisions contained in this volume.

Princeton   C. R. F., Jr.
April 1969

The following are the official rates of exchange as of December 31, 1967.

1 U.K. pound sterling $=$ US$2.40
1 Nigerian pound $=$ US$2.80
1 Ghanaian cedi $=$ US$0.98[1]
1 East African pound $=$ US$2.80
1 Indian rupee $=$ US$0.13
1 Colombian peso $=$ US$0.06
1 Brazilian cruzeiro $=$ US$0.70[2]

[1] On July 19, 1965, the old cedi was set at 5/12 of the old Ghanaian pound and therefore was equivalent to US$1.17. On February 23, 1967, it was replaced by the new cedi, equivalent to 1.2 old cedis (US$1.40 or 10 Ghanaian shillings). In July 1967, the new cedi was reset at US$0.98 or 7 shillings.

[2] As of February 13, 1967, the new cruzeiro is equivalent to 1000 old cruzeiros.

PREFACE TO FIRST EDITION

This volume was suggested by a gap in the availability of reading materials for second-year students at Makerere University College taking a year's course in quantitative economics, taught jointly by both authors.

Since the book was originally conceived with students at an African University in mind, it is oriented toward African problems and examples. In particular, we attempt to provide an awareness of the lack of complete data, the shaky assumptions used to derive aggregate figures from the limited data available and therefore the care and ingenuity which must be exercised in using such material for economic analysis and planning. Our approach was influenced by some of the peculiar structural characteristics of many less-developed economies, e.g., a heavy dependence on foreign trade and primary exports, a large subsistence sector, a bias of production toward agriculture, and scarcity of capital and skilled manpower.

In drawing up the first draft of this volume, the authors were fortunate to have the help of Clifford Russell who came to Uganda early 1964 before entering Harvard graduate school in economics later that year. Under the supervision of Dr. Van Arkadie, Mr. Russell did much of the drafting of preliminary versions of parts of the manuscript, most of the bibliographical research and the majority of the legwork involved in the earlier stages. It is only because of his absence in the final stage of the writing of the first draft (which was distributed in mimeographed form to students at Makerere and elsewhere in Africa) and during the revision of the first draft (which emerges as this volume) that he is not named as a co-author. Mr. Russell is, of course, not responsible for any defects in the work.

Dr. Van Arkadie conceived the original scope and approach of the book and is mainly responsible for Parts I and III. Dr. Frank is the main author of Parts II and IV. Each author, however, made numerous suggestions and revisions to the other author's work and they are jointly responsible for the entire volume.

It should be noted that with the lapse of time between the original drafting of this volume and its publication many of the descriptions of sources will be already out of date. The main objective of the volume, however, is to serve as a guide to principles. The student should be able to keep abreast of the latest developments in available sources in his area of special interest.

There are a large number of people in Makerere community who deserve our thanks for help in preparation of this volume. Most of all, however, we would like to thank Professor Philip Bell, the general editor of the series of which this volume is part, for his encouragement, support, and suggestions at all stages. We would also like to thank the Rockefeller Foundation and the Economic Growth Center at Yale University for their financial support (of Dr. Frank and Dr. Van Arkadie, respectively) during our two-year stay at the East African Institute of Social Research, at Makerere University College.

New Haven, January, 1966   CHARLES R. FRANK, Jr.
Entebbe, January, 1966   BRIAN VAN ARKADIE

CONTENTS

ix

TABLES

PART

I

BASIC PRINCIPLES OF ACCOUNTING

I

AN INTRODUCTION TO ACCOUNTING

A. Accounting and the Economist

This volume introduces the student of economics to a number of accounting techniques which are likely to be useful in work in applied economics. Very few economists spend most of their time on theoretical work; the majority, whether in government, business, or academic life, have to deal with quite practical problems. To tackle such problems the economist soon finds himself in need of tools which are not part of the subject matter of economics itself. He will have to use statistical methods, with such applications as regression analysis and design of sample surveys. He will also have to use various accounting data, interpreting the reports of businesses and applying the techniques of accounting to raw material he collects himself.

The central themes of the study of economics consist of the examination of general principles regarding the operation of economies and the manipulation of fairly abstract models of economic behavior. The step from such general principles to the practical problems of policy and the analysis of economies as they in fact operate is often a difficult one. The theory must, to serve its purpose, present an oversimplified version of the real world, particularly at the introductory stages. Also, the data the student faces when he comes to tackle his first practical economic problem will often seem quite remote from the economic categories to which he has been introduced in his studies.

The economist has to use data of a diverse nature, often prepared for purposes quite different from those the economist has in mind. In the developing countries, where information is less complete than in more wealthy and industrialized societies, economists must be particularly careful about automatically accepting published figures at their face value. This is not to cast doubt on the honesty or competence of those producing published accounts, but rather to indicate the difficulty of the tasks they face.

The applied economist soon finds himself learning a number of techniques outside the formal limits of his subject. This has become more true as economics has extended beyond its earlier role as a more or less abstract discipline, semi-philosophical in character, to become a quite practical art, used to aid decisions in government and business. Also, academic economists have become more interested in testing their theoretical hypotheses in an increasingly systematic fashion against the evidence provided by economic events.

Thus the following chapters are intended to introduce the student to some of the tools which he will have to use throughout his career as an economist. The central theme is the use of accounting methods to tackle a number of the problems of interest to the economist. Although a wide range of topics is included, it will soon become clear that they have much in common.

The task of accounting is to organize very large quantities of information into forms which will render it useful. In even a simple economy there will be vast numbers of decisions regarding production, distribution, and exchange taking place every day. The individual economic unit—the firm, or even the household—engages in literally thousands of transactions with other units in the economy during the course of a year. Any given economic action will itself have many different characteristics. A simple sale, for example, will involve a buyer and a seller and might be described in terms of the price, the quantity, the value or some other description of the good purchased (e.g. whether a consumer good or an investment good was involved). The purpose of accounting is to select the relevant aspects of economic events, record them and subsequently to organize and to summarize these records for further analysis. The concept of *relevance* is important to grasp and is fundamental to understanding any problem of economic measurement. For the economist, measurement is a tool, the effectiveness of which can only be gauged by its value in tackling specific problems. A particular method or criterion of measurement which may be perfectly valid for one use may be quite inadequate for another.

The professional accountant and the government statistician aim to produce published data with a wide range of uses. They may therefore adopt forms which are compromises, providing a tool with a number of applications, although not quite as effective for each individual function as one of a set of more specialized tools. In criticizing such accounts it is well that the economist recognizes that they are designed for a range of uses. Part of the skill of the applied economist lies in adjusting the tools to the job.

What are the specific tasks for which the economist is likely to use accounting techniques? A useful distinction can be made between three different sorts of problems for which data must be marshalled. First, there is the problem of the individual economic unit—the business, plant, or household. Examination of the activities of the particular firm, planning for the individual project, investigation of the problems of allocation, and choice between alternative projects are all part of that branch of economics which is usually called "micro-economics." For such problems, the data available are likely to be derived from the accounts of individual businesses or even plants.

The second sort of problem which arises concerns the co-ordination of the activities of the separate components of the economy, in particular the examination of the relationship between the various industries which make up the economy. Here the attempt is made to account for whole industries, with the emphasis on the complicated set of inter-relationships which wed the fortunes of any one industry to the performance of a number of others. This subject is known as "inter-industry economics."

The third approach is to consider the aggregate performance of the economy in terms of the total product produced in a given geographical area, total levels of employment, and the distribution of income between major income groups. This is the subject matter of the study of "macro-economics."

These three divisions are not self-contained. Data on inter-industry relationships may be compiled from the accounts of individual firms and plants. Aggregate estimates draw on all sorts of data regarding the household, the individual firm and the industry. With this in mind, the first part of this volume examines the problems of accounting for the individual business or project; the second part builds up from that to the study of inter-industry accounting; the third section treats the aggregate accounts; the final section treats the application of accounting techniques and data to the problems of national planning.

The traditional concern of accounting has been to provide an historical record of economic events. The emphasis on providing a reliable and accurate picture of past events has, in recent years, been augmented by attempts to use the accounting framework to plan and to project future economic activity. The business firm has become increasingly interested in systematically predicting future costs and revenues. Even more important, governments are increasingly interested in influencing economic performance. For the economist in particular, it is interesting to consider the possibilities of using accounting techniques for planning as well as for recording. This aspect of the use of accounts will therefore be a major theme of the volume.

B. Some Basic Concepts

The basic data supplied by the accountant will consist of the various accounts of the individual business enterprises. Individual firms form only one sector of the economy. Households, receiving incomes mostly from the sale of labor services and purchasing goods as consumers, form another important sector of economic activity. The government may itself own and operate businesses. Most of the activities of government, however, might be considered yet another sector, distinct in character from the productive activities of businesses. Much of the theory and practice of accounting was developed to handle the situation of the individual firm. These methods can, with some modification, be applied to other types of economic activity. It will be useful, therefore, to take the example of the firm as the starting point for an investigation of accounting methods.

One comment is necessary. In many less-developed countries the basic unit of operation in agriculture is the peasant small-holding. This unit is unusual in that it encompasses within itself the functions of both the household and the firm. This will become important later when national accounts are examined. These accounts are very much built on the assumption that there is a very clear distinction to be made between household, firm, and government.

Because of the importance of the peasant, commercial accounting records are applied to a much smaller part of total economic activity than would be the case in an industrialized economy, where the dominant form of economic organization is the limited company or the nationally owned corporation. It will be useful, however, to organize information about the units which do not prepare commercial accounts into a similar framework as that used by larger enterprises. Therefore, the study of accounting for the firm will prove basic to the formal treatment of data from economic units which do not, in fact, keep accounts themselves.

How should the firm be viewed from the accounting point of view? To provide a first insight the firm might be viewed as a collection of assets, organized under a single control, for the pursuit of manufacturing or trading activity. The assets will not only consist of physical equipment and raw materials but will also consist of claims on other economic units in the form of debts owed to the firm, or bonds owned by the firm.

There are two methods whereby a firm can initially acquire or subsequently increase the assets at its command. The first is by increasing its liabilities—borrowing money or purchasing goods on credit. The second method is by increasing the contribution of the proprietors, either through a contribution of funds or the retention of profits in the business. Ownership of the firm, in the sense of control over the decisions regarding the utilization of the assets of the firm, lies exclusively with the proprietors. The value of the proprietors' contribution to the business is often known as "the net ownership" or the "net worth."

This brief discussion gives rise to a fundamental identity:

Assets (A) equals Liabilities (L) plus Ownership (W)

$$A = L + W \tag{1-1}$$

(Note that assets which are claims on the assets of others would constitute liabilities for some other economic units.)

This identity will be seen many more times in the course of the text and it is essential to understand it now. The assets of the firm are the resources at its disposal. Some portion of this asset total, the liability interest, is subject to the claims of people or firms who have loaned the business money or goods; the value of the residual assets (those which would be left if all the debts were settled) is the ownership interest. At the beginning of the firm's life, this ownership interest will be equal to the total money paid in by the owners, whether they be partners or the thousands of shareholders of a limited company.

The assets and liabilities of the firm are stocks; the transactions which constitute its dealings with the rest of the society are flows. This distinction is important; it will be worth pausing to ensure that it is understood. Perhaps the best way of clarifying the point is to draw a physical analogy.

Imagine a bath; the amount of water in it at any particular moment is a *stock*. In measuring a stock, units of quantity are used (weight, mass, or volume). In the example, gallons, liters, ounces would be appropriate units. Imagine further that the bath is provided with a tap and a drain. Water running into or out of the bath constitutes a *flow*; indeed, it would be natural to say that the water was flowing in the pipes. Clearly, time is somehow important in the idea of a flow. In the example, the rate at which the bath filled or drained would depend on the volume of water per unit time entering or leaving it, and in order to measure flows, then, it will be necessary to use units specifying a certain unit of quantity per unit of time. In the example, gallons per hour, liters per second or per minute would all be acceptable units. Observe also that stocks and flows are intimately related, for, as in the example, the stock of something will change from moment to moment according to the sizes of the flows into or out of it.

Applying this analogy, two kinds of flows which influence the stocks of assets, liabilities, and ownership of the firm can be distinguished. The first arise from transactions between the firm and other units in the economy (other firms, the government, or members of households). The second category is purely internal to the firm, not involving transactions with outsiders. The latter case includes flows of services from buildings and machines owned by the firm and the use of raw materials acquired in the past.

The task of accounting within the firm involves keeping appropriate records of the size and composition of assets and liabilities, of the transactions conducted by the firm, and of the flows internal to the firm and, finally, relating the flows to the stock.

Every transaction involves change in the structure of assets, liabilities, and net ownership. Transactions involve exchanges. Therefore every transaction has two aspects. Goods may be exchanged for cash, i.e., an exchange of one asset for another. Cash may be transferred in payment of a debt, i.e., an asset is reduced, but so is a liability.

There are, of course, several different basic kinds of transactions in which the firm might involve itself. Each of these will affect the fundamental identity in different ways.

For example:

(i) The firm may purchase goods or services with cash. (The effect on the identity is shown by the arrows; an arrow pointing up means that the item is increased, while an arrow pointing down means that it is decreased.)

$$\uparrow\downarrow A = L + W \tag{1-2}$$

(ii) It may sell goods or services for cash or on credit.

$$\downarrow\uparrow A = L + W \tag{1-3}$$

(iii) It may purchase goods or services on credit.

$$\uparrow A = \uparrow L + W \tag{1-4}$$

(iv) It may borrow money.

$$\uparrow A = \uparrow L + W \tag{1-5}$$

(v) It may pay off an outstanding debt with an asset.

$$\downarrow A = \downarrow L + W \tag{1-6}$$

(vi) It may sell ownership (represented by ordinary shares usually) in the company.

$$\uparrow A = L + \uparrow W \tag{1-7}$$

This is not an exhaustive list, but it will serve to indicate the method which might be used to relate flows to stocks. The fundamental identity represents that account kept by the firm known as the "balance sheet." This account is a statement of the asset and liability structure and the size of ownership interest. For a firm engaged in business with many citizens and other firms, with a continuous flow of purchases, sales, movements of cash, etc., adjustments cannot be made to the balance sheet continuously, as the transactions occur. Instead, the accountant sets up other records which are removed a step from the balance sheet. He can then record the individual transactions as they occur, while being freed of the necessity of making constant adjustment of the balance sheet. At the end of some period (as decided by the managers of the firm) he will undertake to calculate the net effect of that period's flow on the balance sheet.

The firm will be interested in identifying and separating a special category of flows. These consist of the revenues it gains from the sale of its products and the costs which have been incurred in their manufacture. Some transactions do not relate to current production—for example, the purchase of capital equipment for future use. Also, some costs do not result from current transactions—for example, the use of raw materials drawn from an inventory purchased in an earlier accounting period. By isolating costs and revenue the accountant will be able to estimate the profit of the firm.

If revenues are greater than costs then the firm will have made a profit. This profit will accrue to the firm and have a net effect on the balance sheet. This effect is best understood by considering a very simple example. Assume all transactions are for cash. If total revenues during an accounting period exceed total costs then the total receipts of cash will exceed the total payments of cash. Some part of this increase in the asset item, cash, will be accounted for by costs resulting from the use of assets already owned and paid for at the beginning of the period. Any excess over this amount represents an increase in an asset for which there is no corresponding decrease in any other asset, nor an increase in a liability. The fundamental identity is restored by an increase in the ownership interest. This effect of current operations on the balance sheet will take one of two forms, depending on whether a profit or loss has been made:

$$\uparrow A = L + \uparrow W \text{ (Profit)} \qquad (1\text{-}8)$$

$$\downarrow A = L + \downarrow W \text{ (Loss)} \qquad (1\text{-}9)$$

In introducing the idea of the balance sheet it was noted that each transaction affecting the balance sheet has a dual nature. Similarly, the transactions creating sales and costs involve exchanges, while the flows within the firm involve the transformation of an asset or liability from one state to another. The accountant has used this characteristic of transactions to create a system of accounting known as "double-entry." *The essence of this system is that whenever a transaction or internal flow occurs an entry is made to represent both aspects of the exchange.*

This is done by setting up flow accounts which have two sides in a similar fashion to the balance sheet identity. The sides are labelled "credit" and "debit." A number of different accounts are organized on the basis of the principle that any transaction or internal flow should be recorded by a debit entry in one account and a credit entry in another, each representing a different side of the exchange or internal flow. Some examples will illustrate. The student should not worry about the logic of assigning items to the debit or credit side of the accounts.

Examples:

  (i) the *sale* of a good for cash
      outflow of goods = credit to sales account
      inflow of cash   = debit to cash account

 (ii) the *purchase* of a good for cash
      inflow of goods = a debit to the purchases account
      outflow of cash = a credit to the cash account

(iii) the payment of *wages*
      inflow of labor services = debit to wages account
      outflow of cash = credit to cash account.

In this way every expenditure or receipt of cash will have to be explained elsewhere in the accounts.

At the end of the period these various accounts will be used both to calculate profit and to adjust the balance sheet. This will provide a check on the accounts, for the profit resulting from the cost and revenue calculations should equal the addition to the ownership interest in the balance sheet indicated by the increased gap between assets and liabilities, which results from adjustments made directly to the balance sheet from the particular accounts.

An example will make the process clearer:

Consider a trader in a less-developed country who each morning buys bananas in the central market and during the day sells them door to door. Suppose that the going market price for bananas were 20 cents per stem and that the man charged 30 cents per stem on his route. In following through his operations for two days, it will be seen how his operations and the changes in his balance sheet are related.

On the first morning he starts out with $4.00 in cash. His balance sheet then appears thus:

Balance Sheet

Assets		Liabilities and Ownership interest	
Cash	$4.00	Ownership interest ...	$4.00

First he buys 20 stems of bananas at the market price and then he sells them at his price to his customers. The following three accounts will cover these transactions:

Purchase of Bananas

20 stems ...　　　...　　　... $4.00

Sale of Bananas

　　　　　　　　　20 stems ...　　　...　　　... $6.00

Cash

Received ...　　　...　　　... $6.00　　Paid　　　...　　　...　　　... $4.00

Profit is simply calculated as the difference between revenues and cost— $6.00 minus $4.00 = $2.00.

The new balance sheet may be obtained with the aid of the cash account:

Balance Sheet

Assets		Liabilities and Ownership interest	
Cash ...　...　...	$6.00	Ownership interest　...	$6.00

On the next morning the trader decides to borrow $2.00 in order to be able to buy more bananas. Then his starting balance sheet looks like this:

Balance Sheet

Assets		Liabilities and Ownership interest	
Cash ...　...　...	$8.00	Liabilities ...　...　...	$2.00
		Ownership interest　...	$6.00
	$8.00		$8.00

Now, he trades as before, this time buying 40 stems and selling all but 10. In addition he must pay interest of 10 cents per day on the loan. The following five accounts will suffice to illustrate this second day's activity.

Purchase of Bananas

Cash　　...　　...　　... $8.00　　To stock ...　　　...　　　... $2.00

Sale of Bananas

Cash $9.00

Cash

Sales $9.00	Purchases $8.00
	Interest ... ... $.10
	$8.10

Interest Paid

Cash   ...   . $.10

Stock of Bananas

From purchases $2.00

For the second day, the profit calculation is slightly more complicated. The cost of the bananas sold is now important rather than total purchased since part of those purchased are retained overnight.

      30 stems bought at $.20 per stem = $6.00 cost.
      30 stems sold at $.30 sales price per stem = $9.00 revenue.

Note the additional cost of the interest payment. The resulting profit is $2.90 or $9.00 − ($6.00 + $.10).

The new balance sheet may be determined from the cash and stock accounts:

Balance Sheet

Assets		Liabilities and Ownership interest	
Cash $8.90		Loan $2.90	
Bananas, 10 stems @ $.20 $2.00		Ownership interest ... $8.90	
$10.90		$10.90	

The stock of bananas retained is valued at cost. This point will be dealt with more fully in the next chapter.

Note that new ownership interest equals the old ownership interest plus the day's profit. That is,

$$W_1 + (R - C) = W_2 \qquad (1\text{--}10)$$

where R is revenue and C costs.

Up to this point, no attempt has been made to justify the assignment of items to the debit and credit columns of the accounts. This part of basic accounting theory can be confusing. Rather than offering any explanations of the origins of the terms or presenting tricks for remembering what goes where, this text will merely list here certain basic rules of debit and credit which will carry the student through most of the straightforward applications in later chapters.

Debits are:
  (i) Flows into the firm of goods and services (that is, purchases);
 (ii) Increases in the firm's claims on others; and
(iii) Flows into the firm of cash.

Credits are:
  (i) Flows out of the firm of goods and services (sales);
 (ii) Increases in the claims of others on the firm; and
(iii) Outflows of cash from the firm.

II

THE BALANCE SHEET

This chapter and the next introduce some of the problems of accounting for the firm. It is obvious that in such a short space a systematic treatment of accounting theory and method is not possible. Emphasis is therefore placed on the interpretation of accounts, rather than on the practical problems of bookkeeping.

In the last chapter it was suggested that at any point in time a firm could be looked upon as an organization controlling a stock of assets for use in the pursuit of its business. The account which illustrates this aspect of the firm is the balance sheet. The balance sheet attempts to provide a record of the total assets involved in a business from the two points of view suggested above. On the one hand, it attempts to record the claims on the assets of the business, on the other hand, it details the uses to which the assets have been put. The different claims on the assets depend on the source of supply from which the arm obtained control of the assets—whether by contribution from the owners, or accumulating profits, or by borrowing, etc. The liability side of the accounts, therefore, consists of a record of the owners' investment (including accumulated profits), and the liabilities of the business. The asset side of the accounts on the other hand describes whether the assets are being held in the form of cash, equipment, raw materials, etc.

These accounts are kept in terms of monetary units. This is obviously necessary, as the assets are a collection of goods multifarious in nature. The monetary unit provides a common unit of account. The values are recorded as assets are bought or sold, and as new liabilities are accepted. The result is that the balance sheet measures a stock by cumulatively recording the flows which, over time, have created the stock. If either the unit of measurement (that is, the value of money) or the price of a particular asset changes over time then the measurements will be inaccurate. This is a very important point to understand, as it is the basis of many of the difficulties faced in using accounting data.

A. The Assets Side

In order to organize the mass of information recording the hundreds, perhaps thousands of different forms in which the business holds its assets, the accountant utilizes a number of general headings. In so doing, he will often have to allocate an asset under a particular heading in quite arbitrary fashion. Although the distinctions accountants make will apply quite obviously to most assets, there will be cases for which the application will be quite fuzzy.

The three main headings used are: fixed assets, current assets, and intangible assets.

(i) *Fixed assets* are those which are expected to last (and which the firm expects to own) for more than some arbitrary minimum period, usually a year. A sub-division is made into land and fixed plant. The latter includes buildings and machinery.

As machines and buildings get older, accountants will reduce their value as carried on the books. The figure shown in the balance sheet will therefore be a net figure, less than the original cost. Sometimes the gross figure, that is, the original cost of the assets, will be shown. The difference between gross fixed assets and net fixed assets is accumulated *depreciation*. The amount that the assets are reduced in value each year to allow for the effect of age is known as the depreciation charge for that year.

(ii) *Current assets* are those assets which are likely to be turned over during the course of the year. In part, they correspond to the economist's concept of liquid assets, that is cash and things readily convertible into cash. This will not necessarily be true of raw materials and work in progress, however, which may have no ready market at all, but which could be transformed into final goods and sold within the accounting period. Accountants may also include in this category assets which are clearly durable, having an expected life beyond the year, but which the firm has an intention of selling during the accounting period.

Where a firm holds long term assets (such as government bonds) which are not used in the operation of its business, it is useful to include "investments" as an additional major heading in the accounts to cover this category. This is particularly so for some financial assets (e.g., long term bonds) which are held for long periods and are not continuously turned over like the other current assets. They are, however, a potential source of ready cash, for they may usually be marketed or discounted.

One of the most important current asset items is made up of stocks of raw materials and finished and semi-finished products which the business has on hand. Such stocks are unavoidable in manufacturing and trade and are always counted as current assets, no matter how long they have been owned or how long it is expected that they will be kept. In general it is true that even though a specific item may remain in stock (inventory) for a considerable period, the group of which it is a part will be turning over constantly.

Another type of current asset takes the form of claims on other organizations or individuals. Cash itself represents a claim on a currency board or central bank. A large item under this heading is likely to be the trade debts owing from firms who have purchased goods from the business but have not yet paid their bills. The business may also have loaned money or purchased the bonds of another business. An interesting aspect of this form of asset is that as it is a claim on some other business, it will make an appearance in the books of the debtor as a liability. For the economy as a whole, therefore, such assets and liabilities would cancel out if the accounts of all the different economic units were consolidated. Cash, however, is evidently special for it is a claim against the community at large rather than any private organization.

In analyzing the accounts of a business some judgment has to be used in deciding how far current assets are in practice liquid assets. For example, an unwise businessman could allow large amounts of credit to his customers which would appear on his balance sheet as a current asset, but which might not be realizable in cash because of the shaky financial condition of the debtors. For an established business in normal times bad debts will form a fairly small and stable proportion of the credit the firm offers its customers, but in times of general economic depression or when a firm has been acquiring large numbers of new customers a large part of the debts owed to a business may be very far from liquid and may, in practice, only be realizable over a painfully long period of time.

(iii) *Intangible assets* are those which either do not exist in the form of real physical assets (or financial agreements) or, if existing in such form, convey to the owner advantages of an undefined and uncertain value. An important class of intangible assets grows out of the creation or expansion of a business. In these processes many expenditures are incurred which are really part of the cost of future increases in business. These expenses are not properly thought of as connected with only one year's output and so are entered as assets to be written off in subsequent years, or even to be retained throughout the life of the company. In addition, often when other firms are acquired it will happen that the purchase price is more than the recorded asset value of the purchased business. In these latter cases, it is usual accounting practice to enter an intangible asset "good will" in the books of the purchaser. This will equal the difference between the price and the recorded asset value.

B. The Liabilities Side

The other side of the balance sheet will consist of a record of the claims outsiders have on the assets of the business and of the net ownership interest. The ownership interest is equal to the total assets of the business less the liabilities to outsiders. Liabilities are normally fixed at their money value at the time the original debt is incurred, plus any accrued interest not paid. The liability items as shown in the firm's accounts, therefore, represent a true record of the debt in terms of current prices.

The accountant will seek to make similar distinctions to those he made in organizing the assets side of the accounts. Current liabilities will be distinguished from long-term obligations. The criterion for classification is based upon the time the debt falls due, that is, the period after which the firm must transfer some form of asset to its creditor. If that period is less than one year, the liability is generally regarded as current; if it is more than one year, non-current. Examples of current liabilities are accounts payable (the amount due for some good or service received but not yet paid for) taxes due, and notes payable (a *note* is a promise to repay a short term debt). Long term liabilities include property mortgages, long term loans, and issued bonds.

*The ownership interest** may be divided into two parts: the paid-in capital obtained from the original purchasers of shares or the original contributors to a partnership, and the retained earnings of the firm accumulated during its years of operation. This will become clearer in the illustration below.

C. The Two Sides Related

Recall the fundamental identity:

$$A = L + W$$

The balance sheet is, of course, based on this identity and thus may be presented in a number of different ways corresponding to the several transpositions of the equation. Considered in the form above, one side of the balance sheet represents the utilization of resources by the firm (assets), while the other is simply the claims outstanding against the firm whether by outsiders or owners. While it is always true that the two sides are in balance (assured by the definition of net worth), it is equally true that there

---

* The ownership interest is sometimes called the net worth or the equity interest or, in the case of a company, the shareholders' interest.

is no necessary connection between individual items on the two sides. That is, current liabilities, for example, have no connection with current assets, and the two should not, normally, balance each other. This same statement may be made of each individual item and each category and sub-category.

Note that there are four ways in which a firm may add an asset to its stock:

(i) It may reduce some other asset it owns, e.g., it may exchange cash for machinery.

(ii) It may increase its liabilities, e.g., it may take out a bank loan in order to purchase land for expansion.

(iii) It may increase net ownership by selling ordinary shares.

(iv) It may make and retain a profit in the business.

Several things may be observed here. The *first* method does not result in a *net* addition to the assets of the firm, but merely a change in the form in which these assets are held. The *first three* of the methods involve only the transfer within the economy of already existing assets. No change in form is involved for society as a whole, merely a change of ownership. The *fourth method*, on the other hand, represents a net addition to both the assets of the firm and those of society as a whole. This addition is the net effect of the operation of a profit-making and retaining business. The nature of profit is a matter full of difficulties both for the accountant, who must consider its definition in the accounts, and for the economist, who is concerned with the factors which give rise to it. Some discussion of these points will be presented in the next chapter. For the moment, note that the firm will be keeping track of its transactions over the year in order to calculate its profit.

The balance sheet for the firm is here illustrated with the help of a fictitious company, the Acme Cotton Fabric Co., Inc. First, a balance sheet for the firm will be set up which will reflect the firm's position after most of the tasks of establishing it have been accomplished but before the start of operations. The very first balance sheet for the firm would simply show authorized and issued shares (stockholder's interest is the latter figure), and would show the money collected as an asset. It would be probable that no liabilities would yet have been incurred, so net ownership would simply equal the asset total. As various transactions were entered into, the composition of assets would change, liabilities would be incurred. All these would be flow processes and would have their effects on the balance sheet. The net ownership would, however, remain at its initial figure in any event, unless additional shares were sold.

The following assumptions are made concerning the items shown:

(i) All depreciation will be by the straight-line method, that is, the

TABLE II–1

Balance Sheet

For the Acme Cotton Fabric Co., Inc., as of 31st December, 1967

ASSETS		LIABILITIES AND OWNERSHIP INTEREST	
Fixed Assets		*Liabilities*	
		Long term Liabilities	
Land $60,000			
Buildings 160,000		Bank Loan—from American Commercial	
Machinery and Equipment 420,000		Bank 6% $50,000	
Furniture and Fittings 40,000			
	$680,000	Total Liabilities:	$50,000
Current Assets			
Cash with bank $60,000			
	$60,000		
Intangible Assets			
Patents and Licences $90,000			
Processes 160,000			
Formation and Preproduction expenses ... 60,000			
	$310,000	*Ownership Interest*	$1,000,000
Total	$1,050,000		$1,050,000

same percentage of the original cost will be deducted each period over the life of the asset. No depreciation will accrue before the start of operations. The lives of the various assets are assumed to be as follows:

Buildings:	40 years
Machinery and Equipment:	10 years
Furniture and Fittings:	5 years
Patents and Licences:	15 years
Land:	Infinite

(ii) The interest rate on the bank loan is assumed to be 6% per annum on the unpaid balance.

D. The Special Problems of Asset Valuation

Economists, when they study the state of a business, will most likely be interested in the current value of the assets of that business. It is, therefore, necessary to examine at greater length the problems and methods of asset valuation used by accountants. The problem may best be introduced by considering four different categories of assets:

(i) assets with values fixed in money terms;
(ii) inventories of raw materials and work in progress;
(iii) fixed assets in the form of machinery and equipment;
(iv) intangible assets.

1. *Assets with Fixed Money Values*

The most obvious case of an asset with fixed money value is cash itself. Also most debts owed to a business will be stated in terms of some fixed monetary amount.

These items present the least problem, because the current monetary value will be equal to the recorded value in the accounts. Corporate and government bonds will have a fixed monetary value at some future date when they are due for redemption. At any particular point in time, however, the market value of such bonds might be quite different. Because of the existence of markets for such assets, however, and because of their defined and homogeneous nature, it will always be possible to find a current market valuation.

The only difficulty arises when comparisons are made over time. Then, although there will be an accurate estimate of the current monetary value in each time period, the value of the monetary unit itself may be changing between time periods. In any account of the changing fortune of businesses over time, allowance must be made for this change in the unit of measurement.

Also, the business, in making decisions about the disposal of its assets, will be concerned with the future behavior of the value of money. If prices are rising (that is, the value of money is falling) the business will not wish to hold as much of its assets in terms of obligations with fixed monetary values as would be the case if prices were stable. On the other hand, the firm might then find it desirable to extend those liabilities fixed in monetary value.

In relation to this subject it is interesting to note the case of bond issues. These are liabilities in the form of promises to repay some fixed sum at some date in the future and additionally to pay interest at some fixed rate as long as the debt is outstanding. Debts represented by bond issues are incurred by firms in order to raise financial resources, usually with a view to converting the cash into some other form of asset or even paying off another, more pressing, debt. At first it might seem that raising capital by issuing bonds is little different, for the big company, from issuing new shares, that is raising the net ownership through additional subscription. There are a number of important differences, however. First of all, shareholders have voting powers in electing the directors of a company, while bondholders do not. Second, the sale of bonds creates a future obligation to make a regular interest payment. The payment of a dividend on a share, on the other hand, is discretionary. Therefore the expansion of bonded debt causes a rise in future fixed costs of operation. Further, however, the liability is fixed in money terms so that with changes in the value of money there are changes in the real value of the obligation. By contrast, the shareholders have a claim on the residual value of the assets of the business after it has met all its other obligations and therefore a claim on the profits of the business, however much they might be, after all costs have been met. Therefore shares and bonds represent very different obligations (and similarly, very different assets to those who own them).

2. Inventories

The firm's stocks of raw materials, finished and semi-finished goods are generally valued at their cost to the firm. In the case of raw materials this is a straightforward concept if prices are constant although even here, the cost of the goods should ideally include the cost of storage, administration, etc. In practice, these "overhead" expenses are not, because of practical difficulties, allocated to inventories. When dealing with semi-finished and finished goods, the cost basis becomes more complicated. What production and overhead costs should be allocated to inventory items? It would, of course, be most realistic to have these inventories carry a share of the burden of overhead expense, including utilities, executive and administrative effort, and interest payments on debts and bond issues. Again, however practical considerations generally rule out this approach. The allocation of overhead to goods which are at different stages in the production process would be an enormously difficult undertaking. Hence, the normal procedure is to value these stocks on the basis of the cost of raw materials and the direct production labor involved in their creation. These methods produce two sources of distortion for the asset account. First, some distortion intrudes to the extent that the most desirable methods are not followed. Second, the methods of estimation, particularly of the direct labor cost, may be subject to error.

Such problems are overshadowed by those created by changing price levels. Goods are bought at one price level and may be used in production or recorded on balance sheets under entirely different price conditions. The valuation at cost will not represent current market value of the goods. For example, suppose that 100 units of some raw material are bought in period 1 at a price of $1. Suppose that in period 2, fifty of these items are still in stock, but that now the price in the market is $2. Is the value of the inventory most reasonably considered to be $50 or $100. The complexity of the problem increases when one considers the continuous round of purchase and use which is found in practice.

The accountant, when faced with such problems, tends to feel that his primary responsibility is to provide an historical record of what has happened, which he interprets as meaning that valuation should be at a cost recorded in a transaction which actually occurred, rather than a value in some hypothetical transaction which might now take place. One defense for this position is the contention that if assets are valued up or down on the basis of the accountant's judgment whenever it is believed that market prices have changed, then the accounting records become largely a subjective evaluation. This would leave the door open for all sorts of sharp practice. This is of primary importance for the accountant, who sees his first responsibility to be that of ensuring the honesty and literal accuracy of records. For the economist, who is less interested in discovering whether a swindler or embezzler has been at work, but more interested in making the best judgment possible of current market values of assets, this approach seems inadequate.

There are some exceptions to the accountant's unwillingness to adjust values. Perhaps because accountants have felt that their primary responsibility is to creditors and shareholders, they have been willing to admit that there are dangers when the market value of assets falls below the book value, so that the book values represent an overvaluation. In such cases accountants may be willing to write down the value of assets. For the valuation of inventories they sometimes generalize the procedure by adopting the criterion "original cost or market value, whicheves is lower." In this phrase, "market value" means the current price of similar goods in the market in which the firm buys.

However, in the valuation of inventories there is some room for flexibility, even in terms of the conservative principles the accountants adopt. When a producer uses part of his stock of raw materials he will be withdrawing from an inventory purchased at many differing dates in the past. If the materials used were to be valued at their original cost it would be necessary to know the particular transaction through which that particular batch of material was acquired. Of course, this is not usually known. The accountant therefore adopts a convention. The two most standard conventions are to assume that the materials used were the most recently purchased ("last-in first-out" or LIFO) or, alternatively, that it is the oldest materials in stock which are being used ("first-in first-out" or FIFO). The first method will normally value the stock used in production at a cost very near current prices (at least when inventory volume remains constant), but will be using more remote prices to value the stock retained on hand. The second method will use the more remote prices to value material inputs and more recent prices to value the remaining stocks. The objective of LIFO is to provide a more realistic measure of the cost of raw material inputs, particularly so as not to over-value profits during periods of rising prices.

This is the first introduction to a problem where the method of evaluation of a stock will influence the estimates of cost and profits made in the flow of accounts. The relationship may be confusing at first, but should become clearer as the current accounts are discussed in more detail in the next chapter.

3. *Plant and Equipment*

For the economist, perhaps the most interesting part of the balance sheet is that part which records the stock of fixed assets. The buildings, machinery, and equipment items correspond to the capital stock which plays such an important role in the discussion of growth and development.* The capital stock is the tangible evidence of the existence of a business. Also, it often sets the effective short-run limit on the size of the output. This role of capital as the effective short-run constraint on the capacity to produce explains the considerable interest in its measurement.

The problems of capital stock measurement are many. Some of them are taken up in another chapter toward the end of the book, when the problem is examined at greater length from the economist's point of view. The

* This statement simplifies a complex issue. See the subsequent chapter on the measurement of capital stock.

first step, however, must be to understand the problems the accountant faces.

Compare the problem of accounting for a machine with the treatment of a stock of materials. An inventory item remains on the books until it is eventually removed as a result of a sale. The reduction in the inventory coincides with the exchange of a good for cash or some other form of asset. Machinery is different in that it remains in the control of the firm until it is eventually scrapped. When this happens, the machine can no longer be carried as an asset of the business. At the time when the machine is scrapped, however, the only receipts will result from whatever scrap value the old machine commands. Therefore the accountant must either reduce some liability item or reduce the ownership interest. Scrapping a machine has no effect on the liabilities of a company. Therefore, in the absence of any previous provision, the accountant would have to reduce the net ownership of the company by the amount of the intial cost of the machine (less any scrap value). This would have the same effect on the balance sheet as a loss of that amount during the accounting period when the machine is removed. From the accountant's point of view, this is not acceptable. One way of viewing the situation is to see the machine as being used up gradually, although it is eventually scrapped at one point in time. The accountant therefore feels that it is sensible to recognize this gradual exhaustion of the machine throughout its life by recognizing it as a cost which must be met before profits are measured, just like any other cost.

This special sort of cost is the depreciation charge mentioned above. For the accountant, it is a method of allocating the *historical cost* of a machine or building to the various accounting periods during the lifetime of the asset. This is another instance of the relationship between stocks and flows in the accounting system. The reduction in the book value of assets to allow for age results in a cost flow. The accumulation of these flows forms a stock of accumulated depreciation. This stock represents the difference between the stock of net fixed assets (the book value of fixed assets) and the stock of gross fixed assets (the original cost of fixed assets).

Depreciation is a very special sort of cost. Most costs involve payments (wages, interest payments) or the removal of a physical asset (reduction in inventory). The accounting operations involved in a depreciation charge may be viewed as follows. Part of gross profit is used in each period to allow for a reduction in the book value of the fixed assets, rather than as a net addition to the assets of the business. Thus when a machine is scrapped, the net ownership account is not affected because the value of the machine has already been written off through charges against gross profits throughout the life of the machine.

When the machine is retired (that is, scrapped) no adjustment will be necessary to net fixed assets, because that account will have already been reduced by the process of depreciation. However, the original cost of the machine will have to be removed from the gross fixed assets account and the corresponding depreciation will have to be removed from the accumulated depreciation account.

What happens if a machine is retired before it is fully depreciated? If the scrap value is equal to the net fixed assets book value, net fixed assets will be reduced and cash will be increased by an equal amount. Any gap between the scrap value and the book value will be recorded as a loss, resulting in a reduction in the ownership interest.

As the accountant is mainly concerned with the formal necessity of "writing-off" the historical cost of fixed assets over their life time, he is not much concerned whether the registration of a depreciation charge corresponds with the occurrence of decline in value of the asset. In practice, the accountant adopts fairly standardized conventions for calculating depreciation. The most frequently used is the so-called "straight-line" method. Under this rule an equal amount of depreciation is charged during each year of the machine's expected life. For example, if a machine is expected to last 10 years a depreciation charge of one-tenth of the original cost will be made each year. At the end of the ten years the machine will be fully depreciated and although the machine may still be in operation, no further depreciation charges will be made.

In practice, if price levels are constant, the market value of a machine is unlikely to decline by equal amounts during each year of its life. A machine is valued because it can produce things and therefore its current value will depend on the future output expected of it. As the years pass the future life expected of the machine will shorten. In addition, for many machines the best years of operation may be the first—after that it may get less efficient. The value of a machine may, therefore, decline much faster during the first years of ownership, as the "most efficient" years are used up. Sometimes accountants allow for this by charging much more of the depreciation to the first years of the operation of a machine.

The effects of changing price levels are particularly serious in the case of fixed asset accounting. This is because these assets are kept longer than other balance sheet items and therefore the historical costs which appear in the books are much more out of date. Consider the case when a period of rising prices has been experienced. Then it will be true that the current cost of a new machine will be much higher than the original cost of a similar machine as recorded on the books. The depreciated value of the machine as carried in the net fixed asset account may be well below its market value. This will have two results. The stock of assets controlled by the firm will be undervalued. As the liabilities will be valued at current prices, this means that the ownership interest will be undervalued by the same amount as the undervaluation of the assets. The second effect will be that the depreciation charges used to calculate net profits will be based on the old value of the machine, not the higher current values. If the firm sold and repurchased its own machines, its depreciation costs would rise (and net profits, according to the accounts, would fall) although it was still using the same real resources. For this reason economists often feel that accountants should allow for these changes and should record depreciation charges according to the current market value of the fixed assets rather than the historical cost. The economist is interested in current market values and real costs, while the accountant is interested in historical costs and values.

This topic receives more detailed attention in a later chapter which is concerned with the techniques economists use to measure the aggregate capital stock.

4. *Intangible Assets*

It is not difficult to think of numerous items which could fit into the category of intangible assets, at least from the economist's point of view. The reputation of a firm may be as important a part of its business as the machinery and equipment it uses. A patented invention has often formed as solid a basis for many fortunes as the ownership of physical property. It is usually in the nature of an organization that, taken as a whole, it is worth more than a simple sum of the separate parts.

Accountants, however, are conservative enough not to wish to record such values unless it seems quite necessary. They therefore use the concept of intangible assets only to deal with special situations where a cost is incurred which seems clearly unreasonable to charge off against current production and impossible to include in the value of some other asset. For example, if a business buys up a going concern it may well have to pay more than the book value of the firm's physical properties. A certain amount of this premium may be accounted for by valuing certain of these properties at values above their book value, if there is some straightforward method of valuation available. Where this is not possible an entry is made for an intangible asset which can be retained on the books or written off as a cost against future production. Similarly, a firm may be allowed to count some of the initial cost of its own organization and development or that of a new product as an asset, thus avoiding the necessity of counting it all as a cost in estimating profits in the first year of operation.

However, where there is an intangible (but quite real) value in the business which has not been exposed by some transaction and was not the result of initial promotional expenses, then the accountant is unlikely to be willing to recognize this in the accounts. This means that the accountant only attempts to measure a small part of what might be supposed to be the "intangible value" of businesses. Those using the accounts should never expect the intangible assets item on the account to be an adequate measure of the intangible values involved in the business and unrecorded in the other asset accounts.

E. Interpreting the Balance Sheet

This brief description should be enough to provide a basis for understanding the main headings which will appear on the balance sheet. If the student refers to the published statements of large companies he is likely to find numerous sub-headings not specifically explained in this account. Many of these will be self-explanatory and where reference is necessary to additional sources, an understanding of the general framework will make it a much simpler task to solve the particular difficulty.

The meaning of a balance sheet cannot be fully grasped until its inter-relationship with the flow accounts of the business is understood.The published statement of the business will include a profit and loss account, and often a manufacturing account, which are intimately related to the balance sheet and its change from year to year. The next chapter attempts to clarify that relationship.

Chapter IV contains some additional advice regarding the interpretation of published accounts in practice. There is also a chapter in the third section of the volume which contains a further discussion of the problems of measuring the capital stock.

III

THE INCOME AND EXPENSE ACCOUNTS

A firm purchases inputs, organizes them in some productive process, then sells the results. In purchasing inputs it creates incomes for others, which in turn result in purchases on their part. The firm or the individual may also buy or sell assets which are not going to be used in current production. Such assets may be used subsequently as inputs.

The accountant sets out to use double-entry techniques to record these operations. He does this in a number of steps. He records the transactions as they occur in a *journal*, subsequently consolidating under various headings in *ledgers*. Finally, he draws on these ledgers to prepare an account of the success or failure of the firm during the year (or quarter) in an *income account*. The frequency of preparation of income statements is a matter of management decision, but the journal and accompanying ledgers must be kept on a current basis or they lose their usefulness and become open to significant error.

It is important to recognize that the transactions recorded in the journal and the ledgers refer not only to flows arising out of current operations, but also to those which are mainly concerned with future operations (in particular, purchases of capital equipment) or result entirely from past operations (e.g., the repayment of loans). Therefore some of the entries in the journal will have no relevance to the estimation of current costs, revenues, and profit. All transactions, however, will influence the disposition of assets and liabilities; they will all, therefore, have an effect on the balance sheet.

Similarly, there are some flows which are relevant to current operations which do not result from any current transaction. This is particularly the case with capital, where it may seem desirable to impute a cost for the flow of current capital services when the transaction whereby the capital was acquired took place well in the past.

This distinction gives rise to a further point, which is of some importance to an economist. A firm which purchases capital equipment or increases its inventory of materials does not include these transactions as part of its current costs. However, the firm which produces the capital good or raw material will count it as part of its current sales. It is useful to keep in mind that there is a basic distinction to be made between those purchases which enter into current production and so form part of the costs for the period (and give rise to part of the gross revenue) and those purchases which are accumulated for future use.

In attempting to evaluate its own performance, the firm will attempt to estimate the difference between its revenues and costs for the accounting period. Its revenues will result from sales of its services or products. Extending the point made in the previous paragraph, these sales may be divided into:

(i) purchases by households for final consumption;
(ii) purchases by firms for further processing and sale in the same accounting period;
(iii) purchases by the government for its use; and
(iv) purchases by other firms for use in production during subsequent accounting periods.

Although these distinctions are important to the economist, they are of no particular interest to the accountants of the firms making the sales, so that allocation of the sales figures of a firm between these headings must be a judgment based upon knowledge of the nature of the product or derived from the records of the purchasers. This point will be of some importance in later chapters when the consolidation of firm accounts and the formulation of inter-industry accounts are discussed.

The current costs of the firm can be divided into those which involve current transactions and those resulting from previous transactions. The current transactions will consist of:

(i) labor costs;
(ii) cost of materials used (net of any change in the materials inventory); and
(iii) payments for buildings and land rented.

The major costs resulting from past transactions will be:

(iv) depreciation; and
(v) any net reduction in inventory.

In addition, interest costs on outstanding loans and bonds must be paid. This is a special sort of cost, because it does not arise from the use of any specific asset or service. It occurs because part of the total assets involved in the business are financed by borrowed funds rather than being supplied by the owners. If interest payments are treated as a cost, then for consistency, part of the profits of the business should be treated as an imputed cost of the funds the owners have tied up in the business. For the economist, the distinction between interest, profit, and returns for managerial services has often been a controversial one. Perhaps the easiest thing at this stage is to treat profits plus interest payments as a common category, which covers a return on funds invested, payment for the management services of the owners, and any "pure" or "monopoly" profit.

These various costs can be reclassified according to whether they are purchases of direct factor inputs or the products of other firms. The purchase of direct factor inputs would consist of:

(i) labor costs;
(ii) depreciation, and
(iii) profits plus interest.

Depreciation is treated as a direct factor input because it is a cost representing the use of a factor which is not the result of the output of any other firm in the current period. Profits plus interest are usually treated as a return for the services of property plus enterprise. This, of course, might be challenged as misleading by those who claim that a substantial part of profits is in fact not a return for any service rendered but rather a transfer of surplus value or monopoly profits to property owners.

The products of other firms, or "intermediate products," consist of materials and services purchased from other firms which enter the accounts of those firms as sales.

Materials withdrawn from inventory are in an indeterminate category; when purchased they were intended as an intermediate good, but because they were not used in production at that time they did not enter the accounts as part of the intermediate goods used in production.

These distinctions should be kept in mind, for they are subsequently of great use in translating business accounts into categories useful to the economist.

A further important distinction of concern both to the economist and the accountant is the one between direct and overhead cost. Direct costs include the cost of labor whose employment can be attributed to a particular output (i.e., those labor costs which vary directly with the size of the output), and the costs of materials used in production. These costs may be seen to correspond in a rough way to the economist's concept of variable cost. Overhead costs are those which are substantially independent of the level of output, that is they correspond to the concept of fixed costs. The distinction can be slightly ambiguous; as will be pointed out below, accountants tend to use a fairly narrow definition of direct costs, allocating certain costs to overhead which probably are quite sensitive to the level of output.

In attempting to record the profitability of the firm the accountant treats profits at three different stages:

(i) *Gross profit* is, roughly, the difference between gross operating (sales) revenue and the variable costs of production. The definition is rough because a number of costs which might be considered variable are typically not deducted at this stage. This may be true of utility charges, repair and maintenance charges, storage costs and selling costs, all of which will be treated as overhead costs but all of which vary to some extent with output. Even capital equipment may wear out faster the more it is used, which would suggest that a variable capital cost might be included, in excess of the fixed costs already allowed in the form of depreciation.

In practice, gross profit is usually derived by taking the difference between gross operating revenues and the sum of the cost of materials used in production and the direct labor costs.

(ii) *Net profit* is calculated by deducting from gross profits those costs not already included in the direct costs used for the derivation of gross profits. There is not complete agreement whether interest payments should be treated as a cost for this purpose, or included in net profits. The usual practice is to deduct interest payments as a fixed cost of operation. It has already been noted that from the economist's point of view it is as well to treat interest payments as though they were part of net profit.

(iii) *Unappropriated profit* is that portion of net profit remaining after the payment of corporate income taxes and dividends. It adds to the book value of the ownership interest.

A. The Technique of Bookkeeping

It is now time to move on to a summary of the basic techniques used in keeping track of the transactions in which the firm is involved and in calculating from these the results of the operation over the accounting period. No attempt will be made in what follows to deal with more than the simplest issues and most fundamental techniques, for to do more would require an entire volume. The material that is presented has been chosen for its relevance to the remainder of the book and for the aid it gives in making clear the distinction and the connection between stocks and flows within the firm.

1. *The Journal*

It is common practice for firms to keep records, called "journals" for the initial entry of every transaction, from the use of petty cash to buy postage stamps, to the purchase of a major piece of capital equipment. The value of the transaction is entered in the journal both as a debit and a credit, there being appropriate columns provided for this. These dual entries reflect, of course, the two directions of flow observable in each transaction and are fundamental to the success of the double-entry system. The debit and credit for each transaction are assigned in the journal to the appropriate "ledger accounts" which will be discussed next. First, however, it is important to emphasize that the journal entries are made at the time of the transaction; that they are, consequently, maintained in chronological order; and that they include only those flows which are embodied in actual transactions.

2. *The Ledgers*

From the journal, transaction debits and credits are "posted" to the appropriate ledger accounts as determined by the accountant or book-keeper. These accounts may properly be regarded as the fundamental ones in the double-entry system. Here, the two aspects of each transaction are themselves entered in two different ledgers. For example, the cash flows, both into and out of the firm, will be entered in the cash ledger, inflows being debits and outflows, credits. Similarly, the purchases which cash outflows finance go into a purchases ledger as debits, and the sales, from which the inflows result, are credited to the sales ledger.* Also, entries will be made for flows that are not the result of actual transactions, such as depreciation allowances, inventory adjustments, etc.

In order to clarify the process, it is instructive to divide the ledgers into three groups; personal accounts, real accounts, and nominal accounts. Personal accounts record the firm's claims against persons and other firms, and the claims of others against the firm. A debit balance in a personal account is an asset, reflecting a net claim on the assets of others. A credit balance is a liability, reflecting net claims against the firm by others. These accounts may be kept separately for each firm or person with whom the firm does business, or they may be consolidated into overall accounts-receivable and accounts-payable ledgers. The latter method is quite impractical if the firm is involved with a large number of customers and sellers.

* This is somewhat oversimplified. Most firms will find that their lives are complex enough to require keeping separate ledgers for different types of purchases, such as raw materials, office supplies, etc. The multi-product firm will keep separate accounts for each product, and most firms will probably find it necessary to sub-divide sales of even one product in some way; perhaps by customer or by branch recording the sale.

The real accounts deal with other assets such as fixed and intangible assets, inventories, etc. Here a debit entry represents the addition of an asset, and a credit entry represents the loss of an asset through sale, destruction, etc. Thus, a debit balance at the end of the accounting period represents a net addition to the stock of assets. It should be stressed at this point that entries in the ledgers are flows, that is, changes in the ownership of assets in the real accounts, changes in the status of claims in the personal accounts. The link with the balance sheet should be obvious; the balances resulting from the flows of the accounting period are reflected in changes in the balance sheet. This entry of balances gives the same result as would the changing of the balance sheet for every transaction and is infinitely more practical. As an example of this process, if the ledger (real) which recorded the purchase and sale of buildings contained for the year a debit of $10,000 for the purchase of a building, and a credit of $4,000 for the sale of another building, the item "buildings" on the balance sheet would be increased by $6,000, the amount of the debit balance.

It is in the nominal accounts that the accountant attempts to isolate the revenues and costs relating to the accounting period which will form the basis of the ultimate reckoning of profit or loss. Normally, entries in a nominal account will require balancing entries in a real or personal account. The nominal accounts record certain important flows taking place in the year. These flows are related to the various items in the balance sheet through the real and personal accounts. For example, the purchase of labor will involve a debit to a nominal account (labor cost) and a credit to a real account (cash). The use of raw materials during the accounting period results in a debit to a nominal account (material costs) and a credit to a real account (raw material inventory). A sale of the manufactured product will involve a credit to a nominal account and a debit to either a real account (cash) or a personal account (accounts receivable).

Depreciation can sometimes represent a special case. The registration of a depreciation charge as a cost (debit) in a nominal account can be offset by a credit direct to the real account of the particular asset. More often, however, it is credited to another nominal account (the *accumulated depreciation* or *provision for depreciation*).

3. *The Manufacturing and Profit and Loss Accounts*

At the end of the accounting period, the ledgers are "closed to" the accounts which show the state of the firm and the success of its efforts.

Gross profit is calculated in the *manufacturing account*. From the ledgers containing the nominal accounts the records of direct costs and gross operating revenues are extracted. A "balancing entry" is then made which represents the gross profits of the accounting period. The gross profit is then carried down to the *profit and loss account*, in which net profit is calculated as the balancing difference between gross profit and overhead costs. Unappropriated profit is then shown as the residual after allowance for corporate taxes and dividend payment.

This unappropriated profit represents the net increase in ownership interest in the business as the result of the year's operation. The figure arrived at through the calculation of profit and loss should equal the addition to net ownership derived from the balance sheet, into which adjustments of assets and liabilities have been entered directly from the real and personal accounts.

B. An Accounting Example

In order to illustrate the techniques and accounts described above, the Acme Cotton Fabric Co., Inc., will next be followed through its first year of operation. In this example, no attempt will be made to reproduce fully the accounts of the company. Instead, a set of ledgers, their entries being summaries of transactions occurring over the year, will be shown. No journal will be included. After the ledgers have been shown, those relating to operations will be closed to the appropriate income statement. Finally, after the income calculations are complete, the new balance sheet for the firm will be developed from the records of flows.

The following transactions (summarized) are assumed to have been entered into by the firm;

(i) Cotton yarn costing $500,000 is bought during the year. At first, these dealings are strictly cash, but toward the end of the year, confidence in the firm is such that it is granted credit for $20,000 worth. The bill for this delivery has not been paid on 31st December.

(ii) Chemical dyes worth $100,000 are purchased from a foreign firm. At the end of the year, all but $10,000 of this has been paid for in cash. The remaining payment of $10,000 is not due until January of the next year.

(iii) The Company sells its products to four other firms. They are identified only by letter. Firm A buys $100,000 worth; firm B, $200,000 worth; firm C, $500,000 worth; and firm D, $200,000 worth. At the end of the year, firm C is in receipt of $100,000 worth of cloth for which it has not yet paid (part of its total purchases of $500,000). All the other firms have paid cash on delivery of their purchases.

(iv) The firm hires and pays factory workers for the year, the total wage bill is $160,000. It also hires managerial and clerical help, the respective salary bills being $25,000 and $15,000. It pays its salesmen a total of $60,000 over the year.

(v) It pays interest at the 6 per cent rate on the loan outstanding from the American Commercial Bank.

(vi) It becomes liable for and pays taxes on its net profit at the rate of 43.8 per cent resulting in a total tax bill of $60,000.

(vii) It declares and pays a dividend of $4.00 on each ordinary share, a total distribution to shareholders of $20,000.

(viii) It depreciates its assets (buildings, machinery and equipment, furniture and fittings, and patents and licences) as described in the preceding chapter, by the straight-line method.*

(ix) Inventories of raw materials and finished goods are taken at the end of the year and the values found are:
  (a) Raw materials: $10,000 (at cost), and
  (b) Finished goods: $50,000 (cost of raw materials plus direct labor).

It is assumed for simplicity that no stock of semi-finished goods exist at the end of the year.

The letters in parentheses by the ledger titles in Table III–1 indicate what type the ledger is: (P) personal, (R) real, and (N) nominal. Numbers by the individual entries are intended to assist in identifying both halves of each double entry.

TABLE III–1

The Ledgers for the Acme Cotton Fabric Co., Inc., for Calendar Year 1968

RAW MATERIAL PURCHASES (N)

DEBIT		CREDIT
(1) Cotton Yarn	$500,000	
(2) Dyes	100,000	
	$600,000	

SALES (N)

DR		CR
	To Firm A	$100,000 (3)
	To Firm B	200,000 (4)
	To Firm C	500,000 (5)
	To Firm D	200,000 (6)
		$1,000,000

* In accounting, the writing down of intangible assets is called amortization rather than depreciation.

The Ledgers for the Acme Cotton Fabric Co., Inc., for Calendar Year 1968 (*continued*)

FACTORY WAGES PAID (N)

DR		CR
(7) To Factory Labor	$160,000	
	$160,000	

SALARIES PAID (N)

DR		CR
(8) To Clerical Staff	$15,000	
(9) To Managerial Staff	25,000	
	$40,000	

SALESMEN'S SALARIES PAID (N)

DR		CR
(10) To Salesmen	$60,000	
	$60,000	

INTEREST PAID (N)

DR		CR
(11) To American Commercial Bank	$3,000	
	$3,000	

TAXES PAID (N)

DR		CR
(12) To Federal Government	$60,000	
	$60,000	

DIVIDENDS PAID (N)

DR		CR
(13) To Shareholders	$20,000	
	$20,000	

ACCOUNTS PAYABLE (P)

DR		CR	
		To Cotton Co-operative	$20,000 (1)
		To Chemical Company	10,000 (2)
			$30,000

The Ledgers for the Acme Cotton Fabric Co., Inc., for Calendar Year 1968 (*continued*)

ACCOUNTS RECEIVABLE (P)

DR		CR
(5) From Firm C	$100,000	
	$100,000	

DEPRECIATION A/C (N)

DR		CR
(14) Buildings	$4,000	
(15) Machinery and Equipment	42,000	
(16) Furniture and Fittings	8,000	
(17) Patents and Licences	6,000	
	$60,000	

ACCUMULATED DEPRECIATION (N)

DR	CR	
	For Buildings	$4,000 (14)
	For Machinery and Equipment	42,000 (15)
	For Furniture and Fittings	8,000 (16)
	For Patents and Licences	6,000 (17)
		$60,000

FINISHED GOODS INVENTORY (R)

DR		CR
1 Jan. 1967	—	

RAW MATERIALS INVENTORY (R)

DR		CR
1 Jan. 1967	—	

The Ledgers for the Acme Cotton Fabric Co., Inc., for Calendar Year 1968 (*continued*)

CASH (R)

DR		CR		
(3) From Firm A	$100,000	To Cotton Co-operative	$480,000	(1)
(4) From Firm B	200,000	To Chemical Company	90,000	(2)
(5) From Firm C	400,000	To Factory Labor	160,000	(7)
(6) From Firm D	200,000	To Salesmen	60,000	(10)
		To Clerical Staff	15,000	(8)
		To Managerial Staff	25,000	(9)
		To American Commercial		(11)
		Bank	3,000	
		To Federal Government	60,000	(12)
		To Shareholders	20,000	(13)
	$900,000		$913,000	

Now that the ledgers have been presented it is time to look into the process of closing the operating accounts and preparing the various income statements. In what follows, only the ending balances of the ledgers are entered to save time and space. Again, numbers are used to assist in identifying corresponding entries. Note that the balances shown for the end of the year are the results of the double-entry system; they do not require a second entry themselves. When, however, the closing entries are made, a second entry is required, and that is made in the appropriate income statement. Be careful to understand the manner in which the inventory entries are handled. Refer back to the text if necessary.

TABLE III–2

Deriving Gross Profit

RAW MATERIALS PURCHASES

DR		CR		
Year End Balance	$600,000	To Mfg. Account	$600,000	(1)

SALES

DR		CR		
(2) To Mfg. Account	$1,000,000	Year End Balance	$1,000,000	

Deriving Gross Profit (*continued*)

FACTORY WAGES PAID

DR		CR	
Year End Balance	$160,000	To Mfg. Account	$160,000 (3)

RAW MATERIAL INVENTORY

DR		CR	
1 Jan. 1967	—	To Mfg. Account	— (4)

(5) 31 Dec. 1967	$10,000		

FINISHED GOODS INVENTORY

DR		CR	
1 Jan. 1967	—	To Mfg. Account	— (6)

(7) 31 Dec. 1967	$50,000		

MANUFACTURING ACCOUNT

DR		CR	
(4) Inventory of Raw Materials 1 Jan. 1967	—	Total Sales	$1,000,000 (2)
(1) *Plus:* Purchases of Raw Materials	$600,000	*Plus:* Finished Goods Inventory 31st Dec., 1967	(7) $50,000
	$600,000		$1,050,000
(5) *Less:* Inventory of Raw Materials 31 Dec. 1967	$10,000	*Less:* Finished Goods Inventory 1st Jan. 1967	(6) —
Equals: Cost of Raw Material Used in Production	$590,000		$1,050,000
(3) *Plus:* Factory Wages Paid	160,000		
Equals: Cost of Goods Manufactured	$750,000		
GROSS PROFIT	300,000		
	$1,050,000		$1,050,000

Next, from gross profits and overhead expenses is figured net profit for the year. Net profit will appear as a balancing entry in the profit and loss account just as gross profit appeared as a balancing entry in the manufacturing account.

Finally, from net profit, and the taxes and dividends paid ledgers, the accountant calculates unappropriated profit in the income account of the same name.

TABLE III–3

Deriving Net Profit

INTEREST PAID

DR		CR	
Year End Balance	$3,000	To P & L Account	$3,000 (1)

SALARIES PAID

DR		CR	
Year End Balance	$40,000	To P & L Account	$40,000 (2)

SALES WAGES PAID

DR		CR	
Year End Balance	$60,000	To P & L Account	$60,000 (3)

DEPRECIATION ACCOUNT

DR		CR	
Year End Balance	$60,000	To P & L Account	$60,000 (4)

PROFIT AND LOSS ACCOUNT

DR		CR	
(1) Interest Paid	$3,000	Gross Profit (from Mfg.	
(2) Salaries Paid	40,000	Account)	$300,000
(3) Sales Wages Paid	60,000		
(4) Depreciation	60,000		
	$163,000		
Net Profit	$137,000		
	$300,000		$300,000

TABLE III–4

Deriving Unappropriated Profit

TAXES PAID

DR		CR	
Year End Balance	$60,000	To UPA	$60,000 (1)

DIVIDENDS PAID

DR		CR	
Year End Balance	$20,000	To UPA	$20,000 (2)

UNAPPROPRIATED PROFIT ACCOUNT

DR		CR	
(1) Taxes Paid to Federal Government	$60,000	Net Profit	$137,000
(2) Dividends Paid Out	20,000		
	$80,000		
Unappropriated Profit	$57,000		
	$137,000		$137,000

At this point it is possible to prepare the new balance sheet for the firm and it is presented here as Table III–5. Notice that the changes to the old balance sheet take two forms. First there are changes in the asset and liability items due to the flows of the year corresponding to those items (e.g., depreciation flow reducing the current book value of certain assets; flows of cash decreasing the firm's bank account balance). Second, there is the change in ownership interest (net worth) corresponding to the result of the operation over the year (unappropriated profit).

From this presentation, the relationships between the firm's stocks and flows should be clear. Note that total assets have increased by $87,000, made possible by an increase of $30,000 in liabilities and the retaining of $57,000 profit in the business. Within the asset account, current assets have increased by $147,000, made possible by the $87,000 discussed above and a decrease in other assets (due to depreciation) of $60,000. These changes illustrate three of the four methods of increasing assets mentioned in Chapter II. In practice the balance sheet would not be presented in this way; only the depreciated assets would be shown both at original cost and

TABLE III-5

Balance Sheet

For the Acme Cotton Fabric Co., Inc., as of 31st December, 1968

ASSETS

Fixed Assets

	Original Cost	Less Accrued Depreciation	Current Book Value
Land	$60,000	—	$60,000
Buildings	160,000	$4,000	156,000
Machinery and Equipment ...	420,000	42,000	378,000
Furniture and Fittings ...	40,000	8,000	32,000
	$680,000	$54,000	$626,000

Current Assets

	1 Jan., 1964	+ or − Net Flows	Current Book Value
Cash at the Bank ...	$60,000	−$13,000	$47,000
Accounts Receivable ...	—	+100,000	100,000
Raw Materials Inventory ...	—	+10,000	10,000
Finished Goods Inventory ...	—	+50,000	50,000
	$60,000	+147,000	$207,000

Intangible Assets

	Original Cost	Less Accrued Depreciation	Current Book Value
Patents and Licences ...	$90,000	$6,000	$84,000
Processes	160,000	—	160,000
Foundation and Pre-Production Exps.	60,000	—	60,000
	$310,000	$6,000	$304,000
Total Assets			$1,137,000

LIABILITIES AND OWNERSHIP

Liabilities

Long term Liabilities

Loan from ACB ...	$50,000	$50,000

Current Liabilities

Accounts Payable ...	$30,000	$30,000

Total Liabilities		$80,000

Ownership Interest

31 Dec., 1966 ...	$1,000,000	
Plus: Unappropriated Profit for Operation during 1967 ...	$57,000	
		$1,057,000
		$1,137,000

current value, and there would be no indication of net flows for individual items such as cash. There might be presented however, for comparison, figures from earlier years. These would usually be confined to the major divisions such as total current assets. This approach has been adopted here to emphasize once more the connection between stocks and flows before moving on to consider in more general terms some of the ways in which the businessman makes use of accounting data.

IV

ACCOUNTING AND THE BUSINESSMAN

Having introduced some of the basic methods, accounts can now be discussed from the point of view of those using them. Some comments have already been made regarding the different objectives of the professional accountant and the economist. Further insight will be gained by considering accounting from the point of view of a tool to be used in business administration. Under this heading, two separate points of view can be distinguished. On the one hand, the businessman may be interested in evaluating the past performance and current standing of a firm. Alternatively, he may be interested in planning the future and controlling the current operations of his own business. These two subjects are discussed in this chapter.

A. Accounts as a Measure of Performance and Indicator of Current Health

1. *The Value of a Firm's Assets*

A businessman may be interested in the value of his own company, the value of a business which he is thinking of purchasing, or the financial state of a business to which he is considering lending money. In the case of a nationally owned corporation similar questions will be asked by the representatives of the public responsible for their operation.

The record of the firm's assets, liabilities, and net worth is, as illustrated in the previous chapters, the balance sheet of the business. Some of the difficulties of using balance sheets as a basis for estimating the value of a business will already be apparent. The particular asset values shown on the accounts may be very poor estimates of the current value of the assets.

In the case of fixed assets this is because the prices of assets change, rendering the historical book values obsolete, and because depreciation may not measure the decline in the value of fixed assets accurately. Also, the current assets of the business may be different from those shown on the books, if, for example, some of the accounts receivable are of dubious quality.

There is, however, a more fundamental difficulty which should be recognized. When the assets of a business are valued, two different questions might be asked. The first is, "How much would the value of the assets be if they were sold individually, item by item?" The second question would be, "How much are these same assets worth as a group, organized as they are, for a productive purpose?" The answers to these questions will normally be quite different.

The first reason for this difference is that the firm is something more than a collection of separate assets. It is a particular, possibly unique, combination and organization of assets selected for their appropriateness as joint inputs into some productive activity. Their operation as a combination will have been demonstrated in the past, and the element of organization will have been shown to have enhanced the value of the assets. Analogously, it is often true that in a team game the effectiveness of the team lies in the special combination and compatibility of the players rather than the particular distinction of individual stars. Any individual player might be much less useful if combined in a different group. Also, it is interesting to note that the creation of a new business involves more than just the purchase of the right assets—there is a process of learning involved and a need to establish a reputation as an effective organization.

In some cases the reverse might also be true. The firm might be using assets in its business which would have a much higher value if used in another, quite different, line. If this is the case, it would pay someone to buy the entire firm or part of its asset stock and divert the purchases to another use. This may be true particularly where land is involved. A hotel might be using land and possess a building which would be of far more value if converted to an office building. A farmer might be using land which would be far more valuable if used for housing. In such cases, the use of the asset is likely to be changed either by the firm itself or through transfer of ownership. Of course, there are situations where information is imperfect or where the use of an asset in a particular way has some personal value to the owner which is not shared by others and therefore not represented in the market. Such would be the case where an owner has a sentimental attachment to a business and wishes it to be kept in operation despite the possibility of more profitable alternative uses of the assets.

The normal expectation, however, is that the assets of the firm have a value as part of a *going concern* in excess of the value they would command if sold separately. This is known as the difference between the value of a business as a *going concern* and its value if *broken up*. This difference is an intangible value which can be attributed to the existence of the firm. It was pointed out in Chapter II that this value is typically not registered in the balance sheet except perhaps for a firm which has been purchased in which case the intangible value is listed as "good will."

There is another reason for the difference in the value of an asset to the firm and its value in the market. Some businesses operating in less-developed economies might be the only firm, or only one of a very small group, in a given industry. A machine might, therefore, find no local market and might have a second-hand value only if transported considerable distances. Therefore, once having been acquired, it will be reasonable for the firm to keep the machine as long as its value to the firm is at least equal to its value in some distant market, less the costs of dismantling and shipping to that market. When the machine was purchased its value to the firm must have been estimated at the market price plus the transport costs and the costs of installation. In terms of local prices many firms would find there to be a considerable gap between the price at which capital equipment could be purchased and the price at which it could be sold.

The accounting records of the assets of many firms which are already established and are not engaged in major expansion give the appearance of some stability, the balance sheet changing only by small adjustments from year to year. Yet it is interesting to note that the value of a business can change overnight. For example, a textile firm producing for local consumption will be a much more valuable firm if the duty on imported textiles is increased. Alternatively, the value of a firm which has the monopoly of a local market will fall from the time a new firm entered the market and sets up a competitive plant. The pecuniary advantages to be gained from tariff protection and monopoly power do not appear in the balance sheet as an asset and therefore the balance sheet does not register changes in their value. The behavior of the share values of the businesses in the stock market is in considerable contrast to the year-by-year stability of their balance sheets. A share in a business is a claim on a certain proportion of the net worth of the company as a going concern. The behavior of stock markets is notoriously volatile. Part of this volatility is based more on assessments of the fickle attitudes of other stock-holders than on estimates of the value of the shares in any longer-term sense. This speculative element is, however, built up on an underlying fluctuation of opinion regarding the value of the businesses as going concerns.

This fluctuation in opinion results from the fact that the value of a firm as a going concern depends on the future profits which it can earn. Any assessment of the future will be more precarious and more subject to re-evaluation than judgments about the past. The estimated value of the firm as a going concern should be based on a prediction of the future stream of earnings rather than on a piecemeal evaluation of the assets of the business. For such predictions, however, data from the current accounts are likely to be more valuable than that from the balance sheet. Often, therefore, the current accounts provide a better indication of the value of a business as a going concern than the balance sheet record of asset values.

The balance sheet does, however, have its uses. It does provide a cumulative record of past investments in the business, and if this record is adjusted for price changes, it can be used as a basis for the measurement of management performance. In comparing managerial performances, one criterion is the rate of return achieved on the assets sunk into the business. Also, as was pointed out in the previous paragraphs, if this rate of return is too low, there may be a case for transferring the assets to other uses.

For the economist, it may be the case that, in assessing a business performance from the point of view of the economy as a whole, profit rates may be too high. A businessman with a given amount of capital will be interested in maximizing profits on that capital, and as such may be interested in preventing competitive firms from entering the field. From the social point of view, however, it might be of interest to expand investment in this field and by so doing lower the average rate of profit on the capital invested. The businessman is interested in maximizing the return on his own capital. Public policy should be interested in maximizing the rate of return on the investment of the whole society. This can also be important when considering a national corporation which has a monopoly control over a market—it may be possible for such an organization to make too high a profit rate, indicating that output in that field is insufficient. The responsibility of the manager will be to maximize the profit rate on the capital under his control. The responsibility of public policy will be to see there is the right amount of capital in the industry and that it is not underutilized.

2. *Liquidity*

The balance sheet can also be helpful in assessing the liquidity of a business. The ability of a firm to continue operation as a going concern is dependent on its ability to pay debts as they fall due. Failure to do so can lead to bankruptcy. Difficulties in meeting obligations, even short of bankruptcy, can lead to disruption of the normal running of a business.

A firm might have assets which cover its liabilities but which do not provide readily available sources of cash. When some debt falls due for repayment, the firm might find itself with substantial fixed assets and good future profit expectations but no ready source of cash. The degree to which a firm can command sources of cash is known as its state of "liquidity." Liquid assets, therefore, are those assets which are in the form of cash or are readily transferable into cash. Liquid assets typically form part of the current assets and investments items of the balance sheet.

All current assets, however, are not necessarily very liquid. A firm will count its inventory of raw materials as a current asset, but it may well have no ready market, particularly in an economy without a wide range of commodity markets. Also, the current asset taking the form of "accounts receivable" is ultimately dependent on the liquidity of the firm's debtors. It is interesting to note that there is, in a developed business community, a complicated web of financial obligations, with the liabilities of one firm forming part of the assets of others. In normal times, when there is considerable mutual confidence, the structure rests partly on the belief that most firms will meet their financial obligations. A business failure will have effects on the asset situation of a number of other firms. A number of business failures will undermine the expectation that liabilities will generally be met and alter the interpretation that is placed on the balance sheets of firms. A very healthy state of liquidity in normal times may, therefore, appear quite precarious in times of general financial crisis.

The important thing to recognize in assessing the liquidity of a business is that the firm needs to cover a flow of payments as they fall due. The firm must be able to organize to meet any peaks which appear in this flow. The firm is also likely to enjoy a flow of cash receipts, mostly in payment for current and past sales. It must be able to organize its assets so that its reserves of cash can cover any gap between the flows of payments in and out of the business.

The fluctuation in the payment flows cannot be simply deduced from the balance sheet nor the annual income statements. Particularly if a business is seasonal, the payments and receipts may have decided peaks which coincide neither with each other nor with the date for which the balance sheet is prepared. The firm will have to predict these flows from its experience of past patterns of payments. The outsider will have to base his judgment on knowledge of the general characteristics of the industry in which the business operates. The liquidity of a firm can only be considered satisfactory in comparison with the character of the particular business it is engaged in. Some businesses with very predictable cash inflows and outflows, which tend to match each other, might be able to operate quite satisfactorily without a large reserve of liquid assets. On the other hand, a firm where the reverse is true might have to maintain a considerable part of its assets in liquid form.

It is interesting to note that many businesses may have, in normal times, important hidden liquid "assets" in the form of a reserve of unused credit with a bank or other financial institution. This will be particularly true in businesses where trade is highly seasonal, but where the short-run risks are not great and the seasonal character of the trade is quite predictable. For example, firms involved in the business of moving or processing seasonal crops will often be able to call on banks for short-term loans to tide themselves over the period when they pay out cash to the farmer to the time when they sell the crop, perhaps in some more processed state. During that interim period the firm will have to run down its cash and increase its inventory. To defend its cash position it will prefer to cover part of the inventory with a short-term liability in the form of a bank loan. In primary-producing countries the government will have to ensure that the banking system is able to provide adequate liquidity to finance the very large and highly seasonal crop movements which are characteristic of such economies.

The manner in which the need for liquidity depends on cash flows can be illustrated with two simple examples.

First consider a retail grocery store in a large city. This business will experience very small fluctuation in cash inflows and outflows, for the eating habits of the population it serves will not be subject to violent swings. There may be slightly larger turnover during important holiday seasons when big dinners and considerable entertaining are customary. But aside from this possibility, the fluctuations are liable to be weekly, corresponding to the stocking up of food for the weekend or coming week. There may also be a correlation with local pay days in industry, especially if a large proportion of the store's customers are employed in the same firm. The problem of liquidity will be small for the management of such a business. Small cash reserves will be necessary to allow the building of inventories before pay day or the weekend, but the money involved will represent a small fraction of the firm's current assets, much of which will be held in the form of inventory. Flows of cash into the firm will correspond with the peaks in business, unless the firm grants extensive credit. Thus, small peaks in the size of cash outflows will regularly be followed (closely) by small peaks in cash inflows.

This situation has been illustrated in Figure IV–1, the cash flow chart for the firm over the period of one year. It is evident from the chart that the gaps between outflows and simultaneous inflows is never large.

The second example is of a processor of agricultural produce. He is forced to buy up the crops when they are available, that is, immediately after harvest. Assuming a two-crop climate, he is then faced with two peak spending periods every year. His receipts will tend to lag his payments and to be somewhat more regular, since it is assumed that the processed goods have a "shelf-life" considerably longer than the straight produce. (Shelf-life is the period of time the product may be stored without spoiling or

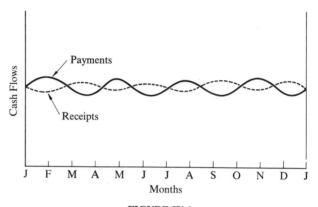

FIGURE IV-1

otherwise becoming useless.) In this case, the gap between receipts and payments grows very large at harvest time twice each year. The firm will have to program its financial position carefully to ensure that it will not be caught short—either without money to buy enough inputs, or unable to meet its contractual obligations and be forced to liquidate other assets under conditions of rush-sale. It would certainly be to the firm's advantage to attempt to even out the flows by borrowing at harvest time and repaying

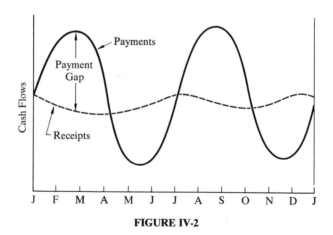

FIGURE IV-2

over the next several months. But if it attempts to meet the problem internally it must keep a considerable amount of its assets in a liquid form and must be extremely careful about building programs, etc. which will tie up its assets in non-salable form. This situation is illustrated in Figure IV–2.

3. *Profitability*

The profits of a firm are estimated in the income statement of the company. In judging past performance, the observer will have to consider how far the profits shown in the accounts are a true estimate of real profits. The estimates of costs as they appear in the accounts may prove faulty if, for example, depreciation is under-estimated. Income statements, just as much as balance sheets, can only be judged against a background knowledge of the nature of the business. If, for example, the firm is opening up new markets, then some part of the costs might be viewed as an investment in the future, although from the accountant's more rigorous point of view the treatment of such costs as the creation of an intangible asset might not be justified.

The profits of a business have to be judged in relation to the size of the investment. Sometimes profits as a proportion of sales has been used as a criterion of performance. This may be appropriate in situations where there is some norm from which to make a judgment, but it is usually a dangerous criterion. Total profits will be maximized when the marginal profit from an additional sale is zero; this must be at a point where average profit per unit of sale is falling. The maximum profit point will *not* therefore, be the same point as that at which average profit per unit of sales (and therefore, profits as a percentage of total sales) is maximized. A firm may, therefore, have too high a rate of profit on sales, as well as too low.

The measurement of profitability as a return on investment involves a number of difficulties. Two will be mentioned here. The profitability of an investment should be compared with the *opportunity* cost involved. The opportunity cost of investing in one business is the return which could have been made in an alternative investment. But which alternative investment should be considered? Here, the difficulty arises that the comparison must be made with an investment of comparable risk. This introduces an additional element of judgment in deciding which are comparable lines of business or investments involving similar risks. The choice of suitable comparisons ultimately requires a certain amount of subjective evaluation.

A second ambiguity arises from the need to specify the investment for which the calculation is being made. A test of managerial performance might well be the rate of return achieved on all the assets invested in the business, irrespective of their source. Such a measure of performance would be to take the profit plus interest payments as a percentage of the value of the total assets as measured by adjusting the balance sheet value for price changes. Alternatively, the same return could be compared to the net worth plus long term liabilities, which together represent the long term investment in the business. The owner will, however, be interested in the rate of profit achieved on his investment; that is, in net profit as a percentage of net worth.

It is interesting to note how these last two ratios will differ. The relationship is extremely simple but sometimes a little confusing at first. The best way to understand it is by way of a simple example. Assume that the net worth of a business is $1,000, and that the net profit for the year is $100. Further assume that the firm has no long term debt. The rate of profit on net worth is 10 per cent. If, instead of this situation, it is assumed that the firm has a net worth of only $500, a long term debt of $500 on which 5 per cent interest is payable, and the same $100 available to provide for the interest plus net profit, the situation is quite different. In this case $25 interest would be paid, after which $75 would remain as a net profit on the ownership interest of $500. This represents a 15 per cent return on the owners' investment. Note, however, that the second case presents a riskier situation than the first. If the sum available to profits plus interest fell to $25, then in the first example the rate of return on the net worth would fall to $2\frac{1}{2}$ per cent whereas in the second case it would fall to zero. By increasing debt the firm may be able to increase the rate of return on the shareholders' investment at the expense of increasing the riskiness of that return. If a firm is faced with highly uncertain profits, large debt issues will be unwise for they entail a fixed, recurring obligation to pay interest. If a business has fairly certain profits, on the other hand, a large proportion of debt finance may be possible. In this way a business, in which the rate of return is low but fairly certain, can increase the rate of return on the ownership interest by financing a considerable proportion of the total investment through long-term debt issue.

The investor assessing the future profitability of a firm will be interested in judging two characteristics of the returns expected. The size of the expected returns and the certainty with which they may be expected are both of interest. Some investors might be willing to accept a return which is certain but low, over a return which is sometimes extremely high but which is quite uncertain. In reviewing past profit performance it is therefore necessary to note not only the level of past profits but the degree to which they have been subject to fluctuation.

B. Accounting as a Management Tool

The use of accounting within the firm as a tool of management has numerous functions; three general, somewhat interdependent, areas of concern can be distinguished: estimating future costs, revenues, and cash flows; controlling current expenses and inventory holdings; and planning the internal consistency of the projected operating plans of the firm. There is a strong contrast between the techniques described in Chapters II and III, with their emphasis on producing an historical record, and the methods necessary for the pursuit of the first objective listed above, with its concern for the future. The decisions which require such forecasts are quite diverse. The following are some of the more obvious:

(i) *fixed investment*—costs and revenues must be forecast for considerable periods ahead.

(ii) *pricing*—estimates must be made of the effects of prices on current and future sales.

(iii) *level of output*—estimates must be made of the level of output which it is sensible to produce.

(iv) *costing for contract bids*—in industries where work is by contract, jobs must be costed for bidding purposes.

(v) *dividends*—the management must decide how much of the net profits should be paid out and how much should be retained in the business.

(vi) *liquidity*—budgets must be made for cash flows, to ensure the future liquidity of the firm.

Such decisions will often have to be made partly on guesswork and judgment based on the accumulated experience of the businessman. However, the existence of uncertainty does not reduce the value of making explicit assessments of prospects.

The most important difference between the accounting discussed in Chapters II and III and managerial accounting for planning corresponds to the distinction economists often make between *ex ante* (i.e., planned) and *ex post* (i.e., realized) economic quantities. The balance sheet and income statement are records of what has happened; the budget statement is an estimate of what will happen. In the past, all is determined. An output has been produced at a certain cost and has created a particular revenue. In the future, much less is determined. There is a range of possibilities. It is the task of management to be aware of these and to make the best possible choice between the alternatives.

When planning for the future the alternatives available to a firm will cover a wider range the longer the time period that is being considered. In the immediate future a firm will be faced with a given stock of fixed assets and raw materials and a number of contractual obligations to its employees. With the passage of time it can build new buildings, acquire new machinery, and free itself from unwanted contractual obligations. Economists often formalize the effect of time on the range of choice open to a firm in the concepts of the "long run" and the "short run." This, of course, makes a much firmer distinction for purposes of illustration than exists in practice.

The simple maximization rules of introductory economics suggest that the management should seek to measure total cost at various output levels, distinguishing the variable costs from the fixed costs. These estimates can then be combined with revenue estimates as a basis for choosing the maximum profit (minimum loss) output. This output will be where marginal cost equals marginal revenue. In the short run, output will be continued as long as there is some output level at which revenues will more than cover variable cost. In the long run the firm must expect to cover variable plus fixed costs.

1. *Break-even analysis*

The problem of output planning is at its simplest in the case of a single product firm. It will be helpful to consider a straightforward case to understand the method involved before some of the complications are introduced. In the simpler cases, a firm can make use of a *break-even chart* to analyze the potential cost, revenue, and profit situation of the firm. The cost data used may come partly from the historical evidence accumulated in the firm's accounts and partly from engineering analysis of the capabilities of the existing plant. The initial problem will be that of determining which costs are to be considered as fixed for the production period over the whole range of output possibilities and which will vary with output size. This may not prove to be as easy as one might expect, for the dividing line may not be clear everywhere. As a first approximation, however, one can certainly assume that the costs of raw materials and of direct production labor will vary with output. Note that these form the direct costs recorded in the manufacturing account. Similarly, many of the items recorded in the profit and loss account will prove to be fixed; for example, interest payments and depreciation charges. The identification of some of the costs will require fairly exact stipulation of the period to be considered. For example, the bill for the salaries of executives will typically be fixed in the short run (say over the next few months of the firm's life). Outside of that period, however, it will be possible to hire or fire in order to bring the managerial staff into line with the intended output. Similar conclusions may be reached concerning the clerical and sales staffs employed. Certain other costs may not vary for a certain range of outputs, but may begin to vary with output after a certain point.

Once the period to be considered has been decided upon, some of the problems mentioned above will be open to solution. Another problem will, however, arise as it may be the case that past experience covers only a small part of the range of potential outputs. Recourse may be had to whatever information is available concerning similar firms operating at other capacity levels in similar plants, but this will offer a limited possibility, especially in the developing economies where firms will often be unique, or one of a very small group. Another approach may be made through engineering analyses which are capable of predicting the capacity of the plant with differing quantities of variable inputs. In particular, some idea may be gained about the amounts of labor which must be applied to the existing plant to produce outputs in excess of those experienced in the past. In addition, estimates of the costs of repair and maintenance bills for machinery may be prepared for a large range of hours of operation per day, week, or month. Finally, the manager will usually be called upon to exercise his judgment based on experience for the estimation of the cost of projected output levels.

Revenue predictions require that management, in effect, predict the demand curve for its output. In the case of farming produce and some other standardized primary commodities a firm will be faced with a competitive market in which it can sell whatever it produces at the going price; its product is too small a part of total supply to effect market price. In this case, however, the price of the product is likely to be highly volatile. Revenue forecasting resolves itself, in this case, into the task of predicting this price.

Many manufacturing businesses, however, face an imperfect market in which they must reduce prices in order to increase sales. This may take the form of decreases in the general price to the consumer, increases in trading margins to particular distributors, or price discrimination. Price discrimination occurs when the firm is able to extend its market by offering lower prices to the marginal customer without changing its prices to the established market. This will happen, for example, when a firm lowers prices in order to sell in some outlying market in which it does not have the protection of transport costs and tariffs which enable it to charge higher prices nearer home. Typically, the manufacturing firm will be faced with much more stable demand conditions than the primary producer, but will have a much more difficult task in estimating the elasticity of demand for its products.

The management may then use the cost and revenue predictions to determine at what level of production it will be most profitable to operate in the short run; at what output level it should cease production, also in the short run; and to estimate the profitability of changing the plant over the long run.

In the short run, management will typically be facing cost and revenue curves somewhat similar to those shown in Figure IV–3 below. A certain set of costs will have been identified as being fixed over the possible output range. Their value will be reflected in the cost-curve intercept on the vertical (cost/revenue) axis. The total cost curve will slope up to the right from here. Perhaps, over some range of output the curve will be a straight line, or very nearly so, but it is likely that at higher output levels, costs will rise at an increasing rate with rising output. This will be true for a number of reasons; diminishing returns will probably set in as more and more labor is applied to the existing plant; unit labor costs will rise as overtime work is scheduled; wear and tear on machinery will increase as it is operated for longer hours and given less preventive maintenance; certain expenses which are fixed in the lower ranges of output may rise with output after a point.

The total revenue curve will start at the origin and have a positive slope upward and to the right. If the firm faces a competitive market for its product, it will be a straight line over the whole range of output. More usually, it will have a decreasing slope. This is the situation portrayed in the Figure IV–3.

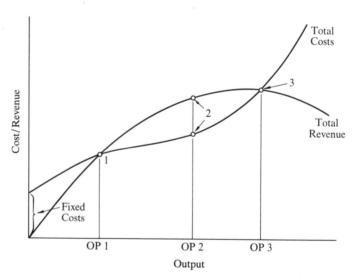

FIGURE IV-3

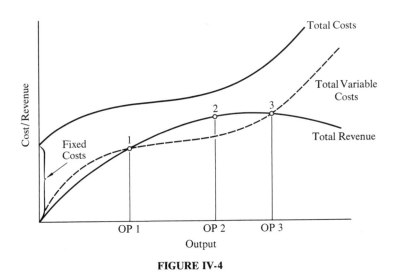

FIGURE IV-4

There are three significant points to be found in the break-even chart. (This should be recognized as a familiar diagram from elementary economics.) Point (1) is the break-even point; at this output the firm will just break even, covering its total costs with its total revenues, but it will not produce a profit. At any output higher than this it will make some profit until it arrives at the output represented by point (3), where it will again break even. The optimum point in the profitable interval between points (1) and (3) is represented by point (2). Here the firm will be maximizing its profit. In terms of the chart, this means that the difference between total revenues (above) and total costs (below) is a maximum. In the language of micro-economic theory at point (2), the marginal revenue is equal to the marginal cost. It is a simple exercise to demonstrate that the two statements are equivalent.

There are, however, situations in which a firm might not be able to make a profit. For example, in Figure IV–4, the total cost and total revenue curves are seen not to intersect. This means that the firm cannot make a profit at any output. Note, however, that the total variable cost curve does intersect with the total revenue curve. At the output of point (1) on this graph, the firm begins just making enough revenue to cover its variable costs. This will be true of every output in the interval between points (1) and (3). At point (2), the total amount earned over and above the variable cost of operation is a maximum. Here, marginal revenue is equal to marginal cost. This point is optimal in the sense that it allows the firm to minimize its losses. By producing at this point the firm will cover its variable costs and make the maximum possible amount towards the payment of the fixed costs of the business. This optimum would be considered by the firm only in the short run and in relation to a view of the future which held forth promise of better earnings. In this situation, the firm would lose more by shutting down than by remaining in production at any point in the 1–3 interval, but even the minimal loss, incurred at point (2), could not be sustained indefinitely.

For the longer run, in which the firm may choose between various possible sizes of plant, it can set up a chart like Figure IV–5 with which to study the alternatives. The revenue possibilities will be assumed to be similar to those in the last example. There are, however, three different total cost curves shown, corresponding to three possible plant sizes contemplated. For this purpose, accounting data accumulated will be of little use if only one size of plant has been operated in the past. A small plant will involve the firm in smaller fixed charges for interest payments, depreciation charges, and the like. It will, however, be subject to a faster rising cost curve as the application of labor to the limited machinery will more quickly result in seriously diminishing returns. The second kind of plant might be larger,

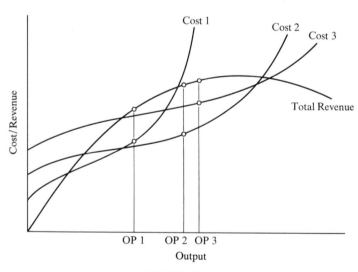

FIGURE IV-5

with attendant higher fixed costs, but the increase in costs with production might be considerably slower. The third might be still larger.

The choice will depend on the shape of the revenue as well as of the cost curves. In the example, the total profit to be obtained from the second possible plant, operating it at output (2), is greater than the alternative possibilities.

2. Difficulties in the Analysis of Costs and Revenues

What are the difficulties? The first difficulty that arises is that the firm is typically a multi-product business. The introductory textbook talks of "the" cost curves for a firm's output. If a firm produces more than one product in a given income period, it may be very difficult to separate the individual effects of each product on total costs. One of the most difficult problems of managerial accounting will be the allocation of costs among products. If there is excess capacity in the plant, so that one product can be expanded without checking the production of another, it will be sensible to expand production as long as the marginal revenue covers the additional direct cost of output. However, as soon as there is some constraint on output capacity so that more of one product means less of another, this rule will no longer apply because part of the costs of expanding one product will be the loss of opportunity to produce the other. If there is one clearly identifiable constraint on output, the rate at which one product can be substituted for another in the total output combination may be readily estimable. For example, if there is a bottle-neck in one department of a firm, but excess capacity in all other departments, then the rate of substitution of product A for product B in the output process will depend entirely on the relative degree to which they require the utilization of the bottle-neck in their production. If there are two or three such bottle-necks, the problem will still be relatively straightforward. (It is, in fact, soluble by the linear programing methods introduced later in Chapter XVII.) If, however, the constraint on output is much vaguer (but none the less real) then the management is likely to have to use its judgment based on experience, and probably translated into certain rules of thumb. This will be the case where the increase in the output of one department causes some diversion of management energies and other common services, which may eventually lead either to an increase in overhead expenses or a fall in the production of other products. In such situations, it may not be possible to place a finger on the precise cost effects of increases in the output of one product. In practice, the costs accountant will use certain rules of thumb, allocating "overhead" costs to a product on the assumption that there is a cost involved over and above the direct costs of increasing output. This overhead allocation may well be ignored in making production decisions in times of slack business when there is excess capacity in the firm, so that the managerial and other general services within the firm are not fully utilized.

When there are products which are strictly joint outputs of a production process, so that the production of one necessarily results in a particular level of output of the other, both the cost and the revenue should be combined in making a production decision. The two products should be treated as one, as the output of one inevitably results in the production of the other.

Even in the case of the single-product firm there will be some ambiguities. It has already been noted that the distinction between variable and fixed cost is not very clear. For example, a cost may be fixed in the sense that it has to be met if the business wishes to continue operation at some future date but would be avoidable if the business were dissolved. The decision whether to continue to incur a fixed cost, therefore, involves a decision about future operations. In this sense, it is also true that many costs which seem variable may be partly fixed. For example, direct labor and raw material costs are usually looked upon as variable. The economic rule suggests that if these costs are not covered then output should be discontinued, thus minimizing the loss. It may well be true that the cessation of operations would minimize the loss in one time period. However, if operations are revived in a subsequent period, there might be considerable costs involved in assembling a new team of workers and even, in some cases restoring the sources of raw material supply.

Similarly, of course, on the revenue side the sales of one product may be intimately linked to those of another produced by the same firm or, alternatively, sales in one period linked to those in another. Thus the firm might find that if it reduces price in this period it can increase sales now, but only at the expense of losing the same sales at some high price in a later period. Alternatively, a firm might find that by selling at a low price now it can establish itself in a market and build a basis for future sales at higher prices.

Many of the problems of accounting for production decisions arise from many characteristics of the production process of firms in practice which are not allowed for in the very simple models of introductory economics. The simple profit maximization rules of economics are, in general, correct, but for their application they require some ingenuity in allowing for the complicated links between various products and time periods which are found in actual production processes.

3. Control and Consistency

The second important function of management accounting is the control of spending and other aspects of the business. Traditional accounting is much concerned with control in the sense of checking honesty. Modern management accounting is very concerned with control in the sense of checking efficiency. This involves much the same sort of procedure as that envisaged in the discussion of costing set out above. By allocating costs to the various activities and departments of a firm some check can be kept on the effectiveness of the various units of operation. Often much can be discovered merely by comparing the cost of one department with those of another. Similarly, by keeping accurate records of the stock and flow of inventories, the size of the inventory load the firm carries may be reduced. For this purpose, the firm will be very interested in setting up a set of internal accounts which provide it with frequent and immediate information on the various parts of the business.

Also, systematic budgeting for costs, revenues, and cash flows will ensure that the various plans the firm is making are internally consistent. A firm will always make mistakes both in forecasting external conditions and in predicting the performance of its own organization. Budgeting can eliminate one source of error, however, which would arise if there is no effective method of checking the implications of various departmental and product-line plans for other parts of the business, and no way of assessing the total implications of the many small decisions being planned in the various parts of a large business.

FURTHER READING FOR PART 1

1. W. T. Baxter and S. Davidson, editors, *Studies in Accounting Theory*, Homewood, Illinois, Richard D. Irwin, Inc., and London, G. B. Sweet and Maxwell Ltd., 1962.
2. F. S. Bray, *The Interpretation of Accounts*, (Stamp-Martin Papers), London and New York, Oxford University Press for the Incorporated Accounts' Research Commission, 1957.
3. F. C. De Paula, *Management Accounting in Practice*, London, Sir I. Pitman and Sons Ltd., 1959.
4. H. C. Edey, *Business Budgets and Accounts*, London, Hutchinson, 1960.
5. E. O. Edwards and P. W. Bell, *The Theory and Measurement of Business Income*, Berkeley and Los Angeles, University of California Press, 1961.
6. W. A. Paton, *Essentials of Accounting*, revised edition, New York, Macmillan and Co., 1959.
7. J. P. Powelson, *Economic Accounting*, New York, McGraw-Hill, 1955.
8. S. W. Rowland and B. Magee, *Accounting: Part I*, London, Gee and Co. Ltd., 1949.

NOTES ON FURTHER READING FOR PART ONE

Paton (6), Powelson (7), and Rowland and Magee (8) are good introductory accounting texts and supply the concepts and mechanics involved in manipulating journals, ledgers, and balance sheets. They should be consulted in connection with Chapter I–III; see also Edey (4), pp. 7–34. Bray (2) and De Paula (3), assume some familiarity with the principles of accounting, as does Edey (4), pp. 35–167, and deal with the use of accounts as indicators of changes in the status of the business and as aids to business planning. Edwards and Bell (5) is concerned with developing a theory to resolve conflicts between the accountant's and the economist's concepts of income, and will be of use in connection with Chapter IV. Baxter and Davidson (1) is an anthology of articles on accounting, including sections on asset valuation and income theory, depreciation, price levels, accounting in the U.S.S.R., published statements and their interpretation, and new techniques (the use of statistical inference and computers in accounting).

PART

2

INTER-INDUSTRY ANALYSIS

V

CONSOLIDATION OF ACCOUNTS AND
THE INPUT-OUTPUT TABLE

The discussion in Part 1 concentrated on the accounts of businesses. In principle, the accounts of all business firms in any particular industry may be consolidated to form a set of accounts for the industry. The industry accounts will have the same format as the business accounts with assets on one side and liabilities and ownership interest on the other or debits on one side and credits on the other. The consolidation of accounts of businesses to form any industry account is accomplished by adding up similar asset, liability, and net worth items or similar debit and credit items and entering the sums in an industry account with a similar format. The accounts of a business enterprise may be rearranged in a certain way to form a source and use account which shows the source of all current inputs into the firm and the use to which the output of the firm is put. The source and use accounts for all firms in an industry may be consolidated to form an industry source and use account. The source and use accounts for several industries may be arranged in a special table called an input-output table, sometimes called an inter-industry account.

The input-output table has numerical entries in the rows and columns which give a picture of the complicated set of flows of goods and services between various industries and other sectors of the economy. The input-output table may be used to determine the requirements of capital, skilled labor, foreign exchange, food, power, and other factors for the whole of any given plan or for any particular project within the plan. The requirements of various factors for the whole plan help in determining the consistency of the plan. For example, if the skilled labor requirement of the plan exceeds the estimated supply of skilled labor forthcoming during the period of the plan, then the plan is inconsistent and has to be altered. If the foreign exchange required for the purchase of imports exceeds the expected foreign exchange earnings from exports plus foreign exchange obtained from grants or foreign borrowing, then the planners must set about altering the plan or seeking out new sources of external finance. Knowledge of the requirements of various factors for individual projects is useful to the planner in choosing among various alternative investment projects. The capital requirements for each of several alternative investment projects are necessary in order to use certain rules of thumb in choosing between them. All requirements of each project are necessary in the application of linear programing techniques in choosing among investment projects.

The main sources of information which may be used in constructing input-output tables consist of the accounts of business activities which were discussed in Chapters II and III. Often the necessary information is obtained from businesses through the use of a manufacturing census or through surveys of various sorts. Additional information will come from government budgets and from engineering data. In order to arrange the information contained in business accounts for use in input-output tables, business accounts must be broken down and combined and consolidated. Concentration on business accounts should not obscure the fact that households and government may also be thought of as account keepers. The usefulness of this notion is not impaired by the general lack of formal accounts within individual households, for it is the possibility of keeping such accounts that is important here.

A. Flows

An input-output table is a summarization of the flows of goods and services between three types of organization and the rest of the world. The three types of organization are (i) households, (ii) productive organizations (firms and farms), and (iii) the government. Those departments of the government which are engaged in producing a marketable output (such as electric power) are, however, considered to be productive organizations. To each transfer of a good or service between any two organizations or the rest of the world, there usually corresponds a cash flow in the opposite direction. For example, if Acme Cotton Fabric Co., Inc. transfers 10,000 yards of cotton fabric to Burke Clothing Factory, Inc., then, unless Acme Cotton Fabric is a charitable organization, Burke Clothing Factory will make a cash payment in return. Cotton fabric goes from Acme to Burke while cash goes from Burke to Acme. The flows of goods and services on the one hand and cash on the other between the three types of organization, and the rest of the world form a complicated set of relationships, the basis of the complex modern economy. Figure V–1 demonstrates the inter-

FLOWS OF CASH

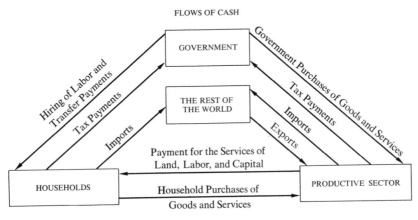

FIGURE V-1

connected flows which take place. The arrows indicate the direction of cash flows while the flows of goods and services, if any, are in the opposite direction.

Observe that all three sectors are purchasers. Households and productive organization are also sellers, while the government uses the revenue from taxation to finance its purchases. The major inter-sectoral flows are cash, goods, and services of factors of productions.

PRODUCT FLOWS

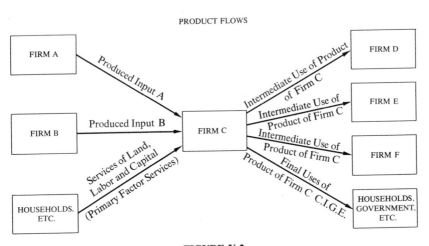

FIGURE V-2

Within the productive sector itself, there will be a large amount of buying and selling. Firms will buy part of the output of other firms and use these products as inputs in the production of other goods and services. The goods or services thus turned out may, in turn, be sold to other firms for use as inputs. In general, when the product of one firm is used as an input in the productive process of a second firm, it is called an *intermediate use* of the first firm's product. From the point of view of the using firm, the purchased good or service is called a *produced input*. These ideas are illustrated by Figure V–2.

All other sales of the output of firms and farms are called sales for *final use*. These uses may be subdivided into consumption, investment, and government purchase.

(i) *Consumption*: Consumption goods are purchases by households of the output of productive organizations for use within the household within the current period.

(ii) *Investment*: Purchases by productive organizations of capital goods, that is, goods intended for use in the productive process over several accounting periods, are included in final uses of the output of the productive sector. Also counted as a final use is the accumulation of stocks of goods (inventory investment). The inclusion of investment purchases here is a matter of convention and is intended as one solution to a difficult problem. Investment goods do not fit nicely into the scheme so far developed. They are, in one sense, produced inputs, for they are certainly used in the production of other goods and/or services. They are not, however, used up within one period but, by definition, last through several periods of production.

As noted in Chapter III, transactions involving investment goods will be included in the income accounts of only one of the transactors involved. The seller of capital equipment will include the value of the sales in his income accounts, but buyers will not show their purchases as operating transactions. This characteristic of capital good transactions ensures that if all business accounts are consolidated, none of the value of investment will be lost due to cancellation.

(iii) *Government*: Purchase by government of the output of productive organizations is considered a final use of that output. Here again, a convention is necessary because of the difficulty of dealing with government purchases within the simple framework outlined above. Goods and services sold to the government are generally used in the provision of services for which no direct payment is received. The problem is compounded by the fact that some of these services are, in effect, inputs for the productive sector. The fact that they are not sold in the market place makes the measurement of their value extremely difficult, and makes it virtually impossible to allocate them between firms.* Government enterprises add another conceptual difficulty. Here the purchased goods and services are obviously used as produced inputs and the outputs of each enterprise are priced and sold in the market to identifiable buyers. If government enterprises are important in the economy, it will be necessary to treat the government, at least partially, as another productive organization, retaining as final use only those government purchases for current use identified with general services.†

(iv) *Exports*: Goods and services purchased by foreigners, whatever their use by foreigners may be, are usually given one final-use classification as exports.

To complete the discussion of flow relationships within the economy it is necessary to consider six additional items:

(i) *Productive Sector Purchases from Households*: Productive organizations obtain some of the inputs for their productive process direct from households. These are called *primary inputs* and consist of land, labor and capital. In return for supplying these, households receive from the productive sector rent for land, wages for labor, and profit plus depreciation as a return on capital. Using profit as a measure of capital services is a convention adopted to provide a complete accounting for expenses and to avoid the manifold difficulties in the way of finding a truly accurate measure of the value of the services of capital. Profit, in the subsequent discussion, is considered to be net profit plus interest, or equivalently as unappropriated profit plus dividends plus interest. Households will receive the return on capital in two forms: first, as an increase in net ownership through the retention of profit within the firm; and, second, as distributed profits in the form of dividends paid to the shareholders.

(ii) *Government Purchases of Labor Direct from Households*: Obviously in the provision of services and in the operation of enterprise, the government must employ members of households. This hiring of labor will constitute a primary input whenever government is included as a productive organization and the labor is hired in this productive effort. Otherwise the hiring of labor by the government will be treated separately as a final use of a factor service.

* A further discussion on the role of government in the economy and its place in the national accounts is contained in Chapter XI.
† In general, all government investment will be included as final use. Chapter XI will deal more fully with this question.

Where the government is considered, by convention, only as a final user, its output is considered to be equal in value to the sum of the cost of goods, services, and labor involved.

(iii) *Tax Payments by Productive Organizations and Households to the Government*: Taxes are usually grouped into one of two classifications: (i) direct taxes and (ii) indirect taxes. Direct taxes are taxes on the income of individuals and on the profits of firms, poll taxes, and taxes on assets such as land and property. Indirect taxes are usually taxes levied on the sale of various goods and services such as import duties, export taxes, licence fees, and excise taxes. These two types of taxes are often treated differently in applications to input-output. The payment of taxes is a flow of cash which does not correspond to an opposite flow of goods and services.* When accounts are summed over the economy, taxes are generally included implicitly as part of incomes (direct) or value of sales (indirect).

(iv) *Transfer Payments from Governments to Households*: When the government makes a payment to an individual without having purchased any good or service, the payment is called a transfer payment. Cash flows related to transfer payments do not correspond to any flow of goods or services. Transfer payments include payment of government pensions, social security payments, payment of unemployment benefits, and other types of welfare payments. Transfer payments by government usually are a much bigger item relative to total cash flows in a highly developed economy than in the developing economies.† Transfer payments are not explicitly added in any summing of total economic activity.

(v) *Sales by the Rest of the World to Productive Enterprises, Households, and Government (Imports)*: Imports by households and government are purchases for final use. Imports by productive enterprises are either investment goods, which are considered to be a final use, or are intermediate products which are consumed by current production. Nearly all imports require a compensating outward flow of foreign exchange.

(vi) *Imputed Values*: The vast majority of transactions are exchange transactions, in which goods or services are exchanged for cash or credit. As previously mentioned, when cash or credit is transferred from one unit to another without an equivalent exchange of goods

---

* Taxes, their effects on costs and prices, and their relation to government spending, are discussed in more depth in the Chapters X and XI.

† Transfer payments may originate in other sectors than government. Clearly business gifts to non-profit organizations, for example, are transfer payments. Similarly, inter-household gifts of money are transfer payments also.

or services, a transfer payment is recorded. When, on the other hand, goods or services are used without any exchange of cash or credit, an *imputed-value transaction* takes place. Subject to the usual cautions about the changing value of money, exchange transactions and transfer payments may be measured in terms of the amount of money which changes hands. Imputed-value transactions are more difficult to measure, the imputation methods being adjusted to fit the particular circumstances.

The relative and absolute importance of transfer payments and imputed-value transactions will vary from economy to economy depending on such factors as the extent of government social welfare schemes, the size of the government debt, the degree to which subsistence farming is prevalent and the size of the stock of owner-occupied housing. Imputed-value transactions form an important part of the economic activity within most developing countries. This is particularly so for those activities in the agricultural sector which result in goods produced and consumed within the household. Such activity is known as *subsistence* activity.

B. Consolidation and Breakdown of Accounts for the Individual Firm

Chapter III was concerned with three different types of flow accounts for the individual firm: (1) the manufacturing (trading) account, (2) the profit and loss account, and (3) the unappropriated profit account. These three types of accounts may be combined and consolidated to give a picture of the flow of goods and services from all other firms, households, and government to the individual firm and the flows from the individual firm to all other organizations.

The manufacturing account (Table II–2), the profit and loss account (Table III–3) and the unappropriated profit account (Table III–4) of Chapter III have been combined in Table V–1 below.

The first two items in the debit side of the account in Table V–1 are from the manufacturing account (Table III–2), the next four items are from the profit and loss account (Table III–3), and items 7, 8, and 9 are from the unappropriated profit account (Table III–4). The first two items on the credit side are derived from the credit side of the manufacturing account. The accumulation of raw material inventories has simply been transposed, with appropriate changes of sign, from the debit side of that account. Thus on the debit side, raw material inventories show up as "beginning balance" minus "ending balance." When transposed to the credit side this becomes, as for finished goods, "ending balance" minus "beginning balance." The item's gross profit and net profit which are included in the accounts in Chapter III are left out of the account in Table V–1 since they appear on

TABLE V–1

Combined Profit and Loss and Unappropriated Profit Account

DEBIT			CREDIT		
1. Cost of materials and services purchased	...	$600,000	1. Sales Revenue		$1,000,000
2. Factory wages		160,000	2. Increase in stock of finished goods		50,000
3. Sales expenses		60,000	3. Increase in stock of raw materials		10,000
4. Administrative and management salaries ...		40,000			
5. Interest paid on bank loan		3,000			
6. Depreciation accrued ...		60,000			
7. Income (profit) taxes paid		60,000			
8. Dividends declared ...		20,000			
9. Unappropriated profit ...		57,000			
		$1,060,000			$1,060,000

both debit and credit sides and hence cancel out. Also item 1 on the debit side has been assumed to include cost of services such as transport, electricity, agents' services, etc., which are used in the manufacturing and sale of the products of the company.*

Some of the items on both sides of the account in Table V–1 must be combined with others, and other items must be further broken down in order to fit into an input-output scheme. For example, item 1 on the debit side of the account, which covers all purchases of goods and services from other productive enterprises, must be broken down by industry and by source, either domestic or foreign. An industry is a group of firms or enterprises which performs a similar type of activity such as all firms which produce chemicals. The definition of an industry is to a large extent arbitrary and presents many theoretical and practical problems which will be discussed later. The breakdown for the Acme Cotton Fabric Co. is shown under item A on the debit side of the account in Table V–2 below. There are four industries from which purchases are made. Industry 1 might be chemicals; industry 2 could be cotton ginning; industry 3 might be transportation; and industry 4 could be utilities such as water and electricity.

* This contrasts with Chapter III where purchases were assumed to include only cotton and dye stuffs.

The entry under item B on the debit side of Table V–2 represents purchases from abroad or imports of goods and services.

Items 3 through 9 in Table V–1 represented payments to the primary factors of production, land, labor, and capital. These payments are conventionally termed the value added and have been grouped under item C on the debit side of the account in Table V–2. Value added is broken down into four categories: (1) wages and salaries (payment to labor), (2) rent (payment to land), (3) profit plus interest (capital costs), and (4) depreciation (charges for the consumption of capital). Wages and salaries have been taken from items 2, 3, and 4 on the debit side of Table V–1. They are entered as debit item C–1 in Table V–2. Profit in Table V–2 (debit item C–3) is taken from debit items 5, 7, 8, and 9 of Table V–1. Since there are no rents recorded in Table V–1, zero entry is made in debit item C–2, Table V–2. Depreciation (debit entry C–4 in Table V–2) is taken from item 6 of Table V–1.

The first item on the credit side of Table V–1, sales revenue, must be broken down into sales to other productive organization (sales of intermediate products) on the one hand, and sales to households for consumption, to government, for export, and as investment goods (final sales), on the other hand. It is assumed, of the sales revenue of $1,000,000, $400,000 represents sales to industry 5; $20,000 is sales to industry 6; households purchase $500,000; and $80,000 worth is sent for export. Sales to industries 5 and 6 are entered under A on the credit side in Table V–2 as representing sales of intermediate products. In the case of Acme Cotton Fabric Co., industry 5 might be the clothing industry, and industry 6 could be the furniture industry. Since cotton fabrics are not usually considered to be capital goods, it is assumed that there are no sales for investment purposes. The increase in stocks of finished goods, item 2 on the credit side in Table V–1, amounts to $50,000 and is placed in the inventory investment category on the credit side in Table V–2. Similarly for the increase in stocks of raw material of $10,000. It is conventional to list changes in inventory under investment. If there has been a decrease in the stock of finished goods or inventories it would have been listed as negative investment.

The account shown in Table V–2 does not correspond to any sort of actual account kept by businesses. It is just a convenient way of arranging the various accounts already discussed in order to make the information contained in them useful for constructing an input-output table. The account shown in Table V–2 can be called the *Source and Use Account* since it shows the source of all the various types of inputs to the firm and shows the various uses of the output of the firm. The exact breakdown of the firm's purchases from the various industries and the breakdown of intermediate sales to various industries can, in principle, be determined from the

TABLE V–2

Source and Use Account

DEBIT			CREDIT		
A. *Purchases of Produced Inputs*			A. *Sales of Intermediate Products*		
			1. To industry 5	$400,000	
1. From industry 1 ...	$23,000		2. To industry 6	20,000	
2. From industry 2 ...	458,000				
3. From industry 3 ...	25,000			$420,000	
4. From industry 4 ...	34,000		B. *Final Sales*		
			1. Consumption	$500,000	
	$540,000		2. Government	—	
			3. Export	80,000	
B. *Purchase of Imports* ...	$60,000		4. Fixed investment ...	—	
	$600,000			$580,000	
C. *Value Added*			C. *Inventory Investment*		
1. Wages and salaries ...	$260,000		1. Raw materials ...	$10,000	
2. Rent	—		2. Finished goods ...	50,000	
3. Profit (gross of dividends and taxes) plus interest	140,000			$60,000	
4. Depreciation	60,000				
Total Value Added ...	$460,000				
	$1,060,000			$1,060,000	

daily double-entry bookkeeping accounts kept by businesses which record every sale and purchase of the firm. All other figures in the source and use account can be gleaned from the manufacturing, profit and loss, and unappropriated profits accounts.

Both sides of the sources and use account in Table V–2 add up to the same total, $1,060,000. The items on the debit side fall into two classifications, purchases of produced inputs (A and B) and value added (C). The items falling under the two classifications on the debit side must equal the sum of the items under the three classifications on the credit side of the account, sales of intermediate products, final sales, and inventory investment. This relationship may be expressed in terms of the following equation:

> Payment for produced inputs (including imports) + Value added = Sales of intermediate products + Sales for final uses + Inventory investment.

C. Industry Consolidation

A source and use account as shown in Table V–2 may be compiled for a whole industry by adding up the total for every firm in the industry for each item on both the debit and credit sides of the account. For example, suppose there are five firms in an industry and the amounts which the five firms have purchased from industry 1 are $45,500, $32,000, $104,000, $38,000, and $46,000. The total amount purchased by the five-firm industry from industry 1 is the sum of the amounts purchased by each firm or $265,500. This amount would be entered under purchases of produced inputs from industry 1 in the source and use account for the five-firm industry. Similarly, totals are derived for the industry for every item in the source and use account. Note that firms in an industry may purchase from and sell to other firms in the same industry. If this is the case, the industry account will show a figure on the debit side for intra-industry purchases, and on the credit side for intra-industry sales.

D. The Input-Output Table

Once a source and use account has been constructed for every industry in the economy, it is possible to construct an input-output table such as that shown in Table V–3. The table is divided into four areas by the vertical and horizontal double lines. Each of the four areas is called a quadrant. They are:

(i) Quadrant I. That part of the table which lies above the horizontal double line and to the right of the vertical double line.

(ii) Quadrant II. That part of the table which lies above the horizontal double line and to the left of the vertical double line.

(iii) Quadrant III. That part of the table which lies below the horizontal double line and to the left of the vertical double line.

(iv) Quadrant IV. That part of the table which lies below the horizontal double line and to the right of the vertical double line.

First consider Quadrant II. Each of the seven columns in Quadrant II (numbered 1–7) corresponds to an industry; i.e., there are seven industries represented in the hypothetical input-output table. Similarly, each row of Quadrant II represents one of the seven industries except for the last one which is an import row. The numbers entered in the boxes under any column in Quadrant II are the total purchases of the industry corresponding to that column from all other industries. For example, let column 7 represent the cotton textile industry. Suppose there are 100 firms in the cotton textile industry and that each firm is exactly like the Acme Cotton Fabric Co., Inc., whose source and use account is shown in Table V–2.

TABLE V-3
A Hypothetical Input-Output Table
($ million)

Use \ Source	1	2	3	4	5	6	7	C	G	I	E	FU	TR
1	5	34	0	52	43	20	2.3	35.7	10	5	43	93.7	250
2	0	14	0	0	10	14.5	45.8	101.7	14	0	210	325.7	410
3	0	8	0	20	5.5	13	2.5	28	0	15	28	71	120
4	15	0	22	0	0	30	3.4	16.6	13	10	10	49.6	120
5	0	2	10	0	3	40	0	43	3	20	14	80	135
6	0	0	18	0	0	2	0	85	15	40	105	245	265
7	0	0	0	0	40	2	0	50	0	6	8	64	106
M	30	72	10	12	2.5	15.5	6	205	85	92	0	381	530
W	60	214	40	21	15	80	26	31	195	0	0	226	682
D	40	11	4	5	5	13.7	6	0	0	0	0	0	84.7
R	10	5	0	0	4	0	0	18	5	0	0	23	42
P	90	50	16	10	7	34.3	14	0	0	0	0	0	221.3
VA	200	280	60	36	31	128	46	49	200	0	0	249	1030
TP	250	410	120	120	135	265	106	614	340	188	418	1560	2966

INDUSTRIES

I — II — III — IV

Key to Symbols

Number 1–7 indicate industries 1–7

M: Imports R: Rent TP: Total Sources I: Investment TR: Total Uses

W: Wages and Salaries P: Profit

The purchases of the entire cotton textile industry from industry 1 are 100 times the purchases of the Acme Cotton Fabric Co., Inc., alone which are shown as the first entry on the debit side of the source and use account in Table V–2. Since Acme Cotton Fabric Co., Inc., purchased $23,000 worth of goods and services from industry 1 (see Table V–2), the cotton textile industry purchases from industry 1 are $100 \times \$23,000 = \$2.3$ million. This figure is entered in the first box of column 7. Purchases of the cotton textile industry from industries 2, 3, and 4 are $45.8, $2.5, and $3.4 million, respectively. These figures are determined by multiplying by 100 the entries A–2, A–3, and A–4 on the debit side of the source and use account in Table V–2, and are entered in the second, third, and fourth boxes under column 7 of the input-output table. The cotton textile industry makes no purchases from industries 5 and 6, and hence a zero entry is recorded in the fifth and sixth boxes of column 7. The seventh box in column 7 represents purchases of some firms in industry 7 (the cotton textile industry) from other firms in industry 7. In this case there are so such intra-industry purchases. The second box in column 2, however, has an entry of 14 which shows that firms in industry 2 have made purchases of $14 million from other firms in industry 2. An example of purchases by one or more firms in an industry from other firms in the industry might arise in the case of the steel industry which uses steel products such as nails, wire, beams, angles, etc., as inputs in the manufacture of steel. The row labelled M in Quadrant II shows the imports purchased by each of the industries for use as inputs. The entry 6 in the row corresponding to imports under column 7 shows that $6 million of imports were purchased by the cotton textile industry. This figure is obtained by multiplying the item B on the debit side of the account in Table V–2 by 100.

The first seven rows of Quadrant II show the breakdown for each industry of its sales of intermediate products to other firms. For example, the row labelled 7 shows the sales of intermediate products of the cotton textile industry. Sales to industries 5 and 6 are $40 million and $2 million, respectively. These figures are obtained by multiplying by 100 the first two items on the credit side of the source and use account (Table V–2) and are entered in the fifth and sixth boxes of row 7. The cotton textile industry makes no sales to other industries so all other entries in row 7 with Quadrant II are zero. In general, Quadrant II gives an overall picture of inter-industry transaction, i.e., sales of intermediate products by each industry to all other industries and purchases of produced inputs by each industry from every other industry and from abroad.

Next consider Quadrant III. Each column of Quadrant III corresponds to one of the seven industries just as in Quadrant II. The rows of Quadrant III, however, correspond to different types of payments for primary-factor services (different types of value added). The first row of Quadrant III refers to wages and salaries, the second to depreciation, the third to rent payments, and the fourth to profit plus interest. The fifth row shows total value added by each of the seven industries. The last row of Quadrant III shows the total payments by each of the seven industries for purchases from other firms and for purchases of primary inputs. As an illustration, consider the seventh column of Quadrant III which represents the cotton textile industry. Wage payments are $26 million; depreciation amounts to $6 million; there are no rent payments; and profits plus interest come to $14 million. Again these figures are derived from the debit side of account in Table V-2. Total value added, $46 million, is obtained by adding up wages and salaries, depreciation and interest, rent and profits. Total payments by the cotton textile industry amount to $106 million and include both purchases of produced inputs amounting to $60 million and the $46 million of value added.

The first seven rows of Quadrant I show the disposition of the sales of each of the seven industries among the four types of final use, consumption, government, investment, and export. The last row of Quadrant I is labelled M and gives an account of the disposition of imports for direct final use by households for consumption purposes, by government, and for purposes of investment. The column labelled FU in Quadrant I gives the total final uses of the products of each of the seven industries and the total of imports for final use. The last column of Quadrant I shows the total uses of each of the seven industries which are comprised of sales for intermediate use and sales for final use plus inventory investment. The last entry of the row labelled M shows total imports whether for use as inputs by business or for final use. Examination of the seventh row of Quadrant I shows that final uses of the product of the cotton textile industry amount to $50 million for consumption, $8 million for export, and $6 million inventory accumulation. Again, these figures are derived from items B and C on the credit side of the source and use account in Table V-2 as discussed above.

Quadrant IV shows direct purchases of primary factors for final use. The first column, labelled C, in Quadrant IV shows purchases of labor by households (say payments for domestic help) of $31 million in the first box, and rent payments of $18 million by households in the third box. The total value added by households, shown in the next to last box of the column labelled C, is the sum of wage and rent payments by households and amounts to $49 million. The column labelled G in Quadrant IV shows the purchases of labor ($195 million), and rent payments ($5 million) by government. The total value added by government from direct purchases of primary factors is the total of these two amounts, $200 million, and is entered in the next to last box of the government column. The column labelled FU in Quadrant IV shows the total of each type of direct primary factor purchase of government and by households. The first box in Quadrant IV in column FU shows total wages and salaries ($226 million) paid and the third indicates total rent payments ($23 million) by government and households. The next to last box of the FU column gives the sum of wages, salaries, and rents paid by government and households. The very last row (TP) in Quadrant IV gives total consumption expenditures in the first box, total government expenditures in the second box, total investment in the third box, and total exports in the fourth box. Each of these figures is determined by adding up all the entries in the column above except for the next to last entry in the column. The last box of the FU column shows total expenditure for final use of $1,560 million. This figure is obtained in two ways: (1) It is obtained as the sum of the previous four TP-row entries which show total consumption expenditure, total government purchases, total investment, and total exports; (2) it is also the sum of all the entries of the FU column above the last two entries. The last column (TR) in Quadrant IV gives total wage payments by all industries, households, and government in the first box; total depreciation in the second box; total rents in the third box; and total profits plus interest in the fourth box. The next to last box of the last column gives the total of all wages, rents, profits (plus interest), and depreciation. The last box of the last column gives total transactions which include all purchases of intermediate goods plus all purchases for final use by all seven industries, all households, and government. It is the sum of all entries of the last column of the input-output table except for the last two entries, and it is the sum across the bottom row (except for the last two entries).

The last row (labelled TP) and the last column (labelled TR) are especially important. Each entry in the last row is the sum of all entries above the next to last row in its column. Each entry in the last column is the sum of all entries in its row to the left of the next to last column. Note that the first seven entries of the last column are exactly equal to the first seven entries of the last row. The reason for the equality is simply that for each industry, total uses equal total sources (illustrated in Table V–2 for industry seven). That is, total production equals total costs. For example, the entry in the last row for column 7 is $106 million. This is the sum of all entries in the seventh column above the next to last row, namely $2.3 million of purchases from industry 1, plus $45.8 million of purchases from industry 2, plus $2.5 million of purchases from industry 3, plus purchases of $3.4 million from industry 4, plus purchases of $6 million of imports, plus payments of $26 million, in wages and salaries, plus depreciation accrued equal to $6 million, and plus $14 million in profits, all for industry 7. These figures, as shown above, may be obtained from the debit side of the account in Table V–2 by multiplying each entry by 100. Now the number of the last box of the seventh row is also $106 million, the same as the entry in the last box of the seventh column. This figure is obtained by adding the entries of the seventh row to the left of the next to last column, namely $40 million of sales to industry 5, $2 million of sales to industry 6, $50 million of sales for consumption purposes, $8 million worth of exports, and $6 million in investment. These figures are all obtained from the credit side of the account in Table V–2 by multiplying each item by 100. Since the figures in the seventh *column* are derived from the entries on the *debit* side of the account in Table V–2, and since the figures in the seventh *row* are derived from the entries on the *credit* side of the same account it is no wonder that each adds to the same total of $106 million. They balance for the same reason that accounts must balance. Similarly, every one of the other six columns corresponding to an industry is in effect a representation of the debit side of a source and use account for the industry. Every row corresponding to an industry is a representation of the credit side of the industry source and use account.

To sum up, Quadrant I shows how the output of each industry (and imports) are distributed among the various types of final uses. Quadrant II is a summary of the sales of intermediate products by each industry to other industries and of the purchases of each industry from other industries and from abroad. Quadrant III above the TP row shows the value added by each industry and the breakdown into different primary factor shares of this value added. Quadrant IV (above row TP and to the left of column TR) shows the direct purchases of different types of primary inputs by government and households. Quadrant I could be called the final use quadrant, Quadrant II the inter-industry flow quadrant, Quadrant II the value added quadrant, and Quadrant IV the direct purchases quadrant.

E. The Colombia Input-Output Table of the Manufacturing Sector

The compilation of an actual input-output table often involves many compromises, because of the limited availability of data. To illustrate some adjustments that may be made in moving from the theoretical input-output Table V–3 to a concrete matrix for a less-developed country, an actual input-output table of the manufacturing sector of Colombia, Table V–4, will be examined.* Let us note some general points of difference between the hypothetical matrix (Table V–3) and the Colombian table.

First, note that the Colombian table is not complete. The table provides complete inter-industry flows only for the industries in the manufacturing sector of the economy. The transport and distribution sectors are not

* The figures in Table V–4 are an aggregation of the original matrix and *they should not be quoted* without reference to their source.

explicitly included at all. Agriculture and livestock, and mining are considered only insofar as they supply raw materials to manufacturing industries. Their purchases of inputs and the distribution of the final goods they produce are not analyzed in detail.

The exclusion in the Colombian table of non-manufacturing sectors—mainly transport and trade—results in over-estimation of sales of domestically produced intermediate products. For example, the foodstuffs industry (column 3) purchases domestically 10.8 million pesos of inputs from the textile industry (row 6) but this sum includes transport and distribution costs. Therefore, the sales of the textile industry of 10.8 million pesos is over-estimated because they include sales actually made by the transport and distribution sectors which are not contained in the Colombian table. In addition, the over-estimation of the domestic sales of intermediate goods tends to produce under-estimates of sales for final uses. The value of domestically produced final goods for each industry is determined by deducting intermediate sales at market prices from the total value of production at ex-factory prices. For example, the total value of domestic production by the textile industry (column 24 and column 25, row 6) in the Colombian table is 480.3 million pesos. Subtracting from this total the sum of the over-estimated domestic intermediate textile sales, we obtain a residual of 317.3 million pesos (column 24, row 6) which is an under-estimate of final sales.

The second important difference between the hypothetical matrix and the Colombian table is the treatment of imports in the latter. It is often desirable in less-developed countries to show imports in considerable detail. Quadrant II of the Colombian matrix details inter-industrial transactions in both domestic and imported products and a similar classification is shown for final demand in column 25 of Quadrant I. The classification of imported final goods in column 25 of Quadrant I enables one to analyze changes in final demand of a given industry on the basis of a breakdown into demand supplied through imports and that supplied through domestic production. The former would have little effect on intermediate demand (except on demand for certain services). The listing of imported intermediate goods by industry of origin in Quadrant II provides the possibility of analyzing the effects of a policy of import substitution of intermediate goods on inter-industry flows. Note that the total value of imported inputs in row 20 is generally greater than the sum of imported inputs in rows 1 through 18. The import entries in rows 1 through 18 are valued at prices in the country of origin to facilitate an analysis of the effects of import substitution. The total figures in row 20 are valued at prices at the point of destination which include transport and distribution costs associated with the process of importation.

TABLE V–4

Colombia Input–Output Table of the Manufacturing Sector, 1953

RAW MATERIALS AND INTERMEDIATE PRODUCTS

(Million Pesos) Producer Industry		Consumer Industry	Foodstuffs	Beverages	Tobacco	Textiles	Footwear and Clothing	Wood and Cork
			3	4	5	6	7	8
1. Agricultural and Livestock Production	Domestic		1,188.1	37.3	30.6	60.9	11.7	9.2
	Imports		34.9	9.0	0.3	36.5	—	—
2. Mining	Domestic		0.8	—	0.1	0.1	—	—
	Imports		0.1	—	—	—	—	—
3. Foodstuffs	Domestic		97.7	15.3	—	—	—	—
	Imports		12.5	0.2	—	—	—	—
4. Beverages	Domestic		—	37.8	—	—	—	—
	Imports		—	6.2	—	—	—	—
5. Tobacco	Domestic		—	—	—	—	—	—
	Imports		—	—	—	—	—	—
6. Textiles	Domestic		10.8	2.1	0.1	16.7	115.8	—
	Imports		0.2	—	—	19.8	10.7	—
7. Footwear and Clothing	Domestic		—	—	—	—	—	—
	Imports		—	—	—	—	—	—
8. Wood and Cork	Domestic		0.3	0.6	0.8	—	1.0	16.6
	Imports		—	—	—	—	0.1	—
9. Wooden Furniture	Domestic		—	—	—	—	—	—
	Imports		—	—	—	—	—	—
10. Pulp and Paper	Domestic		7.8	—	0.6	0.7	0.5	—
	Imports		0.6	0.1	1.9	—	0.2	—
11. Printing and Engraving, etc.	Domestic		0.4	1.3	2.6	1.2	—	—
	Imports		—	—	—	—	—	—
12. Leather	Domestic		—	—	—	—	50.2	—
	Imports		—	—	—	—	3.0	—
13. Rubber	Domestic		—	—	—	—	1.5	—
	Imports		—	—	—	—	—	—
14. Chemicals	Domestic		3.8	2.1	—	40.3	0.8	0.1
	Imports		6.9	5.2	0.5	17.1	0.2	—
15. Petroleum Derivatives and Coal	Domestic		—	—	—	—	—	—
	Imports		—	—	—	—	—	—
16. Cement, Ceramics, Glass, etc.	Domestic		0.1	8.2	—	—	—	—
	Imports		0.1	0.5	—	—	—	—
17. Mechanical and Metallurgical	Domestic		0.8	6.9	—	—	1.0	0.1
	Imports		1.6	5.2	0.8	—	0.5	0.7
18. Other Industries	Domestic		0.1	0.2	—	0.4	2.2	—
	Imports		—	0.8	—	—	0.5	0.1
19. Domestic Inputs: Total			1,310.7	111.8	34.8	120.3	184.7	26.0
20. Imported Inputs: Total			118.8	53.1	5.9	118.0	30.5	1.8
21. Fuel and Energy			14.9	10.3	0.2	8.4	0.8	0.6
22. Value Added			287.4	303.8	55.8	233.6	145.6	21.0
23. Gross Value of Production			1,731.7	479.0	96.7	480.3	361.6	49.4

TABLE V–4 (*continued*)

Colombia Input–Output Table of the Manufacturing Sector, 1953

RAW MATERIALS AND INTERMEDIATE PRODUCTS *continued*

	Wooden Furniture	Paper	Printed Matter	Leather	Rubber	Chemicals	Petroleum Derivatives and Coal	Cement, Ceramics and Glass	Metallurgic Industries	Other Industries
	9	10	11	12	13	14	15	16	17	18
1.	0.5	0.2	—	26.4	1.4	12.7	—	—	0.1	—
	—	—	—	—	5.9	2.9	—	—	—	—
2.	—	—	—	—	—	4.1	62.8	17.2	0.1	—
	—	—	—	—	0.1	0.5	—	4.3	—	—
3.	—	—	—	—	—	0.6	—	—	—	—
	—	—	—	—	—	0.1	—	—	—	—
4.	—	—	—	—	—	1.6	—	—	—	—
5.	—	—	—	—	—	—	—	—	—	—
6.	0.4	0.3	0.1	1.1	3.2	0.2	—	—	0.1	—
	0.5	0.3	0.1	0.1	4.6	0.4	—	—	—	—
7.	—	—	—	—	—	—	—	—	—	—
8.	13.1	—	—	—	—	2.0	—	0.4	2.6	—
	—	—	—	—	—	—	—	0.2	0.5	—
9.	—	—	—	0.2	—	—	—	—	—	—
10.	—	1.3	10.7	0.1	—	2.8	—	4.9	1.5	—
	—	5.9	16.9	—	—	2.3	—	0.3	0.3	—
11.	—	—	—	—	—	1.3	—	—	—	—
12.	0.6	—	—	9.0	0.1	—	—	—	—	—
	—	—	—	0.1	—	—	—	—	—	—
13.	—	—	—	—	0.2	0.1	—	—	0.3	—
	—	—	—	2.5	0.5	—	—	—	0.4	—
14.	0.6	0.3	—	4.0	0.1	9.6	—	4.4	1.2	—
	0.2	0.4	1.6	—	1.4	20.2	0.2	1.8	1.7	—
15.	—	—	—	—	—	0.5	—	—	0.1	—
	—	—	—	—	—	4.8	—	—	—	—
16.	0.3	—	—	—	—	1.8	—	5.9	—	—
	—	—	—	—	—	3.7	—	1.7	—	—
17.	0.7	0.1	0.1	0.5	—	1.5	—	—	0.2	—
	0.5	0.1	0.4	0.4	0.3	0.4	—	—	7.9	—
18.	—	—	0.1	0.3	0.6	0.7	—	1.5	0.3	6.4
	0.1	0.1	0.3	0.9	0.9	0.6	—	0.1	1.8	3.0
19.	16.2	2.2	1.3	41.6	5.6	39.4	63.0	34.3	14.6	6.4
20.	2.7	10.3	27.0	9.6	21.0	54.5	0.3	13.0	60.2	5.3
21.	0.3	1.5	0.6	0.8	1.1	4.8	1.1	16.4	3.5	0.5
22.	26.6	16.4	42.3	31.8	34.9	108.5	16.8	114.0	95.2	17.6
23.	45.8	30.4	71.2	83.8	62.6	207.0	81.2	177.7	173.5	29.8

TABLE V–4 (*continued*)

Colombia Input–Output Table of the Manufacturing Sector, 1953

SALES TO FINAL DEMAND SECTORS

	Exports	Capital Goods	Durable Consumer Goods	Non-Durable Consumer Goods	Fuels and Lubricants	Total Final Use	Imports of Final Goods	Availability: Domestic Production plus Imports less Exports
	19	20	21	22	23	24	25	26
1. Agricultural and Livestock Production								
2. Mining								
3. Foodstuffs	806.0	—	—	797.8	—	1,603.8	127.9	925.7
	—	—	—	11.8	—	11.8	12.8	24.6
4. Beverages	—	—	—	437.3	—	437.3	41.7	479.0
	—	—	—	7.2	—	7.2	6.2	13.4
5. Tobacco	—	—	—	96.7	—	96.7	—	96.7
	—	—	—	2.7	—	2.7	—	2.7
6. Textiles	2.1	—	—	315.2	—	317.3	163.0	478.2
	—	0.6	0.3	11.0	—	11.9	36.8	48.7
7. Footwear and Clothing	0.4	—	—	361.2	—	361.6	—	361.2
	—	—	—	3.2	—	3.2	—	3.2
8. Wood and Cork	0.1	7.2	—	3.0	—	10.3	39.1	49.2
	—	0.5	0.8	2.0	—	3.3	0.8	7.1
9. Wooden Furniture	—	10.8	35.0	—	—	45.8	—	45.8
	—	—	—	—	—	—	—	—
10. Pulp and Paper	—	—	0.5	8.7	—	9.2	21.2	30.4
	—	0.3	0.4	3.5	—	4.2	28.6	32.8
11. Printing and Engraving, etc.	—	—	4.0	60.2	—	64.2	7.0	71.1
	—	—	1.1	2.9	—	4.0	0.1	4.0
12. Leather	3.1	1.0	19.7	—	—	23.8	60.0	80.7
	—	0.4	—	0.8	—	1.2	3.2	4.4
13. Rubber	—	31.4	13.0	16.0	—	60.4	2.2	62.6
	—	6.2	2.2	2.2	—	10.5	0.9	11.4
14. Chemicals	0.5	11.3	—	125.7	—	137.5	69.5	206.5
	—	5.7	1.2	40.0	—	46.9	74.8	121.6
15. Petroleum Derivatives and Coal ...	0.7	—	—	—	79.9	80.6	0.6	80.5
	—	—	—	—	57.2	57.2	4.8	62.1
16. Cement, Ceramics, Glass, etc. ...	1.3	140.4	19.7	—	—	161.4	16.3	176.4
	—	8.4	7.7	0.7	—	16.9	6.3	23.1
17. Mechanical and Metallurgical ...	0.4	115.8	37.4	0.3	—	153.9	19.6	173.1
	—	501.0	98.1	4.4	—	603.5	51.8	655.3
18. Other Industries	—	—	—	16.4	—	16.4	13.4	29.8
	—	1.4	15.1	5.1	—	21.6	9.8	31.4
19. Domestic Inputs: Total	814.6	317.9	129.3	2,238.5	79.9	3,580.2	581.5	3,346.9
20. Imported Inputs: Total	—	661.8	208.7	190.7	107.2	1,168.3	559.7	1,558.2
21. Fuel and Energy	—	—	—	—	—	—	—	—

Source: United Nations Economic Commission for Latin America, *Analysis and Projections of Economic Development III: The Economic Development of Columbia*, Geneva, United Nations Department of Economic and Social Affairs, 1957, pp. 242–45.

A third general difference in the Colombian matrix is the treatment of the fuels sector. Sales by the industry, petroleum derivatives and coal (row 15), include only products utilized directly as raw materials; those used as fuels or lubricants are excluded. Final sales of fuels and lubricants are in a special column (column 23). Fuels and lubricants purchased as intermediate goods are allocated to a special row, fuel and energy consumption, (row 21). In this row, no distinction is made between imported and domestic products. There is no justification for this treatment other than purely practical reasons derived from shortage of data.

Note that the Colombian table does not include a government final demand column. Government purchases are allocated to the other final demand columns.

Finally, value added is not broken down into its various components. The reason for this treatment is the lack of reliable data on wages, salaries, and profits. Value added is estimated as a residual. That is, total purchases; domestic inputs (row 19) plus intermediate imports (row 20), plus fuel and energy consumption (row 21), are subtracted from gross production (row 23), to obtain value added (row 22).

In summary, an actual input-output table may differ in some respects from a theoretical matrix (Table V–3). However, actual tables all follow the same basic rules of accounting. In using input-output tables for planning purposes, their limitations must be kept in mind. Many of the entries are often derived from various sources, some or all of which contain very wide margins of error.

VI

USING AN INPUT-OUTPUT TABLE

A. Aggregation

As mentioned in the last chapter, input-output analysis has two major uses in planning. The first is to help determine the consistency of a plan, that is to determine whether the requirements of primary factors and other inputs are within the limits of the amounts available. The second is to aid in choosing among various investment projects. Before the planner begins to construct an input-output table, he must make the decision as to what degree and type of aggregation or consolidation of accounts is desirable. That is, he must decide on the number of industrial classifications and the way in which various enterprises are to be grouped under these classifications. The decision must be based on many elements, among them the simplicity or complexity of the table which is desired, the form in which information used to construct the table is available, type of primary factors or inputs which are likely to be scarce, the industries which are the most crucial in determining the general level of economic activity, and the way in which industrial groupings may or may not cause the basic assumptions of input-output analysis to be violated. The first part of this chapter will involve a brief discussion of some of these problems. Some examples of the way in which calculations of input requirements are performed will follow.

1. Degree of Aggregation

At the one extreme, complete aggregation or consolidation of the accounts of all productive enterprises would result in an input-output table which was merely a statement of the way in which the total output of the productive sector was disposed among the various uses, consumption, government, investment, and export, and the way in which factor payments were distributed among wages, rents, depreciation, and profits. No information on intermediate product flows or inter-industry purchases would be provided.* At the other extreme each firm could be classified as a separate economic activity and given its own industrial classification. The resulting input-output table would give a complete picture of inter-industry flows but would clearly produce confusion by its sheer complexity. The problem then is to determine the degree of aggregation which will provide the best balance between large amounts of information on the one hand and simplicity of the table on the other.

2. *Type of Aggregation*

Up to this point, the discussion has centered around a basic unit of production called the firm. In actuality a firm may be a very large corporate entity engaged in the production of a multitude of different items, using a different technology and different input combinations in the production of each. It will be clear from what follows that the planner will often be concerned with the firm itself only if that firm engages in the production of a very narrow range of products which are either close substitutes or have similar production technologies. In many other instances he may want to limit his attention to one plant or factory of a multi-plant firm or even one section of a very large diversified plant. In any case he is more likely to be concerned with the *establishment* as distinguished from the *firm*, the establishment being defined roughly as a single firm or part of a firm that produces only the narrow range of products mentioned above. An *industry* is normally a group of establishments engaged in supplying goods or services that are similar in nature and for which a common output measure is available. In some instances, however, it may be desirable to combine establishments which produce quite different commodities under the same industry classification. Several rules are useful as guidelines in performing these groupings:

   (i) *The Rule of Exclusive Use.* This rule allows aggregation of two establishments one of which is the exclusive user of the product of the other. For example, one might combine oil refining and crude oil production or sugar cane production and sugar manufacture.
   (ii) *The Rule of Identical Input Structure.* This rule permits aggregation of two or more establishments which have similar input structures,

---

* This extreme consolidation produces, in effect, the national accounts discussed in Chapters IX *et. seq.*

i.e., whose purchases of each type of input are the same proportion of the total value of production.

(iii) *The Rule of Demand Complementarity.* This rule allows aggregation of two or more establishments if the demands for their products rise and fall together.

3. *Aggregation and Sources of Data*

Industrial classification and the degree of aggregation are to a large extent dependent on the statistical sources available. The most useful sources, of course, are the industrial census, the census of agriculture, and the census of distribution, provided that each census has been taken in such a manner as to give sufficient detail on sources of inputs. The census itself usually provides a convenient industrial classification. Although this classification may not be ideal from other points of view, it may be extremely difficult to reclassify on the basis of the information which is provided in the census itself. In some instances, census data may be combined with engineering data on the structure of inputs, and information on output and input structure provided through direct inquiries; trade publications; governmental reports in publications which give sources of tax revenue, especially the income tax, excise taxes, and other indirect taxes; and through other publications. For some industries, information from sources other than the census will be in very great detail. This may be true particularly if the industry is large, and there is a large degree of government concern about the industry, either because prices are controlled, government has a financial stake in the industry, the industry is heavily taxed or subsidized, or the industry has such a significant impact on the whole economy or in a particular area that governmental officials regard detailed information about it as necessary to the formulation of cogent public policies. If a great deal of supplementary information is available, then the industrial classification can be much finer. In those areas of economy where detailed information is lacking, broader industrial groupings will be necessary.

4. *Aggregation and the Purpose of the Analysis*

The final industrial grouping must also be related to the particular problems for which the analysis is being conducted. In general the planner will most likely want to set up a separate industrial classification for those industries:

(i) which because of their size or type of activity play an important role in formulating public policy;

(ii) for which the government has a substantial financial interest;

(iii) which are major sources of tax revenue;

(iv) which are expected to be the crucial industries which conceivably could put a serious constraint on the maximum attainable rate of growth.

Any one of the above factors may be important depending on the purpose of the analysis and the particular country in which the analysis is being applied.

B. Fixed Factor Proportions

One of the most crucial assumptions of the theory of input-output analysis is that input proportions are fixed.* That is, if labor inputs are valued at one fifth of total output for a particular industry in the past, then generally it is assumed that this will be true in the future. Whether the assumption of fixed input proportions is justified or not depends on several other conditions being satisfied. Whether these other conditions are satisfied or not depends, in part, on the degree and type of aggregation.

First, it must be true that relative input price changes cause very little substitution of one input for another. This means either that price changes must be sufficiently small so that there is little substitution, or that the relative proportions of different inputs are fixed by technological considerations. A very fine classification of industries will result in closely substitutable produced inputs being put into different industrial categories and would more likely result in price changes causing the output of one industry to be substituted for that of another in the input combination of a third. Broader aggregation on the other hand is likely to result in close substitutes being grouped into one industrial classification, so that there would be less chance of significant substitution of the produced inputs of various industries.

Secondly, it must be assumed that there is no significant excess capacity within any industry. With excess capacity or very large inventories of certain inputs, it may be possible for output to be increased without proportional increases in all inputs because present facilities could be worked more intensively or stocks of materials could be depleted. A large degree of aggregation would mean that excess stocks of inputs by some establishments would tend to be cancelled out by depleted stocks of other establishments.

Thirdly, indivisibilities are neglected. It is assumed that it is not necessary, at certain output levels, to increase the amounts of some factors by unusually large amounts for small increases in output, the new level of input sufficing over a range of outputs. Again a greater degree of aggrega-

* Fixed factor proportions are crucial to most of the theory of input-output. Variable factor proportions may be introduced in practical applications, but the factor proportions can vary only a finite number of times which implies fixed factor proportions for certain ranges of output.

tion will tend to cancel out errors introduced by indivisibilities. Some firms will be in the position of having just hired the specified increase of an indivisible input necessary to increase output, and will be able to undergo a certain amount of expansion without further purchases of that input while other firms will need to hire the specified amount for small increase in output. On the average, the amount hired on the indivisible input for a given expansion of the industry will tend to be more proportional to the increase in output if there are a large number of establishments in the industry.

Fourthly, the assumption of fixed factor proportions ignores technical change. The greater the degree of aggregation, the less likely it is that a technical innovation by a single enterprise will significantly change the input structure of the industry.

Fifthly, it must be assumed that there are no differences in technology among different firms, or if technology does differ among firms then the right combination of firms take part in any expansion of the industry so that the effects of different technologies cancel out and factor proportions remain unchanged. The broader the industrial classification, the more likely it is that the effects of different technologies will cancel out. Note, however, that finer classification could allow less room for differences in technology in the first place.

Sixthly, it must be true that there are no significant economies or diseconomies of scale, either internal to the firm or the industry or external to the industry. A broad aggregation means that economies internal to *firms* would tend to cancel out. Aggregation, however, will have little effect on economies which are external to the firm but internal or external to the *industry*.

Finally, it must be considered that depending on the degree of aggregation, each industrial classification will cover a range of different products. Either it should be assumed that each product within the industry classification has the same input structure or that an expansion of the industry results in an equi-proportionate increase in all products within the classification. In this case, the degree of aggregation is a two edged sword. On the one hand a very fine industrial classification would tend to guarantee a homogeneous input structure. Greater aggregation, however, would allow for increased possibilities of the cancellation of distorting effects.

These assumptions are justified or not depending on the errors which will be tolerated in any estimate of input requirements. If the assumptions are violated in a crucial way, however, all is not lost, since in many cases it is possible to adapt the input-output table to take care of changes in the ratio of purchases of any factor to the value of output. The discussion in this chapter will proceed on the basis of an assumption of fixed factor proportions for the sake of simplicity.

C. Determining Fixed Factor Proportions

The usual way of estimating fixed factor proportions for input-output analysis may be illustrated by using the hypothetical input-output model in Table V–3. The first seven entries in the last row of the table are the respective total values of output for each of the seven industries in the economy. The ratio of purchased inputs to total value of output for any one industry is calculated by dividing the first seven entries of the *column* representing that industry by total output, the last entry in that column. The ratios of purchases of imports (M), wage payments (W), profits, interest and depreciation (P + D), and rents (R) to total value of production for any industry are determined by dividing the eighth through twelfth entries of the column by total output. The result of performing these operations for all seven industries is shown in Table VI–1. (Note that profits, interest, and depreciation have been consolidated.) The entry of .02 in the first column and first row of the Table VI–1 is obtained by dividing the entry in the first row and first column of Table V–3, namely 5, by the last entry in the first column of the Table V–3, namely, 250. The fourth entry of the first column in Table VI–1 is obtained by dividing the fourth entry in the first column of Table V–3, namely 15, by the last entry in the first column of Table V–3, namely 250. Similar operations were performed to obtain all the other entries in Table VI–1.

The entries in any column of Table VI–1 show the number of dollars of purchases of the output of each industry (or the number of dollars paid in wages, capital costs or rents) *per* dollar of output for the industry represented by that column. For example, the entries in column 3 indicate that industry 3 makes no purchases from industries 1, 2, and 3; but for every dollar of output, industry 3 incurs .18 dollars of purchases from industry 4, .08 dollars of purchases from industry 5, .15 dollars of purchases from industry 6, no purchases from industry 7, .08 dollars of purchases of imports, .33 dollars of payments in wages, and .17 dollars of capital costs and no rents. Note that by definition, the column sums in Table VI–1 are all equal to one.

1. *Forward and Backward Linkages*

The entries in Table VI–1 are called factor proportions or alternatively input coefficients. Using these input coefficients, one may determine the capital, labor, or foreign exchange requirements of a particular investment project. Calculating these requirements is not as simple a task as one might expect; for the project in question may have not only direct requirements but indirect requirements as well. For example, suppose the annual output of the textile industry is expected to be $200 million by the end of a five-year

TABLE VI–1

Input Coefficients

Source / Use	1	2	3	4	5	6	7
1	.02	.08	.00	.43	.32	.08	.02
2	.00	.03	.00	.00	.07	.05	.43
3	.00	.02	.00	.17	.04	.05	.02
4	.06	.00	.18	.00	.00	.11	.03
5	.00	.01	.08	.00	.02	.15	.00
6	.00	.00	.15	.00	.00	.01	.00
7	.00	.00	.00	.00	.30	.01	.00
M	.12	.18	.08	.10	.02	.06	.06
W	.24	.52	.33	.17	.11	.30	.25
P+D	.52	.15	.17	.13	.09	.18	.19
R	.04	.01	.00	.00	.03	.00	.00
	1	2	3	4	5	6	7

planning period. The direct annual import requirements may be estimated by looking at the column of Table VI–1 which corresponds to the textile industry (this is still assumed to be column 7) to find the ratio of purchases of imports to the total value of output. For column 7 this ratio is .06 and is found at the intersection of row M and column 7. Then total annual *direct* import requirements amount to .06 multiplied by the expected output of the textile industry or .06 × $200 million = $12 million. In addition to the direct import requirements of $12 million, however, one must take into account the indirect import requirements which arise from the fact that the cotton textile industry makes purchases from other industries of produced inputs and that these other industries also have their import requirements. For example, the cotton textile industry certainly uses the services of the transport industry in getting the cotton from the ginnery to the factory, in getting the finished products to consumers and to other firms. The transport industry is a heavy import user in many less-developed countries, especially if fuel and lubricants must be imported.

    The sum of the direct annual import requirements and the indirect annual import requirements gives the total annually recurring import needs of a cotton textile industry which produces $200 million worth of cotton textiles per annum. In addition to the annually recurring import requirements, one must take into account the import content of the investment in plant and equipment which will be required to increase the capacity of the textile industry to $200 million per year. (The investment in plant and equipment is a non-recurrent expense, at least during the useful life of the new plant and equipment.) The import content of the investment will also have a direct and indirect component. While some of the investment goods will be imported directly from abroad, others will be manufactured locally. The import content of the locally manufactured investment goods is regarded as the indirect import content of the investment in the textile industry. The annual indirect import requirements and the indirect import content of the investment in plant and equipment arise from what the economist calls backward linkages. An industry whose purchases from other industries in the economy are a large proportion of the total value of output is said to have good backward linkage. An industry with a great deal of backward linkage is industry 5 as shown in Table VI–1. Its proportion of purchases from other industries is determined by adding up the entries 1 through 4, 6, and 7 of column 5; this comes to .73. That is, 73 per cent of the output of industry 5 is comprised of purchases from other industries in the economy. Imports and value added amount to 25 per cent of the total value of output, while intra-industry purchases account for the remaining 2 per cent. At the other extreme is industry 1 whose purchases from other industries in the economy amount to only 6 per cent of total value of output. Value added and imports comprise 92 per cent and intra-industry purchases 2 per cent of the output of industry 1.

Beyond the import requirements which arise from backward linkages, further import requirements may come about because of forward linkages. Increasing the output of the cotton textile industry may result in an expansion of the industries which use its output. The expansion of these using industries will require direct and indirect imports. The amount of forward linkages is dependent upon the proportion of total output which is sold to other industries rather than for final uses. For example, industry 1 has a great deal of forward linkage although it has very little backward linkage. Its product is sold as an intermediate input to all other industries save number 3. Products of industry 1 constitute 8 per cent of the total inputs of industry 2, 43 per cent of those of industry 4, and so on. Contrast this with the situation of industry 6 which sells its products only to industry 3; its products accounting for 15 per cent of that industry's total inputs. The industry with the least amount of forward linkage in Table VI–1 is industry 6.

Basic industries such as steel, electricity, and mining tend to have a great deal of forward linkage and at the same time very little backward linkage. Some consumer goods industries such as food processing and electrical appliances will have a great deal of backward linkage and not much forward linkage. Industries which produce intermediate goods such as transportation will have much forward linkage and backward linkage as well. Nearly every industry, however, will have both forward and backward linkages to some extent.

D. Approximating Annual Import Requirements

There are two basic methods for calculating the total direct and indirect annual import requirements, the method of successive approximations and the simultaneous equation approach. The method of successive approximations gives a better insight into the nature of backward linkages and will be discussed in this chapter.*

The annual direct requirements for the cotton textile industry when final use demand is $200 million are shown in Table VI–2.

In order to produce the postulated $200 million of output, the textile industry will have to purchase certain quantities of intermediate inputs, of intermediate-use imports and of factor services. The assumption of fixed input coefficients says that these new inputs will be the same proportion of the new total output as were the old inputs of the old level of output. This, then, allows the use of the input coefficient matrix, (Table VI–1) in the calculation of the new required levels of the various inputs. The calculation is shown in Table VI–2 of the intermediate inputs required directly by industry 7 in producing the new output. Thus, for example under the assumption and given conditions, $86 million of the product of industry 2 is required by industry 7 for the production of $200 million of output.

Were the calculation of direct input requirements all that were necessary in tracing the implications of planned outputs, the task would be simple indeed. Note, however, that the new direct input needs of industry 7 involve new output levels for the supplying industries (1, 2, 3, and 4). These new output levels imply, in turn, new input requirements for those industries. New input levels for industries 1 to 4 imply new output (and hence input) levels for their suppliers. The whole process, then is tremendously complex, and will be more so to the extent that more extensive backward linkages exist. In passing from the direct input requirements of industry 7 at its new output level to the total production, import and factor service requirements of the economy in the new situation, the method of successive approximations is used. This technique may at first seem confusing. It should, however, be remembered that nothing more is involved than the postulating of some planned output for one or more industries and then the successive application of the fixed input coefficients on this basis to

* For a treatment of the simultaneous equation technique see the appendix to this chapter.

TABLE VI-2

Direct Requirements of an Annual Output of
$200 Million for Industry 7

Direct Requirements from Industry	$ million		$ million
1	4	=	.02 × 200
2	86	=	.43 × 200
3	4	=	.02 × 200
4	6	=	.03 × 200
5	0	=	.00 × 200
6	0	=	.00 × 200
7	0	=	.00 × 200
Import Requirements	12	=	.06 × 200

determine an approximation to the new total requirements for imports, factor services, etc.

In the interest of concise discussion, terms are adopted to refer to the various states of calculation and to the various sets of requirements obtained. The inputs directly absorbed by industry 7 are called the *direct input* requirements. The input requirements of the industries supplying these direct inputs are termed the *indirect input requirements* for round 1. The input requirements implied, in turn, by the round one indirect requirements become the round 2 indirect requirements. The process is continued as long as is desired, but in the end, the total input requirements created by the new postulated output level are found by adding the direct input requirements to the sums of the indirect input requirements found in each of the rounds. (Note that the process may be carried out to find produced input, import and factor service requirements.) After a large enough number of these rounds have been calculated, the additional indirect input requirements obtained will become smaller and smaller. Given certain assumptions, the total input requirements (direct plus indirect) may be made to approach the correct value to any desired degree of accuracy by calculating enough rounds;* hence the term, *successive approximations*.

The calculation of the input requirements implied by the adoption of a production goal of $200 million for industry 7 will be carried through four rounds in Table VI-3. The first row of round 1 of this table is the set of

* This statement will not be proved.

TABLE VI–3

Calculation of Indirect Requirements for $200 million of Output of Industry 7
($ million)

				Round 1					
Industry		1	2	3	4	5	6	7	
Direct Requirements		4.00	86.00	4.00	6.00	—	—	—	Total
I	1	.08	6.88	.00	2.58	—	—	—	9.54
N	2	.00	2.58	.00	.00	—	—	—	2.58
D	3	.00	1.72	.00	1.02	—	—	—	2.74
I	4	.24	.00	.72	.00	—	—	—	.96
R	5	.00	.86	.32	.00	—	—	—	1.18
E	6	.00	.00	.60	.00	—	—	—	.60
C	7	.00	.00	.00	.00	—	—	—	.00
T	M	.48	1.54	.32	.60	—	—	—	2.94

				Round 2					
Industry		1	2	3	4	5	6	7	
Indirect Requirements from Round 1		9.54	2.58	2.74	.96	1.18	.60	—	Total
I	1	.19	.21	.00	.41	.38	.05	—	1.24
N	2	.00	.08	.00	.00	.08	.03	—	.19
D	3	.00	.05	.00	.16	.05	.03	—	.29
I	4	.57	.00	.49	.00	.00	.07	—	1.13
R	5	.00	.03	.22	.00	.02	.09	—	.36
E	6	.00	.00	.41	.00	.00	.00	—	.41
C	7	.00	.00	.00	.00	.35	.00	—	.35
T	M	1.14	.46	.22	.10	.02	.04	—	1.98

direct requirements as calculated in Table VI–2. Consider, for example, the direct input requirement of output from industry 1 of $4 million, the first entry of the first row of round 1 of Table VI–3. Considering this as an *output* of industry 1, what then are the inputs required for its production? They are, reading down the first column of round 1, $0.8 million of the product of industry 1, $.24 million of the product of industry 4, and $.48 million of imports. These figures are calculated by multiplying the figure at the top of the first column of round 1 by the appropriate input coefficient from the first column of Table VI–1. Each column of round 1 is determined

Calculation of Indirect Requirements for $200 million of Output of Industry 7
($ million) (*continued*)

		Round 3							
Industry		1	2	3	4	5	6	7	
Indirect Requirements from Round 2		1.24	.19	.29	1.13	.36	.41	.35	*Total*
I	1	.02	.02	.00	.49	.12	.03	.01	.69
N	2	.00	.01	.00	.00	.03	.02	.15	.21
D	3	.00	.00	.00	.19	.01	.02	.01	.23
I	4	.07	.00	.05	.00	.00	.05	.01	.18
R	5	.00	.00	.02	.00	.01	.06	.00	.09
E	6	.00	.00	.04	.00	.00	.00	.00	.04
C	7	.00	.00	.00	.00	.11	.00	.00	.11
T	M	.15	.03	.02	.11	.00	.02	.02	.35

		Round 4								
Industry		1	2	3	4	5	6	7		
Indirect Requirements from Round 3		.69	.21	.23	.18	.09	.04	.11	*Total*	*Total All Rounds*
I	1	.01	.02	.00	.08	.03	.00	.00	.14	11.61
N	2	.00	.01	.00	.00	.01	.00	.05	.07	3.05
D	3	.00	.00	.00	.03	.00	.00	.00	.03	3.29
I	4	.04	.00	.04	.00	.00	.00	.00	.08	2.35
R	5	.00	.00	.02	.00	.00	.01	.00	.03	1.66
E	6	.00	.00	.03	.00	.00	.00	.00	.03	1.08
C	7	.00	.00	.00	.00	.03	.00	.00	.03	.49
T	M	.08	.04	.02	.02	.00	.02	.01	.19	5.46

Note: *All Entries rounded to nearest whole number.*

in a similar manner. Then the total indirect requirements of output from each industry for round 1 are found by summing across each row of round 1. These totals are entered in the total column, e.g., the total indirect round 1 requirements of the output of industry 4 is $.96 million. The next step is to take the indirect requirements from the total column of round 1 and enter these in the first row of round 2. The other entries in round 2 are determined by multiplying the figure at the top of each column by the appropriate input coefficient from Table VI-1. The rows are summed to get the total column. The entries in the total column of round 2 are put into the first row of round 3, and so on. The same process is repeated until, as stated above, the total indirect requirements for a particular round become negligible. Depending on the accuracy of the data available and of the information required, the process is carried for a larger or smaller number of rounds. Whenever the process is stopped, the approximate total of indirect requirements for the output of each industry and for imports is the sum of the industry totals for each round. Thus, after 4 rounds in the example, it is determined that total indirect requirements for the output of industry 3 is (approximately) $3.29 million. The total indirect requirements are included in the table in the column headed "total-all rounds." By adding the total indirect requirements to the direct requirements (Table VI–2) the grand total of production of each industry plus total imports required *annually* is obtained. Notice that in the example, the particular linkages existing produce the particular patterns of each round. Thus, the suppliers of inputs to industries 1, 2, 3, and 4 do not include industry 7. Hence, the total indirect requirement for the output of industry 7 in round 1 is zero.

At the end of the approximation process, to find the total import requirements, add the direct import requirements (from Table VI–2) to the total indirect requirements generated in Table VI–3. For industry 7, the total annual direct and indirect import requirement or import content is $12 million + $5.46 million = $17.46 million. Although the direct import content is only 6 per cent of the output of $200 million, the direct and indirect import content is about 8 per cent.

An additional question rising out of this example deals with when to stop; are there any serviceable general rules in this respect? First, experience seems to indicate that reasonable approximations are generally obtainable within 4 rounds of calculation. Second, never *stop* the process after any one of the total indirect requirements increases from one round to the next. Always carry it at least one additional step. For example, observing that indirect requirement for the product of industry 4 increased from round 1 to round 2, one must carry the process at least *through* round 3.

E. Calculating the Import Requirements of Investment

If it is desired by the planners to increase the output of the textile industry from $106 million to $200 million, an additional investment in plant and equipment will most likely be required. The necessary amount of investment depends on the capacity of present plant and equipment. If the capacity of the present textile industry is $120 million of output, then the required investment is the amount necessary to increase capacity by $80 million of output. The capital goods to be used for this investment may be determined from engineering data. Some of the capital goods will be im-

TABLE VI-4

Import Requirements Implied by Investment of $240 Million in Textile Industry

($ million)

	Round 1				Round 2	Round 3	Round 4	Total All Rounds
	1	3	6					
	80.00	30.00	10.00	Total	Total	Total	Total	
1	1.60	.00	.80	2.40	6.57	.78	.55	10.30
2	.00	.00	.50	.50	.56	.61	.16	1.83
3	.00	.00	.50	.50	2.32	.20	.19	3.21
4	4.80	5.40	1.10	11.30	.74	.86	.14	13.04
5	.00	2.40	1.50	3.90	.81	.24	.08	5.03
6	.00	4.50	.10	4.60	.13	.35	.03	5.11
7	.00	.00	.10	.10	1.22	.24	.07	1.63
M	9.60	2.40	.60	12.60	1.92	1.25	.34	16.11

ported and others may be produced domestically. The value of the imported capital goods comprises the direct import requirements of investment. The indirect import requirements of investment are derived from imported inputs in the domestic production of capital goods and may be approximated in a manner similar to that used in calculating the annual indirect import requirements for the new annual output of the industry. First one

TABLE VI-5

Import Requirements for Increase in Annual Textile Output to $200 Million

($ million)

Annual Import Requirements				
Direct	...	...	...	...	12.00
Four Rounds of Indirect	...	...	5.46
				17.46
Investment Import Requirements				
Direct	...	...	...	...	120.00
Four Rounds of Indirect	...	...	16.11
				136.11

calculates the round 1 requirements, then round 2 requirements, and so on.

Suppose the amount of investment required to increase the annual capacity of the cotton textile industry by $80 million is $240 million of which $120 million must be in the form of imported capital goods. The remaining $120 million is assumed to be comprised of purchases of $80 million from industry 1, $30 million from industry 3, and $10 million from industry 6. The calculation of round 1 indirect requirements for imports and intermediate products is shown in Table VI–4. The investment purchases from industries 1, 3, and 6 are given in the first row. The resulting requirements for purchases of imports and of the output of other industries by industry 1 are given in the column 1 (for industry 3 in the second column, etc.). The requirements are determined by multiplying by the appropriate input coefficients as given in Table VI–1. The total first round requirements are given in the last column under round 1 (the "total" column). The last entry in this column is the first round indirect import requirement. The second, third, and fourth round total requirements and the total of four rounds are given in the last 4 columns of Table VI–4. The calculations are not shown, but are exactly analogous to those carried out above.

An estimate of total import requirements including both annual requirements and investment requirements is given in Table VI–5. The direct annual import requirements come from Table VI–2, and the four rounds of indirect annual import requirements from Table VI–3. The investment indirect import requirements are from Table VI–4. Remember that the annual import requirements only recur after the original plant and equipment nears the end of its useful life. Thus the investment requirements only refer to the period during which the investment takes place.

F. Wage Bill and Skilled Labor Requirements

In addition to the annual import requirements, the planner may wish to know the annual wage bill and the annual direct and indirect skilled labor requirements. The skilled labor requirements may be approximated by first calculating the *total* annual labor requirements and then estimating the proportion of the total annual wage bill which represents payments to skilled workers. The calculations already performed in estimating the annual import requirements for a $200 million annual output of the textile industry will be of great help in estimating the labor requirements. The first column of Table VI–6 shows the direct purchases by industry 7, the cotton textile industry, from each of the seven industries in order to produce $200 million of output annually.

The last entry in the first column is the annual wage bill of the cotton textile industry when output is $200 million. This last entry is determined by multiplying $200 million by the input coefficient (.25) for labor found at

TABLE VI–6

Wage Bill for Annual Direct and Indirect Requirements

($ million)

Purchases From Industry	Direct Requirements	Four Rounds of Indirect Requirements	Total Requirements	Wage Bill
1	4.00	11.61	15.61	3.75
2	86.00	3.05	89.05	4.63
3	4.00	3.29	7.29	2.41
4	6.00	2.35	8.35	1.42
5	—	1.66	1.66	.18
6	—	1.08	1.08	.32
7	—	.49	.49	.12
Direct Labor	50.00	x	x	50.00
			Total Wage Bill	62.83

the intersection of column 7 and row W in Table VI–1. It assumes the ratio of wage bill to total output (.25) remains the same. The first six entries of the first column of Table VI–6 are copied directly from Table VI–2. The indirect requirements in the second column are obtained from the last column of Table VI–3 (round 4). Total requirements are the sum of direct and indirect requirements. The total wage bill for each industry producing its required output is given in the final column. For each industry the wage bill is estimated by multiplying the total requirement by the proper input coefficient in row W of Table VI–1. For example, the total wage bill for industry 1 is .24 × $15.61 million = $3.75 million. The coefficient .24 is the first entry of row W in Table VI–1 and is the ratio of wage bill to total output.

The final figure in the last column gives an estimate of the annual direct and indirect labor requirements in terms of the wage bill. A certain proportion of this wage bill represents payments to skilled labor. This proportion may be approximated by the planners by taking the present ratio of skilled labor wages and salaries to the wages of unskilled labor. If 30 per cent of the total wage bill is assumed to be payments to skilled labor then the estimated salary and wage bill of skilled labor is .30 × $62.83 million =

$18.85 million. The actual number of skilled workers required can be estimated by assuming an average wage or salary. Suppose the average salary is assumed to be $7,500. Then the estimated direct and indirect annual skilled labor requirement is about 2,500 workers.

This estimate of 2,500 workers must be regarded at best as a rough guess since the way in which the estimate is calculated depends on several assumptions which may be only roughly correct. As mentioned above it assumed a constant ratio between total wage bill and the total value of output. The ratio between skilled and unskilled wage bills is assumed to remain the same. Finally, the average skilled labor salary can only be approximated and the present average salary may not hold in the future.

The figure of 2,500 skilled laborers is an estimate of the *annual* direct and indirect requirements. This means that in order to produce $200 million of textiles, 2,500 skilled workers must be employed on a continual basis in the economy. Additional skilled labor will be required, however, in order to produce domestically part of the investment goods which will be used to expand the capacity of the textile industry. These workers will only be needed so long as the investment goods are being produced. The requirements of skilled labor for producing the investment goods may be estimated by taking the direct requirements of the investment (from the first row of Table VI–4) and adding to these the indirect requirements of four rounds (the last column of Table VI–4) to get total requirements from each industry. This is shown in the first three columns of Table VI–7. The wage bill of each of the seven industries is shown in the last column of Table VI–7 and is determined by multiplying each entry in the third column by the input coefficients of row W of Table VI–1. The total wage bill arising from domestic production of investment goods is given as the last entry of the fourth column of Table VI–7. Assuming 30 per cent of this is wages and salaries of skilled labor, the skilled labor wage bill would be $12.39 million. Again supposing an average salary of $7,500, the number of skilled laborers required to produce domestically the necessary investment goods is about 1,662. This compares with an annual skilled labor requirement of 2,500 involved in the production of textiles and the required intermediate inputs.

G. Direct and Indirect Requirements of a Final Bill of Goods

Another use of the iterative technique for input-output is that of finding the total direct and indirect requirements of a given "final bill of goods." A final bill of goods is a set of target outputs for each industry for final use, i.e., for consumption, government, investment, and export.

The direct requirements for a hypothetical final bill of goods are calculated in Table VI–8. The final bill of goods has been specified in the first

TABLE VI–7

Wage Bill for Investment Requirements
($ million)

Purchases From Industry	Direct Investment Requirements	Four Rounds Indirect Requirements	Total Requirements	Wage Bill
1	80.00	10.30	90.30	21.67
2	—	1.83	1.83	.95
3	30.00	3.21	33.21	10.96
4	—	13.04	13.04	2.22
5	—	5.03	5.03	.55
6	10.00	5.11	15.11	4.53
7	—	1.63	1.63	.41
			Total Wage Bill	41.29

row of this table. The required purchases from each industry are calculated in the other rows of this table. For example, in order for industry 3 to produce $180 million for final use (the target for industry 3 in the final bill of goods), it must purchase (reading down column 3 of Table VI–8) $32.4 million from industry 4, $14.4 million from industry 5, and $27.0 million from industry 6. These purchases have been determined by multiplying the industry 3 target in the final bill of goods by the appropriate input coefficients from column 3 of Table VI–1. The direct requirements are summed along each row to get the total direct requirements in the last column of Table VI–8.

The indirect requirements of the final bill of goods are calculated in the same manner as the calculations done in Table VI–3 for indirect requirements of $200 million worth of output of the cotton textile industry. The direct requirements are entered in the first row under round 1 and then the first round indirect requirements calculated. As many rounds (iterations) may be computed as is deemed necessary to get a sufficiently good approximation of the total indirect requirements.

This chapter has demonstrated several uses to which an input-output table might be put. The demonstration has been based on the hypothetical table developed in Chapter V, and has been concerned with calculation of

the import and skilled labor requirements implied by a planning decision
to boost the output of the textile industry (industry 7) to $200 million
annually from its current rate of $106 million.

The calculations rested on the assumption of fixed input coefficients
which for the hypothetical model, were displayed in Table VI–1. The
method of successive approximations was used. This was done primarily
because it makes clear the way in which inter-industry linkages extend
requirements for imports and primary factor services beyond the easily
calculated direct requirements of any planned production increase. In
addition, the use of this method made it unnecessary to become involved in
matrix algebra to the extent necessary to present the simultaneous equation
method of applying fixed input coefficients.

The arbitrary nature of the table used in the example indicates that if,
in any economy, sufficient information were available for the construction
of an input-output table, that table might be used in ways similar to those
shown.

TABLE VI–8

Direct Requirements of a Final Bill of Goods
($ million)

Industry	1	2	3	4	5	6	7	Total Direct Require- ments
Final Bill of Goods	375.0	615.0	180.0	180.0	203.0	398.0	159.0	
1	7.5	49.2	.0	77.4	65.0	31.8	3.2	234.1
2	.0	18.5	.0	.0	14.2	19.9	68.4	121.0
3	.0	12.3	.0	30.6	8.1	19.9	3.2	74.1
4	22.5	.0	32.4	.0	.0	43.8	4.8	103.5
5	.0	6.2	14.4	.0	4.1	59.7	.0	84.4
6	.0	.0	27.0	.0	.0	4.0	.0	31.0
7	.0	.0	.0	.0	60.9	4.0	.0	64.9

APPENDIX TO CHAPTER 6

ALGEBRAIC FORMULATION OF INPUT-OUTPUT

In this appendix, we will demonstrate the algebraic formulation of a three industry input-output table. The generalization to an n-industry input-output table is obvious and is left to the reader.

Table VI–A1 shows a three industry input-output table in which the final use columns have been aggregated into one column showing the sum of all final uses (consumption, government, investment, and exports) for each industry. Each of the entries in this schematic input-output table is a letter entry which symbolizes the number entry of an actual input-output table. The notation in the Table VI–A1 should be clear except, perhaps, the notation in parts of the final use (FU) column. M_f represents imports of final goods, W_{hg} and R_{hg} represent wages and rents, respectively, paid by households and government, and VA_{hg} is total value added directly\ by households and government.

Table VI–A2 is a schematic table of input coefficients. Each entry in this table is derived from Table VI-A1 and represents the ratio of payments for various types of inputs to total output. For example, a_{21} is the ratio of payments by industry 1 for intermediate inputs produced by industry 2 to the total value of output of industry 1, i.e.,

$$a_{21} = X_{21}/Z_1. \qquad\qquad\qquad (6\text{–}1)$$

TABLE VI–A1

Schematic Input-Output Table

Use \\ Source	1	2	3	FU	TR
1	X_{11}	X_{12}	X_{13}	F_1	Z_1
2	X_{21}	X_{22}	X_{23}	F_2	Z_2
3	X_{31}	X_{32}	X_{33}	F_3	Z_3
M	M_1	M_2	M_3	M_f	M
W	W_1	W_2	W_3	W_{hg}	W
D	D_1	D_2	D_3	—	D
R	R_1	R_2	R_3	R_{hg}	R
P	P_1	P_2	P_3	—	P
VA	VA_1	VA_2	VA_3	VA_{hg}	VA
TP	Z_1	Z_2	Z_3	Z_f	—

Another example is a_{R2}, the ratio of rent payments by industry 2 to the total value of output of industry 2, i.e.,

$$a_{R2} = R_2/Z_2. \tag{6-2}$$

Each of the other entries in Table VI–A2 may be defined in an analogous fashion.

TABLE VI–A2

Schematic Table of Input Coefficients

Use \\ Source	1	2	3
1	a_{11}	a_{12}	a_{13}
2	a_{21}	a_{22}	a_{23}
3	a_{31}	a_{32}	a_{33}
M	a_{M1}	a_{M2}	a_{M3}
W	a_{W1}	a_{W2}	a_{W3}
D	a_{D1}	a_{D2}	a_{D3}
R	a_{R1}	a_{R2}	a_{R3}
P	a_{P1}	a_{P2}	a_{P3}
VA	a_{VA1}	a_{VA2}	a_{VA3}

Suppose a planner is given a set of final demands for each industry for the last year of a projected five year plan. That is, the target sales by each industry for final uses has been set at F_1^0, F_2^0, and F_3^0 for industries 1, 2, and 3, respectively. The planner may want to ask the question: What is the implication of this set of final demands in terms of the required total outputs (for intermediate use as well as final use) of the three industries? The answer to this question may be determined *approximately* by using the iterative techniques outlined in the text of Chapter VI. The question may be answered *exactly* by using algebraic methods.

Let Z_1^0, Z_2^0, and Z_3^0 be the required total outputs of the three industries which are implied by the given set of final demands. These total outputs may be determined by solving the following set of simultaneous equations:

$$a_{11}Z_1^0 + a_{12}Z_2^0 + a_{13}Z_3^0 + F_1^0 = Z_1^0,$$
$$a_{21}Z_1^0 + a_{22}Z_2^0 + a_{23}Z_3^0 + F_2^0 = Z_2^0, \text{ and} \tag{6-3}$$
$$a_{31}Z_1^0 + a_{32}Z_2^0 + a_{33}Z_3^0 + F_3^0 = Z_3^0,$$

for Z_1^0, Z_2^0, and Z_3^0. These equations are simply an expression of the fact that for each of the three industries

$$\begin{matrix} \text{Intermediate Uses} \\ + \\ \text{Final Uses} \end{matrix} = \begin{matrix} \text{Total} \\ \text{Uses.} \end{matrix}$$

The first three terms on the left hand side of each of the equations in (6-3) represent sales to industries 1, 2, and 3, respectively. The fourth term on the left hand side of each equation is final sales, and the term on the right hand side of each equation is total sales. For example, look at the second equation in (6-3). The first term is intermediate sales by industry 2 to industry 1 which is determined by multiplying the ratio of purchases of industry 2's output to total output of industry 1 (a_{21}) by the total output of industry 1. The second and third terms on the left hand side of the second equation are, of course, purchases by industry 2 from industry 2 and by industry 3 from industry 2, respectively.

In order to solve the equations (6-3), for Z_1^0, Z_2^0, and Z_3^0, they should be rearranged as follows:

$$(1-a_{11})Z_1^0 - a_{12}Z_2^0 - a_{13}Z_3^0 = F_1^0$$
$$a_{21}Z_1^0 + (1-a_{22})Z_2^0 - a_{23}Z_3^0 = F_2^0 \qquad (6-4)$$
$$a_{31}Z_1^0 - a_{32}Z_2^0 + (1-a_{33})Z_3^0 = F_3^0$$

The variables Z_1^0, Z_2^0, and Z_3^0 have been brought over to the left hand side of each of the three equations in (6-4); the variables F_1^0, F_2^0, and F_3^0 to the right hand side; and both sides multiplied by -1. One may use any of the standard techniques for solving simultaneous linear equations to solve the equations (6-4) for Z_1^0, Z_2^0, and Z_3^0, the total outputs of the three industries.*

One may do further algebraic analysis. For example, suppose the planner wishes to get an estimate of total imports. He may use the equation

$$a_{M1}Z_1^0 + a_{M2}Z_2^0 + a_{M3}Z_3^0 + M_f^0 = M^0 \qquad (6-5)$$

This equation expresses the fact that imports by industry plus imports of final goods equals total imports, Z_1^0, Z_2^0, and Z_3^0 have already been solved from the equations (6-4). There are two unknowns in equation (6-5), namely M_f^0 and M^0, imports of final goods and total imports, respectively. If the planner is able to estimate M_f^0 on the basis of various information at his disposal, then M^0, total imports, follows immediately from equation (6-5).

Another example is a situation where the planner wishes to estimate the total wage bill. He may use the equation

$$a_{W1}Z_1^0 + a_{W2}Z_2^0 + a_{W3}Z_3^0 + W_{hg}^0 = W^0. \qquad (6-6)$$

* For a discussion of some of the techniques for solving systems of linear equations, see R. G. D. Allen, *Mathematical Analysis for Economists*, London, Macmillan, 1960, pp. 472-84. One particular method matrix inversion, is discussed briefly below.

This equation expresses the fact that wages paid by industry plus wages paid by households and government equals the total wage bill. The only unknowns in this equation, after Z_1^0, Z_2^0, and Z_3^0, have been solved from the (6–4), are W_{hg}^0 and W^0, wages paid by households and government and the total wage bill, respectively. Wages paid by households and government may be estimated independently and the total wage bill follows immediately from equation (6–6).

The reader ought to be able to specify the equations which might be used in projecting rent, profits, depreciation, and total value added. One must always keep in mind, however, that the use of such projection equations involves an assumption about constant input coefficients.

The matrix inversion method for solving the system of equations (6–4) is of particular interest because of the interpretation of the coefficients of the inverse matrix.* The matrix

$$A = \begin{bmatrix} a_{11} & a_{12} & a_{13} \\ a_{21} & a_{22} & a_{23} \\ a_{31} & a_{32} & a_{33} \end{bmatrix} \tag{6–7}$$

is called the matrix of input coefficients. The matrix

$$I = \begin{bmatrix} 1 & 0 & 0 \\ 0 & 1 & 0 \\ 0 & 0 & 1 \end{bmatrix} \tag{6–8}$$

is called the identity matrix. Equations (6–3) may be written

$$A \cdot Z^0 + F^0 = I \cdot Z^0 \tag{6–9}$$

where

$$Z^0 = \begin{pmatrix} Z_1^0 \\ Z_2^0 \\ Z_3^0 \end{pmatrix} \text{ and } F^0 = \begin{pmatrix} F_1^0 \\ F_2^0 \\ F_3^0 \end{pmatrix}$$

are column vectors of total outputs (Z^0) and final demands (F^0). Equation (6–9) may be rearranged to obtain

$$[I - A] \cdot Z^0 = F^0 \tag{6–10}$$

* For those readers who are unfamiliar with the algebra of matrices and vectors see R. G. D. Allen, *Mathematical Economics*, second edition, London, Macmillan, 1963, pp. 371–402.

which is then equivalent in matrix and vector form of the system of linear equation in (6–4). The total output vector Z^0 may be solved in terms of the given vector F^0 of final demands in terms of the inverse of the matrix $[I-A]$.

$$Z^0 = [I-A]^{-1} \cdot F^0 \tag{6–11}$$

Let us solve for the final bill of goods in Table VI–8 using the input coefficients from Table VI–1. The $[I-A]$ matrix is

$$\begin{bmatrix}
.98 & -.08 & -.00 & -.43 & -.32 & -.08 & -.02 \\
-.00 & .97 & -.00 & -.00 & -.07 & -.05 & -.43 \\
-.00 & -.02 & 1.00 & -.17 & +.04 & +.05 & +.02 \\
-.06 & -.00 & -.18 & 1.00 & +.00 & +.11 & +.03 \\
-.00 & -.01 & -.08 & -.00 & .98 & -.15 & +.00 \\
+.00 & +.00 & +.15 & +.00 & +.00 & .99 & +.00 \\
-.00 & -.00 & -.00 & -.00 & -.30 & -.01 & 1.00
\end{bmatrix} \tag{6–12}$$

The inverse of this matrix is

$$\begin{bmatrix}
1.05 & .09 & .15 & .48 & .38 & .21 & .08 \\
.00 & 1.03 & .03 & .01 & .21 & .09 & .45 \\
.01 & .02 & 1.05 & .18 & .06 & .08 & .04 \\
.07 & .01 & .22 & 1.06 & .04 & .14 & .04 \\
.00 & .01 & .11 & .02 & 1.03 & .16 & .01 \\
.00 & .00 & .16 & .03 & .01 & 1.02 & .01 \\
.00 & .00 & .03 & .01 & .31 & .06 & 1.00
\end{bmatrix} \tag{6–13}$$

The numbers in this inverse matrix leave a special interpretation. Consider the first column of the matrix. This shows the total increased output which is required from all seven industries to obtain an additional dollar of final demand from industry 1 taking into account both the direct and *all* the indirect requirements. Thus, to furnish $1.00 of demand from industry 1, industry 1 itself must produce a total of $1.05 of output; industry 2 must produce $.00; industry 3 must produce $.01; industry 4 must produce $.07; and so on.

To find the total output of all seven industries required to produce the final bill of goods in Table VI–8, we need only multiply the inverse in (6–13) by the column vector representing the final bill of goods, i.e.,

$$\begin{pmatrix} 375.0 \\ 615.0 \\ 180.0 \\ 180.0 \\ 203.0 \\ 398.0 \\ 159.0 \end{pmatrix} \qquad (6\text{--}14)$$

The result of this multiplication is

$$Z_1^0 = 735.7$$

$$Z_2^0 = 792.6$$

$$Z_3^0 = 292.3$$

$$Z_4^0 = 333.5 \qquad (6\text{--}15)$$

$$Z_5^0 = 307.4$$

$$Z_6^0 = 446.3$$

$$Z_7^0 = 255.7$$

These are the total direct and indirect requirements in terms of $ million to produce the final demands (6–14). These figures are more accurate estimates than one could normally obtain by the method of successive approximations discussed in the text of Chapter VI, but the inversion of a matrix with seven columns is extremely tedious and quick approximations may often be obtained by calculating a few rounds of indirect requirements using the method of successive approximations.

VII

A MODIFIED INPUT-OUTPUT TABLE

FOR DEVELOPING COUNTRIES

Dudley Seers has proposed a modified input-output table specially adapted to the use of less-developed countries. The modified format was used to make projections of requirements in Jamaica, Ghana, and Zambia.

The Seers modified version of input-output in many of its aspects is simpler than the tables discussed above because of the lack of data in developing countries and also because of the relative simplicity of a less-developed economy. On the other hand his modified input-output table contains more information on governmental revenues and expenditures and on foreign trade than is usually the case. Government finance is emphasized because of government concern with raising the necessary funds for ambitious development programs. Foreign trade often plays a larger role in less-developed countries, dependent, as they often are, on a rather small range of primary-product exports (agricultural and mineral products) with widely fluctuating prices. A knowledge of the inter-connections between domestic industry and the rest of the world is necessary in order to formulate cogent policies of import substitution.

This chapter will present a thorough discussion of the various rows and columns of the modified input-output table as applied to the Zambia economy. The following chapter includes an explanation of the way in which the modified table can be used to make projections.

A. Industry Rows and Columns

Table VII–1 is a hypothetical modified input-output table for the Zambian economy for the year 1961.* One of the major differences be-

* The figures given in Table VII–1 are *hypothetical* and not actual values. Table VII–1

TABLE VII-1

Hypothetical Input-Output Table for Zambia: 1961

(£ million)	BASIC INPUTS							VALUE ADDED	
	Imports	Import Duties	Electricity and Water	Transport and Communication	Distribution	Other Inputs	Total Inputs	Employees Income	
								Non-African	African
	1	2	3	4	5	6	7	8	9
1. Mining	20.5	0.5	6.5	1.3	0.1	4.1	33.0	21.0	12.2
2. Agriculture	1.2	—	—	0.1	0.3	1.4	3.0	0.8	1.9
3. Food and beverages ...	3.8	0.1	0.1	0.1	—	5.3	9.4	0.7	0.6
4. Textiles	0.8	—	—	—	—	—	0.8	0.1	0.2
5. Metal manufacturing	3.2	0.1	—	0.1	0.2	0.4	4.0	1.5	0.9
6. Other manufacturing	1.2	—	—	0.2	0.1	1.1	2.6	0.9	0.9
7. Construction	8.4	0.2	—	0.6	1.6	3.7	14.5	3.5	3.6
8. Electricity and water	1.3	—	0.9	0.1	0.1	—	2.4	0.5	0.3
9. Transport and communication	1.0	—	—	—	0.1	0.8	1.9	4.1	1.7
10. Distribution	—	—	0.1	2.1	—	1.3	3.5	5.3	1.8
11. Government services	—	—	—	—	—	—	—	7.8	5.4
12. Other services ...	—	—	0.1	—	—	0.6	0.7	4.0	4.3
13. Intermediate products	—	—	−7.7	−4.6	−2.5	−18.7	−33.5	—	—
14. Rest of world ...	−41.4	—	—	—	—	—	−41.4	—	—
15. Government current Account	—	−0.9	—	—	—	—	−0.9	—	—
16. Households: non-African	—	—	—	—	—	—	—	−50.2	—
17. Households: African	—	—	—	—	—	—	—	—	−33.8
18. Savings and investment	—	—	—	—	—	—	—	—	—

tween this table and the hypothetical table presented in Chapter V is the lack of a column for each and every industry which has a row. That is, there are two levels of aggregation. On the one hand, the economy is divided into twelve separate industries and each of these industries is given one of the first twelve rows in Table VII-1. Only three industries, however, have a separate column, utilities (column 3), transport (column 4), and distribution (column 5). The industries which are given rows in the Table VII-1 are not necessarily the industries which would be allocated rows in any developing country. Rather, the availability of data and the importance of an

is based to a large extent on an actual table given in *Report of the UN/ECA/FAO Economy Survey Mission on the Economic Development of Zambia*, Ndola, Falcon Press, 1964, Appendix A, p. vii, but the numbers here have been modified slightly for pedagogical reasons and *should not be quoted as actual figures*.

TABLE VII–1 (continued)

Hypothetical Input-Output Table for Zambia: 1961

| | | VALUE ADDED (cont.) | | | | | | | COMPOSITION OF SUPPLY | |
| | | Mixed Income | | Income Payments | | | | | | |
	Subsistence	Direct Tax	Non-African	African	Home	Abroad	Transfers	Savings and Depreciation	Total Value Added	Gross Output	Imports final (c.i.f.)
	10	11	12	13	14	15	16	17	18	19	20
1.	—	23.5	—	—	2.3	23.1	—	15.1	97.2	130.2	—
2.	20.8	—	2.6	3.8	—	—	—	—	29.9	32.9	0.8
3.	—	0.7	—	—	0.1	0.1	—	1.2	3.4	12.8	10.9
4.	—	—	—	—	—	—	—	—	0.3	1.1	10.1
5.	—	0.5	0.3	0.2	—	—	—	0.5	3.9	7.9	18.2
6.	—	0.3	—	—	—	0.1	—	0.4	2.6	5.2	9.1
7.	—	0.1	0.5	0.5	—	0.1	—	0.4	8.7	23.2	—
8.	—	—	—	—	1.4	1.1	—	1.4	4.7	7.1	1.0
9.	—	0.2	0.3	0.5	0.3	1.5	—	1.9	10.5	12.4	—
10.	—	1.0	2.0	0.6	0.7	0.2	—	2.0	13.6	17.1	—
11.	—	—	—	—	—	—	—	—	13.2	13.2	—
12.	5.2	0.6	4.4	0.3	−1.8	0.4	—	1.1	18.5	19.2	6.6
13.	—	—	—	—	—	—	—	—	—	−33.5	—
14.	—	—	—	—	—	−26.7	+1.6	−3.0	−28.1	−69.5	−56.7
15.	—	−26.9	−2.2	—	−3.2	+0.3	−1.9	+17.0	−16.9	−17.8	—
16.	—	—	−7.9	—	+0.2	−0.2	+0.3	+8.6	−49.2	−49.2	—
17.	−26.0	—	—	−5.9	—	—	—	+5.1	−60.6	−60.6	—
18.	—	—	—	—	—	—	—	−51.7	−51.7	−51.7	—

industry in governmental decision making should dictate the choice of whether an industry should be allocated a separate row. In general, one might say that the same criteria used in Chapter VI in the discussion of aggregation should be used in determining the proper industrial classification for the purpose of allocating rows in the input-output table.

The criteria for allocating a separate column are somewhat different. When there are more industry rows than columns, it is not generally possible to obtain a complete picture of all the flows of intermediate products between all industries. In order to maintain a fairly good idea of the intermediate product flows, however, any industry which makes most of its sales to other industries (produces mostly intermediate products) generally should be allocated a separate column. This is often the case with utilities,

TABLE VII–1 (*continued*)

Hypothetical Input-Output Table for Zambia: 1961

(£ million)	Distribution	Indirect Tax	Total Supply/Demand	Sales to Other Sectors	Exports	Non-Africain	Subsistence	Other African	Government Consumption	Government	Other	Change in
	21	22	23	24	25	26	27	28	29	30	31	
1. Mining	—	—	130.2	−1.4	−113.8	−1.8	—	−0.6	−0.1	—	−5.6	—
2. Agriculture	2.4	—	36.1	−5.8	−4.6	−1.2	−20.8	−1.9	−0.5	—	−0.2	—
3. Food and beverages ...	2.6	2.1	28.4	−0.6	−0.4	−12.2	—	−13.8	−1.2	—	—	—
4. Textiles	2.4	0.6	14.2	—	−0.1	−5.6	—	−8.1	−0.4	—	—	—
5. Metal manufacturing ...	4.3	0.7	31.1	−5.4	−0.2	−5.2	—	−2.0	−0.8	−7.2	−10.2	—
6. Other manufacturing	2.0	0.7	17.0	−3.4	−0.7	−6.3	—	−3.4	−3.3	—	—	—
7. Construction	—	0.1	23.3	−0.9	—	—	—	—	−2.8	−1.0	−18.6	
8. Electricity and water	—	—	8.1	−6.8	—	−1.0	—	—	−0.3	—		
9. Transport and communication	—	0.6	13.0	−4.6	−5.3	−0.7	—	−1.0	−1.4	—	—	
10. Distribution	—	0.2	17.3	−16.2	—	−0.2	—	−0.2	—	—	—	
11. Government services	—	—	13.2	—	—	—	—	—	−13.2	—	—	
12. Other services	—	1.3	27.1	−2.1	—	16.1	−5.2	−3.6	−0.1	—	—	
13. Intermediate products	−13.7	—	−47.2	+47.2	—	—	—	—	—	—	—	
14. Rest of world	—	—	−126.2	—	+125.1	+1.1	—	—	—	—	—	
15. Government current Account...	—	−6.3	−24.1	—	—	—	—	—	+24.1	—	—	
16. Households: non-African	—	—	−49.2	—	—	+49.2	—	—	—	—	—	
17. Households: African	—	—	−60.6	—	—	—	+26.0	+34.6	—	—	—	
18. Savings and investment	—	—	−51.7	—	—	—	—	—	—	+8.2	+34.6	+

COMPOSITION OF SUPPLY (cont.) — *COMPOSITION OF DEMAND* — *Consumption* — *Capital Formation*

transport, and distribution. Thus in Table VII–1 separate columns were allocated to electricity and water, transport and communications, and distribution. Since these industries are *primarily* suppliers of other industries they will be called the intermediate goods industries throughout this chapter and the next. An industry which sells to only one other industry should not be allocated a separate column, but any industry which sells to more than one other industry should be given consideration for a separate column especially if it is suspected that the industry may not be able to grow fast enough to supply other rapidly expanding industries and thus may act as a constraint on development.

There are two reasons for limiting the number of industries which are assigned columns. First, it may be impossible to assign a column to every industry which has a row because of lack of data, or because the data which are available may be so rough and inaccurate that a full-fledged input-output table would be highly unreliable. Second, and more important, the construction of a complete table with all the rows and columns may require unnecessary expenditure of time and manpower. Less-developed economies are often characterized by a lack of complex inter-industry relationships. Further, most of the industries in a less-developed economy produce directly for final uses (usually for either consumption or export) and use mainly primary factors and imports as inputs. The type of industries that one finds are those which produce primary products for exports, which perform simple processing of local agricultural products, and which engage in assembly or final processing of imports such as bicycles and motor cars or oil refining. Because of the lack of inter-industry relationships a table which shows inter-industry transactions in detail may be of little additional benefit.

B. Government Finance

The modified input-output table permits an analysis of government finance by including certain columns which usually are not found in an input-output table. For example, import duties on imports for intermediate use are given a separate column (column 2). Imports are valued before duties are imposed and the duties are entered as a separate item. The direct tax components of profits and wages are entered as separate items in column 11. Indirect taxes on the output of domestic industries for final use and on imports of final-use goods are also given a separate column (column 22). Finally, the government current account is allocated a separate row (row 15). This row shows all receipts by government of taxes and interest on government held securities and all payments by government on current account such as payments for services, payments of interest on government debt, and transfer payments. A receipt by government is a negative entry (a number preceded by a minus sign) in row 15. For example, the second entry of row 15 in Table VII–1 is −0.9. This shows that government received £0.9 million in import duties during the year 1961. Other receipts by government are £26.9 million in direct taxes (shown at the intersection of column 11 and row 15), £2.2 million in mixed income payments (column 12, row 15), £3.2 million in property income (column 14), receipts of £1.9 million in transfer payments (column 16) and £6.3 million in indirect taxes on domestic output and imports of final-use products. A payment by government is a positive entry. The payments by government on current account shown in row 15 are £0.3 million in interest paid abroad (column 15), and £24.1 million for purchases of materials and services (mostly labor) in column 29. The government surplus on current account (total receipts less total expenditures) is also shown as a positive entry (£17.0 million) in column 17.

C. Transactions with the Rest of the World

The crucial role of foreign trade in many under-developed countries makes it desirable to have the table well articulated with regard to transactions with the rest of the world. The predominance of customs revenue as a source of government finance often means that statistics are available to complete that part of the table which refers to foreign trade. There is a separate column for dividends and interest which are paid abroad (column 15) in the modified input-output table. Another novelty of the modified table is column 20 which shows the imports of final-use goods broken down by the industry in which they presumably would have been produced if produced domestically. For example, imports of agricultural products is £0.8 million and this figure is in the second row, the row corresponding to the domestic agricultural sector, of column 20. Column 20 is useful in analyzing the effects of a policy of import substitution. The inclusion of columns 15 and 20 also makes possible an analysis of the transactions between the domestic economy and the rest of the world in row 14. Payments to the rest of the world are entered as negative numbers (a number preceded by a minus sign) while receipts from the rest of the world are positive entries in row 14. Payments to the rest of the world include £41.4 million for imported inputs (column 1), £26.7 million in interest and dividends (column 15), and £56.7 million for imports of final products (column 20). Receipts from the rest of the world are comprised on £125.1 million of payments for exports (column 25), transfer payments of £1.6 million (column 16) and £1.1 million in transferal of funds by expatriates and expenditures by tourists (column 26). The difference between total payments to the rest of the world (£124.8 million) and total payments from the rest of the world (£127.8 million) is called the balance of payments on current account. In this case the balance is negative (receipts exceed payments). This is called a surplus in the balance of payments on current account of £3.0 million and is entered as a negative number in column 17 of row 14.

D. The Inter-Industry Section

The modified input-output Table VII–1 may usefully be divided into four sections: (1) the inter-industry section comprising the first twelve rows and the first seven columns, (2) the value added section comprising the first twelve rows and columns 8 through 18, (3) the composition of supply and composition of demand section comprising the first twelve rows and columns 19 through 32, and (4) the balancing section composed of the last six rows. The inter-industry section is the same as the inter-industry section of our hypothetical input-output table in Chapter V with a few exceptions. The rows show the purchases of inputs of each industry from the various other industries and the columns show the way in which the intermediate sales of each industry are allocated among the various other industries. With the hypothetical input-output table in Chapter V this is reversed. In Table VII–1 imports (column 1) are valued at the borders of the country excluding import duties and the costs of internal transport and distribution in getting the imports to the site of production. Import duties, and distribution costs and transport costs for all inputs incurred by firms in each industry directly and not through internal distribution channels are shown in columns 2, 4, and 5. Purchases by each industry of produced inputs from all industries excluding utilities, transport, and distribution industries are given in column 6. Looking at the construction industry row 7, one sees that the value of imports purchased by the construction industry is £8.4 million of which the import duties resulted in an additional cost of £0.2 million, the value of transport purchased directly is £0.6 million, the costs of distribution of inputs was £1.6 million, and purchases of inputs from all other industries amounted to £3.7 million. The total of all these payments is £14.5 million and this figure is entered in column 7 of the construction row.

E. The Value Added Section

The value added items in the modified input-output table are allocated columns while in the hypothetical input-output table of Chapter V the value added items were given rows. There are several other differences more substantial in nature. Employment income (wages and salaries) is divided into income paid to Africans (column 9) and that paid to non-Africans (column 8). Since the economic behavior of these two groups is often quite different, especially with respect to expenditure patterns, this sort of break-down can be extremely useful in countries with a large expatriate population. A separate value added column is labelled subsistence. Subsistence activity (column 10) is neglected in most well-developed countries but in countries where a large part of the population drives most of its livelihood from subsistence activity, an attempt is usually made to impute a value to subsistence output. It is assumed that the subsistence sector does not make purchases of produced inputs from other industries, and thus all subsistence output is value added, i.e., can be attributed to the use of land, labor, and capital owned by the subsistence producer. Direct taxes on the profits of industrial enterprises are allocated a separate column (column 11). Mixed income may be defined for most purposes to include all profits of unincorporated enterprises (generally small firms) and all rents. Again the division is made between African and non-African recipients. Columns 14 and 15 give distributed profits, interest, and rent payments by incorporated enterprises. They are divided into payments at home and payments abroad. The copper industry in Zambia annually pays a large sum in dividends and royalties abroad as is shown by the very large first entry in column 15. Savings and depreciation (column 17) shows the sum of depreciation and undistributed profits. Row 2 for agriculture shows that non-African agricultural labor and management personnel received £0.8 million; African employment income in agriculture was £1.9 million; the agricultural output of the subsistence sector was imputed a value of £20.8 million; agricultural enterprises paid negligible direct taxes; and rent and profits received by non-Africans was £2.6 million and by Africans was £3.8 million. The total of all these items is total value added (29.9 million) and is entered in column 18 of the agricultural row.

F. Composition of Demand and Supply

The gross output of each industry is the sum of the value of total inputs and total value added. Thus each of the first twelve entries in column 19 is the sum of the corresponding entries in columns 7 and 18 in Table VII–1. The gross output of each industry is valued at the "producer price," i.e., it does not contain expenditures on the distribution of output to the users nor indirect taxes. The distribution costs involved in getting domestic output for final use and imports of final products to users is shown in column 21. Indirect taxes on domestic output and duties on imports of final goods are allocated to column 22. Total supply is the sum of the value of gross output, imports of final goods together with the distribution costs and indirect taxes. This sum is entered in column 23. The way in which the total supply of each industry is allocated among the different uses is shown in the final nine columns. Consumption is broken down into non-African consumption, subsistence consumption and other African consumption. Investment is broken down into real capital formation by government and by private industry and into changes in stocks or inventories.

All items in the consumption of demand section of Table VII–1 are negative entries except possibly in the case of changes in stocks (column 32). The negative sign indicates a receipt on the part of one of the twelve industries. The items in the basic inputs and composition of supply sections are all positive to indicate payments by each of the industries. For example, looking at row 6, other manufacturing, one sees receipts of £3.4 million for intermediate sales, £0.7 million for export sales, £6.3 and £3.4 million for sales to non-African and African households, and £3.3 million for sales to government. Inventories have fallen by £0.1 million which is a positive entry in the last column of row 6. An increase in inventory would be a negative entry. All other entries in row 6 are positive and represent payments for basic factors of production, final imports, distribution, and indirect taxes.

G. The Balancing Section

The last six rows of Table VII–1 represent an innovation in input-output which enables an analysis of the financial impact of any particular pattern of output on the flow of saving and investment, government finance, and the balance of payments. The row which refers to the rest of the world and the row referring to government current account have already been analyzed earlier in this chapter. The intermediate products row 13 gives the total intermediate sales of the utilities industry (column 3), the transport industry (column 4), the distribution industry (the sum of entries in columns 5 and 21), and all other industries combined (column 6). The sum of all these items is entered in column 24, sales to other sectors, of the intermediate product row. The intermediate sales of the utilities industry, the transport industry, and the distribution industry may also be determined from column 24, sales to other sectors. The figures are the 8th, 9th and 10th entries of column 24. Rows 16 and 17 show the payments (positive items) and receipts (negative items) of both African and non-African households. Receipts (income) of non-African households is composed of employment income, mixed income, interest and dividends from abroad, and transfer payments. The payments of non-African households are comprised of direct taxes on income (column 11), interest (column 14), and consumption expenditure (column 26). The difference between receipts (income) and payments (expenditure) is savings. In this case savings of non-African households are positive and are entered as a positive number in column 17. The savings and investment row gives total savings in column 17. It is the sum of all savings and depreciation by each of the thirteen industries (the sum of the first 12 entries in column 17), the government current account budget surplus (column 17, row 15), savings by non-African and African households (column 17, rows 16 and 17), less the balance of payments surplus (column 17, row 14). The way in which savings are allocated among the various types of investment is shown by the last three entries of the savings and investment row.

One of the main features of the rows in Table VII–1 is that, excluding certain columns, if one adds up all the negative items in any given row, the result is equal (in absolute value) to the sum of all the positive items. The entries in columns 7, 18, 19 and 23 are sub-totals and are ignored in adding up the positive or negative items. For example, the negative items in row 16 corresponding to non-African households are employment income (£50.2 million), income from unincorporated enterprises (£7.9 million), and earnings on foreign assets (£0.2 million). The sum of these items is £58.3 million. The positive items are payment of interest (£0.2 million), transfers (£0.3 million), savings and depreciation (£8.6 million), and consumption (£49.2 million). These items also total £58.3 million.

Similarly, one can show that the sum of all negative items is equal (in absolute value) to the sum of all positive items for each *column* of the input-output Table VII–1. A positive item represents a payment and a negative item a receipt. For example, consider column 11, labelled direct tax. The first twelve entries of this row are positive and represent payments of taxes by various business enterprises and their employees and proprietors to the government. The sum of all these items is entered as a receipt, a negative entry of £26.9 million. The single negative item equals (in absolute value) the sum of all the positive items.

VIII

PLANNING PROJECTIONS AND

THE MODIFIED INPUT-OUTPUT TABLE

This chapter will consider the way in which the modified input-output table may be used to make projections into the future of:

   (i) The total output of each industry,
  (ii) Employment and employment income,
 (iii) Import needs and the balance of payments,
 (iv) Tax revenues and the government budget,
  (v) Investment in fixed capital, and
 (vi) Wages and prices.

The first four of these, total industry outputs, employment, imports and tax revenues, can be estimated in whole or part using primarily information contained in the modified input-output table and a variation of the iterative method discussed in a previous chapter. The calculation of the required investment in fixed capital must be based on a knowledge of the capacity of each industry and the investment required to increase that capacity to handle projected increases in output of each industry. Movements in prices and wages can be predicted by noting the projected increase in incomes which is implied by the plan and determining from estimates of income elasticity whether at current prices the projected demand for the output of each industry equals the projected output of final products. If projected demand is greater than projected supply or vice versa for any or several commodities, then one can be reasonably sure that price and wage changes will have to occur if the plan is to be fulfilled, or that the balance of payments will be affected through changes in the demand for imports. If the necessary price modifications are serious, then the process could take an extremely long time and may result in severe misallocations with target rates of output failing to be attained and plant capacity and scarce skills going unused.

A. Contributions to Final Demand and Intermediate Sales

A common planning procedure is to make estimates of the contributions to final demand of each of the industries in the economy for some future year, often five years ahead. The contribution to final demand of an industry is that part of its output which goes for final uses, consumption, government current expenditures, investment (including government investment contained in the non-recurrent or development budget of the government), and exports. This excludes intermediate sales of each industry. The estimates of contributions to final demand at the end of a planning period include implicit policy decisions such as the planned investment in each of the industries during the five-year period and the amount of import substitution.

The contributions to final demand for each of the twelve industries in the Zambian economy for the year 1961 are shown in Table VIII-1. These figures were obtained by subtracting intermediate sales (shown in column 24 of Table VII-1) from the gross output of each industry (shown in column 19 of Table VII-1). The target contributions to final demand for 1966 for each of the twelve industries are also given in Table VIII-1. These target contributions are purely for purposes of illustration and do not represent actual or proposed targets. Actual targets may be determined through consultation with representatives of private enterprise about their investment plans in the case of industries which are predominantly in private hands. Where governments exercises a great deal of ownership or control, the target figures are generally implied in government investment policy. The targets for each industry also imply a rate of growth for the economy as a whole, and this implied rate of growth must be consistent with a planned or a maximum achievable rate of growth.

Many of the other projections which a planner may desire to make are dependent upon his making a projection of the gross output of each industry, the gross output of an industry being its contribution to final demand plus its intermediate sales. The determination of projected intermediate sales and gross output may be divided into two parts. First is the estimation of intermediate sales and gross output of the electricity and water, transport and communications, and distribution industries. These industries, having columns which show their intermediate sales to all other industries, are the major producers of intermediate goods. Second is the estimation of intermediate sales and gross output of all other industries. These industries are not major sellers of intermediate products and thus

TABLE VIII-1

Final Sales, Intermediate Sales, and Gross Output: 1961 and 1966

£ million Column	Contribution to final demand		Intermediate sales		Ratio: Contribution to final demand to gross output (col. 1 ÷ col. 6)	Gross output	
	Actual 1961	Target 1966	Actual 1961	Estimated 1966 (col. 7 ÷ col. 2)		Actual 1961	Estimated 1966 (col. 2 ÷ col. 5)
	1	2	3	4	5	6	7
1. Mining	128.8	150.0	1.4	1.7	.989	130.2	151.7
2. Agriculture	27.1	35.8	5.8	6.7	.824	32.9	43.5
3. Food and beverages ...	12.2	17.0	0.6	0.8	.953	12.8	17.8
4. Textiles	1.1	3.0	—	—	1.000	1.1	3.0
5. Metal manufacturing ...	2.5	3.5	5.4	7.6	.316	7.9	11.1
6. Other manufacturing ...	1.8	2.3	3.4	4.3	.346	5.2	6.6
7. Construction	22.3	35.0	0.9	1.4	.961	23.2	36.4
8. Electricity and water ...	0.3	2.0	6.8	x	.042	7.1	x
9. Transport and communications...	7.8	10.0	4.6	x	.629	12.4	x
10. Distribution	0.9	1.1	16.2	x	.053	17.1	x
11. Government services ...	13.2	18.0	—	—	1.000	13.2	18.0
12. Other services	17.1	20.0	2.1	2.4	.891	19.2	22.4

TABLE VIII–2

Input Coefficients

	Electricity and Water	Transport and Communications	Distribution
1. Mining	.050	.010	.001
2. Agriculture	—	.003	.009
3. Food and beverages	.008	.008	—
4. Textiles	—	—	—
5. Metal manufacturing	—	.013	.025
6. Other manufacturing	—	.038	.019
7. Construction	—	.026	.070
8. Electricity and water	.127	.014	.014
9. Transport and communications ...	—	—	.008
10. Distribution	.006	.123	—
11. Government services	—	—	—
12. Other services	.005	—	—

have not been allocated a column in the input-output Table VII–1. The projection of intermediate sales for these latter industries must necessarily be done in a cruder, more inaccurate, yet simpler manner. The errors, however, introduced by a less precise calculation of the intermediate sales of these industries are usually quite negligible.

The intermediate sales of all industries excluding the three intermediate goods industries may be estimated by assuming that, for each industry, contribution to final demand is a constant proportion of gross output. This ratio may be calculated in the present example for the base year, 1961, by dividing the entries in column 1 of Table VIII–1 by those in column 6. The results of this calculation are recorded in column 5 of the table. For any industry, the planner may then estimate gross output in any future year by dividing his final demand target figure in column 2 by the ratio in column 5. In the example, this calculation is shown for 1966 and the results are entered in column 7 of the table. Intermediate good sales for 1961 and 1966 are shown for each industry in columns 3 and 4. Intermediate sales for 1966 (shown in column 4) are determined, of course, by subtracting contribution to final demand from the estimate of gross output.

The estimate of intermediate sales of the remaining three industries requires a calculation of the direct requirements and then several rounds of indirect requirements. The direct requirements are determined by using the input coefficients given in Table VIII–2. These coefficients equal the ratio of purchases from the three intermediate goods industries to the gross output of each of the other industries. For example, the entries in row 8 of Table VIII–2 show the ratio of purchases from the electricity and water industry to the gross output of the electricity and water industry, the ratio of purchases from the transport and communications industry to the gross output of the electricity and water industry, and the ratio of purchases from the distribution industry to the gross output of the electricity and water industry. The ratios are calculated from the data in Table VII–1. For example, gross output of the electricity and water industry is in column 19 of Table VII–1 while the purchases of the electricity and water industry from the three intermediate goods industries is obtained from the third fourth, and fifth entries of the eighth row of that table.

Table VIII–3 gives the direct requirements for intermediate sales from the three industries, electricity and water, transport and communications, and distribution. For example, the direct requirements for purchases of transport and communications by the mining industry are given as the second entry in the first row. The last row gives the total direct requirements of the three intermediate goods industries. The entries in Table VIII–3 were calculated in two stages. First came the calculation of direct requirements of all industries except the three intermediate goods industries. These direct requirements were determined by multiplying the 1966 *gross output* of each of the industries by the corresponding input coefficient from Table VIII–2. For example, the direct requirements of the construction industry

TABLE VIII–3

Direct Requirements

(£ million)	Electricity and Water	Transport and Communications	Distribution
1. Mining	7.6	1.5	0.2
2. Agriculture	—	0.1	0.4
3. Food and beverages	0.1	0.1	—
4. Textiles	—	—	—
5. Metal manufacturing	—	0.1	0.3
6. Other manufacturing	—	0.3	0.1
7. Construction	—	0.9	2.5
8. Electricity and water	1.8	0.2	0.2
9. Transport and communications ...	—	—	0.1
10. Distribution	—	0.1	—
11. Government services	—	--	—
12. Other services	0.1	—	—
13. Total direct requirements... ...	9.6	3.3	3.7

TABLE VIII–4

Indirect Requirements

£ million	Round 1			Round 2		
INDUSTRY	8	9	10	8	9	10
8. Electricity and water	1.2	0.1	0.1	0.2	—	—
9. Transport and communications ...	—	—	—	—	—	—
10. Distribution	—	0.5	—	—	—	—
Total	1.2	0.6	0.1	0.2	—	—

for purchases from the distribution industry are calculated by multiplying the gross output of the construction industry (given in the last column of Table VIII–1) by the third input coefficient in the construction row of Table VIII–2. The second part of the calculation was the determination of the direct requirements of the intermediate goods industries. This was done by multiplying the 1966 *contribution to final demand* of each of the three intermediate goods industries by the proper input coefficient from Table VIII–2. For example, the direct requirements for purchases of transport and communications by the distribution industry is estimated by multiplying the contribution to final demand of the distribution industry (given in columns 2 of Table VIII–1) by the second input coefficient of the distribution industry row of Table VIII–2.

Table VIII–4 shows the computation of two rounds of indirect requirements of the output of the three intermediate goods industries. The total direct requirements from the last row of Table VIII–3 are multiplied by the corresponding input coefficient from Table VIII–2 in order to obtain any of the entries in the first three rows under round 1. For example, the second entry of the third row under round 1 is calculated by multiplying the second input coefficient (.123) of the distribution industry row from Table VIII–2 by the total direct requirement of the output of the distribution industry (3.7) found in the last row of Table VIII–3 to obtain .123 × 3.7 = 0.5. The total round 1 indirect requirements from the last row under round 1 of Table VIII–4 are multiplied by the proper input coefficient from Table VIII–2 to obtain the entries in the first three rows under round 2 of Table VIII–4. For example, the second entry of the first row under round 2 is determined by multiplying 1.2, the total first round requirement of the electricity and water industry, by the second input coefficient (.014) of the electricity and water row from Table VIII–2. The result, when rounded off to one decimal place, is nil.

B. Composition of Supply and Demand

Up to this point, we have

(i) been given 1966 targets for final sales (contribution to final demand for 1966) for each of the twelve industries,

(ii) calculated the total intermediate sales for all industries except for the intermediate goods industries, electricity and water, transport and communications and distribution,

(iii) calculated part of the intermediate sales for the intermediate goods industries, and

(iv) calculated gross output except for the intermediate goods industries.

All the above calculations are assumed to be net of distribution costs of final goods and net of indirect taxes on output. Total intermediate sales of the intermediate goods industries can only be determined fully after some estimate of the distribution costs of final goods has been made.

We can now begin to make some projections to 1966 in the form of an input-output table for 1966 such as that illustrated by Table VIII–5. We can fill in the gross output column (column 19) of this table immediately (except for the three intermediate goods industries) with the information at our disposal (in column 7 of Table VIII–1). We cannot fill in column 24, sales to other sectors, in Table VIII–5, because we must have sales to other sectors *including* indirect taxes. The intermediate sales as calculated in Table VIII–1 are *net* of indirect taxes. We will proceed to make projections for all the entries of Table VIII–5 in the following manner:

Step 1. All of the items in the composition of demand section and imports of final goods (column 20) will be estimated *net* of indirect taxes and distribution costs *except* for the three intermediate goods industries.

Step 2. Distribution margins on final products and indirect taxes on gross output will then be calculated and entered in columns 21 and 22 of the input-output Table VIII–5 *except* for the three intermediate goods industries.

Step 3. The costs of distribution of final products and indirect taxes on gross output will then be allocated to each of the items in the composition of demand section *except* for the three intermediate goods industries. The entries of the composition of demand section were already estimated in Step 1 net of distribution costs and indirect taxes so that the share of direct taxes and distribution costs can be added and the composition of demand section of Table VIII–5 completed except for the three intermediate goods industries.

Step 4. The direct and indirect requirements from the three intermediate goods industries by the distribution industry in order to distribute final goods is estimated. These requirements are added to that portion of intermediate sales of the intermediate goods industries estimated previously to get total intermediate sales of the intermediate goods industries. Intermediate sales are added to final sales, estimated previously, to get gross output.

Step 5. Steps 1, 2, and 3 are performed, this time for the three intermediate goods industries.

1. *Step 1*

For each industry the items in the composition of demand section may be estimated net of the distribution costs on final products and net of indirect taxes by using the following equation:

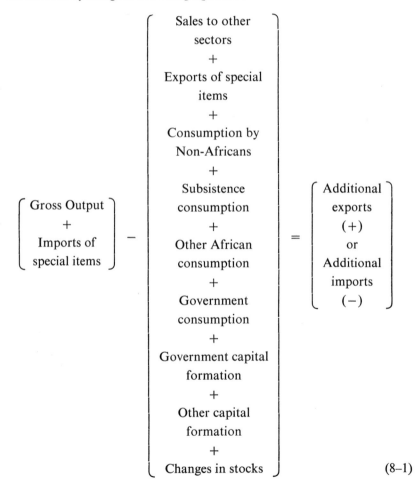

$$\begin{bmatrix} \text{Gross Output} \\ + \\ \text{Imports of} \\ \text{special items} \end{bmatrix} - \begin{bmatrix} \text{Sales to other sectors} \\ + \\ \text{Exports of special items} \\ + \\ \text{Consumption by Non-Africans} \\ + \\ \text{Subsistence consumption} \\ + \\ \text{Other African consumption} \\ + \\ \text{Government consumption} \\ + \\ \text{Government capital formation} \\ + \\ \text{Other capital formation} \\ + \\ \text{Changes in stocks} \end{bmatrix} = \begin{bmatrix} \text{Additional exports} \\ (+) \\ \text{or} \\ \text{Additional imports} \\ (-) \end{bmatrix}$$

$$(8\text{--}1)$$

Each of the items on the left hand side of this equation has either been calculated in Table VIII–1 or must be estimated independently using the available information on income elasticities of African and non-African households, government budget information, and information on planned capital formation. Once all the items on the left hand side have been determined, the item of the right hand side of the equation follows automatically. Total imports net of internal distribution costs and import duties then is the sum of imports of special items on the left hand side of equation (8–1) plus additional imports, if any, from the right hand side. Total exports are exports of special items (from the left hand side) plus additional exports, if any, from the right hand side. The following are some rough guidelines which may be used in estimating each of the various items on the left hand side of equation (8–1).

(i)   Gross output is obtained from the last column of Table VIII–1.

(ii) Imports of special items occur whenever the industrial classification is so broad that they cover some items for which demand is satisfied through domestic production and others which must be imported. Domestic demand may be approximated for these special items by using estimates of income elasticity, and domestic demand less domestic supply is the required import. The sugar manufacturing industry may present such a case. Speciality sugars such as highly refined, cubed, and powdered sugars may be imported even though there may be a large exportable surplus of less-highly refined sugar.

(iii) Sales to other sectors for each industry are contained in the fourth column of Table VIII–1.

(iv) Exports of special items occur whenever the industrial classification is so broad that it contains certain types of products which are not wholly consumed at home and must be exported even though on balance the country in question may be a net importer of the items in the industrial classification. For example, Zambia may export copper handicraft objects and at the same time be a net importer of goods falling within the industrial classification, metal products.

(v)   Consumption by non-Africans may be approximated by using estimates of income elasticity which refer to non-African expenditure patterns.

(vi) Subsistence activity is usually determined by using estimates of population growth and multiplying by an estimated subsistence production per head based on past experience.

(vii) Other African consumption may be determined by using estimates of income elasticity based on African expenditure patterns.

(viii) The allocation to government consumption is largely a political deci-

TABLE VIII–5

Hypothetical Projected Input-Output Table for Zambia: 1966

(£ million at 1961 prices)	BASIC INPUTS							VALUE ADDED Employees Income	
	Imports	Import Duties	Electricity	Transport	Distribution	Other Inputs	Total Inputs	Non-African	African
	1	2	3	4	5	6	7	8	9
1. Mining	24.0	0.5	7.6	1.5	0.2	4.5	38.3	24.5	14.3
2. Agriculture	1.5	—	—	0.1	0.3	1.9	3.8	1.1	2.7
3. Food and Beverages	5.3	0.1	0.1	0.1	—	7.6	13.2	1.0	0.9
4. Textiles	2.2	—	—	—	—	—	2.2	0.3	0.5
5. Metal Manufacturing	4.5	0.1	—	0.1	0.3	0.6	5.6	2.1	1.3
6. Other Manufacturing	1.5	—	—	0.3	0.1	1.4	3.3	1.1	1.1
7. Construction	13.2	0.3	—	0.9	2.5	6.0	22.9	5.4	5.5
8. Electricity and Water	2.4	—	3.2	0.3	0.3	—	6.2	0.7	0.4
9. Transport and Communication	1.3	—	—	—	0.4	1.1	2.8	5.2	2.2
10. Distribution	—	—	0.1	2.9	—	1.9	4.9	7.5	2.5
11. Government Services	—	—	—	—	—	—	—	10.6	7.4
12. Other Services	—	—	0.1	—	—	0.7	0.8	4.6	4.8
13. Intermediate Products	—	—	−11.1	−6.2	−4.1	−25.7	−47.1	—	—
14. Rest of World	−55.9	—	—	—	—	—	−55.9	—	—
15. Government Current A/C	—	−1.0	—	—	—	—	−1.0	—	—
16. Households: Non-African	—	—	—	—	—	—	—	−64.1	—
17. Households: African	—	—	—	—	—	—	—	—	−43.6
18. Savings and Investment	—	—	—	—	—	—	—	—	—

sion and must be based on the assessment of needs for health, education, cultural activities, housing, police and other components of public welfare. Any decision on the amount allocated to government consumption must take into account at least crude estimates of government sources of revenue and the needs for government expenditure on capital formation discussed below.

(ix) Government capital formation is usually based on the estimated investment requirements necessary to obtain some desired rate of growth and assessment of the role which government capital formation will play in achieving the desired investment rate. The proportion of investment goods which each industry will supply for government capital formation depends on some analysis of the

TABLE VIII-5 (*continued*)

Hypothetical Projected Input-Output Table for Zambia: 1966

	VALUE ADDED (*cont.*)									COMPOSITION OF SUPPLY	
			Mixed and Property Income		Income Payments							
	Subsistence	Direct Tax	Non-African	African	Home	Abroad	Transfers	Savings and Depreciation	Total Value Added	Gross Output	Imports Final (c.i.f.)
	10	11	12	13	14	15	16	17	18	19	20
1.	—	27.3	—	—	2.7	27.0	—	17.6	113.4	151.7	—
2.	26.0	—	3.6	5.3	—	—	—	—	38.7	42.5	2.3
3.	—	0.6	—	—	0.2	0.2	—	1.7	4.6	17.8	15.2
4.	—	—	—	—	—	—	—	—	0.8	3.0	12.0
5.	—	0.7	0.4	0.3	—	—	—	0.7	5.5	11.1	21.6
6.	—	0.4	—	—	—	0.2	—	0.5	3.3	6.6	11.0
7.	—	0.2	0.8	0.8	—	0.2	—	0.6	13.5	36.4	—
8.	—	—	—	—	2.1	1.6	—	2.1	6.9	13.1	1.8
9.	—	0.3	0.4	0.6	0.4	1.9	—	2.4	13.4	16.2	—
10.	—	1.4	2.8	0.8	1.0	0.3	—	2.8	19.1	24.0	—
11.	—	—	—	—	—	—	—	—	18.0	18.0	—
12.	6.6	0.7	5.0	0.3	−2.0	0.4	—	1.2	21.6	22.4	8.4
13.	—	—	—	—	—	—	—	—	—	−47.1	—
14.	—	—	—	—	—	−31.9	−2.5	+6.3	−28.1	−84.0	−72.3
15.	—	−31.6	−2.8	—	−4.7	+0.4	+2.0	+7.7	−29.0	−30.0	—
16.	—	—	—	−10.2	+0.3	−0.3	+0.5	+16.7	−57.1	−57.1	—
17.	−32.6	—	—	−8.1	—	—	—	−1.3	−85.6	−85.6	—
18.	—	—	—	—	—	—	—	−59.0	−59.0	−59.0	

specific types of projects included under government capital formation. Estimates of needed supplies from local industries for government investment may, however, be based on an examination of past ratios of supplies by each industry to total government capital formation with certain adjustments for possible import substitution.

(x) The amount allocated to other capital formation depends on the role which private industry is willing to take in achieving the desired rate of capital formation. This role may be assessed partly through consultation with representatives of private industry and depends to a great extent on proposed government policy concerning taxation; provision of ancillary services such as training schools, transport, police protection, medical services, housing, market surveys,

TABLE VIII–5 (continued)

Hypothetical Projected Input-Output Table for Zambia: 1966

(£ million)	Distribution	Indirect Tax	Total Supply/Demand	Sales to Other Sectors	Exports	Non-African	Subsistence	Other African	Government Consumption	Govern-ment	Other
	21	22	23	24	25	26	27	28	29	30	31
1. Mining	0.1	—	151.8	−1.7	−140.6	−2.1	—	−0.7	−0.1	—	−6.6
2. Agriculture	3.4	—	48.2	−7.5	−5.7	−3.2	−26.0	−4.2	−0.9	—	−0.7
3. Food and beverages	3.5	3.0	39.5	−0.8	—	−13.9	—	−22.8	−2.0	—	—
4. Textiles	3.0	0.8	18.8	—	—	−6.1	—	−12.0	−0.7	—	—
5. Metal manufacturing	6.4	1.1	40.2	−7.6	−0.2	−6.0	—	−3.1	−1.2	−2.1	−20.0
6. Other manufacturing	2.4	0.9	20.9	−4.3	−1.0	−6.0	—	−4.3	−5.3	—	—
7. Construction	—	0.1	36.5	−1.4	—	—	—	—	−5.8	−18.4	−10.9
8. Electricity and water	—	—	14.9	−11.1	—	−2.1	—	−0.2	−1.5	—	—
9. Transport and communication	—	0.8	17.0	−6.2	−7.3	−0.7	—	−0.7	−2.1	—	—
10. Distribution	—	0.2	24.2	−22.9	—	−0.5	—	−0.3	−0.2	—	—
11. Government services	—	—	18.0	—	—	—	—	—	−18.0	—	—
12. Other services	—	0.9	31.7	−2.4	—	−18.0	−6.6	−4.7	—	—	—
13. Intermediate products	−18.8	—	−65.9	+65.9	—	—	—	—	—	—	—
14. Rest of world	—	—	−156.3	—	+154.8	+1.5	—	—	—	—	—
15. Government current Account	—	−7.8	−37.8	—	—	—	—	—	+37.8	—	—
16. Households: non-African	—	—	−57.1	—	—	+57.1	—	—	—	—	—
17. Households: African	—	—	−85.6	—	—	—	+32.6	+53.0	—	—	—
18. Savings and investment	—	—	−59.0	—	—	—	—	—	—	+20.5	+38.2

and research; the role of government in providing power and other basic inputs; government control of private industry; and investment in competing or complementary industries. The amount supplied by each industry depends, of course, on whether the output of that industry is composed of final goods, investment (producer) goods, or both. It also depends on the nature of the presumed projects included under non-government capital formation.

(xi) Planned changes in stocks or inventories may occur for strategic reasons, for price stabilization purposes, or because of a gradual overall increase in inventories necessary to support growing retail and wholesale trade activities.

If the first two of the above items are greater than the last nine, then the balance is the additional exportable surplus beyond the export of special items. If the opposite is true then the balance is the additional required imports beyond the required imports of speciality items.

2. Step 2

It still remains to calculate for each industry the distribution margins on final products and the indirect taxes on gross output and imports of final goods which go in columns 21 and 22 of the input-output Table VIII–5. One possible assumption that may be used is that distribution margins for the year 1966 are the same as the margins for the base year 1961.

$$\begin{array}{l}\text{Distribution of final} \\ \text{products (1966) of an} \\ \text{industry}\end{array} = \frac{\begin{array}{c}\text{Distribution of final} \\ \text{products (1961) of an} \\ \text{industry}\end{array}}{\begin{array}{c}\text{Contribution to final} \\ \text{demand by the industry} \\ +\text{imports of final pro-} \\ \text{ducts (1961)}\end{array}} \times \begin{array}{c}\text{Contribution to final} \\ \text{demand by the industry} \\ +\text{imports of final pro-} \\ \text{ducts (1966).}\end{array} \qquad (8\text{–}2)$$

All the items on the right hand side of this equation are contained in Table VII–1 above. Similarly, one may assume that indirect taxes are a constant proportion of gross output and imports of final products. Then

$$\begin{array}{l}\text{Indirect taxes on gross} \\ \text{output and imports} \\ \text{of final products} \\ \text{(1966)}\end{array} = \frac{\begin{array}{c}\text{Indirect taxes on gross} \\ \text{output and imports of} \\ \text{final goods (1961) of an} \\ \text{industry}\end{array}}{\begin{array}{c}\text{Gross output of the} \\ \text{industry}+\text{imports of} \\ \text{final goods (1961)}\end{array}} \times \begin{array}{c}\text{Gross output of the} \\ \text{industry}+\text{imports of} \\ \text{final goods (1966).}\end{array} \qquad (8\text{–}3)$$

Alternatively, one may estimate indirect taxes for 1966 on the basis of a knowledge of specific proposed tax rates if the 1966 tax rates are expected to differ significantly from those of 1961.

At this point it is possible to fill in all entries in the composition of supply section of Table VIII–5 (columns 19 through 22) and in column 23 (Total supply/demand) for all industries except the intermediate goods industries (electricity and water, transport and communications, and distribution). Gross output (column 19) is taken from the left hand side of equation (8–1). Imports of final goods (column 20) is the sum of imports of speciality items from the left hand side of equation (8–1), plus additional imports, if any, on the right hand side of the same equation. Distribution and indirect taxes (columns 21 and 22) are determined from equations (8–2) and (8–3). Total supply/demand, of course, is the sum of all items in columns 19 through 22.

3. *Step 3*

A proportionate share of indirect taxes on gross output and imports of final goods as calculated from equation (8–3) and of distribution costs on final products as calculated from equation (8–2) must be allocated to items in each of the columns 24 through 32 since the values given in equation (8–1) are net of distribution costs and indirect taxes. Thus indirect taxes and distribution costs would be allocated for each industry as follows: Total demand net of distribution costs and indirect taxes (NTD) is given by

$$
\begin{aligned}
& \text{Sales to other sectors} \\
& + \\
& \text{Exports ($=$ exports of speciality} \\
& \text{items$+$additional exports, if any)} \\
& + \\
& \text{Consumption by non-Africans} \\
& + \\
& \text{Subsistence consumption} \\
& + \\
\text{NTD} = \; & \text{Other African consumption} \\
& + \\
& \text{Government consumption} \\
& + \\
& \text{Government capital formation} \\
& + \\
& \text{Other capital formation} \\
& + \\
& \text{Change in stocks.}
\end{aligned}
\tag{8–4}
$$

All items on the right hand side of equation (8–4) are net of distribution costs and indirect taxes and have been calculated in Step 1. Then the share of distribution costs allocated to non-African consumption, for example, is

$$
\begin{array}{l}
\text{Distribution costs of} \\
\text{non-African con-} \\
\text{sumption (1966)}
\end{array}
=
\frac{\begin{array}{c}\text{Non-African consump-}\\\text{tion (net of distribu-}\\\text{tion costs and indirect}\\\text{taxes) (1966)}\end{array}}{\begin{array}{c}\text{NTD—Sales to other}\\\text{sectors (net of distri-}\\\text{bution costs and in-}\\\text{direct taxes)}\end{array}}
\times
\begin{array}{c}\text{Total distribution cost}\\\text{of final products (1966)}\\\text{of the industry and of}\\\text{imports of final pro-}\\\text{ducts.}\end{array}
$$

(8–5)

The share of indirect taxes allocated to non-African consumption is

$$
\begin{array}{l}
\text{Indirect taxes} \\
\text{on non-African} \\
\text{consumption (1966)}
\end{array}
=
\frac{\begin{array}{c}\text{Non-African consump-}\\\text{tion (net of distribution}\\\text{costs and indirect taxes)}\\\text{(1966)}\end{array}}{\text{NTD}}
\times
\begin{array}{c}\text{Total indirect taxes on}\\\text{gross output of the}\\\text{industry and imports}\\\text{of final products (1966).}\end{array}
$$

(8–6)

The share of indirect taxes and distribution costs allocated to each of the items on the right hand side of equation (8–4), except for sales to other sectors, is determined by substituting each of them in turn into equations (8–5) and (8–6) instead of non-African consumption. The share of distribution costs and indirect taxes is added to each of the items and the result entered in the appropriate row of one of the columns 24 through 32 except in the case of sales to other sectors. Only indirect taxes are added to sales to other sectors since its share of distribution costs is contained elsewhere in the table.

4. Step 4 and Step 5

This completes the discussion of all the industries except the intermediate goods industries (electricity and water, transport and communications, and distribution), as far as the composition of demand and composition of supply sections are concerned. From Table VIII–5, the sum of costs of distribution of final products is £18.8 million. In order to provide this amount of output of the distribution industry, however, it requires inputs of the services of the three intermediate goods industries. These direct

TABLE VIII–6

Requirements for £18.8 Million of Output of the Distribution Industry

£ million	Electricity and Water	Transport and Communications	Distribution
Direct requirements of purchases by the distribution industry	0.1	2.3	—
Indirect requirements — Electricity and water	—	—	—
Indirect requirements — Transport and communications	—	—	0.3
Indirect requirements — Distribution	—	—	—
Indirect requirements — Total indirect	—	—	0.3
Total direct and indirect	0.1	2.3	0.3

requirements are determined by multiplying the £18.8 million by the input coefficients of the distribution row of Table VIII–2. The results are shown in Table VIII–6. In addition, Table VIII–6 shows one round of indirect requirements. The calculation of indirect requirements is done in the same manner as that used earlier in determining the entries in Table VIII–4. The gross output of the three intermediate goods industries may now be determined. It is composed of the sum of contribution to final demand as given in column 2 of Table VIII–1, the direct requirements from the last row of Table VIII–3, the two rounds of indirect requirements in the last row of Table VIII–4, the total requirements in the last row of Table VIII–6, plus £18.8 million output of the distribution industry for distributing final products. Then sales to other sectors net of indirect taxes and distribution costs is the balance between gross output and contribution to final demand. All other entries in columns 20 through 32 are determined for the inter-mediate goods industries in the same manner as for all the other industries discussed above.

C. The Inter-Industry Section

The filling in of the entries of the inter-industry section of Table VIII–5 is relatively straightforward. Imports of materials and services to be used as inputs are assumed to be a constant proportion of gross output. Thus the first column entries for each industry may be calculated by using the following equation.

$$\frac{\text{Imports of inputs (1961)}}{\text{Gross output (1961)}} \times \frac{\text{Gross output}}{(1966)} = \frac{\text{Imports of}}{\text{inputs (1966).}} \qquad (8\text{–}7)$$

Then import duties may be calculated as a constant proportion of imports of inputs.

$$\frac{\text{Import duties (1961)}}{\text{Imports of inputs (1961)}} \times \frac{\text{Imports of}}{\text{inputs (1966)}} = \frac{\text{Import duties}}{\text{(1966)}} \qquad (8\text{--}8)$$

Alternatively, import duties may be estimated from a knowledge of proposed tariffs and the composition of imports used as inputs. This is certainly a better approach if there are to be significant changes in import duties during the planning period.

The inputs of the products of the three industries, electricity and water, transport and communications, and distribution into all industries except the three intermediate goods industries may be filled in using the figures from Table VIII–3. For example, columns 3, 4, and 5 of the construction row of Table VIII–5 may be filled in by taking the three entries from the construction row of Table VIII–3. The construction industry makes negligible purchases from the electricity and water industry, purchases of £0.9 million from the transport and communications industry, and purchases of £2.5 million from the distribution industry. Columns 3, 4, and 5 of the distribution industry row of Table VIII–5 are obtained by taking the three entries of the distribution row of Table VIII–3, adding to each of these items the corresponding entries in the distribution row under round 1 and round 2 of Table VIII–4 and in the direct requirements row and the distribution row under indirect requirements of Table VIII–6. For example, the purchases of the distribution industry from the transport and communications industry (shown as the fourth entry of the distribution row of Table VIII–5) is the sum of £0.1 million (the second entry of the distribution row of Table VIII–3), £0.5 million and £0.0 million (the second and fifth entries of the distribution row of Table VIII–4), £2.3 million (the second entry of the first row of Table VIII–6), and £0.0 million (the second entry of the distribution row under indirect requirements in Table VIII–6) or £2.9 million. Columns 3, 4, and 5 of the electricity and water, and transport and communications rows of Table VIII–5 are obtained by taking the sum of corresponding entries in those rows of Table VIII–3 under round 1 and round 2 of Table VIII–4, and under indirect requirements of Table VIII–6.

The calculation of other inputs (column 6 of Table VIII–5) for each of the twelve industries may be based on a constant proportions assumytion by using the following equation:

$$\frac{\text{Other inputs (1961)}}{\text{Gross output (1961)}} \times \frac{\text{Gross output}}{\text{(1966)}} = \frac{\text{Other}}{\text{inputs (1966).}} \qquad (8\text{--}9)$$

Each entry in column 7 of Table VIII–5 is the sum of the entries in the previous six columns for each of the twelve industry rows.

In order that the projections for the inter-industry inputs section be consistent with the projections in the composition of demand and composition of supply sections of Table VIII–5, it may be necessary to make a slight adjustment. Because of the crude way in which the intermediate sales for all the industries except electricity and water, transport and communications, and distribution were estimated, the sum of all purchases of other inputs (the sum of all items in the first twelve rows of column 6) may not equal the sum of sales of intermediate goods by all industries except the three intermediate goods industry (the sum of rows 1 through 7, 11, and 12 in column 24). Since by definition these two sums must equal, it may be necessary to make slight upward or downward adjustments of the items in column 6.

D. The Value Added Section

The value added column (18) is filled in for each industry by subtracting total inputs from gross output which have already been determined. The subsistence column of the value added section is taken directly from the subsistence column in the composition of demand section. Each of the other entries in the value added section is calculated by assuming a constant proportion of value added less subsistence. That is, for each row one uses the following equation:

$$\frac{FP\ (1961)}{\text{Value added (1961)} - \text{Subsistence (1961)}} \times \frac{\text{Value added}\ (1966) - \text{Subsistence}\ (1966)}{} = FP\ (1966). \qquad (8\text{–}10)$$

where FP (1961) stands for non-African employees' income in 1961, African employees' income in 1961, direct taxes in 1961, etc. in order to calculate FP (1966), non-African employees' income in 1966, African employees' income in 1966, direct taxes in 1966, etc., respectively.

The calculation using equation (8–10) assumes that wage rates, productivity, and direct taxes as a percentage of employees' income will be the same at the end of the five-year period, that wage rates and productivity will grow at the same rate and direct taxes as a percentage of employees remain the same, that wage rates will grow faster than productivity but that taxes will increase, or that wage rates will grow slower than productivity but that taxes as a proportion of income will decrease. The calculation also assumes that the proportion of employees' wages going to Africans remains constant. A policy of Africanization would make this assumption dubious.

The planner, however, may have information about future tax rates, wages, productivity, and Africanization policy which cause him to want to reject these assumptions. If, for example, he has reason to believe that wage rates and productivity will probably grow at the same rate but that taxes as a proportion of employees' income will increase, then he must make the appropriate downward adjustment in employees' income (net of taxes) and an upward adjustment in the direct taxes column. Similarly, the planner may know from a knowledge of the make-up of the capital stock and the dividend policy of corporations that one can expect an increase in the savings and depreciation proportion of value added. This figure must be adjusted upwards and the other components of value added appropriately adjusted downward.

E. The Balancing Section

The projections of the rows of the balancing section of the projected input-output table are relatively straightforward. Some columns need special mention. Column 7 is the sub-total of the first six columns; column 18 is the sub-total of columns 8 through 16; column 19 is the sub-total of columns 7 and 18; and column 23 is the sub-total of columns 24 through 32 and also of columns 19 through 22. These sub-total columns can be filled in automatically once the individual items in each of the sub-totals have been determined.

Column 12, mixed income paid to non-Africans, has two entries in the balancing sector, one showing that portion of total payments which accrues to non-African households and the other showing that portion of payments which accrues to government. Both of these entries are negative numbers, representing receipts, and together they equal (in absolute value) the algebraic sum of all the entries in the first twelve rows. The proportion of payments which accrues to government may be estimated by assuming that a constant proportion of net payments (the algebraic sum of the first twelve rows) goes to government. Alternatively, the portion accruing to government may be estimated independently from projected government budget data. The remainder, of course, goes to non-African households.

Columns 14 and 15, payments of interest and dividends at home and abroad, present special problems with respect to the government current account and non-African households rows of the balancing section. If government or non-African households are net recipients of dividends and interest from local residents or from abroad, then this requires a negative entry in column 14 or column 15 of the appropriate row. Otherwise, a positive or zero entry must appear indicating that government or non-African households are net players of interest (dividends being paid only by incorporated enterprises), or that receipts equal payments. The projection of these net receipt or payments items is normally difficult and must be done using independent knowledge, such as governments' plans for future non-tax finance, and good judgment. With column 14, once the estimate of government net receipts or payments is determined, the net payments or receipts by non-African households follows automatically and is the algebraic sum of all the other items in column 14 since, for the economy as a whole, income receipts must equal income payments. With column 15, however, the net receipts or payments by both households and government must be estimated independently. The net payment or receipt of dividends and interest for the rest of the world then is the algebraic sum of all other entries in column 15.

Net transfers (column 16) are also usually extremely volatile and difficult to estimate especially for the rest of the world and non-African households. Government transfer payments are more predictable and may be estimated from budget forecasts. The method of projection must fit the circumstances. In any case, a negative entry is a projection of net receipts of transfer payments and a positive entry represents a net payment of transfers. The net receipts shown in column 16 must equal net payments.

Column 26, non-African consumption, has two entries, consumption by tourists shown in the rest of the world row and consumption by local non-Africans shown in the non-African households row. Tourist expenditure may be estimated independently from statistics of the past rate of growth of tourist trade by taking into mind planned efforts to stimulate tourist trade. Consumption by resident non-Africans is determined immediately when tourist expenditures are estimated since these two items must equal (in absolute value) the sum of all the negative items from the first twelve entries in column 26.

The projections for all of the other columns except column 17 in the balancing section of the input-output Table VIII–5 follow automatically. There is only one entry in each of these columns and this entry is equal to the negative of the algebraic sum of all entries in the first twelve rows. The row in which this entry is placed is in every case obvious. For example, the algebraic sum of all items in the first twelve rows of column 25 of Table VIII–5 is -154.8. This figure represents total export proceeds and is a payment by the rest of the world to local residents. The negative of the algebraic sum is $-(-154.8) = +154.8$ and this number is entered in the rest of the world row. Similarly, the algebraic sum in column 11, direct taxes, is 31.6. The negative of this is -31.6 and is entered as a recept in the government current account row.

The determination of the entries in column 17, savings and depreciation, is the last step in the projection analysis. The entry in the intermediate row is always nil. The entry in the rest of the world row is the balance of payments on current account, i.e., the difference between all receipts by the rest of the world and payments to the rest of the world. The sum of all the negative entries (receipts) in the rest of the world row of Table VIII–5 except for those entries in the sub-total columns 7, 18, 19, 23 is $-55.9 + (-31.9) + (-2.5) + (-72.3) = -162.6$. The sum of all positive entries (payments) except for that in column 17 and the sub-total columns is $154.8 + 1.5 = 156.3$. Since the receipts of £162.6 million are greater than payments of £156.3 million, the difference of £6.3 million is entered as a positive number in column 17. If payments are greater than receipts then the difference is entered as a negative number in column 17. Similarly, the entries in column 17 of the government current account, African and non-African households, and savings and investment rows are the difference between payments and receipts. If payments are greater than receipts, a negative number is entered; otherwise a positive or zero number is entered.

F. Final Projections

Table VIII–7 gives a comparison of the gross output for the base year 1961 (taken from column 19 of Table VII–1) and for the projection year 1966 (taken from column 19 of Table VIII–5). The difference between the two values for each industry represents the amount of new capacity, assuming full capacity in 1961, for which investment must be found during the five year period if the 1966 projections are to be attained. If the amount of investment per unit of increased capacity is known for each of the

TABLE VIII–7

Comparison of Gross Output
(£ million)

	1961	1966	Increase
1. Mining	130.2	151.7	21.5
2. Agriculture	32.9	42.5	9.6
3. Food and beverages	12.8	17.8	5.0
4. Textiles	1.1	3.0	1.9
5. Metal manufacturing	7.9	11.1	3.2
6. Other manufacturing	5.2	6.6	1.4
7. Construction	23.2	36.4	13.2
8. Electricity and water	7.1	13.1	6.0
9. Transport and communication ...	12.4	16.2	3.8
10. Distribution	17.1	24.0	6.9
11. Government services	13.2	18.0	4.8
12. Other services	19.2	22.4	3.2

industries, then the total necessary investment during the five year planning period is determined by multiplying the difference in gross output in the last column of Table VIII–7 by the investment per unit of increased capacity for each industry.

Total projected employment income for 1966 is the sum of all entries in columns 8 and 9 of the first twelve rows of Table VIII–5 or £107.7 million. This compares with employment income in 1961 of £84.0 million. The difference is £23.7 million or a 28 per cent increase between 1961 and 1966. The projected labor force for the year 1966 is estimated by dividing total employment income by some estimate of the average wage.

The government surplus on current account (receipts less payments) is taken from the savings and investment entry of the government current account row and is £7.7 million. On the other hand, planned government capital formation (the sum of the items in the first twelve rows of column 30) is £20.5 million. The difference of £12.8 million must be financed through loans or other grants.

In making the projections it was assumed that if any domestic demand for the products of various industries was not met through domestic supplies, the difference was made up through imports. The 1966 projection, however, shows that if the estimates of income elasticities which were used to project consumer demand are correct, then domestic demand will grow at a rate which exceeds the rate of domestic supply. This is made evident by comparing the balance of payments surplus of £3.0 million in Table VII–1 (the entry in column 17 of the rest of the world row) with the projected balance of payments deficit of £6.3 million in Table VIII–5. This may mean a tendency for domestic prices to rise during the five year planning period. This rise in prices may reduce consumption somewhat, provided that wages and real money balances do not rise accordingly, and the balance of payments deficit may be reduced to a limited extent. The deficit, however, will probably remain despite the rise in prices, which implies that foreign investment must rise or the appropriate monetary and fiscal policies must be implemented to reduce consumption and imports and correct the deficit situation.

G. Conclusion

The reader should remember that the projections shown in Table VIII–5 are hypothetical and may be based on assumptions which are not true about the Zambian economy. This exercise on making projections, however, brings out some of the problems encountered, techniques used, and necessary assumptions. There are an infinite number of variations on the above method of making projections and the exact way in which projections should be made depends on the individual circumstances of each country. The making of such projections requires an experienced analyst intimately familiar with the economy of the country in which he is working. It must be emphasized that projection is an art rather than an exact science. The reader must also remember that projections are not infallible. They are based on assumptions which may or may not hold throughout the planning period. The best a projection analyst can say is that if his assumptions are correct his projections are implied by these assumptions. The value in making careful projections, however, lies in the fact that the assumptions which are made must be fully stated, the full implications of any set of assumptions come to light, and the effects of a modification in any one of the assumptions can be traced clearly.

FURTHER READING FOR PART TWO

1. O. Aukrust and the Research and Planning Division of the Economic Commission for Europe, "Input-Output Tables: Recent Experience in Western Europe," *Economic Bulletin for Europe*, Vol. VII, No. 1 (May, 1956), pp. 36–53.

2. T. Barna, editor, *The Structural Interdependence of the Economy*, New York, Wiley, 1956.

3. H. B. Chenery and P. G. Clark, *Inter-industry Economics*, New York, Wiley, 1959.

4. R. Dorfman, P. Samuelson and R. Solow, *Linear Programming and Economic Analysis*, New York, McGraw-Hill, 1958.

5. C. R. Frank, Jr., "The Seers Modified Input-Output Table: Some Projection Techniques," *The Review of Income and Wealth*, Series 14, No. 1, March, 1968.

6. W. Leontieff, *The Structure of the American Economy, 1919–39*, 2nd edition, New York, Oxford University Press, 1951.

7. W. H. Miernyk, *The Elements of Input-Output Analysis*, New York, Random House, 1966.

8. National Bureau of Economic Research, *Input-Output Analysis: An Appraisal*, Vol. 18 of Studies in Income and Wealth, Princeton, Princeton University Press, 1955.

9. D. Seers, "The Use of a Modified Input-Output System For an Economic Program in Zambia," I. Adelman and E. Thorbecke, editors, *The Theory and Design of Economic Development*, Baltimore, The Johns Hopkins Press, 1966.

10. C. R. Taskier, *Input-Output Bibliography, 1955–60*, New York, United Nations, 1961. St/Stat 17); *Input-Output Bibliography, 1960–1963*, United Nations, 1964 (St/Stat/Ser. M139); and *Input-Output Bibliography, 1963–1966*, United Nations, 1967, Series M, No. 46.

11. United Nations Economic Commission for Africa and Food and Agricultural Organization, *Economic Survey Mission on the Economic Development of Zambia*, Ndola, Falcon Press, 1964.

12. United Nations Economic Commission for Latin America, *Analysis and Projections of Economic Development III: The Economic Development of Colombia*, Geneva, United Nations Department of Economic and Social Affairs, 1957.
13. United Nations Seminar on National Accounts, *Input-Output Table and Analysis*, New York, United Nations Statistical Office, 1959.
14. United Nations, *Problems of Input-Output Tables and Analysis*, Series F, No. 14, New York, United Nations Statistical Office, 1966.

NOTES ON FURTHER READING FOR PART TWO

The books by Chenery and Clark (3) (Chapters 2, 3, and 4), Dorfman, Samuelson and Solow (4) (Chapters 9, 10, and 11), and Miernyk (7) contain very good expositions (the first two at a somewhat more advanced level than this volume) of the basic theory of input-output models and the techniques of solution. Both these works show the relation between input-output and linear programing techniques while the latter demonstrates how the system can be made into a dynamic model with capital coefficients.

Seers (9) discusses the methodology of his modified input-output table, and Frank (5) contains a rigorous algebraic derivation of some projection techniques for the modified table.

Wassily Leontieff is considered to be the pioneer in the development and application of input-output techniques. His classic work (6) presents the first large scale attempt to formulate an empirical input-output model together with some selected applications of input-output.

The volume edited by Barna (2) and that put out by the National Bureau of Economic Research (8) are collections of articles dealing with data collection, problems of aggregation, and applications of input-output. Chenery and Clark (3) (Chapters 5–12) and the United Nations volume (14) deal with the same topics in a systematic fashion.

The two empirical studies for Zambia and Colombia discussed in this section are contained in (11) and (12). Anyone interested in other empirical input-output studies should consult the 1963–66 bibliography by Taskier (10) which contains a comprehensive list of countries and dates for which input-output tables have been compiled. O. Aukrust (1) contains a description of input-output studies in various countries of Europe and the U.N. volume (14) lists countries in which current and planned input-output work is being undertaken.

The bibliographies compiled by Taskier (10) are very comprehensive and an indispensable aid to anyone who would like to do research on input-output theory, techniques, or applications on an inter-regional, regional or country basis.

PART

3

NATIONAL ACCOUNTS

IX

THE NATIONAL ACCOUNTS: AN INTRODUCTION

This chapter introduces the section of this volume which examines problems of aggregate economic accounts. This subject has sometimes been known as "social accounting" but more usually the accounts are referred to as the "national accounts." The national accounts are concerned with the measure of aggregate product originating within a given geographical area, or alternatively produced by factors of production owned by citizens of a certain nation. The most typical accounts are concerned with estimating the annual flows of income and product, although some countries with more elaborate statistical services may produce quarterly estimates.

The desire to produce aggregate estimates of output may be traced back to the work of the first economists. However, extensive work along the lines currently used grew up mainly in the period after World War I, initially through the work of academic economists and subsequently through official government agencies. Some examples of the early work on national accounts are those of A. L. Bowley and Colin Clark in Britain, Simon Kuznets in the United States, R. Simon in Chile, F. Eppenstein in Turkey, F. Shirras and V. K. R. V. Rao in India, and S. H. Frankel in South Africa. During and immediately following World War II, progress has been gained on two fronts. From time to time there have been attempts to estimate national income of particular countries for particular years. Such efforts as those of Prest and Stewart in Nigeria, Peacock and Dosser in Tanganyika, Phyllis Dean in Rhodesia, and F. Benham in the West Indies and Malaya were preliminary to the establishment of official, continuous, time series estimates of national income. It has only been since World War II that systematic efforts have been made to produce official government estimates of national income on a continuing basis, although the United States has been producing an official income series since 1934.

The work on national accounts has been especially difficult for the less-developed countries, because of the limited personnel available and because the concepts being applied are often not very well tailored to local conditions. However, as a result of these efforts there are now national accounts available for a number of countries.

As this piecemeal development has proceeded, there have been some differences in the methods applied in various countries, the approaches adopted in the French and English speaking countries differing considerably, for example. Recently, attempts have been under way to standardize the concepts in use throughout the world and to suggest a sensible procedure for developing a set of comprehensive national accounts. This attempt at co-ordination has been through the agency of the United Nations.

The economist working in most areas of the world can expect to have available, to an increasing degree, national accounts in some form or other. The behavior of national income and product will be used increasingly as a measure of economic performance. In many countries "gross domestic product" or "national income" have become the major indicators in the public mind of the success of an economy in achieving economic growth. Comparisons are often made between the levels of *income per capita* achieved in different countries, such comparisons being formulated as *domestic product per capita in country A is four times that in country B.* National accounts have become the most important popular basis for measuring and comparing levels of welfare. It is, therefore, important that the professional economist should be well aware of the nature of such accounts and of their limitations in the uses to which the public, politicians, and even economists, put them.

The national accounts are useful in providing the aggregate basis for assessing plans. Although the broad aggregates involved in the accounts make them inappropriate tools for the detailed planning envisaged in the last section of this volume, much of the policy in less-developed countries must be limited to influencing broad aggregates. In particular, the use of fiscal policy, with adjustment of government spending and programing of taxation, is potentially a powerful policy weapon in situations where the planning mechanism is not strong enough to bear the burden of detailed direction and control of much of the economic activity of the nation.

Both the value and the danger of national accounts derive from the fairly simple methods used to gain a crude overall picture of economic performance. Typically, it will be possible for a small statistical department to produce at least part of the national accounts long before it is feasiale to draw up a detailed input-output table with its considerable degree of disaggregation, or to utilize the programing techniques envisaged in the last section of this volume. At the early stages of development planning the government may well have to concentrate on broad aggregates. It will concentrate on the effects of the overall balance of government spending and taxation on the utilization of resources and the level of aggregate investment. Even where more detailed programing is attempted, the level of disaggregation of the initial planning objectives may not be detailed below the major sectors. At such a stage, the main quantitative tool is likely to be the national accounts.

The results of a plan will need to be summarized in terms of the aggregate effects on the national economy. Ultimately, it is likely that a judgment on the degree to which the economy is reaching the right level of commitment to growth objectives will be based on aggregate estimates of the proportion of total output being devoted to investment in machines, buildings, and human resources.

Much of the available evidence on the patterns of growth throughout the world describes movements in the relationship of broad aggregates. There is an increasing amount of data being collected, describing the development of economies over fairly long periods of time within a national accounts framework. Although the concepts involved and the quality of some of the data, are open to much legitimate criticism, some of which is offered in this volume, there is no doubt that much is being learned about the character of growth which may provide some empirical basis for the adoption of development strategies. At least it can provide a conception of what is practicable and what is unreasonable. The work of Simon Kuznets, in particular, shows how valuable an historical tool national accounting can be if used by an interpreter with a deep understanding of its strengths and weaknesses.

In the developed economies, the expansion of interest in the national accounts paralleled the development of the Keynesian economic analysis, with its emphasis on macro-economic behavior. In the developing countries, with economies of a much less homogeneous nature, such macroeconomics is not readily applicable, and aggregate totals such as *national income, consumption* and *investment* have less validity. Therefore, although national accounts are a useful (and virtually inevitable) part of the policy apparatus, they do have their special dangers. The worst of these dangers are those which are implicit in the use of all averages. To say that average income is $1,000 per year in a certain town can mean one thing when all incomes are equal and quite another when incomes are divided so that 10 per cent of the population earns more than $8,000 per year and 90 per cent earns less than $200. A society undergoing the process of industrialization is not only divided horizontally between classes, but is also divided between sectors according to the degree to which modern techniques have penetrated economic activity. The peasant, using traditional techniques, lives in a quite different environment from the industrial workers in the town. Aggregate data must be handled with caution in such economies, where the whole character of the economic life is undergoing a fast process of change, and averages are likely to mask the diversity of the society.

The national accounts attempt to provide an estimate of the output of all the economic units operating in an economy. But what is output? Firms produce to sell to end consumers and to other firms for further processing; this distinction has been made before in Chapter III and in the chapters on the Input-Output table. If the output of a firm is counted as being its total sales the problem arises that part of the sales which become the intermediate inputs of another firm during the same accounting period will be counted as part of the value of the sales of that other firm. Total sales is obviously too gross a concept. If the purchases of intermediate inputs are, however, subtracted from the sales of a firm, the residual may be viewed as the *value added* to output by the productive activities of the firm. If these value-added outputs are summed then there will be a measure of total output in which output is only counted once. This is the basic concept of national accounting.

A simple example will illustrate the reason for using the value-added concept. If a large bottle of beer is purchased for $.50, this represents the value of the end product to the consumer. The bottle will, however, have gone through a number of stages before it reached the consumer. It might have been sold to the retailer for $.40, while the brewer might have paid $.10 for the materials used to produce the beer. If the total product were calculated by summing the gross sales at each of the three stages of manufacture and trade, the value of the product would have been $.50 plus $.40, plus $.10, or $1.00. If the value-added method is used the results would be a sum of $.10 (the gross profit margin of the retailer, representing his value added or total sales minus intermediate inputs); plus $.30 (the brewer's value added—his gross profits and other factor costs); plus $.10 for the farmer who supplied the raw materials to the brewer. (It is assumed that the farmer purchased no intermediate goods himself.) The total of these three value-added figures is $.50, the value of the final product.

The basic nature of the national accounts can be quickly grasped if a very simple version of the process is first investigated. For this purpose, assume an economy without government and with no relations with foreign countries. The only economic units are firms and households. The firms sell goods partly to other firms and partly to households. Sales to other firms are either intermediate goods or final goods in the form of investment (in fixed assets or inventory accumulation). Sales to households are all final goods.

The sales revenue are allocated to gross profit or costs by the firm. The costs are either payments for intermediate goods or primary factor inputs, or represent reduction in stocks. If gross profits are treated as a return for a factor service, then the two sides of the manufacturing account of the firm can be represented:

Current Accounts of the Firm

Total Costs Plus Gross Profit	Total Sales
1. Intermediate goods (X_p)	1. Intermediate goods (X_s)
2. Primary factor input costs (F_s)	2. Consumer goods (C)
3. Reduction in stocks (J_v)	3. Investment goods (fixed capital) (I_c)
	4. Investment goods (increases in stocks) (I_v)

For each firm, the two sides of this account are equal. Therefore for all firms combined:*

$$\Sigma X_p + \Sigma F_s + \Sigma J_v = \Sigma X_s + \Sigma C + \Sigma I_c + \Sigma I_v \qquad (9\text{--}1)$$

For the economy as a whole, intermediate good purchases ΣX_p equal intermediate good sales ΣX_s. We therefore can subtract this total from each side of (9–1) to arrive at the following equation:

$$\Sigma F_s + \Sigma J_v = \Sigma C + \Sigma I_c + \Sigma I_v. \qquad (9\text{--}2)$$

Shifting ΣJ_v to the right side of the equation, a term for net investment in inventories is obtained $\Sigma(I_v - J_v)$; so that:

$$\Sigma F_s = \Sigma C + \Sigma I_c + \Sigma(I_v - J_v). \qquad (9\text{--}3)$$

This simple relationship is derived from the equality of costs plus gross profit and sales revenues in the current accounts of the firm. Both sides of the relationship are expressions for value added. The left hand side indicates that value added is the sum of factor payments. The right hand side shows that value added may also be expressed as the sum of consumption and investment (both fixed investment and investment in inventories).

Now consider F_s. These factor payments could be treated in two ways. First, the total primary factor payments can be calculated for each industry,

* The Greek letter, *sigma* (Σ), when placed before an item in an account, indicates that the particular item is to be summed over accounts of all firms or households.

to provide an estimate of the value-added output in each industry. Secondly the total for the economy can be analyzed according to the income flows resulting from it. That is, let wage payments be denoted by W, rents by R, depreciation by D, and interest and dividend payments by P. Then either

$$\Sigma F_s = F_{s1} + F_{s2} + \ldots + F_{s3}, \tag{9-4}$$

where F_{s1} are factor payments by industry i or

$$\Sigma F_s = W + P + R + D. \tag{9-5}$$

The three methods, (9–3), (9–4), and (9–5), of treating the same total form the three basic forms of social accounts: final sales, the right hand side (r.h.s.) of (9–3), form the *expenditure accounts*; the breakdown of primary factor payments between industry, the r.h.s. of (9–4), forms the *product or value added by industry of origin* accounts; and the analysis of factor payments by income share, the r.h.s. of (9–5), forms the *income accounts*.

Besides the three basic accounting identities in (9–3), (9–4), and (9–5), one other very important accounting identity is that between savings and investment. The receipts of households (H) are derived from the sale of factor services. A large part of the costs of firms, therefore, becomes the income of households. This will take the form of wages (W), rents (R), interest payments and dividend payments (P). A certain amount of gross profits, however, will stay with the firms. This will consist of depreciation (D) and retained profits (S_b). The households receiving incomes may spend them on goods (C) or may save part (S_h). The flows involved are shown in Figure IX–1.

In terms of the symbols, the above analysis may be set out:

$$\Sigma F_s = \Sigma(W + P + R) + \Sigma S_b + \Sigma D = \Sigma C + \Sigma I_c + \Sigma(I_v - J_v). \tag{9-6}$$

But $\Sigma(W + P + R)$ is total household income (ΣH). Households either spend on goods or save, so that

$$\Sigma H = \Sigma(W + P + R) = \Sigma(C + S_h). \tag{9-7}$$

Applying this above, we obtain

$$\Sigma F_s = \Sigma C + \Sigma S_h + \Sigma S_b + \Sigma D = \Sigma C + \Sigma I_c + \Sigma(I_v - J_v). \tag{9-8}$$

The familiar savings and investment identity is derived from (9–6) by eliminating household spending (consumption) from both sides.

$$\Sigma S_h + \Sigma S_b + \Sigma D = \Sigma I_c + \Sigma(I_v - J_v). \tag{9-9}$$

In practice, part of C will be counted as investment since households will be investing in residential housing. This involves an adjustment to both sides of equation (9–8), part of the household consumption being counted as savings on the left hand side and as investment on the right hand side of the equality.

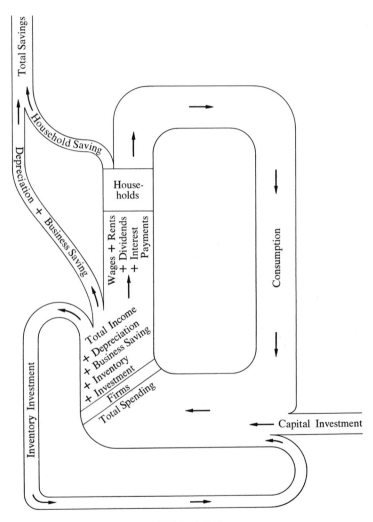

FIGURE IX-1

X

A SYSTEM OF NATIONAL ACCOUNTS

This chapter presents a basic system of national accounts. The treatment is quite formal and attempts to relate the system both to the accounts of firms and to the input-output framework presented in Chapters V through VII.

A. The Formal System

In the previous chapter an economy without government and foreign trade was assumed. Those assumptions are now dropped, although it is not until later chapters that the problems of the government sector and of foreign payments flows are dealt with in great detail.

The simplest way to treat the government is as a final user of goods and services. Its activities are either consumption on the part of the society as a whole or, if goods are purchased for use by the government in subsequent periods, investment.

The foreign sector will be treated at this stage merely by considering exports and imports. Exports are, from the accounting point of view, a final use for the exporting economy.

The final complication that must be noted is that in the real world the rigid distinction between firms and households suggested in the previous chapter tends to break down. Households can sell services directly to the final user, by-passing firms in the process. This is true of many personal services and may also be true of much household renting. A very important form of direct consumption of household services is the purchase of labor by the government, treated here as a final use which does not form part of the input-output flows of the business sector.

The following basic notation will be used throughout this chapter:

(i) Domestic expenditure on final goods and services:

C = total consumption spending by households including intra-household purchases of factor services (wages and rent).

I = total fixed investments, gross of depreciation, including household investment in residential construction.

G = total government current spending, including purchases from businesses and directly from households (wages and rents).

E = total exports.

V = net increase in inventories.

F = final sales.

C_i, I_i, G_i, E_i, V_i, and F_i = expenditure on consumption, on investment, by government, on exports, on net increase in inventories, and on all final sales, respectively, utilizing the products of industry i.

C_b, I_b, G_b, V_b, and F_b = expenditure on consumption, on investment, by government, on net increase in inventories, and on all final sales, respectively, utilizing the products of all businesses.

(ii) Foreign resources used:

M = total imports of goods and services.

M_x = imports of intermediate goods and services.

C_m = imports of consumption goods.

G_m = expenditure on imports by government.

V_m = imports of goods into inventories.

M_{xi} = imports of intermediate goods and services by industry i.

(iii) Domestic resources used:

W = total wages.

R = total rents.

P = total profits and interest.

D = total depreciation charges by businesses.

W_i, R_i, P_i, and D_i = wages, rents, profits, and depreciation of industry i.

W_b and R_b = wages and rents paid by all businesses.

W_h and R_h = direct wage and rent payments by households.

W_g and R_g = wage and rent payments by government.

(iv) Income disposal:

P_d = payments of dividends and interest to households by businesses.

S_b = net business saving (unappropriated profits, after provision for depreciation and payments of interest and dividends).

S_h = household saving.

T_b = direct taxes paid by businesses.

T_h = direct taxes paid by households.

(v) Expenditure on intermediate products and value added:

X_b = total sales of intermediate products by businesses.

X_i = total purchases of intermediate products by industry i.*

VA_i = value added by industry i.

VA_h = value added by households.

VA_g = value added by government.

1. *Product Account*

Using the notation set out above, one may show how the three different types of national accounts, product, expenditure, and income, may be constructed. The *product account* is simply the sum of value added by each industry plus value added directly by households and government. The value added of an industry may be approached from two points of view, (i) as the sum of the factor payments by that industry (wages, rents, profits, and depreciation), or (ii) as the total sales plus net inventory increase of the industry less the intermediate purchases from both domestic and foreign industries. The two points of view are equivalent because of the accounting identity between purchases of intermediate products plus payments for factors of production (including profits) on the one hand and total sales plus net inventory increase on the other. Algebraically, this identity may be expressed as follows:

$$M_{xi} + X_i + W_i + R_i + P_i + D_i \equiv F_i + V_i, \text{ or} \tag{10–1}$$

$$W_i + R_i + P_i + D_i \equiv F_i + V_i - (X_i + M_{xi}). \tag{10–2}$$

On the one hand, value added may be treated as the sum of factor payments which results in the following expression for value added for an industry:

$$VA_i = W_i + R_i + P_i + D_i. \tag{10–3}$$

From the identity (10–2), it is obvious that value added of an industry may also be treated as final sales plus inventory change less intermediate purchases, or

$$VA_i = F_i + V_i - (X_i + M_{xi}). \tag{10–4}$$

The value added by governments and households directly is composed of the wages paid to government employees and to household domestic

---

* Sales of intermediate products of industry i is not the same as purchases of intermediate products of industry i, although for the whole economy, sales of intermediate products of domestic business equals purchases of domestic intermediate products by businesses.

workers and rents paid by governments and households for occupancy of homes and buildings. Included in rent payments is *imputed* rent on *owner-occupied* homes and buildings. For example, if a man occupies a building owned by himself, the rent which he would have to pay if the building were owned by someone else is imputed rent and is included in rent payments by households. The value added by governments and households directly, then, is

$$VA_h + VA_g = W_h + W_g + R_h + R_g. \qquad (10\text{--}5)$$

Product is defined as the sum of value added for all industries plus value added directly by households and government:

$$\text{Product} = \Sigma VA_i + VA_h + VA_g, \qquad (10\text{--}6)$$

where VA_i may be obtained either from (10-3) or (10–4).

2. *Expenditure Account*

The expenditure account includes the total expenditure on all types of final uses, consumption, government, investment in fixed capital, net increase in inventories, and exports, less total expenditure on imports. Algebraically,

$$\text{Expenditure} = C + G + I + V + (E - M). \qquad (10\text{--}7)$$

The term $(E - M)$ is often referred to as net foreign investment.

3. *Income Account*

The income account is the sum of wages, rents, profits, and depreciation, or

$$\text{Income} = W + R + P + D. \qquad (10\text{--}8)$$

The income total may be further analyzed in terms of the manner in which the income is disposed. Profits are either distributed to the owners of businesses, paid out in the form of taxes on profits, or retained in the business in the form of savings. Thus,

$$P = P_d + T_b + S_b. \qquad (10\text{--}9)$$

The income of households is composed of wages, rents, and distributed profits and is either spent on consumption, put into savings or paid out in taxes. Algebraically,

$$W + R + P_d = C + S_h + T_h. \qquad (10\text{--}10)$$

Equations (10–8), (10–9), and (10–10) may be combined to show the disposal of income.

$$\text{Income} = C + S_h + S_b + T_h + T_b + D. \qquad (10\text{--}11)$$

4. Equivalence of Accounts

The three types of accounts, product, expenditure, and income, are equivalent. Each is just a different way of looking at the same total. First, let us demonstrate that product is equal to expenditure. Substituting (10–4) into (10–6), one obtains

$$\text{Product} = \Sigma(F_i + V_i - X_i - M_{xi}) + VA_h + VA_g$$
$$= F_b + V_b - X_b - M_x + VA_h + VA_g. \tag{10–12}$$

Now total final sales of all industries may be divided into sales to consumers, to government, for investment, as exports, and as intermediate goods and services. That is,

$$F_b = C_b + G_b + I_b + E + X_b. \tag{10–13}$$

If one substitutes (10–13) into (10–12), the result is

$$\text{Product} = C_b + G_b + I_b + E + V_b - M_x + VA_h + VA_g \tag{10–14}$$
$$= (C_b + VA_h) + (G_b + VA_g) + I_b + E + V_b - M_x.$$

Note that the X_b in (10–13) cancels with the X_b in (10–12). The reason for this is the equivalence of the sum of all *purchases* of intermediate products from domestic businesses and the sum of all *sales* of intermediate products by domestic businesses when all industries are taken together.

Consumption expenditure may be divided into expenditure on the products of domestic businesses, on imported goods and direct payment for factor services, government expenditure may be divided into the same three categories. Expenditure on investment and in increasing inventories can be divided into expenditure on the products of domestic businesses and on imports. These observations may be expressed algebraically:

$$C = C_b + C_m + VA_h,$$
$$G = G_b + G_m + VA_g,$$
$$I = I_b + I_m, \tag{10–15}$$
$$V = V_b + V_m,$$

or

$$C_b + VA_h = C - C_m,$$
$$G_b + VA_g = G - G_m,$$
$$I_b = I - I_m, \tag{10–16}$$
$$V_b = V - V_m.$$

Substituting the expressions in (10–16) into (10–14), one obtains

$$\begin{aligned}
\text{Product} &= C - C_m + G - G_m + I - I_m + E + V - V_m - M_x \\
&= C + G + I + V + E - (M_x + C_m + G_m + I_m + V_m) \qquad (10\text{–}17) \\
&= C + G + I + V + (E - M) \\
&= \text{Expenditure.}
\end{aligned}$$

This proves the equivalence of product and expenditure.

It is much easier to prove the equivalence of product and income. Substitute (10–3) and (10–5) into (10–6).

$$\begin{aligned}
\text{Product} &= \Sigma(W_i + R_i + P_i + D_i) + W_h + W_g + R_h + R_g \\
&= (W_b + W_h + W_g) + (R_b + R_h + R_g) + P + D \qquad (10\text{–}18) \\
&= W + R + P + D \\
&= \text{Income.}
\end{aligned}$$

Since Product equals Expenditure and Product equals Income, it follows immediately that

$$\text{Expenditure} = \text{Income.} \qquad (10\text{–}19)$$

5. Equivalence of Savings and Investment

The equivalence of savings and direct taxes on the one hand and investment (including inventory investment and net foreign investment) and government expenditure on the other is the result of an accounting identity and is related to the equivalence between income and expenditure. Since income and expenditure are equivalent, (10–7) and (10–11), expressions for expenditure and income, respectively, may be equated.

$$\begin{aligned}
&C + G + I + V + (E - M) \\
&= C + S_h + S_b + T_h + T_b + D. \qquad (10\text{–}20)
\end{aligned}$$

Eliminating C from both sides of this equation results in the familiar savings (plus taxes)—investment (plus government) identity.

$$G + I + V + (E - M) = S_h + S_b + T_h + T_b + D. \qquad (10\text{–}21)$$

6. Aggregate Accounts and Input-Output

The relationship between the aggregate accounts and the input-output table can be shown by taking a simple three-industry input-output table such as that shown in Table X–1. Each of the three different types of accounts, product, expenditure, and income, may be derived from this simple input-output table.

TABLE X–1

Three-Industry Hypothetical Input-Output Table

Use \ Source	1	2	3	C	G	I	V	E	Total Sales plus Inventory Increase
1	53	105	82.6	137.4	24	4	1	253	660
2	25	60.5	88.9	87.6	16	50	−5	52	375
3	0	58	4	135	15	39	7	113	371
M	102	24.5	21.5	205	85	90	2	x	530
W	274	76	106	31	195	x	x	x	682
R	15	4	0	18	5	x	x	x	42
P	140	33	48.3	x	x	x	x	x	221.3
D	51	14	19.7	x	x	x	x	x	84.7

The product account may be derived in two different ways: (i) as the sum of factor purchases (wages, rents, profits, and depreciation) for each industry, households, and government, or (ii) as the sum of total sales plus inventory increase less purchases of intermediate products for each industry plus factor payments by households and government. The first approach may be shown as follows:

			Wages		Rents		Profits		Depreciation		Value Added
Industry 1...	...	...	274	+	15	+	140	+	51	=	480
Industry 2...	...	...	76	+	4	+	33	+	14	=	127
Industry 3...	...	...	106	+	0	+	48.3	+	19.7	=	174
Households	...	...	31	+	18					=	49
Government	...	...	195	+	5					=	200

Total Product = 1030

Each of the sums in this table is arrived at by taking the sum of the wages, rents, profits, and depreciation entries for the columns corresponding to each of the three industries, and the columns corresponding to households and government.

The second approach to the product account may be demonstrated as follows:

	Total Sales plus Inventory Accumulation	Intermediate Purchases		Value Added
		Local (Industries 1, 2, and 3)	Imports	
Industry 1 ...	660	53 +25 + 0 = 78	102	480
Industry 2 ...	375	105 +60.5+58 = 223.5	24.5	127
Industry 3 ...	371	82.6+88.9+ 4 = 175.5	21.5	174
Households	—	—	—	49
Government	—	—	—	200

Total Product = 1030

The numbers in the first column of this table, total sales plus inventory accumulation are from the last column of input-output Table X–1. Intermediate purchases from local industries by industry 1 is the sum of the first three items of the industry 1 column of Table X–1. Similarly for industries 2 and 3. The imports column of the above table is taken from the import row of Table X–1. Value added is obtained by subtracting intermediate purchases from total sales plus inventory accumulation.

The expenditure account is taken from Table X–1 by summing the consumption, government, investment, inventory, and export columns and then subtracting the sum of the import row.

Column	Sum	
Consumption	137.4+87.6+135+205+ 31+18 =	614
Government	24 +16 + 15+ 85+195+ 5 =	340
Investment	4 +50 + 39+ 90 . =	183
Net inventory increase...	1 − 5 + 7+ 2 =	5
Exports	253 +52 +113 =	418
Less:		
Imports ...	102+24.5+21.5+205+85+90+2 =	530

Total Expenditure = 1030

Finally, the income account is determined by summing the wages, rent, profits, and depreciation rows of the Table X–1.

Row					Sum	
Wages	...	...	...	...	$274 + 76 + 106 + 31 + 195 =$	682
Rents	...	...	...	...	$15 + 4 + 0 + 18 + 5 =$	42
Profits	...	...	...	...	$140 + 33 + 48.3 \quad\quad =$	221.3
Depreciation		...	...	...	$51 + 14 + 19.7 \quad\quad\quad =$	84.7

Total Income = 1030

Note that each of the totals, product, expenditure, and income, are the same even though each is derived in a different manner.

B. National and Domestic Aggregates

Total output of the private sector is derived as the sum of the outputs of the firms and households making up the economy. In practice, a very important question can arise in deciding which firms and households to include in such calculations. Thus far, it has been implicitly assumed that the measurements concerned only those elements located within a single country. The firms thus located may be owned by the residents of the country or by residents of other countries. Similarly, the residents may own firms outside the country. Some of the wages paid by those firms may go to non-residents, and some residents may earn wages outside the country. The difference in the product of firms located within the country and those owned by residents is sometimes great; similarly, the difference between the wage bill paid to residents and that paid to labor employed within the country may be significant. The fact that aggregate economic activity as measured by the location and ownership criteria will rarely be the same has given rise to an important distinction between two alternative concepts.

1. The Domestic Concept

If the desire is to measure the activity within some geographic area, interest is centered on the location of the factors employed in production. Accounts designed to measure the output of factors located in an area, irrespective of ownership are called *domestic* accounts.

In the domestic accounts, the intrusion of the rest of the world is seen purely in terms of the volume of exports and imports. Other links between the nation's economic activity and foreign nations and individuals are excluded from consideration.

2. The National Concept

If interest is expanded to take in the ownership of the factor operating within the nation, quite different measurements may result. Income may flow out to non-resident owners of factors of production (to owners of firms and to migrant laborers), or it may flow in to resident owners of factors located in other countries. Accounts designed to measure aggregate economic activity including the effect of these flows are called national accounts.*

The importance of the distinction between location and ownership lies in the simple fact that flows of factor income directed out of the country produce benefits elsewhere. The receivers of that income will be unlikely to spend it on the purchase of the output of the country from which it came. The money will be spent in the countries of residence of the receivers, and it is to these countries that the benefits of the productive effort of the factors owned by their residents will accrue. In some countries the flows thus set in motion are relatively unimportant, the absolute magnitudes being small or the flows in and out being nearly in balance. In many developing countries, on the other hand, where a large part of the capital stock is foreign-owned, these flows may be relatively quite large and predominantly directed out of the country. This will be particularly true of nations with large extractive industries such as Chile, Venezuela, and Zambia. In such cases, a significant part of the domestic income might become part of the national income of another country.

In many less-developed countries there are also important examples of the international flows of wage payments, since migrant labor is very important in certain countries. Much of the unskilled labor of the cities of East and Central Africa, of the mining work forces and even, in some areas, of agricultural labor is migrant. This migration may be international, as when citizens of Malawi work in the Zambia copper-belt, or when workers from Rwanda are employed by Ugandan coffee farmers.

The relation of the domestic to the national accounts is perfectly straightforward in principle; the former are merely corrected (by subtraction) for net factor income paid abroad. Net income paid abroad is defined as follows:

Wages paid to non-residents by domestically-located firms

Plus: Rent paid to non-residents by domestically-located firms and by residents.

Plus: Interest payments to non-residents by domestically-located firms.

---

* The word "national" is used in two senses in reference to aggregate accounting systems. As used up to this point it is simply a generic term for such accounts. As defined in this section, it refers to accounts which reflect international flows of factor income. Both uses will continue to be met in the remainder of the text. No confusion should result as the proper meaning will be clear from the context.

Plus: Profits (gross of depreciation) accruing to non-residents as the owners of domestically-located capital.

Minus: The sum of the factor payments (wages, rent, interest, and profits gross of depreciation) paid or accruing to residents as the result of their ownership of factors of production located abroad (in the case of labor, as the result of employment abroad).

The figure thus arrived at may be subtracted from each of the domestic aggregates in order to arrive at figures for the corresponding national aggregates. It would be preferable to adjust all of the components in each account in accordance with the definition, but the task may be virtually impossible in practice.

Even when undertaken on the aggregate basis just discussed, correction is far from simple. First, it is necessary to adopt some arbitrary standard with which to determine the residence of laborers, and owners of other factors of production. The standards in use vary considerably, the dividing line between resident and non-resident varying from 6 months to 2 years. The matter of the ownership of firms is an even more complicated subject, solved in practice through the application of fairly arbitrary rules.

The second, and perhaps more significant, problem is caused by the difficulty of gathering data on net factor payments moving abroad. The difficulty may come from a variety of sources, e.g., the reluctance of firms to reveal profit transmittal figures and the lack of control over migrant labor at the borders.

The distinction between national and domestic accounts will be dealt with more formally below.*

---

* Some workers in the national accounting field advocate a system of accounts having three distinct measurement bases. These are: the geographic basis, the domestic basis and the national basis. Sample definitions, included below, are taken from G. C. Billington's article in *African Studies in Income and Wealth*, entitled "A Minimum System of National Accounts for Use by African Countries and some Related Problems."

The geographic product may be defined as the product of all producers within the geographic boundaries of a country, the domestic product as the product attributable to factors of production supplied by normal residents.

The difference between geographical product and domestic product is, briefly, the addition of the product of resident producers located abroad less the product of non-resident producers located within the geographical boundaries of the country. Resident producers located abroad include ships and aircraft operated abroad by domestic carriers, domestic government agencies and missions abroad and travelling salesmen, whilst non-resident producers within the geographical boundaries of the given country will include ships and aircraft operated by foreign carriers, foreign government agencies and missions and travelling salesmen.

The difference between the domestic product and the national product is equal to net factor income from the rest of the world, or the factor income of resi-

3. *The Net Accounts*

The accounts presented thus far have reflected the economic activity of the nation before any charges for depreciation are deducted. The aggregates include, as part of the value of current output, the value of the capital services consumed in the production of that output. It is desirable to have accounts which show the output net of capital consumption charges.

The net aggregates are derived from the corresponding gross aggregates as follows: depreciation is deducted from gross profit to arrive at net profit in the income account; depreciation is subtracted from gross domestic investment in the expenditure account, giving net domestic investment; charges for the consumption of capital are made against the product of each industry in the product account.

At this point it is, then, possible to distinguish 12 different aggregates; they are set out in Table X–2.

These different aggregates will often be confused in public discussion. It is, for example, widespread practice to refer to all gross national measures of activity as GNP; similarly for gross domestic activity as GDP.

4. *Estimates at Factor Cost and at Market Price*

It is necessary at this point to deal with a discrepancy which arises from the activity of government in the economy. The discussion earlier in this chapter suggested that the same total would be arrived at if expenditure on final products, value-added product, and factor incomes, were each measured for the whole economy. The final prices of goods and services will not all, however, result in factor payments as so far defined, because of the existence of indirect taxes and government subsidies. Indirect taxes include sales and excise taxes and customs duties. Their effect is to make the price paid in a transaction different from the actual receipts of the factors of production involved. (Note that direct taxes do not have the

---

dents embodied in the product of non-residents less the factor income of non-residents embodied in the product of residents.

The importance of the transactions of these agents (resident producers located abroad and non-resident producers located within the geographic boundaries) will vary from country to country and will seldom be altogether insignificant, especially from a balance of payments point of view. In practice, however, it is likely that African countries will find it more convenient to compile their first estimates in terms of the geographical product rather than the domestic product, mainly because the identification and estimation of the transactions of resident producers located abroad and non-resident producers located within the geographic boundary present special practical problems. The minor, improvements to be gained, bearing in mind the overall accuracy of the estimates are, in the early stages, just not worth the time and effort involved.

TABLE X–2

Types of Accounts

Domestic	Gross domestic product (GDP)	Net domestic product (NDP)
	Gross domestic income (GDI)	Net domestic income (NDI)
	Gross domestic expenditure (GDE)	Net domestic expenditure (NDE)
National	Gross national product (GNP)	Net national product (NNP)
	Gross national income (GNI)	Net national income (NNI)
	Gross national expenditure (GNE)	Net national expenditure (NNE)

same effect since they do not impinge directly on transactions but are levied directly on the income, in the form of individual wages or company profits.) Therefore, gross expenditure will differ from gross income, while gross product will be calculable in two different ways, either through measuring *factor cost* (in which case it will equal gross income) or by measuring sales less intermediate purchases, all at *market prices* (in which case it will equal gross expenditure). Subsidies paid to producers will have the opposite effect; they will tend to lower the value of sales of the product below the level of factor payments involved in its production. They will thus tend to make the income aggregates larger than the expenditure aggregates.

The choice between the use of gross product at factor cost and gross product at market price is usually made on grounds of expediency, depending on the ease with which the two alternatives can be compiled. It has sometimes been argued that factor cost measures are better because indirect taxes are, in some sense, related to the intermediate services of government to business, while direct taxes are a measure of final services of government. Such an argument is without merit. Indirect taxes will be part of the general revenue of government as will all other taxes. This revenue often will be spent without reference to the type of tax from which it came. The only reason for the existence of the GNP at factor cost concept is the convenience of the factor cost approach. In presenting the accounts, however, income *net* of all tax payments will be quite a useful concept to identify.

5. *Other Income Aggregates*

Now that the basic accounting aggregates have been derived, it is possible to look into some of the important subsidiary aggregates and accounts which have been developed in order to extend the usefulness of the national accounts.

In addition to the gross and net domestic and national income aggregates, a series of subsidiary measures of income have been introduced. Starting with net national income, one may derive in succession private income, personal income on an accrual basis, personal income on a cash basis, and disposable personal income.

a. *Private Income*

Private income is a measure of the income of individuals plus the amount of profit retained by firms (the increase in the ownership interest of individuals). It is derived from NNI by adding the sum of government transfer payments (e.g., interest payments on the national debt, social security payments) and business transfer payments (e.g., gifts and grants) and subtracting all wage supplements not paid to employees (e.g., payments into provident funds) and profits of government enterprises.

Transfer payments result from transactions which do not give rise to the

TABLE X–3

Accounts at Market Price and at Factor Cost

GDE (market price) = GDP (market price) = GDP (factor cost)+indirect taxes net of subsidies.

= GDI (factor cost)+indirect taxes net of subsidies.

GNE (market price) = GNP (market price) = GNP (factor cost)+indirect taxes net of subsidies.

= GNI (factor cost)+indirect taxes net of subsidies.

NDE (market price) = NDP (market price) = NDP (factor cost)+indirect taxes net of subsidies.

= NDI (factor cost)+indirect taxes net of subsidies.

NNE (market price) = NNP (market price) = NNP (factor cost)+indirect taxes net of subsidies.

= NNI (factor cost)+indirect taxes net of subsidies.

exchange of commodities or factor services for money. A payment of money is made without a corresponding flow of goods or services in the opposite direction. Examples of transfer payments are unemployment insurance payments and retirement payments. It is general practice to consider in the national accounts only payments which are in exchange for goods or services as contributing to output, so transfer payments are not shown in the major accounts as an addition to total product. The value of transfer payments to households shows up in the income aggregates discussed below as they form part of the disposable income available to households. Although not a payment for factor services rendered, by influencing the distribution of incomes they can influence the level of total spending and therefore the level of total product.

Wage supplements are additions to the wages of labor which are normally included in the wage bill of the economy, but which do not actually accrue to individuals. These include employer contributions to pension and social security funds and to employee welfare schemes.

b. *Personal Income—Variant One (Accrual Basis)*

Personal income on an accrual basis is a measure of the income actually accruing to individuals during the current period. It is derived from private income by subtracting from that figure the retained earnings of firms gross of direct taxes and depreciation.

c. *Personal Income—Variant Two (Cash Basis)*

Personal income on a cash basis is intended to measure only that part of the income accruing to individuals which is his to spend. It is derived from the variant one by subtraction of the total of employee contributions to social security, pension funds, and the like which are compulsory.

d. *Disposable Personal Income*

But even the above subtractions are not sufficient to derive individual income actually available for spending. Disposable personal income is derived from personal income on a cash basis by the subtraction of direct (income) taxes paid by individuals. It is a measure of the amount of money in the hands of individuals and available for their consumption or savings.

C. The United Nations and Its System of National Accounts

National income accounting practices have varied considerably in the past from country to country. The United Nations in recent years has advocated a standardized System of National Accounts (SNA).* The SNA

* See United Nations, *Studies in Methods: A System of National Accounts and Supporting Tables*, Series F, No. 2, Rev. 2, 1964; and United Nations, *Proposals for the Revision of the SNA*, E/CN. 3/356, August, 1967.

is based largely on national accounting practices in North America and western Europe. It embodies a number of recommendations concerning the sectoral breakdown of product accounts, the treatment of government revenues and expenditures in the accounts, methods of estimating depreciation of capital assets, defining the production boundary (discussed in the next chapter), techniques of estimating net factor payments abroad, etc.

The United Nations also suggests the compilation of appropriation accounts for various individual sectors of the economy, a rest of the world account, and a consolidated capital account as supplements to the basic standardized system. An example of a sectoral appropriation account is discussed below. The rest of the world account is basically a form of a balance of payments account; balance of payments accounts are discussed in a later chapter. A suggested format for a consolidated capital account is shown as Table X–4. The consolidated capital account shows on one side the gross domestic capital formation of the economy and on the other the saving of the various sectors of the economy which made that investment possible. Capital formation may be presented in a number of ways, by type of investor, by type of asset, by the industrial use. In each case, the

TABLE X–4

Consolidated Capital Account

A. Own account capital formation of rural households	A. Savings of households
	(1) rural households
B. Other gross domestic fixed capital formation	(2) other households and private non-profit institutions
C. Increase in stocks	B. Saving of public and private corporations
(1) of primary goods produced and retained by rural households	C. Saving of general government
(2) of other goods	D. Deficit of the nation on current account
	(1) net decrease in reserves and other external balances
	(2) net borrowing from the rest of the world and errors and omissions
	(a) net decrease in other assets abroad
	(b) net increase in liabilities to the rest of the world
	(c) errors and omissions
Gross domestic capital formation	Finance of gross domestic capital formation

figures will include estimates of fixed capital and inventory investment, and in many developing countries might profitably include estimates for the capital formation of rural households. The savings figures will include the savings of households (this may be broken down between rural and other households); the gross saving of firms, including public enterprises; the saving of the general government (capital investment financed out of current government revenues); and the borrowing of the nation abroad (the deficit of the nation in its current account dealings with the rest of the world). The capital account might also be prepared net of charges for depreciation of fixed capital. The usefulness of this account for the developing country is obvious. Unfortunately, it may prove difficult to complete the account, especially the saving side.

Although the U.N. has promoted the adoption of the SNA, the organization has recognized the need to adapt recommended practices to the particular needs of less-developed countries and the availability of data in these countries. Consequently, the United Nations Economic Commissions of Africa (ECA), Asia and the Far East (ECAFE), and Latin America (ECLA) formed working groups to recommend adaptations of the basic SNA to the needs of the countries in their respective geographical areas.* The working group proposals include expansion of some of the accounts, addition of others, and abandonment of certain details in still others.

Some of the specific recommendations of the working groups are set out below.

1. *Non-Monetary Transactions*

All three geographical working groups recommended a wider inclusion of subsistence activities in the national accounts. The ECA group recommended the extension of the production boundary to include not only production of goods for own-account consumption as with SNA but also own-account construction, investment in land-clearing and inventory

---

* For detailed discussions of the working groups' initial proposals see Economic Commission for Africa, *Report of the Working Group on the Adaptation of the U.N. System of National Accounts to Africa*, E/CN. 14/221, 1965; United Nations Economic Commission for Asia and the Far East, *Use of National Accounts in Asia and the Far East*, E/CN. 11/ASTAT/NA L.I., 196 ; and United Nations Economic Commission for Latin America, *National Accounts and Development Planning*, E/CN. 12/671, 1963. For later proposals see United Nations Economic Commission for Africa, *Report of the Working Group on Problems of National Accounts for Africa*, E/CN. 14/319, 1965; United Nations Economic Commission for Asia and the Far East, *Report of the Working Group of Experts on National Accounts*, E/CN. 11/L. 171; and United Nations Economic Commission for Latin America, *Report of the Working Group on National Accounts*, E/CN. 12/801, 1967.

accumulation. The ECA group also stressed the need for attempts to include own-account services such as firewood gathering, water carrying, etc. Both the ECA and ECLA groups recommended that subsistence output be valued at both retail and at producer (ex-farm) prices and that the difference between the two measures be assumed to reflect the value of the services (transportation, processing, etc.) performed on primary output by the household.

2. *Rural Household Sectoral Accounts*

Perhaps the most significant difference between the basic U.N. model and the geographical working group recommendations is the inclusion of a sectoral account for rural households. The rural household sector

TABLE X–5

Rural Households Account

Total disbursements	Total receipts

A. Consumption
  (1) on goods produced and consumed by the rural households sector (including purchases and barters within the sector)
  (2) on goods and services purchased from other sectors
B. Fixed capital formation
  (1) own account rural construction and landwork
  (2) goods and services purchased from other sectors
C. Increase in stocks of primary goods produced and retained by rural households
D. Intermediate goods and services purchased for production from other sectors
E. Factor income paid (wages, rent, interest, dividends)
F. Indirect taxes paid to the government
G. Direct taxes and transfers to the government
H. Transfers to other sectors
I. Hoarding and/or net lending to other sectors
	A. Primary commodities sold to other sectors
	B. Primary commodities retained for consumption within the rural households sector
	  (1) for own consumption
	  (2) sold or bartered
	C. Rural household services
	D. Other goods and services sold either within or outside the sector
	E. Own account rural construction and landwork
	F. Increase in stocks of primary goods produced and retained by rural households
	G. Factor income received (wages, rent, interest, dividends)
	H. Transfers from other sectors

account was deemed especially important for those countries where peasant small-holdings were an important part of total economic activity. A sample format for the rural household account is shown in Table X–5. This is primarily a subsistence sector account but also includes transactions of members of rural households which impinge on the cash economy. The detailed data needed to complete an account of this type are extremely difficult to compile in most less-developed countries. Thus, the format of Table X–5 may have to be modified if such an account is to be constructed.

3. Government

All the working groups stressed the need for a government appropriation account with considerable detail. The ECAFE group suggested that taxes be divided into taxes on income, taxes on expenditure, taxes on wealth, etc., instead of using the traditional classification of direct and indirect.

4. Depreciation

Both the ECA and ECLA groups suggested that because of the great difficulties in obtaining accurate estimates of depreciation, most countries should provide only accounts gross of charges for capital consumption rather than attempt estimates of net income aggregates based on bogus estimates of depreciation. The ECAFE group, on the other hand, noting that most countries in the region used the net concept in their product accounts, recommended that the published accounts provide further detail and clarification of procedures for estimating consumption of fixed capital.

5. Domestic and National Aggregates

The ECA group, because of the difficulties in the estimation of net factor income paid abroad, advocated the use of domestic aggregates as opposed to national aggregates.

6. Inventory of Human Resources

The ECA group proposed an inventory of human resources. This would essentially be an industry-by-industry census of the working population, and would show totals for wage earners, self-employed and unpaid family labor. It would, of course, have to be compiled with the aid of a population census of the nation, but would, after its presentation, provide information of independent value in such problems as the estimating of wage bills for various industries and manpower needs and availability.

7. *Total Product*

The ECA and ECAFE groups recommended that the total product of the economy be shown by industry of origin from either or both the income or commodity flow point of view. The commodity flow approach should prove easier for the earlier estimates, but as the availability of data increases and the skill and experience of the statisticians grow, a country might wish to add the income approach, too. The income approach in this context would be nothing more than the calculation of value-added (factor payments) for the industry. The commodity flow approach would show total sales minus the purchase of goods and services from other firms for each industry. The ECAFE group noted that in many countries a combination of approaches are used. While the production approach is predominant in agriculture, mining, manufacturing, and construction, the income approach is more commonly used in the service industries. The group suggested that when different methods are used, care should be used to ensure comparability of the two types of estimates.

The ECLA group proposed exploratory studies toward establishing regional estimates of national accounts and related statistics to be used both for planning by geographical region and for administrative decision and policy recommendations on intra-regional problems. With a gradual implementation by other regions, interesting insights might emerge between regions even if derivation of total product did not prove feasible initially.

XI

SOME CONCEPTUAL PROBLEMS

A. The Major Methods of Estimation

Three different methods of estimation of national accounting figures may be usefully distinguished. These are briefly described below.

1. *Income Analysis*

Income analysis concentrates on the measurement of the flows of payments for factor services. To do this it is necessary to estimate wages, gross profits, rents, and the incomes of the self-employed. There is also some interest in distinguishing that part of gross profits which takes the form of depreciation. The task of compiling the accounts, by this or any other method, involves piecing together data from numerous sources, diverse in character and containing gaps which must be filled by approximation. For example, wage payments are typically obtained from an annual survey of employment. Profit might be estimated from tax returns (an unreliable source where the tax administration is at all lax) or by assuming a standard profit share, derived from some past survey of industry. Gross profits for trading firms may be imputed from turnover figures in distribution aided by the results of a survey of distribution if available. Output figures plus input data from surveys of agriculture are likely to be used to derive the incomes of the agricultural sector. Rent estimates are likely to be based on some measure of the value of the existing housing stock. Depreciation estimates might be based on some knowledge of business depreciation charges, but more likely they will be an assumed proportion of total product or the total estimated capital stock.

172

From such estimates some picture of income flows and product at factor cost can be gained.

2. *Expenditure Analysis*

Expenditure analysis attempts to estimate final expenditure in as direct a fashion as possible. Consumer spending may be estimated from the results of surveys of household spending, from retail trade data and from output information supplied by producers of consumer goods. Investment goods spending might also be tackled from both the demand and supply side. The demand for investment goods may be estimated from surveys of business, reports of business spending, and public accounts. Investment goods production may be estimated from a few basic commodity flows, such as imports of machinery and building materials and domestic output figures for cement. This method will be important in developing countries, partly because of the unusually high dependence on imports for investment goods.

Inventory investment requires better data availability for its estimation than exists at present in most developing countries. This volatile element in the expenditure side of the accounts is therefore likely to be neglected.

The government's spending will be available from the official accounts, but these figures will often not be classified as between investment and current spending in a fashion suitable for the accounts. Also, insofar as some investment spending has been calculated from the supply side care must be taken not to count part of government investment spending twice.

3. *The Product Accounts*

The "value added by industry of origin" can be calculated either by estimating primary factor payments or by calculating value added by a commodity-flow method. Commodity-flow methods attempt to estimate the value added for an industry by subtracting *purchases* of intermediate products from total sales. For the economy as a whole this will sum to sales of final product; for a given industry this will not be so for its purchases of intermediate goods will not equal its sale of intermediate goods (whereas for the economy as a whole, of course, these two totals will be equal). The commodity-flow method will give an estimate of product at market price, while the valuation of primary factor payments provides an estimate at factor cost.

Where commodity-flow methods are used, two methods of crude estimation are sometimes adopted. Where input flows are known (e.g., from import data), value added might be calculated as a fixed ratio to these inputs, the assumed ratio being derived from some past survey, or, where data are more complete, from an input-output table for some past year.

Alternatively, when sales are known similar assumptions might be made regarding the ratio of value added to total sales for the industry.

4. *The Methods in Practice*

In principle it would be desirable to tackle each of the three major accounts with a different method, systematically estimating income from as direct an observation of factor payments as possible, expenditure from surveys of final spending and the product accounts from estimates of output and intermediate input. The results would then provide a check on each other.

Even in developed countries with elaborate statistical services an independent compilation of all parts of the three accounts is not likely to be possible. In developing countries, at the initial stages of creating an accounting system, the best that can be hoped for is that accounts can be pieced together with a mixture of methods. A typical attempt would consist of the creation of a product account from a mixture of income data (providing estimates of payments for primary factor services), final expenditure information (from which value added will be estimated for some sectors), and flows of inputs and outputs. A fully integrated system of accounts is still a distant goal in many less-developed countries.

B. The Significance of the Accounts: Value and Costs

The accounts which have been described have been built up on the basis of the accounts of firms, households, and the government. These accounts of individual economic units are based on prices prevailing in the nation's markets. The justification for use of the accounts as estimates of "value" or "welfare" or "production," either in the aggregate or for particular sectors, depends on the acceptability of market price criteria of measurement.

The product accounts illustrate the dual nature of the market value criteria. Market price is a measure of the value of sales to the consumer; it is also a measure of the value of the factor services to which the product can be attributed. A convention of the accounting system is that all output can eventually be attributed to some factor service and that a suitable measure of the factor service is the payment received by the factor.

It is possible to use national accounts without making such a strong commitment to this particular interpretation. As an organized record of particular types of transactions, the accounts are of considerable interest irrespective of the special interpretation which is placed on the results.

Although this is true, it must be admitted that a value interpretation is usually placed on the accounts by both economists and the public at large who use the accounts. It is therefore necessary to consider with some care how far a value interpretation is justified.

The first and perhaps most fundamental difficulty is that, at best, market prices measure relative scarcity and represent value at the margin. When comparing situations with two different price systems it is not easy to say whether there are more or less goods. The change in relative scarcity represented by a change in price might result from a change in taste and therefore a change in the value placed on the goods by the consumer. Of course, if there were more of all goods in situation *1* than situation *2*, or if it could be demonstrated that more of all goods could be achieved with the resources in use in situation *1*, then it would be reasonable to say that situation *1* is superior to situation *2*. If this cannot be demonstrated then output must be compared, although valued at differing relative prices. The method of comparison in this situation must necessarily be somewhat arbitrary. The attempt must be made to translate the two price systems into some common denominator.

It should be noted that the difficulties involved in making statements like "Situation *1* is superior to Situation *2*," although great, are much less than those arising when a comparison is made of the sort "Situation *1* is twice as good as Situation *2*." The latter statement involves a *cardinal* measurement whereas the former merely involves *ordinal* comparison. The difficulties involved in cardinal comparison may be grasped if they are examined in the simplest situation. Assuming that a consumer has twice as much of all goods in situation *1* as in situation *2*, and it is known that his tastes have not changed, is he twice as well off? If his wants are stable, and he experiences diminishing marginal utility from the consumption of goods in general, then it will not be true, for his valuation of additional goods will be declining, and the value he places on intra-marginal consumption at situation *1* will be greater than that he places on the same quantity of goods added to his consumption between situation *1* and *2*.

In practice, despite the dubious nature of the implicit assumptions, product and income estimates will be used to make such comparisons. In many such comparisons the quantity of goods is so much larger in one of the situations being compared that a common sense conclusion of extraordinary superiority is legitimate (e.g., incomes are obviously very much higher in the United States or the U.S.S.R. than in Bolivia). The difficulty arises when the attempt is made to convey the difference with precision, as when a lecturer in the United States states that the "*per capita* income in Bolivia is less than $200 per year" or, conversely, a Bolivian is told that "*per capita* income in the United States is more than $2900 per year." The precise impression conveyed by such statements is misleading.

The difficulties are compounded by the dangers of making average comparisons. The distribution of national income may be as important a criterion of comparison as its size. Economists sometimes tend to treat the two questions as separate, arguing that if a higher output can be achieved then it could be redistributed to whatever pattern is considered preferable. This presumption is often illegitimate, because the size of the product may be partly dependent on the distribution of income. Where there are sharply delineated classes or communities in a society, the total and average figures may mask very strong differences between these groups. For example, during the 1950's it was possible to say that average *per capita* income in Uganda was less than in Kenya while in Kenya it was very much less than in Britain—but whose *per capita* income? During that period, the data suggests that the *per capita* income of Africans was higher in Uganda than in Kenya, while the *per capita* income of Europeans in Kenya was higher than that of Europeans in Britain!

Also, in evaluating the welfare situation between two countries, many observers would feel that the standard of living of the poorest group in the community is an important criterion. A society in which average income is high but in which the poor live in wretched conditions might be judged inferior to one with lower average income but a higher minimum standard. (Conversely, the judgment could be made that a society with a very wide range of incomes and very great rewards and penalties for *success* or *failure* is preferable.)

These points touch on a complex set of issues which go well beyond the scope of this volume. The arguments raised should suggest to the reader, however, that reading value and welfare meaning into income and product measures is a controversial activity at best, and certainly involves value judgments of quite a complicated nature. This is not to say that such value judgments are inappropriate but rather to suggest that they cannot simply be derived from market data.

The interpretation of the income and product accounts at factor cost as an estimate of the value of the flow of factor services involves difficulties comparable to the market valuation of goods and services discussed in the preceding paragraphs. In particular, it is dubious how far the particular factor payment can be said to provide a measure of services rendered in a situation in which the competitive market equilibrium of the economist's simple model is not operative.

The gross profit share recorded will be a measure of entrepreneurial return, monopoly profit, interest payment, and rents arising from factor immobility. It will not necessarily be a good measure of the opportunity costs involved in factor employment. There are theories explaining factor shares in national income which would hold that factor payments are measures of the productivity of the factors of production, the wage rate and the profit rate being equated with the marginal productivity of labor and capital respectively. There are alternative theories, however, which claim that the marginal productivity theory of factor shares is inadequate and that the profit share is to be explained by the degree of monopoly power or that the saving propensities of capitalists and workers are the determining factors.

The value interpretation placed on the recorded factor shares is therefore still a point of some controversy, and is likely to remain one, because of the complex technical questions involved, and because of the ideological implications of alternative theories of income distribution.

These comments might sound quite remote from the practical problems of the accounts but the ambiguities involved are an important cause of the difficulties which arise in measuring a number of components of income and product. This is particularly true of the difficulties involved in the valuation of subsistence sector activities, government services, and the treatment of changing price levels. Where market transactions can no longer be used as an "objective" criterion of measurement then the accountant is forced to consider precisely what the market prices were supposed to measure, and to attempt to provide an alternative measurement in their absence.

C. Difficulties in Applying Market Price Criteria

In practice it is not always possible to obtain measurements based on current market price, of the type discussed in the previous section of this chapter. The rest of this chapter deals with national accounting problems in situations where there is no market transaction to provide a suitable basis for measurement and with situations in which it is considered desirable to exclude certain transactions from the estimates of income and product.

1. *Imputed Values*

The discussion so far has dealt primarily with transactions conducted in the market and involving the exchange of money for goods or services. Certain implicit transactions have been mentioned, for example, the transfer of goods to inventory within the firm and the charging of depreciation. The instances discussed share the common property that some value for the implicit transaction is recorded in the firm's books. It will, however, be true that some implicit transactions will have no value attributed to them by the participants, but that the national accountant will wish to measure them. This will involve the accountant in the business of *imputation*, that is, the attributing of some value to transactions which are implicit and unrecorded. Two prime examples of this technique may be given here, but the most important will be postponed to the discussion of the subsistence sector.

First, the owner of a house who occupies his own property would have to pay rent in other circumstances and could receive a rental income if his house was occupied by a tenant. Since he does not pay rent, there is no measure of the value of the services being provided by his house. Yet were he to move to rented quarters currently owner-occupied and rent his own home to someone else, the product of the economy would go up by the value of the two rents; this is clearly an unreasonable result. Thus it is necessary to impute rent as part of the income of house-owners. The imputed rent might be charged at the rate being charged for similar quarters in the local area. It may, in some cases, require estimation direct from the assessed value or initial cost of the housing, assuming some standardized rate of return.

A second example of imputed value-transactions concerns commercial banking. Normally, commercial banks do not charge their demand depositors fees large enough to cover the costs of providing the services given them. At the same time, the bank does not credit to its depositors' accounts any interest payment by the bank for the use of that money. It may be assumed that the interest earned by depositors on their money exactly covers the cost of demand deposit services, plus the gross profit of the banking firm. To allow for this situation, both interest payments and additional fees should be imputed to commercial banks. Thus, it should be assumed that the bank pays its depositors interest and charges them fees which cover fully the cost of services rendered plus gross profit. This results in a more realistic evaluation of the product of the economy. In practice such adjustments are likely to be made only in the most sophisticated sort of accounting system.

2. The Production Boundary

Once the possibility is accepted of imputing values in situations in which market transactions do not occur, the decision as to what should be counted as production becomes an open issue. Further, as the practice of national accountants is examined, it becomes apparent that not only are some values imputed when no transaction occurs, but that in some circumstances transactions which do occur are excluded from the accounts. The major difficulty involved here is posed by the existence of households which produce and consume independently of the market economy. This sector of effort is commonly referred to as the *subsistence* sector and will be discussed further shortly. There are, however, other activities which cause trouble. Two of the most significant are the unpaid services of housewives and the illegal and immoral activities of the citizens of the nation.

3. *Housewives' Services*

It has been argued that the services of the housewife, performed in her own home without pay, should be valued because most of them are available in the market through the hiring of domestic help. Thus, as Pigou pointed out, if a man married his housekeeper, national income declines! Though this is an inconsistency, it is not at all clear that the expenditure of effort and the solution of the problems of imputation involved in the estimation of the value of housewives' services would produce returns of any real value.

Attempts have been made in certain African countries to measure the value of the services of wives on the basis of the bride price. This is an ingenious idea, but is based on a misleading view of bride price, resulting from the English translation, which is as legitimate as using the dowry typical of many countries as a measure of husband's services (or perhaps the negative value of the wife's services).

The problem of housewives' services is similar, in principle, to that posed by the subsistence sector but is typically neglected because of the belief that the values involved are small enough, relative to the total economic activity of households in the monetized sector, for the oversight to be unimportant, particularly in the light of the extreme practical difficulties of attempting such a valuation.

4. *Illegal Activities*

Crime, prostitution, and the output of illegal products may involve transactions of considerable magnitude in money terms. The problem here is often one of data collection, for understandably comprehensive statistics on all criminal activity are not usually available. In a number of areas, crime may offer well defined services, such as the gambling facilities provided illegally in the United States. Whether such activities should be considered productive effort is a controversial question. Even in the case of prostitution, some national accountants have argued for inclusion, although the difficulties of data collection and the controversial nature of the activity prevents such measurement in practice.

D. Accounting for Subsistence Economic Activity

In the development of national accounting techniques in the context of the developed economies many of the decisions made about method have been made on a pragmatic basis rather than through the exercise of abstract principle. Much of the ease with which a consensus emerged was probably the result of the similarity of economic environment in which the principles were developed (although even in those circumstances competing systems emerged and issues were left unresolved). Moreover, the techniques were applied to economies with enough continuity of structure to make inter-temporal comparison on the basis of social accounts a sensible activity.

By and large, social accounting became an accounting system for cash transactions. The section of the economy in which a large proportion of production was used directly in the sustenance of the actual producers was small enough for its treatment to be a marginal consideration. Of course, those occupied in full-time paid employment in such economies may engage in leisure time production for their own consumption to such a degree that the absolute value of their output might be very considerable— greater in absolute *per capita* terms than subsistence output in those economies where such activity is the exclusive concern of a sizeable proportion of the population. In the developed economy, however, there is some likelihood that such activities are *proportionally* only a small part of the total productive output and a stable proportion at that. Neither of these two assumptions can be made about the importance of subsistence activity as a source of economic welfare in many less-developed countries. What is a marginal issue in the case of the developed countries becomes a potential source of serious difficulty in developing economies.

In the face of this difficulty practice has varied. As will be pointed out below, different techniques of subsistence accounting are used. This is an area where no satisfactory consensus seems to be emerging.

Most writers have not doubted the wisdom of including *some* estimate of subsistence activity. There has been, however, considerable controversy concerning what activities to include in subsistence estimates. The United Nations experts, in their System of National Accounts (1953) advised that:

> In the case of primary producers, that is those engaged in agriculture, hunting, fishing, mining and quarrying, all primary production whether exchanged or not and all other goods and services produced and exchanged are included in the total of production. . . . As a result of these rules there is omitted from production the net amount of all non-primary production performed by producers outside their own trades and consumed by themselves. Non-primary production may be defined broadly as the transformation and distribution of tangible commodities as well as the rendering of services.

This was a pragmatic set of criteria, apparently designed for economies experiencing a high degree of division of labor in which the distinction between the activities conducted in the pursuit of a producer's trade and other activities had a clear common sense boundary.

A number of economists have felt that such criteria are insufficient in dealing with economies with a low degree of division of labor, where the cash economy has only achieved very limited penetration into the lives of the populace. This is particularly the case when one of the purposes of the accounts is supposed to be the international or the inter-temporal comparison of welfare. This is the motivation of the decision made by Haseeb to include subsistence construction in his estimation of the Iraq national product. Abraham makes a similar adjustment in the Phillippine national accounts. G. C. Billington (at one time responsible for the Rhodesian accounts) has argued for very inclusive estimation in the belief that it is necessary for planning purposes, suggesting that building construction, land works, processing, storage, transportation, and distribution of the primary products in the subsistence sector should all be measured, so as to minimize the risk of under-counting. He accepted the neglect of processing of goods purchased and other households services. On the other hand, P. Okigbo, re-casting the Nigerian national accounts, felt that there had been an overconcern with welfare measures which had resulted in dubious techniques of estimation; he therefore opted for a very narrow definition of subsistence output.

Just as the removal of the cash criterion imposes the necessity of introducing other arbitrary definitions of the boundary of measured production, so also does it remove the straightforward basis of valuation, requiring a choice between valuation at some market price (the more inclusive measure) and valuation at *ex farm* prices. The difficulty also arises, if a broad definition of subsistence output is used, that there might be some items (e.g., rural huts) for which there are no comparable cash prices.

Faced with these differences, the U.N. has suggested that the boundary of production should include, in addition to all goods and services sold:*

(i) All other agricultural, forestry, and fishing products;
(ii) Own account building, construction, and landworks by households;
(iii) Processing, storage, transportation, and distribution of non-primary output by rural households.

The main interest of such estimates is to provide a record of resources which could be mobilized for development purposes.

However, a few economists have argued for the exclusion of subsistence measurement entirely. On the one hand, the subsistence sector is self-balancing and can be expected to have minimal effects on the rest of the economy. On the other, they claim that subsistence income is but a small percentage of total national income. However, the second claim is dependent

* United Nations, *Proposals for the Revision of SNA* E/CN. 3/356, August 1967, pp. 212–14.

on the validity of the very accounts the utility and meaning of which they are doubting.

The recent trend has been for the economic statistician concerned with these questions to move away from the attempt to measure levels of welfare; they state that they desire to produce figures which will be of utility in the planning process. However, there seems to be little clear idea of how the existing or suggested estimates could, in practice, be utilized by a planner.

If the issues of principle have been a source of conflict, the practical difficulties of estimation have been an even greater barrier to the achievement of meaningful estimates of subsistence product. The efforts so far have involved the manipulation of numerous estimates, each individually subject to errors the magnitude and direction of which can only be guessed.

To conclude the discussion of this subject, it will be useful to consider a little more explicitly why these figures are needed and whether there are practical means whereby such needs can be met.

The easy answer to those who seek to conduct international or intertemporal comparisons of welfare is to point out the dubious foundations on which any such project must rest, even in principle. Nevertheless, it may well be that the statistician is not a free agent in this matter, in that willy-nilly his figures will be used for such purposes, and that therefore he should make some effort to ensure that such comparisons are not subject to excessively gross distortion.

In so far as the exercise of measurement is undertaken for the purposes of welfare comparison, the relevant measure would be an estimate of the money income that would be necessary to achieve comparable standards in a monetized economy as in fact are achieved in the subsistence situation. For this purpose the cost of the subsistence output, either in terms of expenditure of effort or in opportunity cost terms, is irrelevant. If, for example, food is a free good in a particular community this is not to be valued at zero for welfare comparisons. What is required is a measure of consumption standards, not inputs of factor services nor even a measure of the market value of the goods consumed if they were marketed in the existing conditions. Thus it might well be that a rural hut which provides services essentially similar to a city dwelling could command not even a nominal rent in the countryside. Now, it could be argued that the market price criterion of value should result in both being valued at rents which could be obtained if the facilities were offered for rental; in the East African case, the services provided by a simple town dwelling might be valued at $56 or so per year, while those of the rural dwelling would be valued at a near zero value. This is the logic of the procedure most often adopted. However, to achieve full consistency with other social accounting practices another step should be included—the value figures should be adjusted for differences of price level; if commodities are valued at the low market prices operating in the countryside, then for comparison, the resulting series should be expanded by price indices allowing for the differentials in the level of prices between the rural and urban sectors.

In can be safely asserted that existing estimates of subsistence output in national accounts do not provide a basis for sensible welfare comparison. The implication of the accounts as they are currently produced is that, for a large proportion of the population, income levels are almost identical with the consumption of food, and even that is valued at very low prices. This may be a true estimate of the standard of welfare in some cases, but as a general picture it is certainly incorrect, undervaluing the welfare derived from self-constructed homes and numerous craft activities. This conclusion is derived without considering the implications of the failure of social accounts to register differences in the consumption of leisure; in an economy predominantly given over to a 40 hour week and 50 week working year this is no serious problem; in comparing welfare in an industrial and a subsistence economy it is a very important issue.

The conclusion must be that it is the responsibility of the economic statistician vigorously to assert the impossibility of making meaningful comparisons of welfare in money-value terms. More would be gained by short verbal descriptions of the character of life in the subsistence sector, supplemented perhaps by crude indexes of health and food intake, than by attempts to conjure up monetary estimates of subsistence consumption standards.

One use of subsistence estimates might be to complete the data necessary to make estimates of changes in productivity over time. Without estimates of subsistence output it would be impossible to distinguish improvements in productivity over time from the results of increased monetization. Unfortunately, the data currently available in no sense make this possible. From existing estimates of subsistence economic activity, it is not possible to tell whether the increases in cash output are at the expense of subsistence production or the result of increased supply of effort or of improved productivity. Similarly, it is not possible to tell whether the movement of labor to the town has resulted in any diminution of subsistence output. This is because the current subsistence estimates are often not based on any real information about subsistence activity, but are rather the result of assumptions and surmises concerning the very things about which it is desirable to have hard facts. If more information were available it would probably be of more use in its original state than in dubious transformations into monetary figures.

E. The Contribution of Government in the National Accounts

Thus far, consideration of the nature of government's peculiar role in the economy has been avoided by implicitly adopting a view of government closely analogous to that of the business firm. This allowed the development of the basic accounting system without undue confusion and diversions. There are difficult issues resulting from the unique position of government, however, which deserve close attention.

The role of government in the economy is essentially different from that of firms and households. To cite only a few characteristics behind this difference, the government offers services to both enterprises and consumers, yet in most cases it receives no payment for them (or if it does receive payment, the sum is likely to bear little or no relation to the value of the service to the user); many of its services apply equally to all citizens whatever their individual feelings about the worth of those services; it often acts to alter the distribution of incomes. Such a list of characteristic activities could with ease be extended greatly, but in the context of the national accounts it will be most useful to consider the difficulties raised by the government's action in four major roles: as a purchaser of goods and services and a provider of services; as the taxing power; as a transfer agent for income; and as a subsidiser of business activity. The most interesting issues are raised by the first two of these roles and the discussion below will concentrate on them. There is a substantial amount of agreement on the meaning and treatment of transfer payments and subsidies, while on the other hand, the closely related problems raised by government's activities as purchaser, taxer, and provider of services have still not been solved to the complete satisfaction of economists, even though a number of conventions have been adopted and have gained authority, if only through familiarity.

How should the many services of the typical modern government be treated in the national accounts? Should they be considered to be all intermediate services, serving merely to create a social framework allowing the attainment of a certain level of economic activity by the other transactors? Or should they all be counted as final services, in addition to the goods and services produced by enterprise? Or does the best view lie somewhere between these two poles, some services being identifiable as final and some as intermediate?

There have been proponents of each of these views. The arguments they have used have rested primarily on differing views of the role of government and, more subtly, on divergent feelings about the goals of social and economic activity. In certain cases, however, economists have espoused one or the other view because of more practical considerations arising out of the difficult problems of identification and allocation of benefits and costs.

1. *Government Services as Intermediate Goods*

The view that all government services are intermediate has been the least popular of the three, currently having little support. The activities of government, in this view, serve only to create the conditions in society which make other economic activity possible. If this were true, then the value of these services would already be included in the value of total production; it would be double-counting to attempt to introduce another measure of them.

This approach to the valuation of government services is consistent with the *laissez-faire* view of the role of government, in which the government is seen as providing the minimum framework of services within which the economy can operate. Such an approach is inadequate in situations where a large part of the government's activity provides services of direct benefit to the welfare of the individual. To view health, education, sanitation, and other public utility services as intermediate goods maintaining the work force is no more legitimate than to consider the provision of food and clothing to workers as a similar intermediate good!

2. *Government Services as Final Good*

The view that all government services should be treated as final goods has great currency in practice, although more for pragmatic reasons than because of support on grounds of principle.

Some commentators argue strongly for the treatment of government services as final product on the grounds that all the services of government create real final consumption value for a nation's citizens. For example, to the value of the automobile produced by enterprise, government adds its own contribution in the way of roads, traffic safety efforts, etc.

This view has also been adopted by many who reject the philosophical position but who are driven to it by despair over the practical problems involved in sorting out final and intermediate services in the government's total activity.* This approach has been persuasive and a good deal of present practice springs from it.

The legitimate criticism of this position is that some part of government services in fact only maintain the framework for productive activity, the value of which is already being included in the product estimates.

Once it is agreed to include government services as part of total national

---

* The word "despair" is used by Kuznets in referring to J. R. Hicks who adopted this position for precisely these reasons.

product a number of questions arise. For example, what is to be the rule for government purchases from business: are they to be all final, all intermediate, or mixed? The purchases of a business firm producing final services are, of course, intermediate products. If this approach were adopted with respect to government, however, it would be necessary to find methods for valuing the services themselves. Thus, if government purchases from business are counted as intermediate products, government will not appear in the expenditure account unless value is imputed to all its final services. This is far from simple conceptually or practically. Consider the manifold difficulties of placing a monetary value on, say, police services. The more fruitful line of attack seems to be the use of costs as a basis of valuation. The general method adopted is to value government services on the basis of the cost of producing them, in terms of wages paid and purchases from business.

Rents may also be imputed for the buildings owned and occupied by the government. It has also been suggested that interest payments on the national debt should be included in the valuation of government services as a measure of the cost of capital in use, analogous to the interest payments of businesses. So much of the national debt, however, is likely to have been acquired in the past to finance expenses which were essentially current (particularly the military expenses of war time) that it does not seem reasonable to treat the national debt as a suitable measure of the services of the existing capital stock of government. Interest payments on the government debt are therefore usually located as transfers rather than payments for current flows of factor services.

The treatment of government services as a final good, valued at cost, is the most widely used method in practice. Its operation in relation to the three basic accounts is quite straightforward. In the *expenditure account* the government contribution consists of its purchases from firms, plus the government wage bill and government rent payments (including imputed rents). In the *income account* the government wage bill forms part of the total wage share and government rent payments part of the rent share, but there is no government contribution to the profit share (excluding government enterprises). In the derivation of personal income, adjustments are made for transfers (including government interest payments) and subsidies. In the *product account* the value added contribution is equal to the government wage bill plus rent payments.

A further question which must be answered once government contribution to final product is admitted is how to treat the various forms of government capital formation. If all government services are considered final, it is only logical to include all government capital formation in gross domestic capital formation. When some mixture of final and intermediate services is conceded, it is necessary to consider whether part of government capital formation should not be excluded as unrelated to final production.

3. *The Measurement of Government Services—A Compromise View*

After the above discussions it should be clear that there is an excellent case for a third view of government services, that is, that some are final, some intermediate. It certainly seems reasonable to hold that part of government's efforts go into maintaining a social framework within which economic activity is possible. It also seems important to recognize that a large (and probably fast growing) share of these services is directed at individual welfare. Unfortunately, this view creates a whole new problem area: the development of criteria for distinguishing a final from an intermediate service. It also requires that some decisions be made about the content of government capital formation.

The most important example of the use of this approach is provided by the work of Simon Kuznets. He begins by assuming that the goal of economic activity is to satisfy the wants of individual consumers who are citizens of a country, both present and future citizens. It must be stressed that this is only one of a large number of possible (and reasonable) goals. This goal stresses the importance of the individual, although it might be decided that the goal could be the extension of national power and prestige, or the creation of a particular kind of society.

The criteria developed by Kuznets for the recognition of final current services of government are summarized below. Other sets of criteria would be necessary under other definitions of goals.

(i) The recipient of a final service must either receive it free or pay only a token price for it. This, of course, is designed to eliminate from consideration instances of government acting as a business. Such activities would be included in the accounts in the same way as would a business, that is by the inclusion of the value in the market of the services it sells.

(ii) The service in question must be available only on an individual's overt initiative; that is, it must not fall to him automatically on the basis of his membership in society or in any particular group within society. This criterion eliminates the great majority of the "social-framework" type of activities such as police protection, legislative work, etc.

(iii) Finally, there must be a widespread analogue to the service available in the private market. This criterion was added to eliminate certain cases, such as court appeals in which there is overt individual initiative but from which it did not seem reasonable to conclude a final product flowed. The "widespread" qualification was inserted to preclude such inclusions as that of police activity based on an analogy with private body guards.

What would constitute final services under these criteria? First, of course, public education and medical services are included where they are not on a fee-paying basis. Also included are public libraries and museums and public-sponsored events in the performing arts (subject, of course, to the first criterion). Then would come the whole range of technical assistance and advice activities in such fields as agriculture and business. The provision of interest-free loans to individuals would also count as a final service. Indeed, the list could be lengthened considerably but these examples should suffice. The criteria governing the inclusion or exclusion of government capital formation are:

(i) Government capital formation (of real assets) is included whether it is designed to produce intermediate or final services. Thus, courthouses and military installations are included, though the services which they help to produce are intermediate. This criterion is, of course, strictly analogous to those used in judging private capital formation, where blast furnaces, for example, are considered part of capital formation though pig iron is strictly an intermediate product.

(ii) Excluded from estimates of government capital formation are additions to stocks of intangibles. In the case of government this criterion is primarily useful in excluding attempts to measure the value of changes in the stock of educated citizens, of patriotism, national prestige, and so on.

(iii) Included in the estimates are all changes in government's international claims and liabilities.

Thus, the criteria for the inclusion or exclusion of government capital formation are closely analogous to those for private investment.

Accounting for government's contribution under the above criteria is formally a relatively simple matter, though as mentioned earlier, its pratical application may prove quite difficult.

In the expenditure account, investment includes all government capital formation allowed under the criteria, and similarly, government current spending includes both wages of employees and value of purchases from business contributing to the final services as defined above.

F. Taxation, Transfer, and Subsidies

1. *Taxation*

In the accounts, indirect taxes are treated differently from direct taxes because the former do not enter into factor cost estimates of product or estimates of national income. If it were decided to view some government services as intermediate then it would be appropriate to eliminate part of the tax bill from the estimates of income on grounds of principle, rather than the current situation in which indirect taxes are eliminated from some of the accounts purely because of the method of calculation. In such a case some part of the tax bill would be viewed as a payment for intermediate services and should therefore be eliminated from the estimates of primary factor income. There are no grounds, however, on which such a deduction could be associated with any particular tax.

2. *Transfer Payments*

The government, of course, is involved in other activities in addition to those discussed above. Two of the most important of these are the redistribution of factor incomes and the correction of certain inequities and hardships. These two activities may be, for convenience, lumped under the heading "Transfer Payments." Specifically included in this category are interest payments on government debt, unemployment compensation, social security payments, pensions to government employees and servicemen, etc. It is general practice not to add such transfers to the national income totals as they are considered unrelated to any productive activity.

Some transfer payments result from funds into which come compulsory contributions from employers and/or employees. In these cases, general practice is to include employer contributions as part of total wages and, if employee contributions are made, to count these as part of personal saving. Payments made from the funds are, of course, not added to national income aggregates.

3. *Subsidies*

The final aspect of government activity to be examined is the subsidy. This is actually another form of redistribution of factor incomes, but is treated separately for convenience. Its slightly different nature requires a different method of handling in the accounts.

Subsidies come in three major varieties:

(i) As government purchases of products from private enterprise at or above market price and subsequent resale at a lower price.

(ii) As export bounties (payment for the exporting of goods to bring the price received for the exports up to home level or above).

(iii) As direct cash payments to producers; such payments are essentially similar to transfer payments and are treated as such in the accounts.

Subsidies represent an income to factors of production above the payments made for final goods and services in the market. They must therefore be added to the estimates of product at market price to get to factor cost estimates, and subtracted if the movement is from factor cost to market price.

G. The Significance of the Accounts

The national accounts are useful both as descriptions of the level of well-being in the society and also as tools in planning operations. Most of the debate regarding accounting methods has tended to concentrate on the first function and the advocates of particular positions have tended to refer back to welfare criteria in support of their points of view. Recently, however, there has been an increasing concern over the second function.

As planning is likely to have as its objective the increase in levels of welfare, defined in one manner or another, the existence of the separate functions need not lead to fundamental conflicts. In practice, however, the planner is likely to be less interested in the niceties of welfare measurement and more interested in the utility of the data in assessing the feasibility and consistency of his plans. For this purpose he may well be more interested in the accuracy of the data for a few strategic sectors than their completeness of coverage. Thus estimates of capital formation may be more important than attempts to evaluate subsistence consumption and local market cash transactions.

Although the ultimate goals of the plan may be stated in welfare terms, the immediate objective will be defined in terms of the performance of particular sectors which are believed to be of importance for the subsequent improvement of welfare.

The manufacturing sector, capital formation, and export performance will all be particularly important. Knowledge of spending on particular classes of goods, such as consumer durables, may be more useful than overall estimates of consumption standards. Measures of income will be more important as a basis for measuring the potential taxable capacity, than for the purpose of estimating welfare.

Despite the frequent acceptance of the ascendancy of planning needs, little work has been done to modify the framework along lines which would produce maximum return in the face of the special objectives, the limited personnel and peculiar data problem of the developing countries. The various U.N. regional economic commissions have begun such work by suggesting a standardized set of accounts, but more radical ventures might be in order which provide a sanction for official accounts which place less emphasis on comprehensiveness but more on detailed, specialized, sectoral data.

This could be important in countries just setting up statistical services or in countries in which the limitations on the supply of statistical personnel make it impossible to maintain a worthwhile set of comprehensive accounts on an annual basis. In such situations a more limited set of data, available in a systematic form and with greater reliability than the comprehensive figures, might be compiled without the considerable delays involved in the preparation of income and product estimates. If work was pursued in such a direction then there would be far less interest in the valuation and welfare issues which have been so much of the concern of this chapter, and far more concern with investigating the potential contemporary uses of the accounts. With the passage of time such comments will become less and less relevant, for statistical services will expand, so that it will become increasingly feasible to maintain reliable and prompt accounts on a comprehensive basis.

XII

NATIONAL ACCOUNTS

UNITED STATES, EAST AFRICA, AND INDIA

This chapter outlines the techniques of national accounting applied in practice in three different areas of the world. The chapter is intended to indicate the diversity of methods which have been applied in practice. The descriptions of method are taken from the basic published sources. In some cases the statistical departments may have adjusted their methods as more and better data have become available. The official statisticians will be working continuously to improve the estimates. The object of the description is to provide insight into the way some of the problems outlined in Chapter X have been tackled in practice, rather than to provide a completely up-to-date report on methods.

A. The U.S. Accounts

1. *Introduction*

As early as 1920, a number of private research organizations in the United States, mainly the National Bureau of Economic Research, initiated substantial work on the compilation of U.S. national accounts. A major early publication, the work of Simon Kuznets on *National Income and Capital Formation, 1919–35*, appeared in 1937.

Work on government estimates was begun in 1932. Since 1934, the official estimates have appeared regularly in the *Survey of Current Business* published by the Office of Business Economics of the U.S. Department of Commerce. Important revisions of the accounts were made in methods in 1947, 1954, 1958, and 1965. Discussions of the later revisions are contained in supplements to the *Survey of Current Business*.

The accounts of the United States are the most detailed set of accounts available for any individual country. They are compiled from a bewildering variety of primary statistical sources and government conducted surveys. As currently published, they include nearly 100 supporting tables providing analyses and breakdown of the major accounting items.

Two basic approaches are used to arrive at a Gross National Product aggregate—the income approach and the product approach. Different statistical sources are used to compile the expenditure and income items to arrive at separate totals for Gross National Product. The two totals are reconciled by a statistical discrepancy (errors and ommissions) item which accounted for only one-tenth of one per cent to four-tenths of one per cent of the Gross National Product between 1960 and 1967.

The U.S. accounts, because of their detail, the quality of the primary statistical sources used, and the considerable effort made to provide reliable estimates of income aggregates, provide a standard of comparison for the accounts of other countries.

TABLE XII–1

Expenditure on Gross National Product of the United States

($ billions)

ITEM	1960	1961	1962	1963	1964	1965	1966	1967
Gross national product	503.8	520.1	560.3	590.5	631.7	681.2	743.3	785.0
Final purchases	500.2	518.1	554.3	584.6	627.0	672.1	729.9	779.8
Personal consumption expenditures ...	325.2	335.2	355.1	375.0	401.4	431.5	465.9	491.7
Durable goods	45.3	44.2	49.5	53.9	59.4	66.1	70.3	72.1
Non-durable goods	151.3	155.9	162.6	168.6	178.9	190.6	207.5	217.5
Services	128.7	135.1	143.0	152.4	163.1	174.8	188.1	202.1
Gross private domestic investment ...	74.8	71.7	83.0	87.1	93.0	106.6	118.0	112.1
Fixed investment	71.3	69.7	77.0	81.3	88.3	97.5	104.6	107.0
Non-residential	48.4	47.0	51.7	54.3	60.7	69.7	80.2	82.6
Structures	18.1	18.4	19.2	19.5	21.0	24.9	27.9	26.8
Producers' durable equipment...	30.3	28.6	32.5	34.8	39.7	44.8	52.3	55.7
Residential structures	22.8	22.6	25.3	27.0	27.6	27.8	24.4	24.4
Non-farm	22.2	22.0	24.8	26.4	27.0	27.2	23.8	23.9
Change in business inventories ...	3.6	2.0	6.0	5.9	4.7	9.1	13.4	5.2
Non-farm	3.3	1.7	5.3	5.1	5.3	8.1	13.7	4.8
Net exports of goods and services ...	4.1	5.6	5.1	5.9	8.5	7.0	5.1	4.8
Exports	27.2	28.6	30.3	32.3	37.0	39.0	43.0	45.3
Imports	23.2	22.9	25.1	26.4	28.5	32.0	37.9	40.6
Government purchases of goods and services	99.6	107.6	117.1	122.5	128.9	136.2	154.3	176.3
Federal	53.5	57.4	63.4	64.2	65.2	66.8	77.0	89.9
National defense	44.9	47.8	51.6	50.8	50.0	50.1	60.5	72.5
Other	8.6	9.6	11.8	13.5	15.2	16.7	16.5	17.4
State and local	46.1	50.2	53.7	58.2	63.7	69.4	77.2	86.4

Source: U.S. Office of Business Economics, *National Income Product Accounts of the United States, 1929–1965*, Washington, U.S. Government Printing Office, 1966, Table 1.1, pp. 2–3. U.S. Office of Business Economics, *Survey of Current Business*, July, 1967, Vol. 47, No. 7, Table 1.1, p. 13. *Survey of Current Business*, June, 1968, Vol. 48, No. 6, p. S–1.

2. *Expenditure on Gross National Product*

The expenditure estimate of Gross National Product might more appropriately be called Gross National Expenditure. It is compiled on a market price basis. Estimates for the years 1960 to 1967 are shown in Table XII–1.

For *consumer goods* two basic data sources are used: (i) the Bureau of the Census annual sample surveys of manufacturers' shipments by type of commodity, and (ii) sample surveys of retail sales by type of store (Bureau of the Census) and by type of merchandise (Federal Reserve Board). The former type of source provides expenditure estimates at factory prices which must be corrected by adding estimates of distribution and sales mark-ups to obtain estimates on a retail market price basis. Use is also made of (i) unpublished compilations of state sales tax data, (ii) sales data from trade associations and other private organizations, and (iii) data on Federal excise tax collections.

Consumer services are estimated using a wide variety of sources including trade association data.

Gross private investment may be divided into three parts: (i) construction, (ii) investment in producers' durables, and (iii) inventory changes. The value of new, residential, non-farm construction is based on the number of building permits issued. An adjustment is made on the basis of a sample survey to cover areas not requiring building permits. Estimates of other new construction are based on contract award reports and data compiled by trade associations and government agencies. These estimates of the value of new construction started are translated to value of construction completed during the year on the basis of assumed rates of completion determined from historical evidence.

Expenditure on producers' durables is estimated primarily from producers' shipments determined from surveys and censuses of manufacturing concerns. Assumed mark-ups are added to the value of producer shipments. These estimates are supplemented by analysis of the plant and equipment expenditure surveys undertaken jointly by the Office of Business Economics and the Securities and Exchange Commission.

The net change in business inventories is particularly difficult to determine, since a small percentage error in the estimate of stock of inventories can result in a very large percentage error in the estimated change in inventories. Estimated non-farm inventories at the beginning of a period are based on Internal Revenue Service (IRS) figures on book value. The IRS figures are updated using sample surveys of the Office of Business Economics and the Bureau of the Census and data compiled by the Federal Reserve Board and the Securities and Exchange Commission on department store stocks and working capital of corporations. The estimated changes in terms of book value are converted to a current price basis using price data from various sources. Data on changes in farm inventories are compiled by the Agricultural Marketing Service of the U.S. Department of Agriculture.

The value of *net exports of goods and services* is determined by a slight modification of data reported in the balance of payments prepared by the Office of Business Economics.

Government purchases of goods and services are estimated primarily from the budget records of Federal, state, and local governments. The budget figures must be modified substantially to convert them to a national accounts basis. For example, transfer payments, loans, and other transactions are excluded. The budget data must be adjusted to synchronize the timing of government outlays with the actual production or delivery of goods.

3. *National Income*

The National Income of the United States for the years 1960 to 1967 is shown in Table XII–2. It is compiled on a net basis and at factor cost.

TABLE XII–2

National Income of the United States

($ billion)

ITEM	1960	1961	1962	1963	1964	1965	1966	1967
National income	414.5	427.3	457.7	481.9	517.3	559.0	616.7	650.2
Compensation of employees ...	294.2	302.6	323.6	341.0	365.7	392.9	435.7	469.7
Wages and salaries	270.8	278.1	296.1	311.1	333.6	358.4	394.6	423.8
Private	222.1	225.9	240.1	251.6	269.3	289.1	316.7	337.5
Military	9.9	10.2	10.8	10.8	11.7	12.1	14.7	16.4
Government civilian	38.8	42.0	45.2	48.6	52.6	57.1	63.2	69.8
Supplements to wages and salaries ...	23.4	24.6	27.5	29.9	32.0	34.5	41.1	45.9
Employer contributions for social insurance	11.4	11.8	13.7	15.0	15.4	16.0	20.3	22.6
Other labor income	12.0	12.7	13.9	14.9	16.6	18.5	20.8	23.2
Proprietors' income	46.2	48.4	50.1	51.0	51.9	55.7	59.3	58.4
Business and professional	34.2	35.6	37.1	37.9	39.9	40.7	43.2	43.6
Farm ... ... '...	12.0	12.8	13.0	13.1	12.0	15.1	16.1	14.8
Rental income of persons	15.8	16.0	16.7	17.1	17.7	18.3	19.4	20.1
Corporate profits and inventory valuation adjustment	49.9	50.3	55.7	58.9	66.6	74.2	82.2	79.6
Profits before tax	49.7	50.3	55.4	59.4	67.0	75.7	83.8	80.7
Profits tax liability	23.0	23.1	24.2	26.3	28.4	31.2	34.5	33.2
Profits after tax	26.7	27.2	31.2	33.1	38.7	44.5	49.3	47.5
Dividends	13.4	13.8	15.2	16.5	17.3	19.2	21.5	22.8
Undistributed profits	13.2	13.5	16.0	16.6	21.3	25.3	27.8	24.7
Inventory valuation adjustment ...	.	−.1	.3	−.5	−.4	−1.6	−1.6	−1.2
Net interest	8.4	10.0	11.6	13.8	15.5	17.8	20.2	22.4

Source: same as Table XII–1. *National Income Product Accounts of the United States, 1929–1965*, Table 1.10, pp. 14–15. *Survey of Current Business*, July, 1967, Table 1.10, p. 15. *Survey of Current Business*, June, 1968, p. S–2.

The primary sources for the estimates of *wages and salaries* are based on statistics of payrolls reported to Federal and state agencies for the purposes of the Federal Old Age and Survivors Insurance program and state unemployment insurance programs.

The non-farm component of *proprietors' income* is based largely on income tax data tabulated by the Internal Revenue Service (IRS). This is supplemented by information for censuses of business and the population. Figures for farm net income are provided by the U.S. Department of Agriculture.

Rental income is estimated in a manner similar to that of proprietors' income.

Corporate profits are derived largely from IRS data on the corporate income tax. To avoid double-counting these are adjusted to account for corporate profits originating from dividends on stock held by corporations. An adjustment is also made to estimate non-reported profits on the basis of additional profits disclosed by the auditing of income-tax returns by the IRS.

Inventory valuation adjustment is the difference between inventory changes on a book value basis and inventory changes on a current price basis. This adjustment removes from business profits the bookkeeping profit or loss which results when the book cost of goods removed from inventories differs from the current replacement cost.

Net interest payments by businesses are based on income tax returns. Interest is imputed to consumer checking accounts on the assumption that actual interest is not paid, since the full cost of services is not charged to depositors.

4. *Relation of Gross National Product, National Income, and Personal Income and Savings*

Table XII-3 shows the relation between five different aggregates, Gross National Product, National Income, Personal Income, Disposable Personal Income, and Personal Saving.

Since National Income is on a net, factor cost basis, one must subtract capital consumption and indirect taxes less subsidies from Gross National Product to arrive at National Income. Business transfer payments and surpluses of government enterprises are also deleted from Gross National Product. The former is subtracted, since transfers reduce income of businesses. The latter deletion reflects a basic philosophy which holds that profits of government enterprises are not to be considered as payments for factor services. Rather they are treated as very much akin to indirect taxes.

Personal Income is derived by subtracting profits less dividends and social insurance contributions from National Income. Transfer payments

TABLE XII–3

Relation of United States Gross National Product, National Income, and Personal Income and Saving

($ billion)

ITEM	1960	1961	1962	1963	1964	1965	1966	1967
Gross national product	503.8	520.1	560.3	590.5	631.7	681.2	743.3	785.0
Less: Capital consumption allowances	43.4	45.2	50.0	52.6	56.0	59.6	63.5	67.0
Equals: Net national product	460.4	474.9	510.3	537.9	575.7	621.6	679.8	718.0
Less: Indirect business tax and non-tax								
liability	45.2	47.7	51.5	54.7	58.5	62.7	65.1	69.7
Business transfer payments ...	1.9	2.0	2.1	2.3	2.5	2.6	2.7	2.8
Statistical discrepancy	−1.0	−.7	.5	−.3	−1.4	−1.6	−2.6	−3.0
Plus: Subsidies less current surplus of								
government enterprises ...	.2	1.4	1.4	.8	1.3	1.0	2.2	1.7
Equals: National income	414.5	427.3	457.7	481.9	517.3	559.0	616.7	650.2
Less: Corporate profits and inventory								
valuation adjustment	49.9	50.3	55.7	58.9	66.6	74.2	82.2	79.6
Contributions for social insurance	20.7	21.4	24.0	26.9	28.0	29.2	38.2	43.0
Plus: Government transfer payments ...	26.6	30.4	31.2	33.0	34.2	37.1	41.2	49.1
Net interest paid by government								
and consumer	15.1	15.0	16.1	17.6	19.1	20.6	22.3	24.1
Dividends	13.4	13.8	15.2	16.5	17.3	19.2	21.5	22.8
Business transfer payments ...	1.9	2.0	2.1	2.3	2.5	2.6	2.7	2.8
Equals: Personal income	401.0	416.8	442.6	465.5	496.0	535.1	584.0	626.4
Less: Personal tax and non-tax payments	50.9	52.4	57.4	60.9	59.4	66.0	75.2	81.7
Equals: Disposable personal income ...	350.0	364.4	385.3	404.6	436.6	469.1	508.8	544.7
Less: Personal outlays	333.0	343.2	363.7	384.7	412.1	443.4	479.0	505.9
Personal consumption expendi-								
tures	325.2	335.2	355.1	375.0	401.4	431.5	465.9	491.7
Consumer interest payments ...	7.3	7.6	8.1	9.1	10.1	11.3	12.4	13.4
Personal transfer payments to								
foreigners	.5	.5	.5	.6	.6	.6	.6	.8
Equals: Personal saving	17.0	21.2	21.6	19.9	24.5	25.7	29.8	38.7

Source: same as Table XII–1. *National Income Product Account of the United States, 1929–1965*, Tables: 1.9, 2.1, p. 12, p. 32. *Survey of Current Business*, July, 1967, Tables: 1.9, 2.1, p. 15, p. 20. *Survey of Current Business*, June, 1968, Tables: 4, 10, pp. 4–5.

by government and business and net interest paid by government and consumers are added to national income. This latter item is added because it has traditionally been excluded from National Income estimates.

The derivation of the remaining three aggregates, Personal Income, Disposable Personal Income, and Personal Saving, is straightforward.

5. *Income by Industry Divison*

Only two separate approaches, income and expenditure, are used in estimating the national accounts of the United States. The third general method, the product approach, is not used, although estimates of income by industry of origin are derived as by-products of the estimation of National Income. These are shown in Table XII–4. One of the major sources of inaccuracy in these breakdowns derives from the difficulties of classifying income accruing to business firms which produce products in a number of different industrial classifications.

6. Reconciliation between U.S. System and United Nations SNA

The basic United States definitions are in close conformity with those of the United Nations system. There are, however, certain differences in concepts and classifications. Net incomes of United States government enterprises are treated as an offset to subsidy payments by government. In the United States accounts there is no imputation of rent on govern-

TABLE XII–4

National Income of the United States by Industry Division at Factor Cost
($ billion)

	1960	1961	1962	1963	1964	1965	1966
All industries, total	414.5	427.3	457.7	481.9	517.3	559.0	616.7
Agriculture, forestry, and fisheries	16.9	17.9	18.5	18.6	17.7	21.0	22.7
Mining and Construction	26.5	27.2	28.5	30.2	32.4	34.8	38.3
Manufacturing	125.8	125.1	137.0	143.8	155.1	170.4	192.1
Non-durable goods ...	52.2	52.8	55.6	57 5	61.5	65.6	73.2
Durable goods	73.6	72.3	81.4	86.3	93.6	104.8	118.9
Transportation	18.2	18.3	19.1	20.0	21.4	22.9	24.8
Communication	8.2	8.6	9.3	9.8	10.5	11.2	12.4
Electric, gas, and sanitary services	8.9	9.4	9.7	10.3	11.1	11.6	12.1
Wholesale and retail trade ...	64.4	66.2	70.3	73.4	79.1	83.6	90.8
Finance, insurance, and real estate	45.8	48.0	50.7	53.6	57.1	61.0	65.6
Services	44.5	47.2	50.7	54.1	58.9	63.0	69.3
Government and government enterprises	52.9	56.6	60.7	64.7	70.0	75.2	84.6
Rest of the world	2.4	2.9	3.3	3.4	4.0	4.3	4.2

Source: same as in Table XII–1. *National Income Product Accounts of the United States*, 1929–1965, Table 1.11, p. 16. *Survey of Current Business*, July, 1967, Table 1.11, p. 16.

ment buildings. Public capital formation is lumped together with government consumption expenditure and is not estimated separately.

B. The East African Accounts

1. *Introduction*

The first official estimates of income and product for Kenya, Uganda, and Tanzania* were published by the East African Statistical Department for the years 1947, 1950, and 1954 respectively. Peacock and Dosser produced estimates for Tanzania for 1952–1954 derived in a fashion similar to that of the subsequent official estimates. In each of the three countries consistent series are available from 1954, although the series for Tanzania runs only through 1962. A new series of income and product estimates starting from 1960 is now compiled for Tanzania.

Techniques used in Tanzania for the 1954–1962 series were influenced by the original work of Peacock and Dosser and therefore vary in some important particulars from those used in other parts of East Africa. As in the other two territories the estimates are of domestic rather than national product and are at factor cost. An unusually wide coverage of subsistence production was attempted; in particular, subsistence construction activity and some craft industry are included. The techniques of estimation used in the present series beginning from 1960 are more similar to those of Uganda and Kenya.

Kenya provides gross product estimates with a similar industrial classification as that used in the Tanzania accounts. In the case of Kenya the manufacturing estimates and the non-African agriculture estimates are built on a foundation of survey data which is more detailed than that yet existing elsewhere in East Africa. The subsistence sector estimates are restricted to primary output of agricultural produce and do not include subsistence construction or craft industries.

In the case of Uganda the estimates of the manufacturing sector are constructed without the aid of the results of a survey of industry.† Tax returns are used to derive the information on which the estimates of the non-wage component of value added are based. A large part of total economic activity is represented by the export crops serviced by marketing boards, a reliable source of data.

* Throughout this chapter, we will use the term Tanzania, although the data which we discuss refer to the former country of Tanganyika, the mainland part of what is now called Tanzania.

† A Census of Industrial Production is now available for Uganda for the year 1963.

2. *The Fundamentals*

Because of available data and statistical sources, the estimates for all three countries aim basically at only one of the many aggregates defined in Chapters X and XI. In each case this is gross domestic product at factor cost. The most complete accounts are presented on the basis of value added by sector of origin. Kenya and Uganda both present supplementary tables showing gross domestic income, also at factor cost, on the basis of factor shares. Tanzania includes an estimate of gross domestic expenditure (at market prices) plus imports. These totals in all cases include estimates of subsistence as well as of monetary activity. The subsistence totals are shown separately and then added to the monetary totals. In the discussion that follows, consideration of the subsistence estimates will be postponed and all comments may be assumed to concern the cash area unless otherwise stated.

As will become obvious in the detailed discussion to follow, there are numerous differences in the approach to the estimation of the various sector totals between the three countries (and even within the same sector in a single country). It is useful, however, initially to ignore these and to consider generally what approach is used within each of the major sectors. Accordingly, in the following Table XII–5, the approach which is characteristic of the three accounts is listed and no mention is made of individual differences.

3. *Detailed Discussion*

The following discussion deals in more detail with the methods used in estimating the products of the major sectors. Certain sectors which contribute small amounts to GDP are not mentioned. The reader should refer to Tables XII–6, 7, and 8.

TABLE XII–5

Basis of Accounts

Major Sector	
1. Agriculture	Net Output—Sales minus inputs
2. Manufacturing	Factor Share—Wages plus gross profit
3. Transport, Storage and Communications	Factor Share—Wages plus gross profit
4. Wholesale and Retail Trade	Factor Share—Wages plus gross profit
5. Government	Factor Share—Wage Bill only

TABLE XII–6

Kenya Gross Domestic Product at Factor Cost by Industry of Origin

(£ million)

	1960	1961	1962	1963	1964	1965	1966*
Recorded Monetary Economy							
Agriculture (including services) ...	29.44	28.33	28.46	33.14	36.72	32.89	38.66
Livestock	9.22	8.97	9.62	9.59	9.50	9.71	10.08
Forestry	.81	.90	.97	.78	.92	.76	.78
Fishing and Hunting	.53	.52	.81	.88	.87	1.01	1.37
Total	40.00	38.72	39.86	44.39	48.01	44.37	50.89
Subsistence							
Agriculture	36.10	34.21	46.43	47.87	49.75	45.60	52.10
Livestock	10.99	10.44	11.86	12.80	12.13	13.00	16.33
Forestry	2.94	3.08	4.74	5.79	6.45	6.54	6.64
Fishing and Hunting	.16	.16	.19	.20	.20	.21	.25
Total	50.19	47.89	63.22	66.66	68.53	65.35	75.32
Recorded Monetary Economy							
Mining and Quarrying	1.09	.85	.83	.89	.75	.84	.82
Manufacturing	21.62	22.73	23.04	24.38	29.38	32.03	34.60
Construction	7.86	7.80	6.76	4.89	4.38	5.09	6.05
Electricity and Water	2.79	2.84	3.29	3.60	3.47	3.72	4.49
Transportation, Storage, and Communications	20.34	21.15	22.26	24.62	26.30	29.63	33.14
Wholesale and Retail Trade	28.96	29.56	30.06	31.92	34.06	35.37	38.17
Banking, Insurance, and Real Estate	3.54	3.88	4.01	4.17	4.49	4.63	5.23
Rents (including imputed rents on owner occupied dwellings) ...	8.70	8.14	8.43	9.36	9.54	10.26	10.49
Total	94.90	96.95	98.68	103.83	112.37	121.57	132.99
Government Services							
Civil Departments	18.33	21.63	22.02	20.86	20.21	24.04	25.38
Local Authorities	3.35	3.49	4.11	5.90	11.34	11.91	12.32
Defence	1.37	1.75	1.83	1.86	1.65	2.16	2.78
Overseas Governments (local employees)	.12	.14	.16	.18	.91	.48	.24
Total	23.17	27.00	28.12	28.80	34.11	38.59	40.72
Services	17.25	14.14	14.21	15.41	18.30	18.37	18.93
Total for Recorded Monetary Economy	175.32	176.81	180.87	192.43	212.79	222.90	243.52
Plus Subsistence	50.19	47.89	63.22	66.66	68.53	65.35	75.32
GDP AT FACTOR COST	225.51	224.70	244.09	259.09	281.32	288.25	318.84

* Provisional estimates.

Source: Government of Kenya, *Economic Survey, 1967*, Nairobi, Government Printer, Table 1.2, p. 7.

a. *Agriculture*

Kenya, for statistical convenience, divides its agricultural estimates between African and non-African farms. (Within the former group, an estimate is made of subsistence activity.) For non-African agriculture, a census, which is carried out annually, provides data on acreage. Costs are based on separate estimates per acre for each crop and are not varied from year to year, with the exception of employment costs which are obtained from the annual employment census. Sales data are obtained from reports of the various marketing boards (e.g., coffee) from the Board of Agriculture, or from the Kenya Farmers Association. The product of the livestock industry is obtained from figures supplied by the Kenya Meat Board and the Kenya Co-operative Creameries. An overall cost deduction is made for the entire industry. Within African agriculture, crop turnover is estimated on the basis of acreage and yield data contained in the District Gazetteers prepared by the Department of Agriculture. Prices are at local market levels and the assumption for purposes of valuation is that all African crops are sold in these markets. From the total turnover figure thus derived, the Department of Agriculture's figures for the sales of African cash and food crops are subtracted. The remainder is the estimate of subsistence crop production. Livestock production is estimated in three ways: by the offtake method, the reproduction method and the hides-sold method. The offtake method of calculating livestock production involves three estimates: an estimate of herd size for some base year; an estimate of the rate of growth of the herd; and an estimate of the rate at which cattle are slaughtered expressed as a per cent of herd size. The hides-sold method simply requires obtaining an estimate of the offtake of cattle each year. The reproduction method estimates herd size based on the percentage of

TABLE XII–7

Uganda Gross Domestic Product at Factor Cost by Industry of Origin

(£ million)

	1960	1961	1962	1963	1964	1965	1966*
Recorded Monetary Economy							
Agriculture	49.54	48.69	44.03	57.44	60.53	56.89	69.50
Forestry, Fishing and Hunting ...	2.30	2.03	2.43	2.39	2.40	2.44	2.56
Total	51.84	50.72	46.46	59.83	62.93	59.33	72.06
Subsistence							
Agriculture	36.36	39.87	42.61	40.73	47.26	63.77	58.92
Forestry, Fishing and Hunting ...	4.95	5.37	6.13	6.60	7.06	9.52	10.88
Total	41.31	45.24	48.74	47.33	54.32	73.29	69.80
Recorded Monetary Economy							
Cotton Ginning, Coffee Curing, Sugar Manufacture	3.88	4.16	3.57	5.68	5.75	5.50	6.27
Mining and Quarrying	2.23	2.30	2.61	2.78	5.30	7.26	5.69
Manufacturing of Food Products ...	1.23	1.29	1.28	1.26	1.72	1.92	2.34
Miscellaneous Manufacturing ...	4.81	4.97	4.93	5.45	6.20	8.54	10.28
Electricity	1.94	2.21	2.46	2.72	2.92	3.28	3.84
Construction	3.90	3.55	3.91	3.48	3.48	4.60	4.53
Commerce	14.39	14.52	14.46	18.39	19.56	20.99	25.54
Transport and Communication ...	6.19	5.89	5.82	6.16	6.16	6.54	7.34
Government (Administration and Miscellaneous)	4.16	4.23	4.90	4.62	6.01	6.49	7.05
African Local Government	2.36	2.40	2.36	2.38	2.85	3.24	2.82
Miscellaneous Services	10.90	11.56	11.55	12.09	13.98	17.49	20.14
Rents	3.35	3.52	3.64	3.76	3.93	4.33	4.86
Total Recorded Monetary Economy ...	110.81	111.17	107.93	128.60	140.79	149.51	172.76
Plus Subsistence	41.31	45.24	48.74	47.33	54.32	73.29	69.80
GDP AT FACTOR COST	152.12	156.41	156.67	175.93	195.11	222.80	242.56

* Provisional Estimates.

Source: Uganda Government, *1967 Statistical Abstract*, Entebbe, Government Printer, 1968, Table UN. 1 p. 82.

TABLE XII-8

Tanzania Gross Domestic Product at Factor Cost by Industry of Origin

(£ million)

Recorded Monetary Economy	1960	1961	1962	1963	1964	1965	1966*
Agriculture	40.6	37.0	40.6	51.9	57.8	61.9	57.2
Livestock Products	5.7	5.3	5.2	5.4	5.7	6.1	7.1
Forest Products	1.1	1.1	1.0	1.1	1.1	1.2	1.2
Hunting and Fishing	1.2	1.2	1.4	1.7	2.1	2.0	2.4
Total	50.5†	46.8†	50.5†	62.8†	68.7†	74.0†	70.8†
Subsistence							
Agriculture	48.4	54.0	60.9	62.2	55.0	51.7	58.0
Livestock Products	12.0	11.3	11.7	12.6	13.6	13.9	14.6
Forest Products	1.5	1.5	1.5	1.6	1.6	1.7	1.7
Hunting and Fishing	.4	.4	.5	.5	.5	.5	.6
Total	62.4	67.3	74.6	76.9	70.7	67.8	74.9
Recorded Monetary Economy							
Mining and Quarrying	5.2	5.5	5.1	4.4	6.1	6.1	7.2
Manufacturing	5.5	7.0	7.9	7.8	9.7	11.1	13.6
Construction	4.6	5.8	6.2	6.2	6.2	7.7	8.6
Public Utilities	1.2	1.4	1.5	1.6	1.8	1.8	2.4
Commerce	20.9	22.1	25.2	25.9	30.0	32.9	38.3
Rent	8.0	8.4	8.8	9.3	11.1	12.3	13.3
Transport, Storage, and Communications	8.7	8.6	9.5	9.9	9.8	10.8	12.3
Services	18.1	20.8	22.9	23.4	25.4	28.5	31.2
Total Recorded Monetary Economy ...	122.7	126.2	136.8	151.3	168.8	185.2	197.7
Plus Subsistence	62.4	67.3	74.6	76.9	70.7	67.8	74.9
GDP AT FACTOR COST	185.0	193.5	211.4	228.2	239.5	253.0	272.6

* Provisional Estimates.
† Includes contribution of public sector to agriculture, livestock, forestry, and hunting and fishing.
Sources: United Republic of Tanganyika and Zanzibar, *The National Accounts of Tanganyika, 1960–62*, Dar es Salaam, Central Statistical Bureau, The Treasury, 1964, Tables 4 and 5, pp. 9–10; and Tanzania, *Background to the Budget, 1967–68*, Dar es Salaam, Government Printer, Tables 2, 3, and 5A, pp. 10, 11, and 16.

cows in the herd and a guess at the number of calves per cow per year. It is then necessary to translate herd size into production via some offtake figure. The estimate provided by the first method is ultimately used in the calculation of turnover. To it are applied prices from the records of the African Livestock Marketing Organization. These prices are adjusted for quality in valuing subsistence output, the size of which is again a residual, the result of subtracting recorded sales in the marketing organization records from the total offtake.

In *Uganda*, the great bulk of the product of agriculture originates in the cash crops, cotton and coffee. Figures from these two areas are readily available. In the agricultural sector, only an overall allowance is made for purchased inputs in the accounts. Sales of food crops to rural employees, urban Africans, and to non-Africans are estimated on the basis of *per capita* dietary information multiplied by population figures and by appropriate prices derived from town prices. Livestock production is estimated on the basis of hides sold as computed by the Veterinary Department. The quantity of meat thus implied is divided arbitrarily between cash and subsistence sectors. The entire product is valued on the hoof at local auction prices in the district of production.

Tanzanian estimates of the gross product of crop agriculture are divided into cash crops and all other production. Data on cash crop sales is obtained from the appropriate marketing organizations, the Ministry of Agriculture, trade reports, or other sources. A deduction is made for purchases from other sectors (including imports). Livestock's contribution to GDP is estimated mainly on the basis of statistics provided by the Veterinary Division on sales at organized auctions plus rough estimates of local sales and sales by large estates to Tanzania packers. Valuation is at producer prices. Forestry products are mainly firewood, building poles, timber, and export items such as honey and beeswax and wattle bark extract. The export items are estimated by subtracting an assumed transport and distribution margin from exports as recorded in the annual trade reports. Firewood is estimated on the basis of an F.A.O. wood consumption survey while other forestry products are estimated by inquiries to firms. Estimates of fishing production are also based on an F.A.O. survey with a deduction for inputs, mainly fishing nets.

b. *Industrial Activity*

In *Kenya*, value added for manufacturing, mining, and road transport are estimated by applying a fixed ratio from the censuses of industry to an estimated wage bill derived from the annual survey of employment. Building and construction activity is estimated by using government contracts, returns on buildings completed in the six main townships and information on non-African farm building derived from the annual survey of non-African agriculture. Own-account building is not included under building and construction with the exception of the construction activity of some government departments.* The value-added estimates for construction are made by adding 10 per cent of gross turnover to the employment costs estimated from the annual employment surveys.

In *Uganda* the value-added contribution of non-African enterprises and public services is estimated by adding employment cost estimates from the annual employment survey to the surplus component as derived from tax data. The industrial classification of the annual employment survey and that of the tax data differ so that the tax data are re-allocated. An estimate is made of the contribution of self-employed non-Africans. African transport

---

* "Own-account construction" is building undertaken by a business unit for its own eventual use through the direct employment of labor and materials rather than the use of a contractor.

is estimated from the data contained in a report on the Uganda road transport system.*

In *Tanzania* the basic method for estimation of value added of industrial activity is to estimate the wage bill from the annual enumeration of employees and the gross profits from an examination of income tax declarations. Since only part of industrial activity is covered by income tax data and by the annual labor enumeration, the basic method is supplemented by information from the 1961 Census of Industrial Production, population censuses, social surveys of towns and rural areas, and other sources. Mining and quarrying is very much dominated by one large firm; so profits are obtained directly from its accounts. The profits of the small mining firms for 1961 are obtainable from the 1961 industrial census and are assumed to be roughly constant in other years. Many small manufacturing and construction firms are not subject to income tax. The profit to wage ratio of such firms from the 1961 industrial census is applied to the wage bill as estimated from the annual labor enumeration. Urban, very small scale construction is estimated by applying a *per capita* construction figure from a social survey to urban population figures. Estimates of road transport activity are based on number of licences issued by the Transport Licensing Authority and an assumed average value of vehicle, rate of return, one driver and one turnboy per vehicle, and average wage.

Transport and communication services supplied by the East African Common Services Organization are allocated between the three countries on the basis of the wage bill derived from the annual employment surveys within each country and the division into three equal parts of the operating surpluses of the various services.

c. *Distribution, Commerce, and Rents*

In *Kenya* the surplus derived from trade is obtained by applying estimated trading margins to figures for gross turnover derived from import and domestic production data. The trading margins used are calculated with the aid of data from the 1952 South African Census of Distribution. (The results of the 1960 Kenya Survey of Distribution are not yet incorporated in the domestic product calculations.) Rents are computed as an assumed percentage of the estimated original cost of the property.

In *Uganda*, the incomes of African traders are estimated on the basis of the number of trading licences issued and on assumed surplus per trader. For food retailing an estimate is made of total surplus by applying an assumed margin to estimated food sales. Non-African distribution is estimated in the same manner as the contribution of other non-African

* Hawkins, E. K., *Roads and Road Transport in an Under-Developed Country, A Case Study of Uganda*, London, Her Majesty's Stationery Office, 1962.

enterprises. Rent of government property is imputed at a fixed percentage of historical costs; private rents are either taken from tax returns or imputed on the basis of the current taxable value of the property.

In *Tanzania*, the basic method of estimating wages from labor enumeration data and profits from tax returns is used for large scale wholesalers and retailers except for cotton and coffee co-operatives where trading profits are derived directly from published accounts. The number of small traders is estimated from statistics on trade licences issued and an assumed rate of turnover and rate of return is used for each category of licence. Paid rents are estimated from tax data rated up for non-response. Imputed rents on African urban housing and on mission buildings are estimated as an assumed percentage of an estimated original value.

d. *Government*

The value-added contribution of the government is estimated from the government wage bill, the value of wages spent on own-account construction, however, being allocated to the value-added contribution of construction. Kenya provides a more detailed analysis of the functional breakdown of the value-added contribution in the product accounts than either Tanzania or Uganda. Much more detail is provided in the annual data published on the government's revenues and expenditures in all three cases, but this is not incorporated into the national accounts, because of the lack of detailed income and expenditure tables.

In the Tanzanian expenditure tables there is a breakdown of total government spending into current and capital account items. In the Tanzanian gross domestic product by industry of origin accounts, the government contribution is allocated to various industries rather than listed separately.

4. *Other Accounts*

a. *Capital Formation Accounts*

Although the expenditure side of the accounts is not completed, all three countries present estimates of gross domestic capital formation. None of the three estimates include figures for the accumulation of stocks, all being confined to showing investment in fixed assets. In all three cases the estimates are given at market prices and adjustments must be made before the figures may be compared with those for GDP which are at factor cost. Within this generally similar framework there are differences of inclusion and exclusion and method of measurement which are briefly discussed below. The Tanzanian capital formation series, like the product estimates, dates from 1960 although an earlier series from 1954 to 1962 is available.

TABLE XII–9

East African Accounts

Gross Domestic Capital Formation by Type of Asset

(£ million)

A. KENYA

	1960	1961	1962	1963	1964	1965
Residential Buildings ...	6.81	4.47	3.05	2.39	1.86	2.42
Non-Residential Buildings	6.42	4.41	3.65	3.04	5.20	3.82
Construction and Other Works	10.06	9.42	12.10	9.27	8.52	10.85
Transport Equipment ...	10.72	6.21	7.59	8.25	11.13	11.60
Machinery and Other Equipment	7.56	7.59	7.21	7.89	8.95	9.49
All Assets	41.55	32.10	33.60	30.85	35.65	38.19

B. UGANDA

	1960	1961	1962	1963	1964	1965	1966
Construction	10.7	10.2	9.9	10.2	11.1	15.7	14.7
Transport Equipment ...	2.6	1.3	2.0	2.8	2.7	4.2	5.8
Machinery and Other Equipment	5.3	6.5	5.8	7.0	10.4	12.4	10.2
All Assets	18.6	18.0	17.7	20.0	24.2	32.3	30.7

C. TANZANIA

	1960	1961	1962	1963	1964	1965	1966*
Dwellings	4.48	4.12	3.45	3.40	5.05	6.10	4.85
Non-Residential Buildings	4.27	4.67	4.22	5.00	5.25	6.60	7.80
Water Supply	1.14	1.27	1.07	1.00	1.25	1.90	1.75
Communications	1.42	1.81	1.58	1.45	1.30	2.85	3.95
Railways and Harbors ...	1.18	3.23	1.89	1.20	1.20	1.20	1.25
Other Construction Works	1.25	2.03	3.26	3.25	4.45	6.80	6.15
Transport Equipment ...	4.09	2.23	2.97	2.95	4.45	5.50	8.45
Machinery and Other Equipment	5.35	7.16	5.97	6.00	7.15	10.95	12.95
All Assets	23.18	26.52	24.40	24.25	30.10	41.90	47.15

* Provisional or Preliminary Estimates.

Sources: Government of Kenya, *Statistical Abstract, 1967*, Nairobi Government Printer, Table 137, p. 137. Uganda Government, *Statistical Abstract 1967*, Entebbe, Government Printer, 1968, Table UN. 7, p. 84, and Government of Tanzania, *Background to the Budget, 1967–68*, Dar es Salaam, Government Printer, Table 48, p. 74.

TABLE XII-10
Kenya GDI at Factor Cost
(£ million)

	1958	1959	1960	1961	1962	1963	1964	1965	1966*
Paid Employment									
Public	34.36	35.42	39.31	42.17	43.85	42.97	48.54	54.15	57.95
Private	51.14	52.95	56.86	56.77	56.32	58.88	64.96	68.48	72.86
Total Employment (Wage Bill)	85.50	88.37	96.17	98.94	100.17	101.85	113.50	122.63	130.81
Operating Surplus									
Public Enterprise	2.69	3.09	3.06	3.00	2.93	3.77	3.39	4.30	5.42
Private Enterprise	59.81	62.26	67.39	66.74	69.34	77.47	86.37	85.70	96.81
Total Operating Surplus (Profit Share)	62.50	65.35	70.46	69.74	72.27	81.24	89.76	90.00	102.23
Public Enterprise and Government	1.63	1.75	1.80	1.93	2.05	2.14	2.22	2.28	2.35
Private Enterprise and Households	5.88	6.30	6.90	6.21	6.38	7.22	7.32	7.98	8.14
Total Rent	7.51	8.05	8.70	8.14	8.43	9.36	9.54	10.26	10.49
Total Monetary Income	155.50	161.76	175.32	176.81	180.87	192.43	212.80	222.90	243.52
Total Product of Subsistence Sector	52.59	53.03	50.19	47.89	63.22	66.66	68.52	65.35	75.32
GDI	208.10	214.79	225.51	224.70	244.09	259.09	281.32	288.25	318.84

* Provisional Estimates.

Source: *Government of Kenya, Economic Survey, 1967*, Nairobi Government Printer, Table 14, p. 9.

TABLE XII–11

Uganda GDI at Factor Cost
(£ million)

	1958	1959	1960	1961	1962	1963	1964	1965	1966*
Recorded Monetary Income									
Paid Employment	31.74	33.19	36.54	37.86	39.17	39.46	44.48	51.60	56.55
Operating Surplus	71.53	71.60	70.92	69.95	65.12	85.38	92.38	93.58	111.35
Rental Surplus	2.66	3.19	3.35	3.36	3.64	3.76	3.93	4.33	4.86
Total Monetary Income	105.93	107.98	110.81	111.17	107.93	128.60	140.79	149.51	172.76
Total Product of Subsistence Sector ...	40.46	40.99	41.31	45.24	48.74	47.33	54.32	73.29	69.80
GDI	146.39	148.97	152.12	156.41	156.67	175.93	195.11	222.80	242.56

* Provisional Estimates.

Source: Uganda Government, *Statistical Abstract 1964*, Entebbe, Government Printer, 1965, Table UN. 3, p. 82. *Statistical Abstract 1967*, Table UN. 3, p. 83.

TABLE XII–12

Tanzania NNI at Factor Cost

(£ million)

Recorded Monetary Income	1960	1961	1962	1963	1964	1965	1966*
Peasant Monetary Income	31.0	28.6	30.0	31.8	36.4	40.4	47.4
Compensation of Employees ...	48.4	54.0	56.3	60.2	65.7	70.9	77.9
Property Income	2.6	2.6	2.7	4.3	4.8	5.3	5.7
Other Surpluses of Enterprises ...	22.4	22.5	28.1	31.3	40.4	34.7	36.5
Government Income from Property and Entrepreneurship	5.7	6.1	6.5	6.5	7.8	8.6	9.5
Total Monetary Income	110.1	113.8	123.6	134.1	155.1	159.9	177.0
Total Product of Subsistence Sector ...	62.4	67.3	74.6	76.9	70.7	67.7	74.9
NNI	172.5	181.1	198.2	211.0	225.8	227.5	251.9

* Provisional Estimates.

Source: Tanzania Government, *Budget Survey*, *1967–68*, Dar es Salaam, Government Printer, Table 1, p. 9.

The Kenya and Uganda series of capital formation estimates date from 1954.

In *Kenya* both the commodity flow and expenditure methods of measurement are used for estimates of private capital expenditure. The former is used in obtaining figures for the purchase of transport equipment and plant and machinery. The latter is used in obtaining figures for construction. Within the public sector, data on an expenditure basis is obtained from the published accounts of the various departments and agencies. Private motor cars are included in capital formation.

In *Uganda* government capital formation is taken from budget accounts. The estimates for the non-government sector for plant, equipment, and vehicles are based on import value from which rough estimates of installed value have been made. Estimates exclude rural construction, land improvement and the establishment of plantations. Private motor cars are *not* included in estimates of capital formation.

In *Tanzania* methods of estimation are similar to those of Kenya in obtaining the figures. Ten per cent of private motor purchases are included in gross capital formation, this being the assumed portion purchased for commercial purposes.

b. *Income-expenditure Accounts*

While it has not yet proved feasible to complete a fully developed set of triple-entry, accounts for East Africa, Kenya, and Uganda do show domestic product divided into factor shares, produced as a side product of the value-added output estimates while Tanzania statistics include Net National Income accounts (see Tables XII–10, 11, and 12).

Gross Domestic Product in Tanzania is calculated on a mixed commodity flow and factor income approach. The commodity flow estimates provide a basis for compiling a gross expenditure account (see Table XII–13). Estimates of depreciation are compiled as a by-product of the factor income approach. These estimates are used to derive a net national income aggregate which is also shown in Table XII–13.

Consumption expenditures are divided into private consumption and general government consumption. The former is obtained as a residual —the result of subtracting government consumption, gross capital formation, and exports less imports from Gross National Expenditure.

TABLE XII–13

Tanzania Expenditure on Gross National Product at Current Market Prices

(£ million)

	1960	1961	1962	1963	1964	1965*
1. Private Consumption Expenditure ... ... (1)	148.5	154.0	174.1	182.0	183.3	184.8
of which Non-Monetary ...	62.4	67.3	74.6	76.8	70.7	67.7
2. General Government Consumption Expenditure	19.8	24.0	26.7	27.8	31.7	35.2
3. Gross Domestic Fixed Capital Formation	23.2	26.5	24.4	24.3	30.1	36.9
of which Non-Monetary ...	—	0.9	0.9	0.9	0.9	1.0
4. Increase in Stocks ... (1)	—	—	—	—	—	—
5. Exports of Goods and Services	63.0	59.7	59.8	73.4	83.9	80.0
6. *Less* Imports of Goods and Services	58.5	59.1	61.6	63.6	69.9	77.2
Expenditure on Gross Domestic Product	196.0	205.1	223.4	243.9	259.1	259.7
7. Net Factor Income from Abroad	−3.4	−2.6	−3.0	−5.5	−3.8	−3.7
Expenditure on Gross National Product	192.6	202.5	220.4	238.4	255.3	256.0
8. *Less* Indirect Taxes	11.2	11.8	14.3	16.8	19.0	20.7
9. *Plus* Subsidies	0.3	0.2	0.3	0.3	0.2	0.2
10. *Less* Provisions for the Consumption of Fixed Capital	9.2	9.7	10.1	10.8	12.2	12.6
Net National Product at Factor Cost = National Income ...	172.5	181.2	196.3	211.1	224.3	222.9

* Provisional Estimates.

(1) Increase in Stocks included in Item 1 which is obtained as a Residual.

Source: United Nations, *Yearbook of National Accounts Statistics, 1966*, New York, 1967, p. 557.

5. Gaps in the Accounts

a. Rest of World Accounts

A particularly serious aspect of the general lack of income and expenditure accounts is the absence of a set of accounts to explain international and interterritorial income and expenditure flows. It is true that there are excellent data, in very fine detail, on the balance of visible trade between East Africa as a whole and the rest of the world. This data is published in full in the East African *Annual Trade Report* and summarized in the East African Statistical Department's quarterly publication, the *Economic and Statistical Review*. There is on the other hand little reliable data on "invisible" trade or on transfers of factor income, resulting from foreign ownership of domestic assets. Tanzania, however, does attempt some rough estimates of factor income flows and invisible trade as does Kenya albeit these first attempts are very crude.

It is difficult even to translate the trade data into accurate estimates of the territorial balance of visible trade with the rest of the world, particularly because Uganda's exports are valued at Mombasa and, also, interterritorial transfers of imported goods are incompletely reported. Interterritorial trade is generally under-reported because of inadequate records of movements of goods via road and on the hoof.

b. Estimates of Real Domestic Product

Official estimates of real domestic output are not available for Kenya. Data on the terms of trade and on the cost of living in Nairobi, Kampala, and Dar es Salaam are available. A private effort to use this fragmentary data to deflate the series for monetary GDP has been published.* In May, 1964 and June, 1964, annual series for the deflated gross domestic product of Tanzania (1960–1962) and of Uganda (1954–1962), respectively, were published. (Chapter X will deal more carefully with the problems and techniques involved in deflating income series and in working with the terms of trade.)

6. The Subsistence Sector

The difficult problems raised by the existence of subsistence activity have been met in different ways in each of the three countries. There are variations not only in estimation techniques but also in the definition of the sector itself even though all three countries profess to follow U.N. guidance in this matter.

* C. P. Haddon-Cave, "Real Growth of the East African Territories, 1954–1960," *East African Economics Review*, Vol. 8, No. 1, June, 1961 and comments in Vol. 8, No. 2 and Vol. 9, Nos. 1 and 2.

On the basis of the U.N. definition, *Kenya* includes in its estimates of subsistence activity only agriculture, livestock production, and certain forestry activities (firewood collection and the production of poles used in hut construction). No value is imputed to the process of hut construction or to any craft industries. Perhaps most significantly, the home production of beer has been excluded. The method of obtaining the subsistence output of food crops and livestock was explained in the discussion of African agriculture. Recall that in both areas local market prices facing producers were the basis of valuation. Figures for the value of subsistence forestry are obtained by assuming that all such work is done by women, by obtaining the population of adult women in African districts, by valuing their labor at an annual wage taken from the employment survey and finally by attributing a percentage of this to forestry. No value is imputed to any part of forestry but the labor of collection on the assumption that all the trees grow wild and that an insignificant amount of labor is expended in forest cultivation. The total gross product of the fishing industry valued at producer's prices, has been divided into 90 per cent cash and 10 per cent subsistence. A lump sum estimate of £100,000 is made to cover subsistence hunting, poaching and crocodile hunting.

Uganda, working from the same U.N. definition as Kenya, has derived a slightly different production boundary for the subsistence sector. In the Ugandian estimates, the production of beer for home consumption is included. The figures for staple crops are obtained by multiplying a population estimate by dietary data based on a 1956 World Health Organization nutrition survey. This production total is then multiplied by an estimated producer price for each commodity. Subsistence livestock production is estimated as discussed under Ugandan agriculture. It is basically derived as a residual in the subtraction of estimated sales from total production. Similar methods are used in obtaining figures for milk and fish. Valuation in the first case is at 50 per cent of rural retail price and in the second is based on estimates of the Game and Fisheries Department. Beer production was valued only on the basis of raw materials used which were assumed to be worth 60 per cent of the retail price. No account was taken of alleged differences in alcoholic content between city and country. Quantity figures were based on estimation of gallons consumed per person times population and were divided between cash sales and subsistence on an arbitrary basis, though account was taken of observed district differences in this respect. Firewood and house-pole gathering is valued on the basis of estimates of consumption per head, population data, and prices. The valuation is intended to cover the cost of the labor of gatherers.

Tanzania had adopted the widest definition of subsistence production of any of the East African countries in their earlier estimates (1954–1962).

In addition to those activities included in the Uganda estimates, African hut construction and craft industries were valued. For the more recent series (1960), the production boundary was narrowed and made similar to that of Uganda, with beer brewing included. Agriculture, livestock, and hunting and fishing output in the subsistence sector are in most cases derived as residuals from total production estimates with either cash sales known or assumed on the basis of rural survey data. Valuation is at producer prices. Only the value of raw materials used in beer is included and is assumed to be 50 per cent of the retail price of beer.

The above discussion should make clear to the student the many practical difficulties of measurement which face the estimator who would include subsistence activity within his figures for the income of the typical developing country. The fact that ingenious methods have been devised to make use of available data should not obscure the very tenuous nature of the resulting figures.

C. The National Accounts of India

1. *Introduction*

Efforts at estimating the national income of India have a longer history than in most less-developed countries. The first attempt—a very rough one—dates to 1876. Several other attempted estimates followed, including the one of Shah and Khambata for 1921. In 1939 V.K.R.V. Rao published the most elaborate estimates to that date for the years 1925–29. Rao followed this with a very comprehensive study based on the census year 1931–32.

In 1949 the government set up a National Income Committee with responsibility for the accounts. Since 1951 official estimates have been published regularly.

National income estimation in India is complicated by the sheer size of the country and the considerable decentralization of governmental responsibilities to state and local agencies. For example, in small countries as in East Africa, the responsibility for marketing the major food and export crops will often be in the hands of a single country-wide marketing board (e.g., cotton and coffee in Uganda, and maize and sugar in Kenya). In India, however, there are a plethora of state agencies responsible for crop marketing. Furthermore, unlike in India, small less-developed countries will have only a few firms in many industries. For example, until recently there was only one textile firm, one small steel plant, and only a handful of companies producing electricity in all of East Africa.

On the other hand, India is faced with the same problems in estimating national accounts as other less-developed countries, a lack of primary sources and a paucity of resources to conduct sample surveys and to gather and compile the requisite information. Thus, there is generally a great delay in the official publication of national income estimates. To satisfy the needs of policy makers and researchers, the Indian government has published a series of "quick estimates" of national income which are available before the official estimates are compiled.

2. The System of Accounts

The basic series is Net Domestic Product at factor cost by industry of origin. To these figures are added net factor income from abroad to obtain Net National Product at factor cost (see Table XII–14). The methods used are a combination of commodity flow (production) and value added, depending on the particular industry.

3. Agriculture, Forestry, Hunting and Fishing

The production approach is used to estimate the net output of agriculture. Estimates of production for major crops are obtained from sample surveys made by the Directorate of Economics and Statistics. Some crop estimates, especially the minor crops, are not available on an up-to-date basis but are extrapolated forward on the basis of changes in acerage estimates which are obtained from sample surveys. Output is valued at wholesale prices on a state-by-state basis. From the gross value of output is subtracted charges for seeds, fertilizer, repair and maintenance, and irrigation water. The cost of these inputs is estimated from a variety of sources. For example, irrigation charges are determined from data kept by public water authorities. An assumed proportion of repair and maintenance is deducted

TABLE XII–14

India Net Domestic Product at Factor Cost

(billion rupees)

	1958*	1959*	1960*	1961*	1962*	1963*	1964*
1. Agriculture, Forestry, Hunting, and Fishing	62.4	62.5	68.9	69.6	70.0	81.7	102.7
2. Mining	1.4	1.4	1.6	1.7	1.9	2.3	2.2
3. Manufacturing, Construction, and Public Utilities	20.3	21.8	24.4	27.1	28.9	31.0	33.8
4. Transport, Communication, and Trade	20.2	20.9	21.8	22.9	24.4	25.7	26.8
5. Banking, Insurance, and Real Estate	1.3	1.4	1.6	1.9	2.1	2.4	2.8
6. Ownership of Dwellings	5.0	5.2	5.3	5.5	5.6	5.8	6.0
7. Public Administration and Defense	7.3	7.9	9.0	10.0	11.3	12.8	14.8
8. Services	8.3	8.7	9.3	10.0	10.6	11.3	12.1
Net Domestic Product	126.2	129.8	141.9	148.7	154.8	173.0	201.2
Net Factor Income from Abroad ...	−0.2	−0.3	−0.5	−0.7	−0.8	−0.9	−1.1
Net National Income	126.0	129.5	141.4	148.0	154.0	172.1	200.1

* Fiscal year beginning April 1.

Source: Central Statistical Office, *Estimates of National Income, 1964–65*, New Delhi, 1966, Table 2, p. 2.

from gross output. This proportion is obtained from past sample surveys.

The value of livestock production is determined from various marketing reports issued by the Directorate of Marketing and Inspection. These reports are usually not available on an up-to-date basis and estimates for prior years are projected forward on the basis of a five-year growth rate for each category of livestock. Production is valued on a state-by-state basis and deductions for non-factor inputs are made in the same manner as for agriculture.

Income from hunting is obtained by multiplying the number of persons listed as hunters in the latest population census by an assumed average income.

The gross value of forestry and fishing is obtained from reports of central government agencies concerned with them. An arbitrary deduction of 5 per cent is made to account for non-factor costs. Fishing output is up-rated by an arbitrary 25 per cent to allow for non-licensed fishing.

4. Mining

Mining output statistics are gathered by the Indian Bureau of Mines. Output is valued at "pit head" prices. From this is subtracted 5 per cent for purchases from other sectors, and depreciation, the latter estimated by an analysis of balance sheets of mining companies undertaken by the Reserve Bank of India.

5. Manufacturing, Construction, and Public Utilities

The value added in establishments employing more than ten persons (more than twenty persons for establishments not using power) is estimated on the basis of a national annual sample survey of establishments. For small manufacturing enterprises and construction activities, value added is estimated on the basis of numbers employed in each manufacturing and construction category as reported in the decennial censuses of population. These numbers are extrapolated to the present. From these figures is deducted the number employed in large scale enterprises obtained from the annual sample survey of establishments. The average annual income per worker in each group is determined from a variety of sources. This estimate of wages and salaries is increased by 20 per cent to allow for other factor income. The 20 per cent figure is derived from a 1949 survey of cottage industries.

6. Banking, Insurance, and Real Estate

Banking income is derived from Reserve Bank statistics. The insurance industry is nationalized and data are provided by the Life Insurance Corporation of India.

7. Transport, Communications, and Other Service Industries

Estimates for communication are based on the annual accounts of the Department of Posts and Telegraph. Estimates for railways are taken from annual reports of the Railways Board and the budgets of the government railways. Income originating in cooperative societies is provided by statistics compiled by the cooperative movement. Other income from the non-government, service industries is based on an extrapolation of population census data and an assumed average income per person employed.

Government services are obtained as the total compensation of employees from central, state, and local government annual budget statements.

8. Subsistence Income

There are no separate estimates of subsistence production. The methods of estimation for a number of industries, however, include an explicit enumeration of non-marketed output. This is true in agriculture, forestry, fishing, and hunting. On the other hand, subsistence activities in other sectors will not be counted except to the extent that a person's main occupation is recorded in a population census.

9. Reliability of Statistics

A number of major weaknesses are embodied in the Indian accounts estimation. Deductions for non-factor costs are often made on an arbitrary basis. In a number of cases, up-to-date production estimates are not obtainable and estimates for prior years are extrapolated forward on the basis of historical rates of growth. This is a dubious procedure at best. The most glaring weakness, however, is the heavy reliance on population censuses to provide employment estimates on an occupational basis. The census figures themselves are far from accurate. The inaccuracy is compounded when members in each occupational categories are projected forward on the basis of assumed rates of growth. The average income estimates of those employed are then based on average earnings indexes which often do not discriminate regarding the same occupational categories.

It is clear that the Indian accounts should be used with extreme care and any conclusions based on the accounts should be most guarded. It would not be justified to base important policy decisions on detailed conclusions drawn from the national accounts.

XIII

CHANGING PRICE LEVELS

The national accounts discussed in the previous chapters all presented values measured in current prices. The aggregates were sums of a great mixture of goods and services, their relative importance being judged by the rate at which they could be exchanged for the current monetary unit. If the price of a good rises relative to that of other goods, the relative importance of a given quantity of that good's output will also increase. With the passage of time it is likely that the price of many different goods will change, both relative to each other and relative to money. If the rate at which money can be exchanged for goods is subject to change, then the standard of measurement is a fluctuating one. This chapter deals with problems of measurement in the face of such a fluctuating standard.

A. Defining Price Changes

The problem resolves itself into a comparison of the value of money in differing time periods. A similar problem arises when comparisons are made between countries with differing monetary systems, or even between areas within the same monetary system but where there is reason to believe there are regional variations in the value of money. In order for comparisons to be made there must be some method of translating the unit of measurement operative in the one country or area into terms of the unit operating in the other.

Although the problem of fluctuating price levels will be familiar to many readers, others may find it worthwhile to consider a very simple example to illustrate the problem.

Imagine for a moment an economy which consumes only a single final product, cotton cloth. Let it have as its currency unit the dollar, and consider the following record of final expenditure for two time periods, 0 and 1:

Price/yd.		Quantity (yds.)	Total Expenditure
Period 0	$1.00	400	$400.00
Period 1	$2.00	400	$800.00

Now, the expenditure of the economy is twice as great in period 1 as in period 0. Is it possible to say that in any sense the citizens of this economy are twice as well off in period 1 as in period 0? Clearly not, for they are consuming exactly the same amount of final product as before. The question itself arises because the units operating in the two periods are assumed to be the same, which leads to an attempt to compare the expenditure figures directly. That the dollar of period 1 is somehow different from that of the earlier period is evident when one considers that the old dollar would buy one yard of cloth while the new dollar will only buy one-half yard of the same cloth. That such a change in "purchasing power" represents a change in the value of money rests on the simple but fundamental idea that money is of no intrinsic value, that its worth at any time is defined entirely in terms of the amounts of various goods it will command.

It might be helpful here to list several alternative ways of stating the nature of the phenomenon observed in the example as illuminated by the above argument:

(i) prices have doubled.
(ii) a dollar buys half as much as before.
(iii) the dollar's purchasing power has been halved.
(iv) the value of money is half what it was.

These are four ways of stating the same thing and may be used interchangeably.

If the problem faced in practice were as simple as the example above there would be little further difficulty. However, consider the complications which arise when a second consumer good is introduced. The problem would still be simple if relative prices remained unchanged. This case is represented in the table below.

It is easy to see that all prices have doubled, expenditure has doubled,

Commodity	Price	Quantity	Total Expenditure
	Period 0		
Cotton	$1.00 per yd.	400 yds.	$400.00
Maize	$25.00 per bag	20 bags	$500.00
		Total Expenditure	$900.00
	Period 1		
Cotton	$2.00 per yd.	400 yds.	$800.00
Maize	$50.00 per bag	20 bags	$1000.00
		Total Expenditure	$1800.00

but the quantity of consumption is constant. Each individual price has doubled, but the relative price of goods is constant. However, what if relative prices change? This case is represented in the table here, which shows period 1 with new *relative* prices.

Commodity	Price	Quantity	Total Expenditure
	Period 1		
Cotton	$3.00 per yd.	400 yds.	$1200.00
Maize	$50.00 per bag	20 bags	$1000.00
		Total Expenditure	$2200.00

The price of cotton has risen by three times while the price of maize has only doubled. How much have prices risen?

The problem is still relatively simple because the quantities have remained constant, there having been no increase in consumption. Therefore, the rise in expenditure represents a price rise only. It can be said that prices have risen by a factor equal to 2200/900.

It is interesting to note how this figure is arrived at by weighting the two different price rises according to the relative quantities involved. Serious problems arise, however, when the quantities of maize and cloth consumed change, as well as their prices. Consider the example when both new quantities and prices are recorded in period 1.

Commodity	Price	Quantity	Total Expenditure
	Period 1		
Cotton Cloth ...	$3.00 per yd.	300 yds.	$900.00
Maize	$50.00 per bag	30 bags	$1500.00
		Total Expenditure	$2400.00

How much have prices risen in this case? Total expenditure now differs from period 0, but so does the quantity of each good consumed. The rise in prices is an average of the two different price rises.

It will be instructive to consider two different types of average which might be chosen. The first average might answer the question: what would be the change in expenditure necessary to buy the goods purchased in period 0? The answer to this question can be discovered by pricing period 0 quantities at period 1 and then at period 0 prices and comparing the two expenditure totals. This is shown below:

Commodity	Price in Period 0	Quantity in Period 0	Total Expenditure
Cotton	$1.00 per yd.	400 yds.	$400.00
Maize	$25.00 per bag	20 bags	$500.00
			$900.00
	Price in Period 1	Quantity in Period 0	
Cotton	$3.00 per yd.	400 yds.	$1200.00
Maize	$50.00 per bag	20 bags	$1000.00
			$2200.00

The comparison of the two total expenditure items gives a price index of $2200/$900 = 2.444.

A second way to look at the price rise is to ask what is the actual expenditure in period 1 relative to the expenditure which would be required to purchase period 1 quantities if prices had not changed. For this purpose, the goods purchased in period 1 must be valued at period 0 and period 1 prices. This calculation is as follows.

Commodity	Price in Period 0	Quantity in Period 1	Total Expenditure
Cotton	$1.00 per yd.	300 yds.	$300.00
Maize	$25.00 per bag	30 bags	$750.00
			$1050.00

	Price in Period 1	Quantity in Period 1	
Cotton	$3.00 per yd.	300 yds.	$900.00
Maize	$50.00 per bag	30 bags	$1500.00
			$2400.00

The change in price by this criterion is 2400/1050, that is 2.285.

The first method of calculation is known as *base weighting* because price changes are weighted by quantities operative at the base period, and the second method is known as *current weighting*. A terminology in frequent use is to describe a base weighted price index as a *Laspeyres* index and a current weighted version as a *Paasche* index.

It should be noted that the change in prices brings about a second difficulty: how should the change in the quantity of output be measured? Analogous to the price index, a quantity index could be derived which would answer the question: what has been the change in the quantity of output given either base year prices for both periods or current prices for both periods? This index is derived by measuring the value of the two quantities in constant prices. For a simple exercise, such a calculation could be undertaken with the figures given above.

The four different forms of index are to be represented quite simply using the notation:

P_0 = prices in period 0

P_1 = prices in period 1
Q_0 = quantities in period 0
Q_1 = quantities in period 1

Using this notation:

Laspeyres price index   = $\Sigma P_1 Q_0 / \Sigma P_0 Q_0$
Laspeyres quantity index = $\Sigma Q_1 P_0 / \Sigma Q_0 P_0$
Paasche price index   = $\Sigma P_1 Q_1 / \Sigma P_0 Q_1$
Paasche quantity index   = $\Sigma Q_1 P_1 / \Sigma Q_0 P_1$

Examination of these expressions reveals the interesting fact that the multiplication of the Paasche quantity index by the Laspeyres price index results in an index which shows the change in the value of total expenditure. The same is true for the multiplication of the Paasche price index by the Laspeyres quantity index.

This fact should be remembered, for if a value index is divided by a quantity index in order to derive an index of price, the weighting system is reversed: if the quantity index was current weighted then the resulting price index is base weighted, and vice versa.

The typical experience is likely to be that the base weighted consumer price index will give a higher estimate of price level rises than an index with current weights. This is because the consumer will substitute cheaper for more expensive goods in his budget, and therefore the prices which have experienced more than average price rises are likely to decline in importance in the current budget compared with those goods for which the price rises has been less than average.

The proposition in the previous paragraph was based on the belief that changes in quantities consumed will be *negatively* correlated with changes in relative price. That this is not necessarily the case will be obvious if the reader thinks of a situation in which prices change purely as a result of shifts in demand. In this case changes in quantity consumed are likely to be *positively* correlated with changes in relative price and current weights will give higher estimates of price rises than base weights.

B. Problems of Application

In practice, in most situations where index numbers are applied, the number of commodities involved will be very large. It is impractical to measure all prices at all times. Therefore some method of selection must be adopted. The most typical method is to select a group of commodities in some base year and to price these, rather than all commodities. The group chosen must be large enough to be representative but small enough to be manageable.

This involves the necessity of *sampling*, that is choosing a collection of goods the behavior of which will provide a satisfactory representation of the behavior of the much larger population of which it forms part. The problems of sampling theory and the statistical methods involved are not discussed in this volume. However, some of the problems involved can be understood in very simple terms, without reference to the theoretical problem of samping as such.

1. *The Choice of the Right* (*"Basket of Goods"*)

One of the most important purposes for which price indexes are calculated is to measure changes in the "cost of living." There is considerable interest in translating the incomes people receive into terms of "real" welfare by attempting to measure the quantity of goods the income can buy. Also, it is often the case that attempts are made to adjust wages to match changes in the price level.

The difficulty that arises is that different people consume different combinations of goods. As long as these differences are fairly small then it is sensible to take an average of the various spending patterns to use as a basis for an index. However, the differences can be so large as to make such averaging absurd. For example, in Uganda the spending patterns of the senior civil servant, living in Kampala, and the peasant producing tobacco in West Nile will differ so much that there will be no meaningful average. There is no "cost of living index" which could sensibly record the changes in the purchasing power of the incomes of such different groups. Differences in income, cultural background, and geographical location are the most important reasons why such averages are inappropriate in estimating changes in "the cost of living."

Statistical offices attempt to deal with this problem by producing more than one index of the price level, attempting to tailor the index to the particular spending patterns of identifiable groups in the society. The degree to which such groups can be isolated is limited, if only because there are limits to the number of indexes a statistical department can produce. In East Africa, for example, indexes are calculated for the African urban employee and for the urban middle class. Because of the base years from which these data are drawn the urban middle class is an expatriate group. Thus in Uganda a cost of living index is published for Kampala which is intended to measure the cost of maintaining the standard of living prevailing among European government servants with a basic salary, in 1951, of some £700 per year. The method of weighting in this case is to modify the expenditure weights used for the similar Nairobi index, which was, in turn, based on a survey undertaken in 1947.

In order to measure the price level facing these two groups, indexes have been constructed for wage-earners' cost of living in Nairobi, Kampala, and Dar es Salaam, and indexes for the cost of living of European civil servants in Nairobi and Kampala. There are no indexes for numerous other categories which could, with equal legitimacy, be considered. For example, there is no index for the costs of either civil servants or peasants in rural areas, and urban dwellers of Asian origin (numerically much more important than the Europeans) are neglected. It would be highly unlikely that the spending patterns of any one of these groups correspond closely enough with the urban wage-earner or the middle rank European (in Nairobi in 1947) to justify the use of the existing indexes to estimate changes in their cost of living.

Even in a more homogeneous society, the concept of a typical spending pattern is a dangerous one. The deviation from the average pattern is less than is the case in the East African examples mentioned above, but there are large numbers of people for whom it is true that their own spending patterns are quite distinct from the average and their own cost of living therefore may behave in quite a different fashion than "the" cost of living index.

2. The Collection of Prices

If a representative basket of goods has been chosen, it is then necessary to obtain prices for goods in the basket. Here a number of practical difficulties arise. For many goods the choice of time and place of purchase will make great differences to the price. Market prices for foodstuffs can fluctuate even during the day and can vary from market to market within the same town. Also, the manner of purchase makes a great difference. In highly industrialized societies most commodities are sold at a fixed price. The nature of this price might not always be clear because of discounts of one sort or another, but even these may be standardized. In developing countries far more bargaining is carried on in almost all transactions, and the selling price may depend on the skill of the purchaser.

In setting up the collection procedure, attempts ought to be made to avoid obvious, sources of bias. Prices should not be collected always on the same day of the week, or at the same time of the day, for example. Some attempt will have to be made to ensure that the prices of actual transactions are recorded rather than some nominal price, which is merely the starting point for a bargaining procedure. Because of the costs involved there will inevitably be a very limited amount of collection going on so that the element of judgment in avoiding the most obvious sorts of bias will be extremely important.

3. Changes in the Quality of Goods

In attempting to measure the changes in the price of a basket of goods, the problem arises that the goods originally identified in the base year may change in quality in subsequent years.

In the case of basic foodstuffs, which form such an important part of the price index for urban workers, the difficulty is that although the types of food available may not change with the passage of years, at any given time there will be a wide variation of quality available. For some goods, differences of quality may be standardized so that from the outset it may be possible to define precisely the grade of maize meal or quality of sugar going into the index. The attempt should be made to choose the more widely used grades. The difficulty may arise, of course, that the behavior of the prices of different grades may be substantially different, and that substantial substitution takes place in the consumer budget. This is but another example of the problems resulting from consumer response to price.

For manufactured goods, the problem is likely to be quite different and inherently more difficult. For foodstuffs and the simplest standardized consumer goods, such as cotton textiles, the basic characteristics of the commodity are well defined and improvements in production technique are as likely to lead to a change in the relative price as a change in the character of the product. For more complicated manufactured goods, such as radios, automobiles, cameras, etc., technical progress is likely to take the form of changes in the character of the commodity itself. In this case new models appear, perhaps with new names, perhaps continuing the old name but with substantially changed performance. If the name of the model is changed and the old model disappears the existence of the problem will be readily recognized. In the case of some commodities however, the changes are not so obvious. For example, the Volkswagen car, which is quite an important import item, is continuously subjected to small changes which may improve (or impair) its performance. In such cases it is likely that the index number will, in one sense, exaggerate price increases, for the product being bought, perhaps at a higher price, is of improved quality. Whether this is serious depends on what the purchaser is viewed as buying. If he is viewed as simply buying a new car of a certain size with but minor interest in its detailed specifications, then continuing to use the price of that car without allowance for improvements in quality may be justified. If he is viewed as purchasing so much speed, so much comfort, so much strength, then the price index should be adjusted for changes in such characteristics.

Although the adjustments for quality change are in principle acceptable, in practice they are unlikely to be feasible. The estimation of the qualities of a product is likely to be extremely subjective. If the salesmen were believed, every year's model is a vast improvement over that of the previous year; if commentators of advanced years are consulted, it will be discovered that nothing is quite as good as it used to be.

At the extreme, of course, a change in quality is represented by a complete disappearance in one commodity and its replacement in a particular use by another, perhaps completely different in physical qualities. In countries where many of the more complicated manufactures are imported, some lines may be driven out of the market by the entry of a new competitor.

As goods appear and disappear a judgment must be made whether to introduce a new good or remove an old good from the index. If a good disappears an effort may be made to identify a good which is a close substitute, and introduce that into the basket of goods as a replacement. This is not the same thing as introducing new weights; rather it involves the use of old weights but the choice of a new method of selecting the price to which the weights are applied. There is a case to be made that the statistician should use considerable judgment in adjusting for piecemeal quality changes, short of complete replacement of one good by another. This case will be strong where it seems reasonable to suppose that some clearly measurable characteristic of a good can be identified with its quality. Then, for example, a fall in the alcoholic content of beer might be treated as a rise in its price or a rise in the horsepower of a automobile model might be treated as a fall in price.

The danger in making such adjustments for quality is that the exercise of subjective judgment involved can give rise to great controversy, particularly when matters of public policy hinge on the resulting figures. An astute, if unscrupulous, official statistician might be able to reduce the cost of living at the request of the government merely by identifying an unusually large degree of quality improvements under way.

What has been said about manufactured goods may be applied *a fortiori* to services, where the quality of the performance is even more difficult to define.

C. Deflation of Expenditure Accounts

The deflation of the expenditure accounts is conceptually the least bothersome of the triple tasks facing any statistical department bent on providing real estimates for all three major accounts. This is not to say that the process is without pitfalls, but only that, for several reasons, these are fewer and less severe than in the other accounts.

The major reason for the relatively easy nature of the task is that the expenditure account deals with commodity flows. As will be noted again below, the notion of index numbers for price and quality is far more easily applied to commodity flows than, for example, to flows of factor services. Even the many problems of sampling, quality changes, etc., already discussed, do not serve to introduce conceptual or practical difficulties equivalent to those found in the other applications.

A second important reason is that a large portion of the aggregate expenditure figure will be the result of transactions in fairly well defined markets with measureable prices. Mention has already been made of the qualifications to this statement which must be kept in mind.

Subject to what has been said about heterogeneous populations, it is also true that some argument can be made for the deflation of the large sub-aggregates in the expenditure account by single indexes. This argument rests on the notion that there is some economic sense to be made in speaking of price for investment goods or consumption goods or exports, etc.

In view, then, of the advantages to be gained by tackling this instead of another account, it is not surprising that most of the effort put into the production of real national accounting data typically goes into expenditure estimates.

The consumption figures may be approached through the consumer price index which may well be calculated for its intrinsic value even before it is applied to deflation use. As was noted above, "the" consumer price index may, in reality, be several indexes covering different segments of the population with very different spending habits. Alternatively, indexes for differing commodity groups may be constructed, perhaps covering consumer durables (e.g., refrigerators) or covering all food products, all clothing, etc. The method of approach used is likely to depend on the existing availability of price data in countries where deflation is being attempted for the first time. In any case, once the indexes are chosen, care must be taken that they are applied to the proper figures. A food price index would be useless in deflating estimates of furniture consumption over the years.

Similarly, the investment aggregate may be approached in a number of different ways corresponding to the nature of the investment taking place. If investment is largely in construction and simple machinery, only two series, one for building costs and one for machinery, might be highly satisfactory. As the investment bill becomes more complex, it will probably be necessary to adopt a more detailed approach, perhaps using many indexes (e.g., machine tool prices, electrical generator equipment prices, house building costs, factory building, costs, etc.). One very difficult problem under investment will be the deflation of inventory accumulation. Just how the inventory is valued in current price estimates will depend on what method of inventory valuation is used by business, what proportion accumulated is in raw materials and what in finished or semi-finished goods, what is happening to wage costs, etc. In order to deflate inventory accumulation data on a correct basis an enormous amount of knowledge would be needed. In practice, inventory investment is often deflated with an index of wholesale prices.

The government's purchases from business may be deflated by one or more of the indexes already developed, e.g., by a wholesale price index or by a combination of a wholesale price and an investment good index. The difficulties here will depend on the range of expenditures in which the government is involved.

The government's wage bill may be deflated by some general wage index or by a special index of government wage rates. In either case it is subject to the difficulties of deflating factor services mentioned below.

Deflating imports and exports includes a particular type of problem to which some paragraphs are devoted below. Indexes of export prices are often quite easy to compile because of the standardized nature and narrow (although relative quantities may change very widely) range of export goods involved. Imports, on the other hand can be quite tricky because of the frequent change in the composition of the import bill, some goods appearing or disappearing completely from year to year. Import price indexes are, therefore, often quite difficult to compile and may be subject to error in addition to the usual bias inherent in fixed weighting systems.

There is one point which is worth noting about export and import price indexes. In comparing such indexes, it is important to note the point of valuation. For example, if the exports are valued at point of exit from the exporting country quite a different picture of price changes might be gained than when they are valued at point of entry to the importing country if there are substantial charges for transport and insurance. Particularly over long time periods, in which substantial transformation of the international transport system can take place, it is possible for both the price to the exporter (at point of exit) to rise and the price to the importer (at point of entry) to fall. It is therefore necessary to be quite clear regarding what the index is intended to tell.

D. Deflation of the Product Account

Since the product account may be derived in two ways it is necessary to consider two alternative methods of deflation. If the commodity flow approach is used in deriving product from total sales and purchases of intermediate goods, similar problems to those just discussed are encountered. There are, however, additional issues raised by the form of this account. If, on the other hand, the product account is considered from the point of view of factor incomes (value added) a whole new set of difficulties arises.

If the product accounts are compiled with the use of the commodity flow method, then there is the advantage that a reasonably well-defined array of goods is being dealt with. Two major problems must, however, be solved. Whereas in deflating expenditure accounts it is likely that the same data can be used as would be mobilized for cost of living indexes, for the product accounts such series will be much less applicable. The industries shown in the product accounts are selling both finished and intermediate products. In general, it seems unlikely that the finished goods indexes of consumer and investment goods prices will be applicable to such accounts.

The most difficult problem, however, is that the product accounts computed through the commodity flow method result from the subtraction of intermediate inputs from the sales of the various industries. Each industry will have a unique set of inputs as well as outputs. A number of indexes will have to be constructed for different types of intermediate input. However, because individual industries can often acquire strong bargaining positions as purchasers of intermediate inputs, the prices faced by a particular industry may vary considerably from the average price levels for that commodity throughout the economy.

If, instead of estimating product through the commodity flow method, the estimation of value added from factor payments is used, a different set of difficulties arise. In particular, it will be extremely difficult to decide how the profit share should be deflated, because of the ambiguous nature of the flow factor services for which the profit share is an implied payment. This problem, similar to that involved in deflating the income side of the accounts, is discussed in the following paragraphs.

E. The Treatment of Factor Services

It was mentioned that the problems of measuring the changing quality of services was particularly difficult in computing consumer price indexes. If the income side of the national accounts is considered, the problem arises that the "commodity" being priced is entirely in the form of services, for which there is a derived demand. No serious problem arises if the total gross domestic income is deflated, as the equality of the different sides of the accounts means that the gross deflator could be estimated from the product side. If, however, price deflators are required for particular factor services the problems involved are even more difficult than those involved in the deflation of commodity flows.

There are two alternative approaches. First, it might be felt that incomes are being deflated purely for the purpose of estimating the changing situation of the income receivers. In this case it would be appropriate to deflate incomes by indexes estimating the changes in the price levels facing the income receivers. Thus wages would be deflated by an index for the cost of living of wage earners, and retained profits might be deflated by an index of investment goods prices. If this method is chosen the problem is straightforward.

The second possibility is that it may be considered desirable to estimate the changing cost of purchasing factor services. In this case the problem is much more difficult because of the character of the services being measured. In the case of labor it is quite possible to calculate an index for average earnings per hour or some other measure of changing wage rates. However, the quality of labor inputs can change as much as anything else. In a developing country, in which new entrants are all the time being recruited to the labor force, it is quite likely that the quality of labor can change considerably with the passage of only short periods of time.

The measurement of the wage rate will also be complicated by the fact that the payment of fringe benefits, overtime, and bonuses for efficiency and seniority will all complicate the choice of wage rates to include in the index, as much as the diversity of grades and prices complicated the construction of a commodity index.

The problem of measuring changes in the price of capital services involves difficulties all of its own. Because of the peculiar difficulties involved this problem will not be tackled in this chapter.

F. Terms of Trade Effects

In primary producing countries much of the output of one of the most important sectors of the economy is sold abroad, while a large part of the manufactures consumed domestically are imported. One of the most important external influences on the local economy will be the behavior of export prices, which are notoriously volatile in the case of many primary products. The behavior of export prices is likely to be quantitatively much more important for such economies than that of other prices.

To choose the method that is appropriate to deflate export commodities it is necessary to specify very carefully the purpose for which the deflation is being made. There are two quite different questions which might be asked. Interest might be concentrated on the consumption standards which can be achieved with the exports. Alternatively, interest might be focused on the attempt to measure the degree to which the change in export earnings represents a change in the physical volume of exports and the degree to which it represents a change in prices.

If the latter objective is chosen, then the attempt should be made to calculate an export price index in much the same fashion as any other price index. If the former objective is chosen, then the choice might be quite different. The purchasing power of export earnings is determined by the price level of goods imported. The growth of real purchasing power should then be measured by deflating export earnings by the import price index.

That these two methods can give very different results can be illustrated by the example below.

			Value of exports ($ million)	Export prices	Import prices
Period 0	...	...	50	100	100
Period 1	...	...	36	60	120

In this example the value of exports (in current prices) has fallen 28 per cent between the two time periods. At the same time export prices have fallen and import prices have risen. Using the export price deflator, period 1 exports at period 0 prices come to $60 million, that is an increase in quantity of exports of 20 per cent which was more than offset by a 40 per cent fall in prices.

If the import price index is used the picture is different. At period 0 import prices the value of period 1 exports would be only $30 million, which represents an even greater fall than the decline in the value figures.

The appropriate method depends entirely on the purpose for which the export earnings are being deflated.

G. International and Inter-Regional Comparisons

The problem of comparing values in different regions or countries is similar, in principle, to the problems of comparing values over time. Just as the value of money in one year will differ from that in another, so countries will have different currencies and the same currency may vary in value between regions. With the existence of trade, it might be assumed that some goods (those which are appropriate for trading) will have similar prices in terms of the official exchange rate. Where transport, distribution costs and customs duties are large, however, considerable price differentials may exist even if goods are traded. Services are not so easily transferable from area to area and some goods may, in a practical sense, because of very high transport costs, not be subject to transfer. It is, therefore, quite possible for differing price levels to exist in differing regions of the same country, and even more likely in differing countries.

Therefore, in making comparisons between countries it is necessary to conduct the same sort of adjustments that are made in inter-temporal comparisons. Some index is necessary to provide a method of translating one currency into units of the other and for adjusting for inter-regional differences in the value of money.

In many countries, for example, price levels in the major urban centers are quite different from those in remote rural areas. Some foodstuffs which fetch very low prices in the remote countryside will be quite expensive in the towns, whereas for manufactured goods, the reverse will be true. Mention has already been made of this problem in the discussion of the subsistence sector above.

In making comparisons between countries, the same technical problems arise as in comparing time periods. The combination of goods consumed will be quite different from country to country. Diets differ for cultural and climatic reasons. The consumption of all sorts of durables will be very strongly correlated with the standard of living. Some goods consumed in one situation may be quite meaningless in another—for example, the expensive heating systems which form part of the housing costs of the north eastern United States are not very relevant to many parts of Africa and Latin America where the natural supply of heat is quite adequate.

A particular sort of difficulty arises from the fact that as incomes grow, mechanical devices get introduced to replace labor in all sorts of tasks. The comparison between two societies at different stages of growth will, therefore, involve comparisons between completely different techniques of undertaking numerous routine tasks. The peasant family may cut its own firewood, do the washing in a local stream, carry water from the same stream for home use, perhaps even brew beer and so forth.

Consider the problem of producing an index to explain the value of those services to someone living in New York or London. One method would be to price the services at New York and London prices. However, because labor is so expensive in the more developed countries, this would result in an estimate of the value of such activities at New York prices which would probably suggest that the peasant was extremely well-off. If the bananas, millet, sweet potatoes, and other staples were also priced at New York prices the comparison would be even more favorable to the peasant.

On the other hand, if an index of price were calculated using New York spending weights it might be found that prices were apparently much higher for the peasant producers than in New York. This is because the goods prominent in a New Yorker's budget might be quite unusual in a peasant's budget.

It will generally be true that in making such comparisons, the price level of the country from which the weights are chosen will be underestimated relative to the price level in the other country. In each country consumers will be adjusting their tastes and consumption patterns to the typical price structure and the organization of production will, in turn, be geared to the structure of demand. In the same way that it is true that inter-temporal comparison over long periods of time is likely to be suspect, comparisons between countries with widely differing income levels and patterns of consumption in quantitative terms are unlikely to be meaningful in any precise sense.

H. Examples of National Account Deflation

The following sections of this chapter examine three examples of account deflation. First to be discussed will be the figures prepared by the Central Statistical Office of the former Federation of Rhodesia and Nyasaland. Second, the work of B. Hansen and D. Mead for the National Planning Board of the U.A.R. is examined. Finally, the case of Brazil is examined to illustrate some techniques which have been applied to countries prone to inflation.

In the first example, estimates have been prepared for the period 1954 to 1962 for the gross domestic and national expenditure at 1954 prices. Further, a considerable number of subsidiary accounts are presented in constant prices. In this chapter, only the Federation expenditure accounts will be discussed, although much of what is said will obviously apply to certain of the subsidiary accounts.

The U.A.R. figures are the result of an attempt by Hansen and Mead to make comparable the several estimates of Egyptian national accounting figures covering the period 1939 to 1962. A large part of the published report of their work concerns the reconciliation of different accounts in current prices, which have been prepared with varying approaches. Fortunately, the authors give a complete account of most of their deflation work, too, including in many instances descriptions of the indexes they had available.

The material in this chapter is presented both to introduce some actual uses of the methods which have been discussed in the abstract and to illustrate some of the compromises which must be made and the short cuts which must be taken when the available resources are inadequate.

I. The Federation of Rhodesia and Nyasaland Accounts

The approach used here (see Table XIII–1) is to deflate the figures for gross domestic expenditure item by item, then to apply to the resulting total a deflated figure for net income paid abroad. This new total, called gross national product, is actually gross national expenditure. From this is derived a figure called gross national income, the result of adjusting the GNP for the effect of the changes in the terms of trade. Thus, in the deflated accounts, GNI and GNP involve essentially different definitions.

The methods used in the actual deflation process are briefly described below. The division follows the lines adopted in the accounts as published. In general, price indexes are used wherever available. In some cases, however, quantity indexes are used; in these cases, implicit price deflators are derived and listed along with the ones obtained independently. There are no really satisfactory methods for the deflation of some series, particularly services and net income paid abroad. The price index numbers used are shown in Table XIII–2. They were mainly constructed specifically for the purpose.

1. Exports and Imports

Imports and exports of goods and services are deflated by their respective currently weighted price indexes.

2. Private Consumption Expenditure

Wherever possible, quantity data for the current year is merely matched with price data for 1954. In other areas deflation is by means of price indexes prepared for the Rhodesias, and where African consumption is important, extended to include Nyasaland. *Financial services* and *religious organizations* both have their contributions deflated on the basis of earning indexes for people employed in the field. Residents' expenditure abroad is attacked in quite an interesting way; an index of travel fares and of foreign consumer prices is used. The former is based on fares to the U.K., Union of South Africa, and Europe by air, sea, and rail. The latter is merely a weighted average of the consumer price indexes for the U.K. and South Africa, the weights reflecting estimated expenditure in the respective countries over the period. This method is based on the assumption that the great bulk of resident spending abroad is done by expatriates on leave.

3. African Rural Household Consumption

This area is simply handled by valuing the *per capita* consumption estimates at 1954 prices, multiplying by population figures and adding the 25 per cent markup.

4. Government Current Expenditure

Deflation here is on the basis of an index of average wages of government employees. The wages of employees of the Public Works Department are excluded as they are assumed to be engaged in capital works projects.

5. Gross Domestic Capital Formation

Conversion to constant prices is undertaken by type of asset. Land improvement expenses and deflated by an index of the average earnings of farm labor. Buildings and works estimates are deflated on the basis of an index of building costs which reflects both material costs and wages of construction workers. Expenditures for plant and machinery are approached element by element, the deflator in each case being a currently

TABLE XIII-1

Federation of Rhodesia and Nyasaland Deflated Expenditure Accounts at 1954 Market Prices

(£ million)

	1954	1955	1956	1957	1958	1959	1960	1961	1962
Private Consumption	168.3	182.3	195.3	211.9	217.2	227.6	237.9	242.1	242.6
African Rural Household Consumption...	52.2	53.2	54.3	55.4	57.4	59.8	61.7	64.4	67.1
Government Current Expenditure									
Central	26.2	26.4	30.6	32.3	33.2	36.6	36.7	40.2	42.0
Local	3.5	3.9	4.2	4.6	4.8	5.2	5.3	5.6	5.7
Capital Formation									
Land improvement	0.9	1.4	1.6	1.8	1.3	1.1	1.6	2.3	1.9
Mine development	2.0	2.7	3.7	4.0	2.6	2.3	2.7	2.8	3.6
Building and works	48.2	49.9	59.4	73.0	66.9	58.5	52.8	47.9	38.8
Plant, machinery, and equipment ...	44.2	52.1	63.0	64.6	49.6	47.8	47.7	41.3	31.8
Increase in stocks	−5.5	4.2	16.5	12.2	−1.7	0.2	9.8	14.2	11.5
Export of Goods and Services	183.6	157.5	176.3	202.9	207.8	243.0	263.0	273.6	279.0
Minus Imports of Goods and Services ...	168.5	181.8	201.8	220.8	196.7	199.6	203.4	196.7	186.2

Continued

TABLE XIII-1 (*continued*)

Federation of Rhodesia and Nyasaland Deflated Expenditure Accounts at 1954 Market Prices

(£ million)

	1954	1955	1956	1957	1958	1959	1960	1961	1962
Plus or Minus Statistical Discrepancy	−0.7	+7.1	+4.7	−3.0	+6.6	+8.2	−2.2	−4.2	−8.9
Equals GDE—1954 Market Prices	354.4	358.9	407.8	438.9	449.0	490.0	514.0	533.4	528.9
Less Net Income Paid Abroad	−34.0	−36.4	−42.9	−36.3	−26.4	−36.8	−39.1	−37.8	−40.8
Equals GNE—1954 Market Prices	320.4	322.5	364.9	402.6	422.6	454.0	474.9	495.6	488.1
Plus or Minus Adjustment for Changes in Terms of Trade	—	40.9	27.1	−20.6	−45.4	−27.0	−30.8	−49.5	−54.6
Equals GNI—1954 Prices	320.4	363.4	392.0	382.0	377.2	427.0	444.1	446.1	433.5
Compare GDE—Current Market Prices ...	354.4	410.8	465.2	460.0	458.1	523.7	556.3	566.2	566.6

Source: *National Accounts of the Federation of Rhodesia and Nyasaland, 1954-1962*, Salisbury, Central Statistical Office, June, 1963, Table 11, p. 6.

TABLE XIII-2

Federation of Rhodesia and Nyasaland Price Index Numbers for Expenditure Accounts

	1954	1955	1956	1957	1958	1959	1960	1961	1962
Private Consumption	100.0	101.6	105.2	107.2	109.6	111.3	113.1	114.9	117.5
African Rural Households ...	100.0	103.0	106.6	105.4	103.5	101.8	103.4	101.9	98.2
Government Current Expenditure ...	100.0	108.3	114.1	124.1	132.3	137.2	144.0	152.3	157.3
Gross Domestic Capital Formation ...	100.0	102.4	107.7	111.0	118.7	115.2	116.8	116.8	122.7
Exports	100.0	128.5	120.7	95.7	84.7	93.7	95.2	91.4	89.6
Imports	100.0	102.0	104.6	106.5	108.4	105.4	107.8	111.6	111.4
GDP	100.0	114.5	114.1	104.8	102.0	106.7	108.2	106.1	107.1
Net Income Paid Abroad	100.0	102.0	104.6	106.5	108.4	105.4	107.8	111.6	111.1
GNP	100.0	115.9	115.2	104.6	101.6	106.8	108.3	105.7	106.8

Source: The National Accounts of the Federation of Rhodesia and Nyasaland, 1954–1962, Salisbury, Central Statistical Office, June, 1963, Table 14, p. 7.

weighted index for the type of import. Where an element of expenditure includes goods purchased at home the index for the element takes this into account. Changes in the value of stocks held are deflated by applying 1954 prices to quantity data when such is available. Where it is not, the available value figures are used with an appropriate price index.

6. *Net Income Paid Abroad*

This figure is converted to constant units by dividing current payments by the index of import prices. This approach is intended to give a measure in real terms of the loss of social welfare resulting from the payment abroad of money which otherwise would have been available for use by residents in importing goods and services.

7. *The Effect of Changes in the Terms of Trade*

The correction for changes in the relative levels of import and export prices is done in a straightforward manner. It is effectively equal to the difference between the current value of exports deflated by the import price index and the current value of exports deflated by the export price index. This figure is obviously minus if the import price level has risen relative to the export price level since the base year. Such a relative rise would indicate a worsening of the terms of trade and the correction would rightly be negative in passing from GNP to so-called GNI.

Note that in several areas input indexes, in the form of wage indexes, are used to deflate expenditure figures. Something has already been said concerning the difficulties of constructing reliable factor cost indexes. It is clear that if employee quality differences over time are not accounted for, the resulting real estimates (e.g., building and construction and land improvement) will be seriously distorted. In the case of government expenditure on goods and services, there would seem to be little justification for deflating this solely by an earnings index for government workers for it not only incurs the problems of factor payment indexes but also distorts the series to the extent that prices of goods purchased by the government move in a different direction from that of wages. This last possibility is very real as presumably some substantial portion of government expenditure would be on imports.

J. Hansen and Mead and the U.A.R. (Egypt) Accounts

The second example of the deflation of African national accounts is drawn from the work of Hansen and Mead for the Institute of National Planning in Cairo. The scope of this work is actually larger than will be discussed here, involving both an attempt to reconcile several independent estimates of various domestic and national aggregates covering the period 1939 to 1962 under the GNP concept, and further, the deflation of the GNP figures. Only the conversion to real terms will be discussed in any detail here. The period dealt with is divided into four sub-periods, 1930 to 1945, 1945 to 1954, 1954 to 1958, and 1952/53 to 1961/62. (The last period is not on a calendar year basis because the available data was in terms of the budget year, July 1 to June 30.) Actually the final estimates are not strictly in constant prices over the entire period as the first period is in terms of 1939 prices, those of the next two periods in 1954 prices and those of the last period in terms of 1953/54 prices (see Table XIII–3). Much of the error one must expect in this series will be due to the difficulty of reconciling estimates done by different men on the basis of different definitions. It will be seen that the methods employed tend to be more sophisticated than those just discussed, largely because of the greater quantity of data available.

1. The Period 1939 to 1945

The aggregate net national income at market price is converted into constant 1939 prices by the application of the wholesale price index based on 1939. This is a Laspeyre price index with the weights chosen on the basis of the Egyptian Statistical Department's judgment as to relative importance of commodities in that year.

2. The Period 1945 to 1954

The basis of these figures is a National Planning Committee memo giving estimates for the period in 1954 prices. These were derived by dividing the economy into a large number of sectors and applying to each sector an index either of employment or of physical output. Hansen and Mead, in turn, adjusted these figures to bring them to a total for GNP at market prices (that is, the account being deflated is a product rather than an expenditure account). *Government services* were valued at the value of the government wage bill which had been deflated on the basis of an index of government wages reflecting the changing cost of living. The *agricultural* figures were recomputed based on data published by the Statistical Department which gave agricultural input and output in 1954 prices (for 1950 to 1954 only). For the years before 1954, reliance had to be placed on the output index implied by the Planning Committee figures. Valuation of intermediate inputs as well as outputs is preferable, because the changing pattern of input prices tends to distort figures based solely on output indexes. The third adjustment made was to add a constant figure representing *household services*. Finally an addition was made for *net factor incomes from abroad*.

At this point account was taken of the effect of changes in the terms of trade. First, the current year import and export bills were deflated by their

TABLE XIII-3

U.A.R. Accounts Deflated
(£ million)

A. 1939–1945 (at 1939 prices)

	1939	1940	1941	1942	1943	1944	1945
NNI at Factor Cost-Current Prices	168	191	233	326	390	464	502
Indirect Taxes minus Subsidies	15	15	17	19	16	24	26
NNI at Current Market Prices	183	206	250	345	406	488	528
Wholesale Price-Index (1939 = 100)	100	113	141	189	238	271	288
NNI at Factor Cost (1939 Market Prices)	183	182	177	182	171	180	183

B. 1945–1954 (at 1954 prices)

	1945	1946	1947	1948	1949	1950	1951	1952	1953	1954
Agriculture	303	302	299	328	325	303	304	334	315	312
Industry and Electricity	91	92	101	113	126	133	132	132	134	146
Construction	19	22	25	31	25	22	36	30	37	33
Transportation and Communications (including Suez Canal)	38	43	46	61	72	78	81	81	86	88
Housing, Commerce and Finance	172	193	200	225	249	282	274	261	254	265
Other Services including Government	96	101	110	122	139	148	157	166	166	179
Total GDP at 1954 Market Prices	719	753	781	880	936	956	984	1004	992	1023
Minus Net Income Paid Abroad	8	9	5	3	9	11	13	12	11	13
GNP at 1954 Market Prices	711	744	776	877	927	945	971	992	981	1010
Net Gains or Losses from Terms of Trade Changes	−38	−40	−45	31	10	68	113	9	−25	0
Real GNI at 1954 Prices	673	704	731	908	937	1013	1084	1001	956	1010

respective price indexes as published by the Bank of Egypt. The surplus (deficit) thus arrived at would have ruled, had 1954 export and import prices remained in effect in the current year. The difference between this surplus (deficit) and the actual one for the current year is, then, the result of changes in the terms of trade. For example, if the 1956 surplus at current prices was smaller than the same surplus at 1954 prices, the country has lost the difference as a result of changes in the terms of trade. This gain (loss) is then deflated by the 1954 import price index in order to measure the effect at constant prices.

This procedure has two weaknesses: first, it nowhere takes account of invisibles; and second, the import price index used does not reflect the prices of some important imports, notably machinery and equipment. It is, however, another example of a practical method of accounting for the effects of terms of trade changes.

3. *The Period 1954 to 1958*

The figures for these years are based on estimates prepared by the Department of Statistics and are deflated to 1954 prices. The *agricultural sector* is treated as discussed in the last section, by computing both inputs and outputs in 1954 prices and subtracting to find value added. This is perhaps the firmest estimate of the lot because of the detailed price and quantity information available over the period.

Industrial value added is found on the basis of wage bill and profit margin estimates. It is deflated by means of a weighted average of wholesale prices for 25 important commodities. Note that while value added is, in principle, computed at factor cost, the deflator is at market prices. The bias involved in this discrepancy will depend on the trend of government expenditure (as reflected in indirect taxes charged at the wholesale level over the years). A downward bias will result if such indirect taxes are growing faster than prices as a whole.

Construction and building expenses are estimated from the material side and are deflated by reference to the wholesale price sub-index for building materials.

Value added by *commerce* is calculated at factor cost (wages plus profit margins), but here again, deflation is by a wholesale price (market price) index, this time for 16 important commodities. For *financial institutions* income payments taken directly from the accounts of banks, insurance companies, etc., are deflated by the cost of living index,* and here again the remarks about factor cost and market price hold.

* The cost of living index is a Laspeyre index based on weights from 1939. These were chosen by the Department of Statistics to reflect the spending pattern of a lower middle income Cairo family. Recent consumer surveys indicate the weights are faulty.

For both *housing* and *transportation,* net value added is deflated by the cost of living index.

Government's contribution and that of *other services* are both calculated from wage bills and are both deflated by the cost of living index.

Note that the problems implicit in using market price to deflate the 1954 to 1958 accounts are difficult to avoid when deflating the product side of the national accounts. They might, in principle, be avoided by adjusting the price indexes to a factor cost basis. This would, however, seem to involve a difficult apportionment of indirect taxes between the various goods and services. It might be still feasible to apportion indirect taxes between industries and on this basis correct to market prices. This last method, difficult as it is, might be the only possible solution for developing countries where product flow information is generally inferior to that concerning the wage bill and profit shares. It is, however, not a problem of as large a magnitude as many others facing these same countries and so might safely be ignored for some time.

4. *The Period 1952/53 to 1961/62*

The estimates for this period, which overlaps with the last, were taken primarily from a continuation of the National Planning Committee's work already mentioned above. These basic data, which are available to 1960/61, are supplemented by fixed price estimates (1959/60 prices) for the latest two years. All these data are available at market prices with the exclusion of customs duties. The data for the agricultural sector is again obtained from the work of the Statistical Department. With few exceptions, there is little difference between the methods employed here and those just discussed. The most important of these differences are discussed below.

Value added by *industry* and *electricity* is deflated with an index produced from a combination of two separate sources. From 1952 to 1959 the general production index of the Bank of Egypt is used. It is an index with net value-added weights based on a 1954 census of production. From 1959 to 1960, the value-added for enterprises with 10 or more employees was adjusted by the wholesale price sub-index of industrial products. Hansen and Mead note a number of defects to this procedure apart from the disparate sources of information. The three most important concern the Bank of Egypt index: first, it occasionally substitutes input for output data, disregarding productivity changes; second, it does not include certain new products and industries introduced in the latter half of the 50's; and third, it is an index based on the most important commodities and ignores the less important. The first two of these defects tend to produce an upward bias, while the third has the opposite effect. No attempt is made to say in which direction the resultant bias might be.

Transportation and communications figures are both deflated by an index of Suez Canal tolls and railway fares.

Housing services are not actually deflated at all as the assumption is made that the price level there remained unchanged during the period.

Other services, including *government administration* and *domestic services* were simply deflated on the basis of the assumption that the wage level in the sector had risen a total of 5 per cent over the period.

For *commerce*, two alternative methods were used and the results are shown for both. In one, the sectoral income is deflated by a simple average of the wholesale and retail price indexes. For the other, it is assumed that the real contribution of the commercial sector is proportional to the flows of commodities. Thus the change in real income from commerce and finance is set equal to the rate of increase of real income in agriculture and industry plus real imports including customs duties.

K. The Brazilian Accounts

The first systematic effort to publish national accounts for Brazil was begun in 1947 by the Brazilian Institute of Economics, a division of the Getulio Vargas Foundation. Estimates for the years 1947 to 1959 were published in the September 1951 issue of *Revista Brasileira de Economia*.

In 1954 estimates of real product and income were made and published in 1956. Subsequent estimates have been published annually by the National Income Unit of the Brazilian Institute of Economics.

The methods of estimating the national accounts of Brazil in terms of constant prices contrast sharply with the methods used for the U.A.R. and the former Federation of Rhodesia and Nyasaland. The latter methods, discussed in the two sections above, involve deflation of the expenditure or value added items in money terms by an appropriate price index. The Brazilian techniques follow rather systematically those advocated by the Economic Commission for Latin America (ECLA). The ECLA system involves the use of quantity indexes for each sector. A quantity index indicates the ratio of real output of a sector in the current year relative to the base year of the index. The base year value added in a sector is multiplied by the quantity index to obtain an estimate of the current year value added in terms of base year (constant) prices.

It should be kept in mind that quantity indexes are subject to the same difficulties and ambiguities of interpretation as price indexes. We may also note that estimation on the basis of quantity indexes in principle is equivalent to the use of price indexes with the proviso that deflation using a base weighted price index is equivalent to estimation using a current weighted quantity index.*

The advantage in using a quantity index approach lies mainly in the extreme difficulty of compiling enough information on prices to compile an acceptable price index. This is especially true in countries experiencing severe inflation as is the case in much of Latin America. Quantity indexes

TABLE XIII-4

Brazilian Gross Domestic Product in Current Prices, Constant 1949 Prices, and Indexes of Real Gross Domestic Product

	BILLIONS OF CRUZEIROS or CRS (1,000,000,000)		INDICES OF REAL GDP	
	Current Prices	*1949 Prices*	*1949 = 100*	*Annual Change (%)*
1947	164.3	186.5	86.5	—
1948	186.8	204.2	94.7	9.5
1949	215.6	215.6	100.0	5.6
1950	253.3	226.4	105.0	5.0
1951	306.1	238.0	110.4	5.1
1952	352.1	251.4	116.6	5.6
1953	430.7	259.4	120.3	3.2
1954	558.2	279.4	129.6	7.7
1955	695.1	298.4	138.4	6.8
1956	887.2	304.0	141.0	1.9
1957	1,059.8	324.9	150.7	6.9
1958	1,313.6	346.5	160.7	6.6
1959	1,806.0	371.9	172.5	7.3
1960	2.418.8	396.7	184.0	6.7
1961*	3.498.6	425.6	197.4	7.3
1962*	5,498.0	448.4	208.0	5.4
1963*	9,591.2	455.6	211.3	1.6
1964*	18,867.3	469.8	217.9	3.1
1965*	31,033.7	491.9	228.1	4.7

* Preliminary Estimates.

Source: Fundacão Getúlio Vargas, *Revista Brasileira De Economia*, Vol. 20, No. 1, March, 1966, p. 72.

* This equivalence follows from the property that a base weighted price index multiplied by a current weighted quantity index results in a value index.

TABLE XIII–5

Brazilian Quantity Indexes by Sector

(*1949 = 100*)

	1958	1959	1960	1961	1962	1963	1964	1965
Agriculture	141.3	148.8	156.1	167.9	177.1	178.9	181.3	211.2
Mining, Manufacturing, Construction, and Public Utilities	213.2	240.7	264.8	293.4	316.0	318.2	334.1	318.3
Transport, Storage, and Communications	176.7	188.7	219.1	240.0	256.2	272.2	282.1	284.5
Commerce	171.1	186.9	197.8	209.8	217.8	220.7	227.5	240.3
Ownership of Dwellings ...	137.8	142.8	148.0	153.2	158.8	164.6	170.6	176.8
Administration	123.9	126.9	130.0	133.1	136.3	139.6	143.0	146.5
Other Services	130.9	134.9	139.0	143.2	147.6	152.1	156.7	161.5

Source: United Nations, *Statistical Bulletin for Latin America*, Vol. III, No. 1, March, 1966, Table 38B p. 132.

are often much easier to compile from trade association data and from records of excise taxes, sales taxes, and export levies.

Estimates of Brazilian Gross Domestic Product in terms of 1949 prices are shown in Table XIII–4. These estimates are obtained for most sectors by applying quantum indexes to 1949 estimates of value added by sector. The quantity indexes for each sector are shown in Table XIII–5. The quantum indexes are neither base weighted nor current weighted but chain weighted indexes of various sorts. The quantity indexes are based on statistics which cover only a portion of the production in each sector but important new products can be introduced through the use of the chain weighting system. The indexes are derived from a number of sources. Electricity and mining production, for example, are based on output figures from producers. Construction output is estimated from building licenses granted and on an assumed completion rate. Other quantum indexes are derived from expenditure tax data.

The quantity index approach is modified in the case of four sectors: commerce, administration, other services, and ownership of dwellings. Real value added in commerce is assumed to be proportional to the estimated amount of goods passing through wholesale and retail channels. The estimates of the amount of such goods is based on the quantity indexes for production and on quantum indexes for imports. Administration (mostly government) and other services are estimated by extrapolating the growth of numbers employed in these two categories between the 1940 and 1950 population censuses.

The estimation of value added from ownership of dwellings is the only sector for which estimates of current money values are determined and deflated by a price index to obtain constant price estimates. The value of rentals in urban areas is determined by estimating the value of buildings and assuming some rental rate. The current money value of rents is then deflated by cost of living indexes for the Federal District and the City of São Paulo. Rural rentals are assumed to be proportional to the rural population which is determined by extrapolating the growth rate of rural population between the decennial demographic censuses.

XIV

BALANCE OF PAYMENTS

This chapter contains a short exposition of the general principles involved in compiling and understanding balance of payments accounts. Ghana will be used to demonstrate the way in which balance of payments are compiled, the reliability of estimates, and the interpretation of some typical balance of payments accounts.

A. The Nature of the Balance of Payments Accounts

The balance of payments is a systematic record of all economic transactions and financial transfers between the residents of a country and the residents of foreign countries. Most of the conceptual difficulties in describing a balance of payments account and many of the practical problems encountered in compiling statistics relating to the balance of payments arise because of the somewhat arbitrary nature of the decisions concerning which type of transactions are to be included and which are to be excluded and which individuals are to be considered residents. In principle, at least, *any* transaction which involves the transfer of goods and services from a resident to a non-resident or vice versa with a corresponding transfer of financial claims in the opposite direction is to be included. The balance of payments will also include a record of many purely financial transactions such as the purchase or sale of financial assets or the lending or borrowing of funds. In addition, certain unilateral transfers between residents and non-residents are included. For example, a bursary grant from a donor in a foreign country to a student resident in Ghana will be recorded in Ghana's balance of payments as a unilateral financial transfer involving no corresponding flow of goods, services, or financial assets from the

Ghanaian student to the foreign donor. The balance of payments does not normally include the implied transactions of barter exchange between residents and non-residents.

Residents are defined in substantially the same manner as in the above discussion of the differences between domestic and national versions of aggregate accounts (see Chapter X). Military and diplomatic personnel are considered to be residents of the country whose uniform they wear or of which they are citizens, no matter how long their stay abroad (although local people employed by foreign embassies or consulates are considered to be domestic residents). In the case of corporations, the residence rule is usually that local subsidiaries of foreign firms are themselves residents. At the same time, local branches of foreign firms most often, though not always, are considered as non-residents. The distinction between branches and subsidiaries is based on legal grounds and is usually drawn for the sake of consistency. The distinction is arbitrary and does not necessarily coincide with any differences in economic behavior. As a final observation, note that international organizations like the United Nations and the International Monetary Fund are not considered residents of any nation, but, in effect, are taken to form separate "nations."

B. Accounting Principles and the Balance of Payments

In theory, the balance of payments is kept on a double-entry system similar to commercial accounts.

It is convenient and instructive in first approaching the balance of payments to do so by analogy with the domestic account of a firm. The nation may be viewed as a firm dealing with other firms in the various facets of trade. Consider the two aspects of a normal transaction, the transfer of goods to other firms, a sale, is represented as a credit; the payment, an increase in cash or in accounts receivable, is entered as a debit. A transfer of goods to a firm, a purchase, is a debit; a payment to other firms, a decrease in cash or an increase in accounts receivable, is a credit. For a nation, a transfer of goods out of a country, an export, is classified as a credit, and the resulting payment is called a debit, a capital outflow, or sometimes a capital export. A capital outflow may take several forms:

  (i) an increase in the holdings of foreign currency,
 (ii) a reduction in the holdings of domestic currency by foreigners,
(iii) an increase in debts owed by foreigners to domestic residents, i.e., increased lending to foreigners,
 (iv) a reduction in debts owed by domestic residents to foreigners, i.e., decreased borrowing from foreigners,
  (v) an increase in claims on foreign assets by domestic residents, e.g., an

increase in ownership by residents of foreign firms, real estate, or inventories, and

(vi) a reduction in claims on domestic assets by foreigners.

An import by a nation is analogous to a purchase by a firm and is a debit. The payment or credit is called a capital inflow or capital import. A capital inflow may also take the form of changes in currency holdings, changes in debt holdings, or changes in asset claims in exactly the opposite direction as for capital outflows.

The basic rules of accounting in the balance of payments may be summarized as follows:

Export	Transfer of goods and services to foreign residents	credit
Import	Transfer of goods and services from abroad to local residents	debit
Capital Outflow	Payment by foreigners to residents for exports	debit
Capital Inflow	Payment by residents to foreigners for imports	credit

As an example, suppose that Ghana imports £3,000 of glass from the U.K. and exports £3,000 of cocoa to the U.K. The application of the above rules is perfectly straightforward:

Ghana's Balance of Payments
(£)

	Credit	Debit
Imports of glass		3,000
Capital inflow	3,000	
Exports of cocoa	3,000	
Capital outflow		3,000
	6,000	6,000

Note that the capital inflow and outflow balance each other and that in the final balance of payments figures, only the export and import items would appear, the *net* capital flow resulting from this transaction being zero.

Thus the balance becomes:

Ghana's Balance of Payments
(£)

	Credit	Debit
Imports of glass		3,000
Exports of Cocoa	3,000	
	3,000	3,000

The *net* capital flow in this example is zero only because exports and imports are equal. If exports exceed imports, then the balancing item is a net capital outflow; if imports exceed exports, then the balancing item is a net capital inflow. For example, suppose Ghana's total exports are £35 million and her imports are £42 million. If the only international transactions by Ghana were those involving her physical imports and exports, her balance of payments would be as follows:

Ghana's Balance of Payments
(£ million)

	Credit	Debit
Imports		42
Exports	35	
Capital Inflow	7	
	42	42

This example does not indicate the numerous types of international transactions which in fact are usually accounted for in balance of payments estimates. The diversity of international transactions is so great that it is necessary to maintain a quite elaborate balance of payment accounts. The normal practice is to divide international transactions into the following sub-types: current, capital, monetary gold, and errors and omissions.

C. The Current Account

The *current account* items may be characterized, as a useful first approximation, as including all those transactions which involve physical movement of resources or the provision of services. The current account transactions also have a direct effect on the national accounts, giving rise to current income and contributing to the supply of goods currently being purchased. There are exceptions to this general description, the most important of which are mentioned below.

The current account is broken down into the visible and invisible accounts. The visible account includes the transactions in goods, that is, it encompasses what are normally thought of as exports and imports. Note that one important physical flow, that of monetary gold, is not included in the current account. The invisible items are transactions involving services. For example, the shipping services provided by a nation's merchant fleet are included here as exports; insurance premiums (net of claims and foreign expenses) sold by domestic firms abroad are an export item; the expenditure of tourists for hotels, transportations, meals, etc., are invisible imports when domestic tourists spend abroad and exports when foreigners spend in the reporting country, investment income payments abroad are included as payments for the productive services of imported capital while investment income receipts are an invisible export item. Investment income is here used loosely to include interest, dividends, and other profit distribution. Often included in the invisible account are certain transfer payments such as donations to charitable organizations. Since these do not, in fact, either give rise to or use up national income, they are sometimes placed in an entirely separate account for transfers.

The current account can be represented schematically in the following manner:

Current Account

Credit (Receipts)	*Debit* (Payments)
1. Goods 　(a) Exports	1. Goods 　(a) Imports
2. Services Rendered 　(a) Transport 　(b) Insurance 　(c) Tourism 　(d) Government 　(e) Other	2. Services Received 　(a) Transport 　(b) Insurance 　(c) Tourism 　(d) Government 　(e) Other
3. Income Receipts 　(a) Interest 　(b) Dividends 　(c) Profits 　(d) Wages	3. Income Payments 　(a) Interest 　(b) Dividends 　(c) Profits 　(d) Wages
4. Current Grants and Transfers Received 　(a) Government	4. Current Grants and Transfers Paid 　(a) Government

(b) Charitable Contributions
(c) Pension and Social Welfare
(d) Receipts
(e) Immigrants Transfers
(f) Other
5. Deficit on Current Account

(b) Charitable Contributions
(c) Pension and Social Welfare
(d) Payments
(e) Immigrants Transfers
(f) Other
5. Surplus on Current Account

If the sum of the first four items on the credit side is greater than the sum of these items on the debit side then the balancing item on the debit side is the surplus on current account. If the opposite holds, then the balancing item on the credit side is the deficit on current account.

In order that a full account can be given for item 2 in the above scheme, the value of services such as transport and insurance should not be included in the value of exports and imports. Thus all goods traded should be valued f.o.b. at the port of exit or the frontier of the exporting country. In fact, however, trade statistics of a country usually give exports valued f.o.b. but imports valued c.i.f. at the point of entry into the importing country since the source of the statistics is customs declarations collected at points of entry into the country.

D. The Capital Account

The *capital account* is to be understood as a record of the changes in claims of the reporting country on the rest of the world and of the rest of the world on it. It should be kept in mind that it is the residents of a country including persons, firms, and the government which have claims and liabilities in relation to the residents of other countries, and that therefore the accounts are dependent on the definition of residency.

Capital flows may be subdivided in many ways depending on the point of view and purpose of the accountant. One common breakdown is between short and long term capital. This division is normally done on the basis of the instrument resulting from the flow. For example, changes in bank deposits, treasury bills, and other very liquid financial assets (typically those maturing in less than one year) would be classified as short term movements. On the other hand, changes in holdings of equity shares, treasury bonds, and real estate would be located under long term movements. It should be noted that whether a capital movement eventually turns out to be a long or short term commitment depends on the intentions and actions of the owner. It is quite possible for holdings of cash in a foreign bank to be quite permanent; conversely, real estate and equity shares may change hands quite frequently. Interpretation of balance of payments data therefore requires understanding a considerable part of the background to the figures.

Long term movements into the developing countries are typically some form of aid or loan from public funds, and private profit-seeking investment. The immediate effect of any inflow is to permit an import surplus of that amount. Short term inflows are most liable to be the means of short run equalization of the balance of payments. Loans in foreign exchange crises and sale of sterling assets by Ghanaian financial institutions are typical short term movements. The short term out-flows are liable to be the most volatile section of the capital accounts, typically representing the outflow of private assets into bank accounts abroad.

Capital Account

Credit	*Debit*
1. Short Term	1. Short Term
(a) Decrease in foreign currency holdings.	(a) Increase in foreign currency holdings.
(b) Decrease in holdings of short term foreign assets or an increase in short term debt to foreigners (decreased short term lending to foreigners or increased short term borrowing from foreigners).	(b) Increase in holdings of short term foreign assets or an increase in short term debt to foreigners (increased short term lending to foreigners or decreased short term borrowing from foreigners).
2. Long Term	2. Long Term
(a) Grants received from abroad.	(a) Grants paid abroad.
(b) Decrease in holdings of long term foreign assets or increase in long term debt to foreigners (decreased long term lending to foreigners or increased long term borrowing from foreigners).	(b) Increase in holdings of long term foreign assets or decrease in long term debt to foreigners (increased long term lending to foreigners or decreased long term borrowing from foreigners).

In an actual statement of the capital account for a nation some of the items listed above will be net. For example, increases in foreign currency holdings will not necessarily be listed separately on the debit side and decreases listed separately on the credit side. Rather, a *net* decrease will be listed on the credit side *or* a *net* increase will be listed on the debit side.

E. The Monetary Gold Account

The *monetary gold account* lists movements of monetary gold where such are required in the balancing of accounts. Gold exports are credits and gold imports are debits, corresponding to the rules for current account visibles. This particular item is of small concern for most of the developing nations, particularly those within the sterling areas, but causes particular concern at times among the larger nations within, or trading with, the dollar area.

F. Errors and Omissions

If the balance of payments figures are complete, then the accounts will balance, i.e., the surplus on current account will equal the deficit on capital account plus the deficit (or minus the surplus) of the monetary gold account. In practice, however, the accounts figures will always be incomplete and inaccurate so that balance is not achieved. Thus a balancing item is added, usually to the credit side of the accounts which may be positive or negative and is entitled *errors and ommissions*. This item can be very large when there is a high level of activity involving those types of transactions which are particularly difficult to record accurately, such as short term private capital flows.

G. The Concept of the "Balance" of Payments

The above discussion of the balance of payments accounts, though necessarily brief, has laid the foundation for consideration of the various concepts of the balance of payments. It is obvious that the sum of all the credit items in the three types of account, current, capital, and monetary gold, plus errors and ommissions must equal the sum of all the debit items in the three types of accounts. It is not true, however, that any list of *some* of the debit and credit items must balance. When one speaks of the balance of payments, one is usually referring to the difference between the sum of some of the credit items and the sum of some of the debit items.

One concept of balance in this sense is the difference between the value of exports and the value of imports. This is called the *balance of visible trade* or sometimes just the *balance of trade*. The balance of trade may or may not be significant for the economy. In the absence of large invisible exports or imports (such as an important maritime nation would enjoy through hauling world trade in her ships) it indicates the magnitude of the balancing capital and gold movements needed to maintain ultimate balance. As statistics on exports and imports are readily available and more accurate in nearly all countries than most of the other items in the balance of payments, the balance of trade has the advantage that it is more accurate and available more quickly than other types of balance.

More revealing than the balance of trade in these days of extensive shipping trade, foreign ownership of productive factors, and ever-growing tourism, is the *balance of payments on current account* which is usually defined as the surplus or deficit on current account. The current account

TABLE XIV-1

Ghana

Balance of Payments

Current Account

1950–1963 (£ million)[1]

Net Credit

	1950	1951	1952	1953	1954	1955	1956
Imports	−46	−59	−61	−71	−66	−83	−82
Exports	68	85	77	82	110	91	78
Trade Balance	22	26	16	11	44	8	−4
Gold Sales**	9	9	9	10	10	9	7
Invisibles*							
Travel	—	−1	−1	−1	−2	−1	−2
Transport and Insurance* ...	−4	−7	−7	−7	−7	−9	−9
Investment Income*	−5	−5	−3	−3	−2	−1	−1
Government	1	1	1	1	1	—	—
Donations							
Official	—	—	—	−1	1	—	1
Private*	—	—	—	—	—	−1	−1
Miscellaneous Services*	−2	−2	−3	−3	−3	−3	−4
Total Invisibles	−11	−15	−14	−16	−13	−15	−16
Current Balance	20	19	11	5	41	2	−13

balance includes the effect of invisible trade items, income payments, and current grants and transfers as well as the visible trade items. The current account balance is regarded as important because it indicates the volume of capital inflow and monetary gold exports which are necessary to finance a current account deficit or the volume of capital outflow and monetary gold imports resulting from a current account surplus. In using the current account balance as a policy tool, it is often implicitly assumed that all current account items are *autonomous* while the capital items are *induced*, i.e., the current account items are determined by the demand and supply conditions regarding exports and imports of visibles and invisibles, and by given propensities to make current transfers and grants and to repatriate income payments abroad; while the capital flows automatically take place in response to a current account surplus or deficit in order that balance may be achieved. It is obvious, however, that some capital transfers are autonomous also in the sense that they do not occur automatically in response to deficit items in the current account. For example, a foreigner might desire to invest in a country because of good investment opportunities rather than in response to some deficit item in the current account.

TABLE XIV-1 (*continued*)

Ghana
Balance of Payments
Current Account
1950–1963 (£ million)

							Net Credit						
					1957	1958	1959	1960	1961	1962	1963
Imports	...	...	...	...	89	78	107	122	137	111	120
Exports	...	...	...	...	84	96	102	108	108	103	98
Trade Balance	...	...	...	−5	18	−5	−14	−29	−8	−22
Gold Sales**...	...	...	...	10	11	11	11	10	11	11
Invisibles*											
Travel	...	...	...	...	−2	−2	−3	−5	−5	−5	−2†
Transport and Insurance*	...	−10	−9	−9	−14	−16	−14	−13
Investment Income*	...	...	−1	−1	−1	−6	−5	−5	−9
Government	...	...	...	−1	—	—	—	−1	—	−2
Donations											
Official ...	...	...	...	—	—	—	−1	—	—	−1
Private* ...	...	...	...	−1	−1	−1	−4	−5	−5	−6‡
Miscellaneous Services* ...	...	−5	−5	−3	−1	−1	−2	−2
Total Invisibles	...	...	...	−19	−18	−17	−31	−33	−31	−35
Current Balance	...	...	...	−14	11	−11	−34	−52	−28	−46

¹ In July, 1965, Ghana's currency was decimalized and the basic unit of currency became the Cedi. Throughout this section the unit used is the Ghana £ which exchanged at par with the £ Sterling.

* Figures from 1960 are not comparable with those of earlier years.

** Excluding domestic consumption.

† Excluding personal remittances of expatriate employees.

‡ Including personal remittances of expatriate employees formerly under travel.

Sources: Ghana, *Economic Survey, 1957*, Accra, Ministry of Finance, June, 1958, Table 16, p. 35, and subsequent annual surveys.

Because of the fact that many capital flows are autonomous, some analysts prefer to work with what is sometimes called the *basic balance of payments*. The basic balance is defined as the current account balance plus the balance between the long term capital items in the capital accounts, i.e., the current account surplus (deficit) plus net long term capital inflow. The use of this definition often assumes implicitly that all long term capital flows and current account items are autonomous while all short term capital, currency, and monetary gold flows are induced. Certainly, however, some short term capital flows must be regarded as autonomous. For example, there are frequently short term capital flows when interest rates in one country are raised substantially above those prevailing in other countries as investors switch their funds to short term securities yielding higher interest rates. The movement is not induced by current account surpluses or deficits but occurs independently of the current account items.

Since many of the short term capital flows are autonomous, the basic balance is sometimes used in conjunction with the *overall balance of payments*. The overall balance is obtained from the basic balance by including with the basic balance both net short term capital movements and errors and ommissions. This balance is, then, effectively equal to the net change in gold and foreign monetary assets (currency) needed to make total credits equal to total debits.

There are a variety of other definitions of the balance of payments both in use and proposed. These various definitions arise because of the need for balance of payments statistics as a tool in different areas of policy making. For example, if one wanted a "balance of payments" to aid in the formulation of monetary policy, the criterion for inclusion in the list of items going to make up the balance would be whether an item is "responsive" or not in some sense to monetary policy decisions. Another reason for the use of a particular definition is reliability and availability of the necessary statistical data.

H. The Balance of Payments and National Accounts

Items in the balance of payments accounts enter into the calculation of all three types of national accounts, income, product, and expenditure, and into the national and domestic versions of these accounts. The balance of visible and invisible trade, exports minus imports, is one of the components of gross domestic expenditure. For example, gross domestic expenditure is defined as the sum of private consumption, government current expenditure, gross investment, net increase in inventories, and net foreign investment (exports of goods and services less imports of goods and services). In order to obtain gross national expenditure from gross domestic expenditure, one must subtract net payment of factor incomes abroad. Payments of factor incomes and the visible and invisible trade items are contained in the current account of the balance of payments.

The gross domestic product of an economy may be obtained by subtracting all intermediate inputs into each industry (including imports) from the output of each industry (including output sold as exports) and adding the result for each industry to direct factor payments by government and households. Thus exports and imports of intermediate products enter into the product accounts. Gross domestic income, which is the sum of all factor payments does not directly include any items contained in the balance of payments accounts, but the distinction between domestic and national income (as well as the distinction between national and domestic product) is based on the net factor payments to foreigners.

An important observation to make is that the only items in the balance of payments which affect the national accounts are in the current account. None of the capital account items affect any of the income, product, or expenditure aggregates.

I. The Balance of Payments of Ghana

Estimates of the Ghana balance of payments on current account are available since 1950. Capital account data are much cruder and only cover a shorter period. The current account estimates are comparable up until 1959. From 1960 on, methods of estimation were revised, especially with respect to transport and investment income. Table XIV–1 shows the current account from 1950 to 1963, and Table XIV–2 gives the capital account

TABLE XIV–2

Ghana
Balance of Payments
Capital Account
1956-1963
(£ million)

	Net Credit							
	1956	1957	1958	1959	1960	1961	1962	1963
Private								
Long Term	−1	−4	−4	−2	2	2	5	10
Short Term	—	—	—	8	1	—	2	2
Changes in reserves								
Long Term	—	—	1	−7	19	32	1	24
Short Term	—	—	−6	14	−1	43	—	—
Other Official Capital Transactions								
Long Term**	—*	14*	—	−3	12	−22	19	11
Short Term	15*	−1*	—	—	—	—	2	2
Capital Account Balance	14	9	−9	10	33	55	29	49
Balancing Item	−1	5	−2	1	1	−3	−1	−3

* Includes changes in reserves.
** Includes changes in assets of public corporations.

Source: *The Commonwealth and the Sterling Area Statistical Abstract*, London, The Board of Trade, Nos. 81 (1960)–84 (1963), pp. 47, 49, 50, and 51.

TABLE XIV–3

Ghana

Balance of Payments

1962

(£ million)

CURRENT ACCOUNT

	Credits	Debits
A. Merchandise		
1. Goods trade excluding gold	102.9	110.8
2. Exports of non-monetary gold	11.3	—
Total	114.2	110.8
B. Invisibles	...	
3. Freight and Insurance	1.2	12.0
4. Other Transportation	2.6	5.7
5. Travel	1.4	6.1
6. Investment Income	3.0	7.9
7. Private Miscellaneous	1.1	3.3
8. Official Miscellaneous	0.3	0.5
Total	9.6	35.5
C. Transfer Payments		
9. Private	—	4.9
10. Official	0.3	1.1
Total	0.3	6.0
Total Current Account	124.1	152.3
	Net Credit	
	−28.2	

for 1956 through 1963. The current and capital accounts for 1962 are given in greater detail in Table XIV–3.

1. *The Current Account*

Official grants are included in Ghana's current account rather than the capital account. Merchandise transactions are based on the official trade statistics adjusted for coverage, to value imports f.o.b. rather than c.i.f. and to exclude ships stores and gold exports. Gold exports are listed separately and ships stores and bunker are included under transportation in the current account. Since imports are valued f.o.b., the value of *freight and insurance*

TABLE XIV–3 *(continued)*

Ghana

Balance of Payments

1962

(£ million)

CAPITAL ACCOUNT

	Credits	Debits
D. Government Capital Transactions		
11. Long term loans...	5.0	—
12. Supplier's credit	12.4	—
13. Pension funds	2.0	—
14. Balance of bilateral trade agreements...	1.7	—
Total	21.1	—
E. Net Private Capital Movement		
15. Long term	4.8	—
16. Short term	2.0	—
Total	6.8	—
F. Changes in Reserves of Official and Banking Institutions		
17. Central government and local authorities	4.7	3.8
18. Public institutions	1.3	1.3
19. Central bank	0.1	4.3
20. Other banking institutions	4.9	—
Total	11.0	9.4
Total Capital Account	38.9	9.4
	Net Credit +29.5	
Errors and Omissions	−1.3	

Source: P. P. Van der Wel, "Ghana's Foreign Trade and Balance of Payments, 1956–1962," Legon, University of Ghana, (mimeo), unpublished, June, 1964, pp. 3 and 4.

payments to foreign firms is included as a separate debit. Receipts of the Black Star Line from foreigners are listed as a credit under freight and insurance.

2. *The Capital Account*

Ghana's capital account includes an estimate of suppliers' credit. This covers delayed payment for certain imports, especially for imports of large pieces of capital equipment, e.g., airplanes, ships, complete factories, etc., which may not be fully paid up for three to twelve years. Another item which plays a significant part since the early 1960's in Ghana's capital account is the balance of credit or debit arising from bilateral trade agreements (item 14 in Table XIV–3), especially with centrally planned Eastern European countries. If Ghana imports less from any one of these countries than its exports, under the bilateral agreement no exchange of cash is involved but Ghana's state trading corporation is granted an immediate credit which permits it to import from that country until balance is achieved. The changes in the foreign reserves of Ghana's economy are listed under items 17 to 20 in Table XIV–3. An increase in the reserves (sterling assets and bank balances) of central government, local authorities, public institutions, the central bank, and other banking institutions is a debit and a decrease in these reserves is a credit.

3. *Trends in Ghana's Balance of Payments*

Most of the movements in Ghana's current account balance can be

TABLE XIV–4

Ghana Cocoa Sales and Prices
1947/48–1960/61

	Index of Cocoa Price f.o.b. Accra (1947/48 = 100)	Cocoa Marketing Board Sales (£ million)
1947/48	100	41.5
1948/49	68	37.5
1949/50	89	45.1
1950/51	133	70.3
1951/52	122	51.6
1952/53	115	57.1
1953/54	179	74.7
1954/55	177	77.5
1955/56	110	52.3
1956/57	94	50.7
1957/58	151	62.9
1958/59	136	70.9
1959/60	n.a.	69.9
1960/61	n.a.	71.6

Source: R. H. Green, "Ghana Cocoa Policy: Some Problems and Perspectives," Legon, University of Ghana, (mimeo), unpublished, June, 1964, Tables IV and VI, pp. 58 and 60.

TABLE XIV–5

Ghana Cocoa Exports and Prices

1956–1962

(1956 = 100)

	Volume	Price	Value
1956	100	100	100
1957	111	89	100
1958	84	145	122
1959	107	126	135
1960	129	101	130
1961	173	78	136
1962	180	73	131

Source: P. Van der Wel, "Ghana's Foreign Trade and Payments 1956–1962," Legon, University of Ghana, June, 1964, (mimeo), unpublished, p.18.

attributed to changes in the trade balance and in freight and insurance (which fluctuates roughly in accordance with imports), and most of the movements in the trade balance can be attributed to fluctuations in the world cocoa price. (Cocoa accounts for about 60 per cent of Ghana's exports.) From 1950 to 1955, Ghana had favorable trade balances and current account surpluses (see Table XIV–1). The index of cocoa prices was relatively high, well over 100 (1947/48 = 100) f.o.b. Accra, throughout most of the period (see Table XIV–4). A drop in the cocoa price index below 100 in 1956–57 was accompanied by unfavorable trade balances and current account deficits in those years. The cocoa price recovered for the 1957–58 and 1958–59 seasons, giving a current account surplus and a favorable trade balance for the year 1958. The trend in cocoa prices since 1959 has been downward (see Table XIV–5). The resulting adverse trade balances and current account deficits were very large, and Ghana began to run down its large foreign exchange holdings which it had acquired during the days of high cocoa prices. A crisis was reached in 1961 when the current account deficit reached £52 million. In July of 1961 import duties were raised substantially, very high purchase taxes were levied on consumer durable items, and exchange control was extended to the sterling area as well as the dollar area. In December of that year import quotas were levied through restrictive licensing of imports. Also during 1961 several bilateral trade agreements with their automatic balance provisions were negotiated.

Finally, in 1961 Ghana received a loan of £5 million from the IMF against its drawing rights of £12.5 million. The current account deficit declined in 1962 due to a substantial fall in imports, but rose again in 1963 as exports fell further and imports rose considerably.

XV

THE MEASUREMENT OF

THE CAPITAL STOCK

This chapter considers a difficult but important field of social accounting: the measurement of capital formation and of the size of the capital stock. Many measurement difficulties arise because capital is a *stock*, part of which may be extremely durable. Its measurement, and the estimation of its growth, therefore involves problems not met in the treatment of the income and output flows. This is also one of those areas of economics which, over the years, economists have found very difficult to handle, so that capital theory is one of the more confusing (and perhaps confused!) branches of economic theory.

In practice national accounts usually only attempt to estimate the rate of capital formation (i.e., investment). However, both official and academic economists have been undertaking considerable work in recent years in this field, so that for many countries estimates of the capital stock are now available. In some cases such attempts have been carried to the point of developing *national balance sheets*, with considerable detail regarding the assets of the nation and the various claims on them. Even where capital stock estimates do not exist, economic planners often find it necessary to make inferences about its size for use in crude models of growth. Therefore, both the measurement of capital formation as it usually appears in the national accounts, and the measurement of the capital stock are considered here. A further virtue in tackling both questions is that ambiguities involved in much of the measurement of capital formation only become apparent if the underlying capital stock concepts are understood.

In order to produce a current flow of goods and services, it is necessary to make use of buildings, machinery, and stocks of raw materials and work in progress. Limits on the availability of these resources will often be the critical constraint on the expansion of output. Expansion of output on a particular project, or for the economy as a whole, will usually require growth in such stocks.

In the past some economists have emphasized the importance of this constraint to the point of making it the over-riding factor in limiting the rate of growth in developing countries. Although this emphasis was exaggerated, neglecting problems of organization and skilled manpower, it is certainly true that the stock of capital is always an important actual or potential constraint on development. Less developed countries are poor in part because their capital stock is so small *per capita*. Expanding the capital stock and economizing on its use are therefore crucial objectives of development planning.

In practice this concern over the use of capital arises in a number of contexts. Important examples of situations in which measures of capital formation or capital stock are useful are:

(i) in seeking to check the consistency of output growth objectives with planned rates of capital formation;

(ii) in judging the overall development effort, by estimating the proportion of current output devoted to capital formation;

(iii) in estimating the capital needed or used on a project or in a particular industry.

In some cases the need will be for a measure of capital formation, in others of the capital stock itself.

The relationship between the capital stock and output has been treated in much traditional analysis and by many modern writers through the notion of a *production function*, which specifies some relationship between the flow of capital services (usually assumed to be directly related to the size of the capital stock), the flow of other factor inputs and the level of output. This approach is simplified still further when it is assumed that there is a fixed proportional relationship between the level of the capital stock and feasible output levels. This ratio of capital stock to output is known as the capital-output ratio. When used, it is often assumed to be a constant, unaffected by the supply of other inputs. This is felt to be an acceptable first approximation in less developed countries, because other factors are supposed to be readily available. In this chapter a large number of cautions will be offered regarding such an assumption about the capital-output ratio but, because of the wide use and relative simplicity of the concept itself, it is a useful starting point.

A. The Capital-Output Ratio

To many readers the use of a constant capital-output ratio in simple growth models will be familiar; only a brief recitation is necessary. Using the symbols:

$$K = \text{capital stock}$$

$$Y = \text{output}$$

$$S = \text{saving}$$

$$a = \text{average capital-output ratio } (K/Y)$$

$$b = \text{average propensity to save } (S/Y)$$

The average capital-output ratio a is a constant when capital is needed in some fixed ratio to output. Even where the capital-output ratio is constant at full capacity, it may vary in practice because the capital stock is not fully utilized. That is, *ex ante*, there is a constant capital-output ratio although the realized capital-output ratio might be higher because of under-utilization.

If a is a constant, then a limit on the increase in output is set by the increase in the capital:

$$a = K/Y$$

or
$$Y = \frac{1}{a} K$$

and
$$dY = \frac{1}{a} dK$$

Where dY is an increase in output and dK is an increase in the capital stock, dK/dY is the marginal capital-output ratio; in this case, the average and marginal ratios are the same (this follows from the constancy of the average ratio). That is, an increase in output requires a proportionate increase in capital in a ratio defined by a.

Then the rate of growth of output is set by:

$$\frac{dY}{Y} = \frac{1}{a} \frac{dK}{Y}$$

Capital formation will be limited by the level of savings. At full capacity output, capital formation can only be increased if savings are increased as a proportion of total output. At less than full capacity output expansion in capital formation can be combined with increases in total output, thus allowing savings to increase absolutely without necessarily becoming a greater proportion of total output. In other words, at full capacity, increases in capital formation require an increase in the average propensity to save. At less than full capacity increases in savings can result from increases in output even with a constant average savings propensity.

Considering the full capacity case:

$$dK = S$$

Substituting $\qquad \dfrac{dY}{Y} = \dfrac{1}{a}\dfrac{S}{Y}$

or $\qquad\qquad \dfrac{dY}{Y} = \dfrac{b}{a}$

This suggests that the capital-output ratio and the average propensity to save are crucial factors in development policy. There is a temptation to take an additional step, to assume a is largely determined by technology and then to concentrate attention on the need to raise the savings propensity. Data on capital formation and output growth are then used to estimate actual capital-output ratios. Using such estimates, the rate of saving which would be necessary to achieve desired rates of growth is calculated. The capital-output ratio estimate, in such an operation, would be a key factor in aggregate planning projections.

A simple example will illustrate the method. In an economy, capital formation in the five years 1963–1968 averages $20 billion per year, making a total over the whole period of $100 billion and the gross domestic product rises by $40 billion from the year 1963 to the year 1968, then it may be inferred that the capital-output ratio is $2\frac{1}{2}$. If this were used for projection, then a rate of growth of 6 per cent per year would require an average propensity to save of 15 per cent and a rate of growth of 8 per cent would require an average propensity to save as high as 20 per cent. Such an exercise infers a future marginal capital-output ratio from an estimate of the past marginal ratio. As the total capital stock is not measured there is no inference in this case about the average capital-output ratio.

Such a simple approach would only be adopted by most economists as a first approximation. In general it is necessary to treat the relationship between capital formation and output growth much more cautiously. Some of the difficulties with the capital-output ratio method are suggested by economic theory. In particular, the neglect of other factor inputs is extremely dangerous. In developed countries the scarcity of unskilled labor is likely to be a serious limitation on output growth and may well cause substitution of capital for labor. In less-developed countries, the scarcity of skilled manpower may at times be a more serious constraint than the capital stock. In such situations, raising the rate of capital formation may result in a lower growth in output than past experience would suggest.

Moreover, *aggregate* estimates introduce special dangers because their stability depends both on the nature of the component parts (in this case, sectoral capital-output ratios) and upon the balance between them. This is a point to be watched in all applied macro-economic work. In general it means that the inference of aggregate behavior from sectoral observations, or vice versa, is far from straightforward. For example, the aggregate capital-output ratio could change, even if the capital-output ratios in individual industries remain unchanged, because of shifts in the industrial composition. Similarly, changes in capital-output ratios in individual industries may be offset by compensating changes in the industrial composition of total output. It is important also to recognize that the marginal relationship is potentially much more unstable than the average. The average capital-output ratio will only change slowly, because it embodies the decisions over many past years. The marginal capital-output ratio, on the other hand, embodies the decisions of a single year and can fluctuate widely even if the average relationship is fairly stable.

This difference between the behavior of the average and marginal capital-output ratios introduces an area of crucial difficulty regarding capital measurement. The marginal capital-output ratio compares an addition to the capital stock over a short period with the growth in the flow of output during the period. The average capital-output ratio compares a stock of capital, perhaps accumulated over many years, with the current flow of output.

One simple point which is sometimes forgotten is that because of this comparison of stock with a flow the ratio must have a time dimension— the flow of output must be measured over some defined time period— usually a year.

B. Measuring the Capital Stock

Of course, it is not uncommon to measure collections of commodities with diverse characterstics—to add together a collection of bananas and maize, for example. This exercise is often straightforward. For many purposes interest will be concentrated on the total value of the commodities, and their price may be taken as a basis for measurement. Even in such cases, however, other characteristics than value may be of interest (e.g., it is often the case in transport problems that weight and size are relevant). Even when value is being considered, the index number problem arises because of the need for international or inter-temporal comparison. Capital stock measurement poses a special problem, as it usually involves inter-temporal problems, for even when it is measured at one date it will have been acquired over a number of years. Not only does it have a complex history but its current value derives from an expected flow of services in the future. A stock of capital is rather like the population of a country, composed of people born over many past years and who may be expected to live for differing periods in the future, continuously changing through births, deaths, and aging.

Thus the capital stock consists of a diverse collection of machines and tools, buildings and stocks of materials, which were acquired at different dates in the past and which will survive into the future for differing periods. Because of these two "time dimensions" the measurement of capital stock is not straightforward. As capital formation represents increases in the capital stock, any ambiguities about the latter concept are likely to result in confusion in measuring the former.

To clarify the issues, two concepts must be distinguished:

(i) the value of the capital stock;
(ii) the flow of productive services.

The value of the capital stock will depend on the valuation placed on the expected flow of services in the future. If two machines provide identical flows of current services but one is expected to survive longer than the other, then it will have a higher value. Alternatively, a machine would have a higher value than another of the same expected life if the flow of services in each time period generated by it were higher.

The point is seen more clearly through a simple example. Assume that a small businessman establishes a taxicab business by buying a car which, under the conditions of cab driving, can be expected to last for three years, but which will perform through those three years at a roughly constant standard of performance. This assumption, that the services from a piece of equipment do not decline gradually, but end abruptly at the end of its life, is often called the "one horse shay" assumptions.* In such a case, at the beginning of the second year of operation the value of the cab will have declined because one year of its life was exhausted. However, the owner is still able to offer the same service as during the previous year. The same output is being produced but the value of the capital investment is lower.

In recognition of the fact that the value of capital goods declines though-out their lifetime, whether or not the services provided deteriorate, and that eventually a piece of capital equipment must be scrapped, the accountant *depreciates* them, as was described in Chapter II. As a result of depreciation there are two separate book values for fixed assets on the accounts of firms (although both will not always be published in the public

* This is from an American song, once popular, about a horse carriage that supplied steady service until its eventual disintegration.

reports of the firm). The gross value of the fixed assets will show the original cost of the machinery and buildings, while the net value will reduce this amount by the recorded depreciation. Neither of these figures will necessarily be a good measure either of the value of the capital stock or the flow of capital services available. It is important to understand why this is so.

To distinguish separate elements of the problem two situations may be discussed:

(i) measurements in situation with constant price level;
(ii) measurement with fluctuating prices.

The first situation is an abstraction which will rarely, if ever, be experienced in practice. Consideration of such a situation will clarify some of the issues, before plunging into the difficulties arising from fluctuating prices.

1. Capital Stock Measurement with Constant Prices

a. Gross Fixed Assets

Gross fixed assets is the accounting entry which represents the value of the capital stock at the time it was purchased (without allowance for depreciation). In special cases, where certain simple assumptions seem reasonable, gross fixed assets might be taken as a measure of the available flow of productive services. This would be appropriate in the taxicab example introduced earlier. In this case if the businessman were running a fleet of taxicabs, acquired at the same price level and with the same life expectancy, then the size of the fleet will be directly proportional to the size of gross fixed assets. Moreover, under the "one horse shay" assumption, the flow of productive services will be proportional to the size of the taxicab fleet.

If, however, the services provided by the taxicabs declined throughout their lives, then the flow of productive services would be influenced by the age structure as well as the size of the fleet. In this case the flow of productive services would *not* be proportional to gross fixed assets.

A second difficulty arises if the assets, when acquired, have differing expected lives. A good example of this arises when the fixed assets involved in a project consist of both machinery and buildings. Buildings last longer than machines. When a building is purchased, the purchaser expects a lesser flow of productive services in any one year than if the same expenditure is on machinery, but this flow is expected to continue for a much longer period.

The same thing is true if machines of different expected lives are purchased. Obviously if machine A has an expected life of two years and machine B of ten years but they both cost $1,000, then the flow of services during the two years life of A must be much higher than from B, in order to make the purchase worthwhile.

There are two quite simple ways in which it is sometimes possible to avoid the difficulties raised by the difference in expected lives and to use gross fixed assets accounts as a basis for measuring the flow of productive services. One way is to group assets in some rough way according to their life expectancy at acquisition. The simplest grouping would be to separate building on the one hand from machinery, tools and equipment on the other. There would then be a considerable gap between the expected lives of these two groups. They could then be treated as two separate inputs.

Alternatively, some estimate of depreciation could be used as a measure of the flow of productive services. The amount of depreciation charged each year will depend on the size of the original investment and the number of years over which the investment will last. However, this is not to say that the accountant's measure of depreciation would be acceptable for this purpose, for it is usually based on some convention which makes no claim at measuring either the flow of productive services or the actual decline in the value of the asset during the particular year.

b. *Net Fixed Assets*

Net fixed assets, a concept introduced in Chapter II, are net in the sense that allowance has been made for depreciation. Depreciation is charged so that the removal of an asset from the books can be gradual, throughout its lifetime, rather than abruptly on retirement. Depreciation is, however, usually estimated by a fairly arbitrary application of a conventional method. Typically an expected life is assumed (usually some round figure) and the total initial cost of the asset is charged to depreciation over that notional life according to a standard rule. Two methods frequently used are the "straightline method" and the "diminishing balance" method. The straightline method charges an equal sum in each year of the assumed life. The diminishing balance takes a constant percentage of the remaining *net* value, thus charging much larger amounts in the early life of the asset than in the later years.

Although it is likely that net fixed assets would be better than gross fixed assets as a measure of the value of the capital stock, the data usually available will not be too accurate. For example, equipment will often last much longer than the notional life assigned to it by the accountant. If this happens then an asset will still be in use although its book value is zero. In some cases the decline in value of an asset may be much faster than is allowed for by depreciation, in which case the net book value will be more than the real value.

The net book value would only be a good measure of the available flow of productive services if accumulated depreciation did measure a decline in the performance of the asset. There is no reason why it should. In the "one horse shay" example depreciation is quite appropriate, because the value of the asset declines with the passage of time and because retirement will eventually be necessary, even though the current performance of the asset does not decline during its lifetime. Nevertheless, this decline in value does not represent any decline in current services available but is rather because of the exhaustion of future services.

c. *Gross and Net Investment*

How are these asset concepts related to investment? Gross fixed investment is capital formation measured without any allowance being made for depreciation. Net fixed investment is computed by subtracting an allowance for depreciation from the gross investment estimate.

Gross investment is not quite the same as the increase in gross fixed assets, because of retirements. When machinery is physically scrapped then it is completely removed from the books, thus reducing gross fixed assets. If part of the retired asset is not fully depreciated, then there will also be a reduction in net fixed assets, to allow for the value of the asset retired. In such a case, the growth in net fixed assets will be less than net investment. An addition to gross fixed assets, or gross fixed investment less retirements, involves an increase in the number of machines, buildings, etc. An addition to net fixed assets, or net fixed investment less undepreciated retirements, represents an increase in value. If depreciation is equal to, or greater than, gross fixed investment, which in turn is greater than retirements, then the quantity of capital (that is, the number of machines, buildings, etc.) may increase while its value declines.

To return to the taxicab example. Assume that there is a fleet of 12 cabs. Depreciation is equal to the value of 4 new cabs per year. In a given year, 3 new cabs are purchased and 2 are retired. In this case the number of cabs in operation increases from 12 to 13, but their total value declines because the gross investment is less than the depreciation.

Because of these relationships it is possible for new machines and expansion in capacity (i.e., increases in the flow of capital services) to be financed out of depreciation. The existence of this possibility is sometimes confusing at first. It arises when the decline in value of capital goods recorded by depreciation is greater than the decline in their current productivity. This is because the decline in value will record both the decline in productivity and will also be affected by the exhaustion of the expected life.

After long periods of stagnation, it could be that a large part of the capital stock is ready for retirement and that retirement exceeds depreciation. This would not be the case in a growing economy, unless there were, in some particular year, an extraordinary bunching of retirement. If such a situation did arise, it would mean that even despite positive gross and net investment there might be a decline in gross fixed assets. One virtue of a sustained high rate of growth is that it keeps the ratio of retirements to depreciation at a low level.

When economists discuss production problems they tend to discuss them in terms of the relationship between labor and capital inputs and the level of output. It has already become clear that the use of capital stock data, if available, is not straightforward. In macro-economic work, however, capital stock data are rarely available. Usually the economist must work with estimates of gross capital formation, from which depreciation is deducted, to arrive at a net figure. The depreciation is usually estimated by some standardized formula. Any relationships between capital and output must therefore usually be inferred from capital formation behavior rather than from direct measurement of the capital stock as such. Thus, in the capital-output ratio discussion above, investment over a number of years was used to estimate the increase in the capital stock and this increase was compared to the increase in output to arrive at an inference about the capital-output ratio.

If a long enough capital formation series is available, it will be possible to estimate the capital stock from this series. This may be done by the "perpetual inventory" method. If enough information about the expected life of capital goods is available, then it is possible to estimate which past investments are still in the capital stock. This having been done for a base year, a capital stock series can be estimated by adding new capital formation each year and removing that which has reached retirement age (for gross estimates) or estimated depreciation (for net estimates). Because of the differences in expected lives mentioned earlier, when undertaking such an operation it is advisable to distinguish between buildings with very long lives, and machinery and tools. It may also be necessary to distinguish between differing types of machinery, separating transport equipment, for example, if it is composed of automobiles with an especially short expected life.

If there is a strong upward trend in investment, the perpetual inventory method is likely to be more acceptable; for in that case the earlier years, for which data is likely to be less adequate, will contribute but a small proportion of the current stock. For example, if investment levels are doubling every ten years, then the contribution to the current capital stock of a year's investment twenty years ago will be much less than one-quarter the current year's contribution. Not only is it much smaller, but with the passage of time much of that investment will no longer be in use.

In most less-developed countries, however, it will not usually be possible to estimate capital formation for as long as twenty years in the past. Aggregate measures of the capital stock will therefore not usually be possible.

The pitfalls of inferring very much from investments and output series about the nature of capital-output relationships should by now be clear. A given level of gross investment may to a differing extent be compensating for retirements or declining productivity of the existing stock, or providing for an expansion in available capital series. Even where it is clear that an expansion in available capital services is taking place, the current flow will vary according to the expected life of the new assets. An asset with a very long expected life, such as a solid building, will give a low gross income flow, but also demand a low ratio of depreciation. A short-lived asset will give a much higher gross income flow but also require a high rate of depreciation. In such exercises the question therefore arises as to whether it is net or gross income flows which are being investigated.

The capital-output ratio accounts not only for the output increases generated by a capital investment in the form of the incomes directly attributable to the asset (i.e., gross profits) but also includes in the output measure the income attributable to other inputs employed as a result of the creation of the asset. If there is unemployed labor available, the output generated by an investment will be greater according to the employment incomes it creates. In a fully employed economy the problem becomes highly complex because it must be expected that capital expansion will result in a shift in factor prices rather than a net increase in the employment of other factors, rendering the capital-output ratio of an individual project highly misleading.

In even the simplest work it is therefore necessary to distinguish:

(i) the type of capital goods classified according to age groups;
(ii) whether employment opportunities for idle factors are created by the new assets.

There is one further difficulty, which is particularly important in analyzing specific projects or in the macro-economic analysis of small economies. This is the problem of time lags between the acquisition of a capital asset and its full utilization. This may be discussed under two headings: the problem of the gestation period and the difficulties arising from indivisibility.

A gestation period may be defined as that period during which a capital asset has not yet been brought into full operation, due to difficulties inherent in the process of investment. Thus a new factory, having been installed, will not at once go into full capacity operation, even if the market for its output were readily available. Installation itself may take considerable time. Initial difficulties will have to be corrected in the machinery, a workforce will have to be assembled and trained, the work of those using the equipment will only slowly acquire a sensible team work basis. Of course, to a degree this process will be continuous, with new organizational and utilization methods being introduced throughout the life of the assets. Typically, however, there will be a period when such improvements are very marked, followed by a gradual flattening out. Once a routine has been created, the new machinery understood, initial mistakes corrected and unforeseen difficulties with the machinery ironed out, a standard pattern of output will be established, improvements on which will appear only slowly.

Because of the gestation period, there will be a lag between an investment and resulting output increases. For many reasons this lag may be protracted in less-developed countries. Skills are less readily available, therefore more training is needed. Inadequacies in the machinery itself may be less readily corrected, because of the limited access to spare parts. Also, because projects may often be in completely new industries where experience is only very limited, the potentiality for mistakes at the outset is that much greater. If a country is large enough and the expansion in output and investment fairly steady, such lags can be treated in a general way as a constant factor influencing the relationship between capital formation and output growth. In small countries there is more chance that the aggregate picture will be influenced by the peculiarities of individual projects.

Indivisibility arises when there is a minimum size of an asset. For example, in building a dam or a steel mill there may be a minimum size which is technically feasible or which, in the long run, would be economically sensible to operate. A dam cannot be built in stages as needed. Thus, in the case of the Aswan Dam, the whole river had to be damned at one time although the resulting hydro-electric capacity was not needed for some time ahead.

It will rarely be the case that a project is completely indivisible. Although a dam may be built at one time, it is not always necessary to install all the generators immediately, so that generating capacity may be expanded gradually over the years, as needs expanded.

This type of situation is frequently found in small less-developed countries because, on the one hand, there is a limited (if growing) market, while on the other the available technology is highly adapted to large scale operation in the industrialized countries. Where indivisibility is an important phenomenon, such projects will often form an important element in the total investment bill in the years in which they are undertaken.

In this situation a large capital investment may bring only small initial output increases, but these may continue over a number of years, as capacity utilization expands. Moreover, a central investment having been made, large output increases may be subsequently achieved in response to very small increases in ancillary investment. If an indivisible project is large enough to affect strongly the size of the total investment bill then it will create additional difficulties in the path of inferring relationships between investment and output over short periods and should suggest caution in extrapolating observed relationships.

Both of these problems would be minimized if comparisons are made over fairly long time periods. It should also be noted in passing that such indivisibilities are not always so unavoidable as the technical facts suggest. It may be true that a particular hydro-electric scheme involves substantial indivisibilities but there might be alternative sources of power or some combination of other schemes which would meet the same need without this disadvantage. The necessity to operate at considerable excess capacity for many years should certainly suggest a serious investigation of such alternatives.

The possibility of expanding output without substantial investment also arises when multi-shift operation of an existing plant is introduced. It will often be the case that when a new plant is opened it will operate with a single shift, but as its market grows, a second or even third shift will be introduced. This was the pattern of expansion in the Nytil textile plant at Jinja in Uganda and is typical of projects in manufacturing. In this situation, the utilization of the capital stock was adjusted by increasing the use of other inputs. Output expansion was achieved without additional investment. Yet a fully utilized single shift might often be taken as evidence of the absence of excess capacity.

The difficulties raised in this discussion so far all occur even if there is no fluctuation in prices. It is now necessary to consider the special difficulties of measurement in this area arising from fluctuating prices.

2. *The Effect of Price Changes*

As the capital stock at any point in time is composed of assets acquired over a number of past years, fluctuations in the prices of capital goods introduce special difficulties. The problem may be handled by adjusting all the component parts to a common price, using a capital goods price index. For comparison of investment behavior from year to year it will also be possible to use such an index. However, there are special difficulties about the construction of an index of capital goods prices and additional difficulties in applying it to capital stocks.

When estimating a consumer price index the object is usually to price a "basket of goods." The discussion in Chapter XIII illustrated the possible difficulties of that task because of changes in the composition of consumer spending and the character of manufactured goods. Similarly, there is a continuous change in the composition of capital expenditures and in the character of capital goods.

The machinery and tools included in capital formation will never be the same from one year to the next. The composition of spending will change from year to year. This will particularly be true in a small country, in which a few projects will make up a high proportion of capital expenditures each year. One year a cement plant may be built, the next year a textile factory. In East Africa, for example, the cost of three new VC10 planes for the East African Airways Corporation is well over 5 per cent of one year's gross capital formation for the whole area. If this expenditure is allocated to a single year it would make a noticeable change in the composition of capital expenditures.

The example of the VC10 illustrates a central problem of capital goods price deflation. This aircraft was not in use before 1964. How is the price of this aircraft to be compared with the price of an aircraft purchased for similar duties in 1960 or 1955? Strictly, there were not similar duties, as the VC10 now provides a type of service not available in 1955. What is an obvious dilemma in this case appears in more subtle forms in the case of almost all machinery. Each new model will claim some improvement, will incorporate some innovation. Technical change largely takes place through the embodiment of new ideas and techniques in the latest machine designs.

Construction presents its own problems. Buildings change and may improve in design, but the improvement is usually thought to be slower than in the case of machinery. The difficulty arises, however, that buildings and the other products of the construction industry are quite heterogeneous. Houses now built are rarely replicas of those built in previous years. Even roads will be laid over differing types of country and will vary in their quality.

At its worst, the problem involves the comparison of the price of a new capital good performing a service in part previously unknown with the price of a machine purchased in the past but no longer produced. Frequently it will be necessary to compare the price of a machine with a slightly modified design, providing just slightly different services, with its predecessors.

It is well to be frank here. The problems involved are such that even in those countries with the most elaborate statistical services, satisfactory working solutions and compromises have been very difficult to find. In most developing countries the only sensible view must be that available capital goods price indexes are quite suspect and are to be treated with extreme wariness by the student. Nevertheless, in the interest of future development, it is worthwhile discussing the possible solution to the problem in principle and to note methods which might prove practicable.

In principle there are two courses of action: to deflate for changes in the price of inputs into the capital goods industry, or to measure changes in the price of a given amount of capital services. The former course is difficult in the case of machinery, as in the less-developed countries it will often be imported. This makes it difficult to acquire the relevant information and introduces a further source of difficulty—namely that a shift in the source of supply may change the average price paid. In practice, this has become very important in recent years with the changing foreign trade patterns of the many newly independent countries. The latter course founders because of the difficulties of specifying and measuring capital services.

Quite apart from difficulties in application, however, the two methods will yield quite different results in principle. This will be because they register changes in the improvement in techniques in quite different ways.

The first method, that of deflating for changes in input prices, values the cost of a given set of factor inputs in the capital goods industries. If the price of these inputs rises, then the capital purchase should accordingly be deflated. However, improvements in technique will mean that a given quantity of inputs in the capital goods industry will produce improved capital goods, with a resulting increase in the flow of capital services. In other words, in terms of the deflated series, a given "constant price" expenditure on new capital goods will result in greater real productivity than previously.

The second method will attempt to measure the cost of a given flow of services from the capital goods. Improvements in technique in the capital goods industry would therefore be registered as a fall in the price of capital services, which would offset price rises associated with changes in the general price level. The capital goods price deflator would register price increases less sharply than the first method.

To summarize, the two methods may be compared in an example. If an investment series shows steady growth over a period in which price levels are known to have been rising, it might be useful to estimate what the "real" levels of investment have been by deflating for price changes. One purpose of this exercise might be to compare investment levels with the growth in real output, so as to estimate a marginal capital-output ratio. The first method would tend to suggest that more of the observed rise was due to price increases and that the growth in real investment was lower than would be implied by the second method. As the lower investment would be compared with the same increase in real output, the first method would suggest a lower capital-output ratio and more productive capital stock.

In practice, methods of deflating are likely to be somewhere between the two outlined. Some types of capital goods are more amenable to the application of one method, some to the other. Thus, for standardized machines and tools the effort will be made to price a given machine or tool, but for much building and construction the only feasible deflation method will be through the valuation of inputs. Even where a machine is priced, the result is likely to vary somewhat from the second method. Those changes in technique which result in modifications in the machine rather than changes in its price will not be accounted for. Because of their complicated nature, it will not usually be possible to define an identifiable flow of capital services for which a price might be sought.

Whenever deflated investment series are used, or capital goods price deflators are used to estimate the real value of a capital stock, it must be recognized that the result will be a compromise between two alternative methods of treating improvements in capital good production.

One further difficulty is worth noting. By applying a deflator, estimates of real expenditure on gross investment can be obtained. To use such a series to estimate the real stock of gross fixed assets it is also necessary to estimate the real value of retirements. Also, to estimate either the real net capital stock or net investment it is necessary to estimate the real value of depreciation.

This problem might be handled by estimating the age of retired equipment or depreciated assets. Then the deflator relevant to the years assigned could be applied to the estimates of retirement or depreciation. The difficulty with this is that it requires two types of information not usually available: past investment broken down into types of capital good investment for a long period, and estimates of the life expectation of the various types of capital good. It is likely, therefore, that some kind of crude guess will be necessary. For example, depreciation might be assumed to be some fixed percentage of gross domestic product or of the estimated real capital stock, effects of the age structure of the capital stock being incorporated, as a matter of judgment, in the choice of the appropriate percentage.

C. Practical Questions of Definition

The discussion so far has attempted to introduce the student to some of the fundamental problems of measurement which will provide sources of misunderstanding in this area. In practice, the person constructing national accounts, or studying capital formation problems from the accounts of firms, is likely to be exercised by less profound but quite tricky practical difficulties.

Gross capital formation will be estimated from expenditure, output, or import flow data. So far the discussion has revolved around the question of what should be done with such a series if it were available. Measurement of gross capital formation in current prices, although not involving some of the questions of principle discussed previously, does raise the problem of defining precisely what is a capital good. A first reaction might be that the problem would be simple—machinery and construction are clearly to be included. However, a little experience will indicate that the problem is not so simple. Many commodities will be defined as a capital good if purchased by government or a firm but not if acquired by a private individual. For example, tables, chairs, cars, etc., are all items which would often be classified as investment goods if purchased by a firm, but as durable consumer goods if purchased by an individual. In the case of housing, however, private building is usually incorporated, at least in principle, in the gross investment estimates.

The difficulty can be especially confusing in situations in which a large part of the productive sector is made up of small enterprises often no larger than the family or even the individual. Thus, a sewing machine, purchased by an individual, might be a necessary item for undertaking an important trade. An automobile, acquired initially for private purposes, might eventually be used as a basis for commercial activities. The unlicensed taxi is, for example, a crucial element in the public transport system in many parts of the world. Even the bicycle is very widely used not only as a personal conveyance, but also to ship considerable quantities of goods. Indeed, even if such equipment is used for private (i.e., non-market) purposes, its use may relieve pressure on more obviously commercial capacity.

This might be thought to be a mere quibble over definitions, but it goes beyond that; for often policy implications flow from the definitions chosen. It will often be the case that preferential tariff and import control treatment will be given to investment as against consumer goods. Also success in performance will sometimes be measured in terms of improving investment levels. Particularly in the economic situation in which many developing countries currently find themselves such judgments may be damaging. Business and industrial development must rely to a considerable extent on new initiatives from small scale operators—necessarily small scale because they are such recent entrants to the field of commercial and industrial activities. In this area sharply defined distinctions between private durable consumer goods and investment goods are often inappropriate. Almost any car, bicycle, or sewing machine might be the basis for a small scale commercial or industrial enterprise. On the other hand, some items are clearly for consumption use, such as radio and television sets, which should normally be treated as consumer durables (but if a bar owner installs a television set, should this be taken as an investment?).

As it is often easiest in these countries to measure the investment in machinery from import flows and it is rarely possible to distinguish, on an annual basis, the use to which commodities are put, the allocation of those commodities most likely to be on the margin between investment goods and consumer durables is usually done by the application of some arbitrary division (e.g., all sewing machines of a certain type may be allocated to consumer durable expenditure, or with automobiles 50 per cent may be assumed to be investment and the rest for consumer use). Quantitatively the most important thing to be watched is the treatment of automobiles. In comparing countries, for example, it is particularly important to check that automobile expenditures are treated consistently in comparing investment levels. It will always be worthwhile to keep a check on consumer durables to judge whether sizeable elements are being used to facilitate future production.

Of course, purists might argue that the distinction between consumer and producer durables is irrelevant and that both should be treated as part of the capital stock. However, such a view would only be reasonable if, in the calculation of incomes, services flowing from the ownership of such durables were imputed as part of the total income flow. As this is not usually done it is quite consistent to exclude consumer durables from capital stock and investment calculations.

A second source of difficulty arises in the treatment of "own-account" investment activities. Own-account investment takes place when a firm, public agency, or private individual invests by doing the work of creating the capital good themselves rather than purchasing the equipment or contracting out the construction work. In such cases purchases of investment goods, outputs of the capital goods industries, or imports of capital goods, cannot be used as a basis for estimation.

In manufacturing and trade this sort of investment occurs when a factory extension is undertaken with the ordinary labor force of the firm or when a piece of machinery is converted from one use to another by a maintenance team (e.g., a lorry is modified for use as a bus). Very large organizations, such as railway authorities, are likely to maintain their own construction departments and engineering works to undertake such activities. Similarly, the public works department of the government will do much public construction work, even if major projects are contracted out to private firms. In such cases it might be possible to identify the amount of investment activity by questioning the firm or government department concerned and by examination of existing public accounts. The railway authorities, for example, will keep separate accounts, for internal purposes, of the costs of the railway workshops. For small businesses the task will be more difficult and is often likely to be neglected.

One difficulty of principle which arises concerns the treatment of maintenance and repair expenditures. Usually there is, to some degree, a choice which can be made between incurring high maintenance and repair costs and prolonging the life of buildings and equipment, or reducing such costs and with them the life expectancy of the capital stock. This not only affects the number of years a machine may be expected to operate but also influences the level of performance over their lifetime. There are even circumstances in which repairs involving replacements might expand capacity or improve over the original performance of a piece of equipment. There is therefore a case for including some part of maintenance and repair expenditures in the investment estimates, although this is not usually done.

Omission of own-account investment may not be serious in that the relative importance of the items excluded is small and their behavior may well be similar to that of the things included. However, it must be admitted that there is little solid evidence on this problem to indicate whether such presumptions are right or wrong. There are two areas in which omissions in own account investment are likely to be large—residential construction and agricultural investment. The inadequacies of the treatment of residential construction have already been explored in the discussion of the measurement of subsistence output. The omission is two-fold in that the new construction is usually excluded from the capital formation estimates, while the flow of services from existing self-constructed housing is also missing from the income and output estimates.

Any inadequacy in the measurement of agricultural investment is of the greatest potential importance. Agriculture always forms a very high proportion of the total economic activity, involving as much as 90 per cent of the economically active population in some less-developed countries. Moreover, it is the main foreign exchange earner. Nevertheless, neglect of this sector in basic economic statistics is only too easy, because of certain difficulties of measurement.

Large scale commercial agriculture will purchase machinery inputs which will be as readily noted as any of the machinery purchases of industry. However, a large part of investment will take the form of employing labor to clear land and tend plants in the immature stage. For perennial crops, there will be a number of years before the crop is productive and a necessary part of the capital investment takes the form of tending of the plant during that stage. For plantation crops or large scale mixed farming it is likely that some estimate can be made of the development costs involved from the accounts of the companies involved and from agricultural surveys. For a going concern which is undertaking expansion, however, it will often be difficult to isolate the element of costs attributable to the expansion. In principle, the problem is the kind which can arise in any type of enterprise, but it is likely to be proportionately more important in agriculture.

The most considerable gaps arise from investment in peasant agriculture. In many tropical countries the peasant is an important contributor to agriculture, both growing food and as an export cash crop producer. Peasant production is the backbone of the economy. It is far from being the stagnant sector which the term "peasant" so often brings to mind in the industrialized societies. Particularly in export crops there has been a long record of substained output growth. Moreover, much of this expansion has been in perennial crops—for example, coffee and cocoa in the past and, increasingly, tea in the future. The investment of the peasant in the perennial crops consists of the labor used in planting and tending in the years prior to production, both in the disutility of the effort involved and in the forsaken opportunities of deriving incomes from alternative and more immediate sources (e.g., annual crops or paid employment). Expansion in the capacity to produce annual crops may also require investment activity in clearing and preparing new areas. Thus, both in the production of food and export cash crops there is a very important type of investment activity in expanding acreages and developing perennial crops. In the future it is to be hoped that productivity will be improved increasingly through self-construction irrigation systems and terracing.

Such activities usually involve little purchase of equipment. It is capital accumulation of the simplest form—namely the use of labor on tasks which bear fruit only after the passage of time. The degree to which such activity is pursued will be an important determinant of future economic performance. Yet such activities are rarely measured because of the extreme difficulty of doing so. This difficulty is of two kinds. There are so many peasants, each making individual decisions about a small plot of land, possibly each deciding to plant just a few more coffee trees, for example, that a complete coverage is impossible on an annual basis. The preponderance of very small economic units in some developing countries suggests that in the future statistical improvements will best be achieved by an expansion of the use of sampling techniques in data collection.

Even if the data were available, however, there would be a considerable valuation problem. In the peasant economy it is difficult to construct a method of valuing labor inputs in the absence of a clearly defined pecuniary opportunity cost. Further, it is no easier to impute a value to the investment effort on the basis of expected output improvement both because the earnings expected are quite uncertain (for reasons of price instability and climatic uncertainties) and because a suitable discount rate would be difficult to select.

One consequence of the failure to measure peasant capital formation is the introduction of an additional source of error in the use of aggregate capital-output ratios. Whereas capital formation in this sector is not usually recorded, the resulting output is incorporated in the domestic product estimates. An element of output growth is introduced which is unrelated to recorded capital formation, the behavior which will therefore have quite unpredictable effects on the observed capital-output ratio.

It is necessary to reiterate an obvious truth, which is nevertheless sometimes forgotten. The absence of records of peasant capital formation does not render it unimportant. It remains of considerable importance to investigate and judge what factors influence the behavior of this component of economic activity. It is an area in which it is important to devise indicators of activity which will provide early information on developments, even if these fall short of comprehensive capital formation series.

D. Inventory

Although at the outset of this chapter there was mention of stocks of raw materials and work in progress, the discussion has largely been concerned with fixed assets. In practice it will usually be the case that "capital," as discussed for example in development plans, is usually taken to mean fixed assets. Inventory problems are often neglected, often because of the absence of useful data on the subject. Yet inventories and their fluctuation are of considerable potential importance. This gap in the national accounts is likely to be one of the last to be filled. However, it will be possible to get fragmentary evidence (e.g., for particular commodities) and, wherever possible, that should be used to throw light on inventory behavior.

In order to maintain the flow of economic activity, it is necessary to hold stocks of raw materials, finished goods, and work in progress as the more obvious needs for machinery and buildings. The stocks actually held will fluctuate in part because businessmen change their view about the desirable level of stocks and in part because they find their holdings fluctuating in an unplanned way because supplies or sales behaved differently than expected.

Inventory behavior is of significance under two headings. Adjustments to inventory levels can be an important factor in cyclical behavior. Inventory holdings can also be an important part of the capital stock, utilizing assets which might be diverted to other uses.

Inventory investment can be a source of income fluctuations as stocks are increased and decreased, fluctuating over a positive and negative range. Producers and distributors may seek to adjust their inventories in the light of their expectation of future economic activity and of the current state of their stocks and, in so doing, will themselves generate fluctuations in economic activity.

In many developing economies it is likely that fluctuation in inventory investment could have substantial effects on the import bill (fluctuations on the inventory investments of commodity users in the developed world are also a most important influence on the price and quantity of exports from the less-developed world). The existence of inventories makes possible lags in adjustment of output and import patterns to changes in final spending. Absence of inventory investment data prevents the identification of the behavior of other elements in the total spending pattern. For example, it will not be possible to decide whether imports of consumer goods are being currently consumed or are adding to the inventories of traders.

Neglect of the role of inventories in the process of production and distribution can be a source of serious error in estimating the capital costs of a project. Some types of investment in fixed capital reduce the need to hold inventories and, therefore, involve a smaller capital cost than would be suggested by the observation of the fixed investment involved.

Improvements in the transport system reduce the inventory requirements for two reasons. With an undeveloped transport system there will be a heavy investment simply in goods in transit. Bottlenecks will cause goods to pile up at one point or another, increasing the inventory necessary to maintain a given output flow. Also the uncertainty created by a slow and unreliable transport system will increase the risk that the manufacturer and distributor will be left without the necessary materials and parts, increasing the level of inventories which it is desirable to have on hand.

Similarly, highly mechanized capital intensive methods may economize on the stock of work in progress, if there is an increase in the speed of transformation from raw materials to finished product. On the other hand, a high degree of division of labor will increase the number of points in the production process at which it may be desirable to maintain stocks as buffers to prevent the dislocation of the whole production process as a result of a breakdown at any particular step in the sequence.

Inventory investment is thus another important area in which there is a considerable poverty of available evidence in most developing countries. However, although this, alongside the other deficiencies noted in this chapter, may be unfortunate for the policy-maker, it must be seen as something of a challenge to the student. It is yet another area in which useful research can be done, filling gaps in the data and using ingenuity to derive the maximum information from the little data available.

E. Capital Stock Estimates for Ghana

An ambitious attempt was made by Robert Szereszewski to measure the capital stock of Ghana. It was measured on a cost basis in terms of 1960 prices with one exception, the capital of the cocoa industry. The cost of setting up cocoa farms and plantations consists mostly of labor. Szereszewski felt that an estimation of cocoa on a cost basis would have greatly underestimated the value of cocoa assets which to a large extent reflect the specific contribution of Ghana's climate and other natural resources in enhancing the productivity of investments in cocoa. Thus, cocoa assets were estimated by discounting the value of the future stream of production of cocoa trees, net of labor costs involved in annual cultivation, disease control, and harvesting and net of marketing and distribution costs. Estimates of the number of cocoa trees, the age structure of the trees, and a typical production profile over time were determined from Ministry of Agriculture data. The price of cocoa was assumed to be a constant £200 per ton in the future* and a discount rate of 7 per cent was used to discount the future stream of earnings to the present.†

For some capital assets, direct estimates of physical quantities were available. These included motor vehicles (which are licensed), roads, aircraft, ships, livestock, and canoes. For these, 1960 price data was obtained and used to arrive at a total value for each of these assets.

For other assets, mainly machinery, equipment, buildings, and other constructions, capital stock estimates had to be built up using a version of the perpetual inventory method. Since very little machinery and equipment is produced in Ghana, imports of these items could be used as the basic data source. In the case of buildings and construction, a major ingredient, cement, was largely an import. The advantage of using import data lies in the fact that figures are available for very long periods in the past. Import data were collected in the process of levying customs duties which have a long history in Ghana, stretching back to the early days of colonization.

The import data used were on a value basis and had to be deflated by a price index. The most appropriate index for this purpose was an index of average unit values of producers' equipment calculated by the Central Bureau of Statistics for 1945 to 1961. This index showed some violent shifts from year to year, presumably due to changes in the composition

---

* Recent trends in cocoa prices make this assumption rather optimistic. Cocoa prices from 1961 to 1967 remained below £200 per ton, ranging from about £130 to £190.
† See Chapter XVIII for a discussion of the discount rate. Szereszewski justified the use of a 7 per cent rate as the rate of interest charged by Ghanaian banks on loans with good security.

of imports in the producer's equipment category. This index was smoothed using a three-year moving average. Prices before 1945 were assumed to be constant. Although this assumption is certainly in error, it does not seriously affect the capital stock estimates, since the great bulk of Ghana's capital stock in 1960 was acquired after World War II. The import series for each producers' goods item was deflated using this index to obtain a series by item in terms of 1960 prices. Each member of the series then had to be rated up to include an estimated cost of marketing, distribution, and installation.

The remaining piece of information necessary to use the perpetual

TABLE XV–1

Ghana

Estimated Capital Stock, Mid-Year 1960, by Types of Assets, at 1960 Prices

(£ million)

General equipment		Vehicles		Constructions	
Agricultural machinery	1.4	Cars‡	3.3	Permanent	492.5
Water supply equipment	3.7	Dual purpose vehicles	2.6	"Swish" buildings	44.4
Railway equipment*	25.9	Coaches and		Local roads	30.0
Marine equipment	3.7	omnibuses	4.3		——
Office equipment	4.7	Trucks and lorries	20.1	Total	566.9
Electricity generating and			——		
measuring equipment	9.7	Total	30.3		
Post and telegraph				*Aircraft and ships*	
equipment	4.4				
Machine tools	1.3			Aircraft	2.8
Industrial machinery and				Ships	0.9
engines	42.9				——
Mining and construction		*Rural capital*		Total	3.7
equipment	40.5	Cocoa	361.0		
Tractors and earthmoving		Livestock	13.4		
equipment	4.9	Canoes	0.5		
Miscellaneous†	42.5	Other implements§	2.6		
	——		——		——
Total	185.6	Total	377.5	Grand Total	1,164.0

* Including rails and construction accessories.
† Miscellaneous machinery, scientific instruments, hand tools, stoves and furnaces, containers, etc.
‡ Estimated value of cars used for business purposes.
§ Fishing nets, axes, matchets (cutlasses), shotguns.

Source: W. Birmingham, I. Neustadt, and E. N. Omaboe, *A Study of Contemporary Ghana,* London, Allen and Unwin, 1966, p. 195.

inventory method is the length of economic life for the various kinds of assets. Some rather arbitrary decisions were made. For example, it was assumed that all permanent construction works (dwellings, roads, etc.) had a standard average life of 40 years. The average economic life of machinery and equipment of various types was based on depreciation formulae used by the Railways and Harbours Administration and the Electricity Department.

The resulting estimates of capital stock for Ghana in the year 1960 are shown in Table XV–1. They do not include land improvements, mine development, rubber and coffee assets, and own-account construction and tool making. The exclusion of these assets gives a downward bias to the figures, although the optimistic prices and low discount rate in evaluating cocoa assets should bias the total in the other direction.

The figures in Table XV–1 indicate that cocoa is almost one-third of Ghana's capital stock and construction is nearly one-half. Excluding cocoa, construction is more than 70 per cent. This is high relative to many other less-developed countries. The high proportion of construction, however, reflects the fact that the high cocoa prices of the early 1950's resulted in swollen government revenues as cocoa exports and the resulting imports were highly taxed in one form or another. Much of these funds were allocated to government development projects, most of which took the form of massive investment in social and economic infrastructure. More than 60 per cent of the total 1960 construction assets date from 1951. The town and large port at Tema were built in this period. Hospital beds increased by 160 per cent and the number of paved roads increased by 50 per cent.

Construction investments tend to have a long life but a low output relative to value. Thus, Ghana's average capital-output ratio is 2.5 to 1 which is relatively high compared to most less developed countries.

The comparatively poor performance of cocoa prices in the 1960's and the depletion of Ghana's foreign exchange reserves have resulted in a shift away from infrastructure investments. The structure of Ghana's capital stock will be very different in 1970.

FURTHER READING FOR PART THREE

1. P. Ady and M. Courcier, *Systems of National Accounts in Africa*, Paris, OEEC, 1960.
2. Phyllis Deane, *Colonial Social Accounting*, Cambridge, Cambridge University Press, 1953.
3. Phyllis Deane, editor, *Income and Wealth*, Series II, London, Bowes and Bowes, 1961.
4. H. C. Edey and A. T. Peacock, *National Income and Social Accounting*, London, Hutchinson, 1959.
5. Irving Fisher, *The Making of Index Numbers*, 2nd edition, revised, Cambridge, Houghton Mifflin, 1923.
6. M. Gilbert, editor, *Income and Wealth*, Series III, Cambridge, Bowes and Bowes, 1953.
7. M. Gilbert and R. Stone, editors, *Income and Wealth*, Series IV, London, Bowes and Bowes, 1955.
8. T. Haavelmo, *A Study in the Theory of Investment*, Chicago, University of Chicago Press, 1960.
9. Bent Hansen and Donald Mead, *The National Income of the U.A.R. (Egypt), 1939–1962*, Memo No. 355, The Institute of National Planning, Cairo, July 21, 1963.
10. J. R. Hicks and U. K. Hicks, "Public Finance in the National Income," *The Review of Economic Studies*, Vol. VI, No. 2, (February, 1939), p. 150.
11. J. R. Hicks, "The Valuation of the Social Income—A Comment on Professor Kuznets' 'Reflections,'" *Economica*, Vol. XV, New Series, No. 59 (August, 1948), p. 154.
12. India Central Statistical Organization, *Estimates of National Income, 1963*, New Delhi, 1965.
13. India Ministry of Finance, *First Report of the National Income Committee*, New Delhi, 1951.
14. India Ministry of Finance, *Final Report of the National Income Committee*, New Delhi, 1954.
15. Kenya Colony and Protectorate, *Domestic Income and Product in Kenya*, Nairobi, Government Printer, 1959.
16. Charles P. Kindleberger, *International Economics*, 4th edition, Homewood, Illinois, Irwin, 1968.
17. T. Killick, "Ghana's Balance of Payments Since 1950, Parts I and II," *The Economic Bulletin* (Ghana), Vol. VI (1962), No. 2, p. 3, and No. 3, p. 3.
18. Simon Kuznets, "On the Valuation of Social Income—Reflections on Professor Hicks' Article," *Economica*, Vol. XV, New Series, No. 1 (January, 1948), p. 1.
19. Erik Lundberg, editor, *Income and Wealth*, Series I, Cambridge, Bowes and Bowes, 1951.
20. F. Lutz and D. C. Hague, editors, *The Theory of Capital*, London, Macmillan, 1961.

21. J. E. Meade, *The Theory of International Economic Policy*, Vol. I, *The Balance of Payments*, London, Oxford University Press, 1951.
22. A. T. Peacock and D. Dosser, "Input-Output Analysis in an Underdeveloped Country: A Case Study," *Review of Economic Studies*, Vol. XXV, No. 66 (July, 1957), p. 21.
23. E. Z. Palmer, *The Meaning and Measurement of National Income*, Lincoln, University of Nebraska Press, 1966.
24. J. P. Powelson, *Economic Accounting*, New York, McGraw-Hill, 1955.
25. A. R. Prest, *The Investigation of National Income in British Tropical Dependencies*, Commonwealth Paper No. IV, London, The Athlone Press, 1957.
26. V. K. R. V. Rao, S. R. Sen, M. V. Divatia, and Uma Datta, editors, *Indian Conference on Research in National Income, Papers on National Income and Allied Topics*, Vol. 1, Bombay, Asia Publishing House, 1960.
27. Rhodesia and Nyasaland, Federation of, *The National Accounts of the Federation of Rhodesia and Nyasaland 1954–1963*, Salisbury, Central Statistical Office, 1964.
28. Richard and Nancy Ruggles, *National Income Accounts and Income Analysis*, 2nd edition, New York, McGraw-Hill, 1956.
29. L. H. Samuels, editor, *African Studies in Income and Wealth*, London, Bowes and Bowes, 1963.
30. Dudley Seers, "The Role of National Income Estimates in the Statistical Policy of an Under-developed Area," *Review of Economic Studies*, Vol. XX (1952–53), p. 159, Comment by A. R. Prest and Rejoinder by Seers, Vol. XXI (1953–54), No. 56, p. 223, and Comments by W. C. Hollinger and J. C. Stewart, Vol. XXII (1954–55), No. 59, p. 220.
31. Richard Stone, *Input-Output and National Accounts*, Paris, Organization for European Economic Co-operation, 1961.
32. Richard Stone, *Quantity and Price Indexes in National Accounts*, Paris, Organization for European Economic Co-operation, 1956.
33. Richard Stone and Giovanna Croft Murray, *National Income and Expenditure*, London, Bowes and Bowes, 1961.
34. Richard and Giovanna Stone, *Social Accounting and Economic Models*, London, Bowes and Bowes, 1961.
35. G. Stuvel, "A New Approach to the Measurement of Terms of Trade Effects," *The Review of Economics and Statistics*, Vol. XXXVIII, No. 3 (August, 1956), p. 294.
36. Tanganyika Government, *The Gross Domestic Product of Tanganyika, 1954–57*, Dar es Salaam, Government Printer, 1959.
37. Tanganyika Government, *The Gross Domestic Product of Tanganyika, 1960–62*, Dar es Salaam, Government Printer, 1964.
38. Uganda Protectorate, *The Gross Domestic Product of Uganda, 1954–59*, Entebbe, Government Printer, 1961.
39. Uganda Government, *The Real Growth of the Economy of Uganda, 1954–62*, Entebbe, Government Printer, 1964.
40. United Nations, *Yearbook of National Accounts Statistics*, New York, Annual.

41. United Nations, *National Accounting Practices in 60 Countries, Supplement, to the Yearbook of National Accounts Statistics*, New York, ST/STAT/SER. F111.
42. United Nations, *Studies in Methods: A System of National Accounts and Supporting Tables*, Series F, No. 2, Rev. 2, 1964.
43. United Nations, "Proposals for the Revision of the SNA," E/CN. 3/356, August, 1967.
44. United Nations Economic Commission for Africa, "Report of the Working Group on the Adaptation of the U.N. System of National Accounts to Africa, 1962," E/CN. 14/221.
45. United Nations Economic Commission for Africa, "Report of the Working Group on Problems of National Accounts for Africa, E/CN. 14/319, 1965.
46. United Nations Economic Commission for Asia and the Far East, "Use of National Accounts in Asia and the Far East," E/CN. 11/ASTATINA/L. 1.
47. United Nations Economic Commission for Asia and the Far East, "Report of the Working Group of Experts on National Accounts," E/CN. 11/L. 171.
48. United Nations Economic Commission for Latin America, "Concepts and Methods Used by ECLA" in *Economic Bulletin for Latin America*, United Nations, New York, Vol. 2, No. 2 (September, 1956), p. 30.
49. United Nations Economic Commission for Latin America, "National Accounts and Development Planning," E/CN. 12/671, 1963.
50. United Nations Economic Commission for Latin America, "Report of the Working Group on National Accounts," E/CN. 12/801, 1967.
51. United States Office of Business Economics, *National Income, 1954 edition: A Supplement to the Survey of Current Business*, Washington, U.S. Government Printing Office, 1954.
52. United States Office of Business Economics, *U.S. Income and Output: A Supplement to the Survey of Current Business*, Washington, U.S. Government Printing Office, 1959.
53. United States Office of Business Economics, *Survey of Current Business*, August, 1965.

NOTES ON FURTHER READING FOR PART THREE

Ruggles and Ruggles (28), Powelson (24), Stone (33), and Edey and Peacock (4) are a few of the many good textbooks on national income accounting and analysis. Palmer (23) is a more recent text which summarizes various controversies concerning income accounting techniques. The relationship between national income accounting and input-output is discussed in all of these texts and at length in Stone (31). The articles by Stone in Lundberg (19) and Gilbert (6) deal with the general problem of concepts and methods in national accounts. The special problem which arises in classifying government expenditure is discussed at length by Hicks, (10) and (11), Kuznets, (18) and his article in Lundberg (19), and by Derksen in an article in Lundberg (19). General problems encountered in international comparisons of national accounts are discussed by Gilbert and Kravis in Gilbert and Stone (7) and by Barna in Gilbert (6).

Phyllis Deane (2), A. R. Prest (25), and D. Creamer in Gilbert (6) deal with the special problems encountered in applying national income estimation techniques to less-developed countries. Emphasis is placed on the lack of statistical material and the problem of imputing a value to subsistence production. The difficulties in comparing national income estimates in developed countries with those in less-developed countries because of the special characteristics of less developed economies are dealt with at length in Gilbert (6) in articles by S. H. Frankel, F. Benham, and V. K. R. V. Rao. An interesting controversy concerning the use of national accounts statistics in less-developed countries occurs in a series of articles and comments by Seers, Prest, Hollinger and Stewart (30) and Peacock and Dosser (22). Seers on the basis of his experience with Ross in compiling national income statistics in Ghana suggests that priority should be given to compiling accounts for key industries and sectors in an input-output framework rather than to the compilation of comprehensive national accounts statistics, including the subsistence sector. Seers' argument is that key sector accounts will be more accurate and more useful for policy purposes than comprehensive but inaccurate national accounts statistics. Prest and Stewart, with experience in compiling Nigerian accounts, indicate that priority should be given to the national accounts because of greater applicability to policy problems, especially those concerning welfare and equity in taxation. Peacock and Dosser tell of their difficulties in compiling the data for a set of inter-industry accounts in Tanganyika and suggest that there is a general lack of interdependence in less-developed economies, making the compilation of inter-industry accounts a low priority activity.

The Economic Commission for Africa, (44) and (45), suggests an adaptation of the U.N. System of National Accounts for African countries. Comments on the suggested system are made by G. C. Billington in Samuels (29). Uses of national accounts statistics are described or suggested by Ady, Barkay, and Saxe in separate articles in Samuels (29). The uses of national accounts statistics in the Far East are dealt with by the Economic Commission for Asia and the Far East, (46) and (47). Application of national income data in Latin America is considered in (49) and (50). The ECLA recommendations for real product accounts are contained in (48).

The United Nations *Yearbook of National Accounts Statistics* (40) provides the most convenient summary of national accounts statistics and the supplement to the *Yearbook* (41) is a comprehensive and invaluable guide to national accounting techniques in nearly every country of the world which compiles national accounts statistics. For more detailed discussion of methods of compiling national accounts statistics in countries discussed in the text, see India (13) and (14); Rao (26); Uganda (38); Kenya (15); Tanganyika (36) and (37); United States (51), (52), and (53); and Okigbo (Nigeria), Martin, Kennedy, Ord, and Walker (East Africa), all in Samuels (29).

Fisher's *The Making of Index Numbers* (5) is a classic work in the theory of deflation of accounts. Reddaway and Derksen in Lundberg (19), Part One of

Deane (3), and Stone (32) are general treatments of the deflation problem. Stuvel's article (35) is more technical and deals specifically with changes in the terms of trade. Specific attempts at deflation of accounts are described in detail in Hansen and Mead (Egypt) (9), Uganda (39), and Rhodesia (27).

Meade (21) and Chapters 24–27 in Kindleberger (16) are excellent treatments of the concepts involved in balance of payments accounts and contain discussions of the various types of adjustment processes in the balance of payments. The balance of payments accounts of Ghana are discussed in detail in Killick (17).

For further reading in capital theory, Haavelmo (8) is an excellent but difficult text Lutz (20) is a collection of articles useful as a reference.

PART

4

PLANNING AND ECONOMIC ACCOUNTING

XVI

PLANNING CRITERIA

A. Introduction

To the economist, business accounting, inter-industry accounting, and social or national accounting techniques are of interest as a tool particularly when performing the role of policy adviser and planner. This work is very important in developing countries, where the government and its planning branch assume considerable responsibility for organizing economic activity. The economist involved in this work will have to face many practical decisions, demanding the use of various accounting techniques for their solution. This chapter introduces some of the special problems of accounting for planning decisions and represents a systematic interpretation of the role of the economist in the planning process, which will provide a framework for the discussion in later chapters.

Questions regarding the role of the government in the economy are often controversial. This chapter, however, is not concerned with the role the government *should* adopt, but rather with the situation which is likely to exist in practice. This situation may be described as follows. In many less-developed countries the government will be the biggest single spending unit. Certain industrial enterprises will be publicly owned. The government will also take the initiative in influencing developments in the private sector. It will be particularly concerned to mobilize economic resources to raise the rate of economic growth. There will also be a public responsibility to maintain balance at the national level in a number of different areas— price stability, balance of payments, employment, and the allocation of skilled labor, for example.

The methods used will vary. The degree to which economic planning can be applied in any detail will be limited by the scarcity of planning personnel, if not for other reasons. The degree of involvement of the government in the economy and the character of its objectives will differ from country to country.

Governments, after all, represent differing interest groups and ideologies and have to face a range of economic situations. The desire for rapid economic growth, social justice, national unity, and the maintenance of political power of the ruling party are all likely to play their role in influencing the government in its choice of economic policy objectives.

So far, policies adopted toward the controversial subject of private property ownership have been determined, in many developing countries, on an apparently pragmatic basis, in the light of the other objectives of the government. Therefore, economic planning works within a framework of a "mixed economy," with both private and public ownership.

B. The Inadequacy of Market Prices in Planning

The government must make decisions regarding price, cost, and output both in managing the public sector and devising its policy toward the private sector. What sort of accounting is proper for the examination of such questions? Commercial accounts, inter-industry accounts, and national accounts are built on a foundation of market values. The transference of the system, and the assumptions implicit in it, to the sphere of public economic planning raises a number of interesting issues.

The government has a number of different roles in, and a number of different motives for, involvement in economic activity. The legitimacy of the straightforward application of market criteria in this sphere will depend on the character of the particular activity. Certain general points should be kept clearly in mind. The existence of public ownership, as such, does not prevent the use of market criteria in making economic decisions. For example, if public ownership is extended because private ownership is seen to be incompatible with the desired income distribution and power structure of the society, the resulting public corporations might still be operated in response to consumer demands as expressed through the market. On the other hand, in situations where private ownership prevails, it might be considered desirable to interfere with the operation of the market through some form of rationing or control.

Because part of the purpose of government development programing is to make good the insufficiency of the market mechanism, there are many tasks for which an accounting system based exclusively on market value will be quite an inadequate tool. The reason for this becomes clear if some of the particular causes of the inadequacies of the market mechanism are reviewed. An exhaustive list of such possibilities is not necessary; the following six general headings are suggested to give an insight into the nature of the accounting problem as it arises in development programing.

C. Reasons for the Insufficiency of the Market Mechanism

   (i) For some purposes the use of the market mechanism is technically not feasible, because of the difficulty of charging and collecting a price (e.g., most roads).

  (ii) For many social services, the ability to pay may be viewed as an undesirable basis for judging need (e.g., education and medical assistance).

 (iii) Although price might be viewed as an efficient method of allocation in principle, the price level required by the market might prove undesirable on other grounds (e.g., where skills are scarce and to be acquired mainly through government education programs, it might seem undesirable to allow salaries to rise to the level which would adequately represent the real scarcity. Similarly, if foreign exchange is scarce it might not be desirable to allow its price to rise, that is to devalue).

  (iv) There might be external benefits and costs not registered in the individual firm's calculations of its profit and loss (e.g., the expansion of the market might improve servicing facilities and lower the costs for other firms, or an infant industry might confer benefits in furthering industrialization possibilities).

   (v) The aggregate co-ordination of the various market units might be inadequate (e.g., the aggregate effects of many different investment plans on future outputs and prices might be best estimated at the national planning level).

  (vi) The mobilization of resources resulting from the operation of the market mechanism might be inadequate (e.g., the national planning unit might be able to estimate aggregate capacity and plan for its maximum utilization, while imperfections in the market mechanism might prevent cases of free capacity being represented by declines in price).

In each of these cases, real (or opportunity) cost is not measured by the existing market price, or alternatively, no market price exists. Yet in the practical policy situation, decision must be made which involve "more or less" type judgments—that is, quantitative judgments. No simple rules can be offered which will apply to all the problems of this sort. There are, however, some accounting methods which can deal with this problem by attempting to measure real constraints and returns.*

* The term "constraint" applies to a factor which is in limited supply.

If the market is not to supply the exclusive criteria for economic decisions, even in principle, what alternative view of economic decision-making can be offered to provide a framework for an alternative accounting method?

Much of the content of the traditional economic theory of the market is concerned with the problem of consumer choice. The consumer has numerous ends and only scarce means of achieving them. He must, therefore, make choices between those ends and allocate his scarce means accordingly. The market economy is seen as a means of registering those various choices made by each consumer subject to the limitations set by his individual income. The business translates the choices into production decisions in the pursuit of profit. This is a far from complete view of even a competitive market; however, it does provide an initial understanding of the processes at work in the market system. Similarly, a somewhat idealized view of the planning process can be helpful in providing insight into the logic of the planning process.

The economic plan set out to achieve certain objectives. Those objectives may be chosen in many alternative ways, depending on the political and administrative organization of the society. In the construction of the plan, many choices will have to be made between numerous objectives because of the limited resources available. The society or the political structure from which the planner seeks guidance might be viewed as if it were a person, with similar attributes to those of the individual consumer. In the same way as the individual has tastes, the society may be viewed as having preferences. This set of preferences or "social" welfare function may then be viewed as the guide for making choices in the plan.

The thoughtful reader will see that this description begs many questions about who expresses or interprets "society's" preferences. This is the point at which many of the more profound questions regarding economic planning arise. In practice, the economist will be working in a subordinate capacity to a political structure from which he will take instruction regarding objectives. However, there will be a large job of interpretation remaining with the economist, for the instructions will be in a vague and generalized form at the initial stages of the plan, while at the later stages the political choices are likely to be made from among a limited number of the possible alternatives which are suggested by the planner. Thus the simplifications involved in talking of a social welfare function are of usefulness only if it is accepted as a sort of shorthand description for a quite complex human situation.

The recognition of the limitations of the market and the acceptance of the concept of a social welfare function does not eliminate the market. There may still be a wide area where it is decided that consumer choice

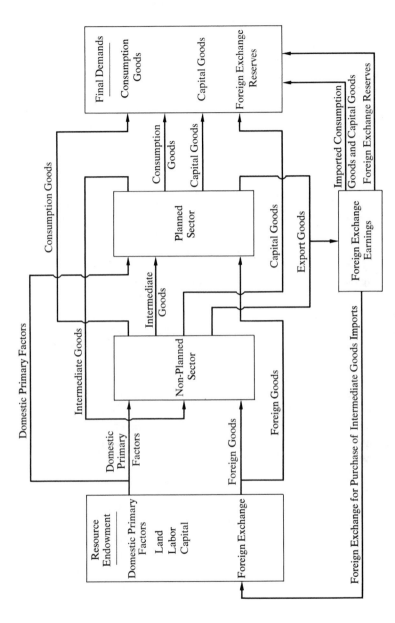

FIGURE XVI-1

shall be made through the market mechanism, either because it is viewed as inherently preferable or because interference would be impracticable. The social welfare function may, therefore, be viewed as operating in two ways. First, there will be a market sector, where the social preference is to be expressed through the choices made by individual consumers (although even here, mainly for taxation purposes, there may be some public intereference with market price). Then there will be a planned sector subject to collective decision. Through the agency of taxation, licensing, subsidy, and rationing there will arise the possibility that the distinction will be much more ambiguous than this description might suggest, for there will be a number of areas where the planning authority will have influence but less than complete control. Also, within that portion of the planned sector which is made up of nationally-owned industries, some part of the activity may be left essentially unplanned, responding to the fluctuating circumstances of market conditions in much the same way as a business completely outside the planned sector.

If the existence of a social welfare function is assumed, the next step is to assume that from this the marginal social utility of various goods can be derived. This concept of the marginal social utility of goods is used throughout the remaining sections of this chapter, which introduces the concept of shadow prices. Throughout, the discussion is subject to the qualification that the concept of marginal social utility is prey to the same weaknesses as the social welfare function from which it is derived.

The discussion in the following sections may seem remote from the practical problems faced by economic planners. It is intended to provide a brief exposition of a formal framework within which to view the planning problem. It is no more than a picture of the skeleton of the relationship involved.

D. The Scope of the Plan

Usually a plan covers a specified number of years. This planning period is likely to be in the range of three to five or even seven years. The plan may concern only a part of the whole economy, such as the government sector or the government sector plus a few key private sectors, or perhaps the whole cash economy excluding the subsistence sector. Even the most extensive plans exclude at least a part of the subsistence sector of the economy.

At the beginning of the planning period, there is a *stock* of resources available. These resources include primary factors of production, such as land, labor, and capital. Foreign exchange may also be treated as a claim on foreign goods and services. The end result of activities in the planned and non-planned sectors of the economy is a set of consumption goods, capital goods, and foreign exchange, which may be called the set of *final demands*. Consumption consists of those goods and services which are consumed during the planning period. Capital goods are those which are held over for future planning periods and constitute part of the stock of resources for the next plan. Export goods earn foreign exchange which may either be used to import goods in the current planning period or held for future use in the form of foreign exchange reserves at the beginning of the next period. The relationships between the planned and non-planned sectors, resources, and the set of final demands is shown in Figure XVI-1.

The inputs into the planned and non-planned sectors include primary factors and intermediate goods. Foreign exchange is an input only in the indirect sense that it finances imported inputs. Intermediate goods are those goods which are used in the production of other goods during the planning period; they are the outputs of one sector which are used as inputs of another sector. The outputs of both planned and non-planned sectors include consumption goods, export goods, capital goods, and intermediate goods.

E. Planning Criteria

A plan can be just a list of projects which seem desirable on a variety of ill-defined criteria. Such a plan may be better than no plan at all. If projects are specified in a planning document, then those responsible for the implementation of the plan have a set of guidelines within which to work and may proceed more vigorously than in the absence of any set of plans. If implemented properly, a written plan may enable individual decision-maker's in various sectors of the economy to have knowledge of the plans for other sectors.

Hopefully, however, a plan can be more than just a list of projects drawn up without a careful consideration of various planning criteria. Throughout this section concern will be confined to three different types of planning criteria, all defined below:

(i) consistency (or feasibility),
(ii) efficiency, and
(iii) optimality.

The *consistency* (or feasibility) of a plan may be viewed as a requirement to be met by a plan in a number of senses.

(i) The investment requirements for each of the projects taken together should be no greater than the maximum amount of savings which can be generated if the target rate of growth for the economy is achieved. Since the individual projects will be drawn up by different committees and different people, there must be some master control over the total investment allocated to each sector in order that a realistic plan emerges in terms of the total investment required.

(ii) Secondly, the amount of foreign exchange used up in investment projects and the recurrent foreign exchange costs of each sector taken together should not exceed the total foreign exchange earnings during the life of the plan. Foreign exchange earnings include receipts from exports and total long term capital imports either in the form of foreign government loans and grants or in the form of foreign private investment. Foreign exchange, of course, is necessary for the purchase of imported goods and materials. For less-developed economies, the foreign exchange cost (import content) of a project is nearly always greater for investment in the form of plant and equipment than for investment in the form of building or construction. Some sectors of the economy will also have high recurrent foreign exchange costs. This may be particularly true of transport, for example, where imported fuel costs may be significant

(iii) The skilled manpower necessary to implement the investment projects plus the skilled manpower used in the day to day operations in each sector should not exceed the skilled manpower available. This seems like an obvious point, but unless there is a central check on the skilled manpower requirements of all projects together, there is no way of ensuring that consistency in this sense will be achieved.

(iv) The government can only raise funds for the implementation of its part of the plan through taxation, loans, and grants from abroad, and loans from local banking institutions. Tax revenues are limited in the sense that political considerations will always place an upper limit on the amount of tax revisions that can be passed through legislative bodies. Foreign loans and grants are limited by foreigners' generosity or desires. Only so much finance can be raised through local banking institutions without raising interest rates to very high levels or risking inflation and consequent balance of payments difficulties which would deter foreign capital investment and might prove to be politically unpalatable. Thus any reasonable plan must take into account the limitations on government finance.

(v) During the planning process each of the committees responsible for drawing up projects for the sectors may be allocated a specified amount of capital and also be given a target rate of output for that sector. The target rate of output must be achievable with the capital allocated.

(vi) Finally, the plans for each of the sectors must be consistent with each other. Investment projects in one sector may only be worthwhile if they are co-ordinated with investments in another sector. The recurrent operation of activities in one sector may require a co-ordinated and constant supply of intermediate inputs from other sectors. This type of consistency may be termed *internal* consistency. Internal consistency is a special problem with reference to the distribution, transportation, and public utilities sectors. The targets for these sectors must be set to ensure internal consistency.

While consistency is important and any realistic plan must contain some implied checks for consistency, over-concern for consistency could result in plans less ambitious than would be possible. A very unambitious plan almost automatically will be consistent. Consistency only becomes difficult to achieve if the plan envisions an attempt to mobilize fully all the resources available in the economy. Targets must be set high enough so that a maximum effort would be required. High but achievable targets may in themselves stimulate the effort and encourage a full mobilization of resources. A plan which is not only consistent but which fully mobilizes resources as well is said to be *efficient*. No plan is efficient which permits unutilized capacity.

Beyond the criteria of consistency and efficiency lies a third criterion, that of *optimality*. There may be many different consistent sets of plans which fully mobilize all resources, but among those sets of plans, one would hope to come up with one that maximizes social welfare, i.e., maximizes the social welfare function. Such a plan would be an optimal plan in the sense that it makes the *best* use of the limited resources available.

F. An Optimal Plan and Shadow Prices

In order that an optimal (best) plan be adopted, it is useful for the planner to have at his disposal a set of prices which differ from business accounting prices in that it reflects society's preferences and the relative scarcity of the various factors. Prices which satisfy these conditions are called "shadow prices" to distinguish them from the prices which are used in business accounts which are market prices. The principles governing the proper shadow prices for the *outputs* of the planned sector differ in some ways from the principles governing the proper shadow prices for the *inputs* of the planned sector. First, consider the outputs of the planned sector, namely consumption goods, capital goods, intermediate goods, and export goods. (See Figure XVI-1.)

G. Shadow Prices of the Outputs of the Planned Sector

1. Consumption Goods

The function of the shadow price is to relate the costs of producing different outputs to the relative valuation placed on these outputs by the society. One of the conditions necessary for the maximization of social welfare will be the equality of the shadow price ratios used in such calculations with the ratio of the respective "marginal social utilities" (*msu*) for consumption goods. This condition may be represented by the following equation:

$$\frac{p_1}{p_2} = \frac{msu_1}{msu_2}$$

The ratio of the shadow prices is shown on the left hand side of the equation, while the ratio of the marginal social utilities is shown on the right. This condition is similar to the condition for maximizing an individual consumer's welfare in the familiar theory of consumer behavior. If there is diminishing marginal social utility, then the shadow price of a consumption good will fall as more of the good is produced in the planned sector.

2. Capital Goods

The shadow price of a capital good output in the planned sector must be related to the output which that capital good will give in future planning periods, since the value of a capital good lies not in its present usefulness but in its future value as a primary input. More specifically, the price of the capital good must be equated with the estimate of its discounted marginal revenue productivities in future planning periods. The marginal revenue productivity is the value of the increase in output in the future which may be attributed to an additional unit of capital. This future output is discounted in the sense that future outputs are valued less than current outputs. The reason for this is that if there is diminishing marginal utility for consumption and if it is generally expected that over the years consumption levels will rise, then future consumption will be valued at a lower rate than current consumption. If the reverse expectation held and it were expected that the social marginal utility of consumption were to be higher in a future period (because of some expected catastrophe, for example), then future outputs would be valued higher than current ones. The usual expectation, however, is that the social marginal utility of current consumption is greater than future. The more current saving is raised and consumption reduced, the more will the current social marginal utility of consumption rise and therefore the more future marginal revenue productivity will be discounted. This is one reason why discounted marginal revenue productivity will decline as current capital formation is increased.

The second reason for the declining value of estimated discounted marginal revenue productivity is that as capital accumulation is increased the more productive projects will be used up. Thus, productivity will decline at the margin because of decreasing returns.

3. *Exports*

The shadow price of an export good in terms of the domestic currency depends on the price of that good in terms of the foreign currency and on the shadow price of that currency in terms of the domestic currency. That is:

$$p_e = p_e^* p_f$$

where p_e^* is the shadow price of the export good in terms of the local currency; p_e is the price in terms of foreign currency; and p_f is the shadow price of foreign exchange. The shadow price of foreign exchange will differ from the market price in situations where there is exchange control and rationing of foreign exchange resources. The shadow price of foreign exchange will represent the domestic productivity of the marginal imports under the exchange rationing system. If either a consumption good or capital good is produced locally, then its shadow price in terms of domestic currency must equal the price of a similar item obtained from abroad times the shadow price of foreign exchange.

4. *Intermediate Goods*

The final type of good which is produced as an output of the planned sector is the intermediate good. An intermediate good produced by the planned sector is any good which is used as an input in the non-planned sector. The shadow price of an intermediate good must equal its marginal revenue productivity in the non-planned sector. That is, the price must equal the addition to the value of the output of the non-planned sector resulting from the increase of one unit in the output of the intermediate good. The shadow price of an intermediate good tends to fall as more of that good is used by the non-planned sector, because of decreasing returns.

H. Shadow Prices of Inputs into the Planned Sector
1. *Primary Inputs*

The inputs into the planned sector are two types: (i) primary factors and foreign exchange which come from the initial stock of resources; and (ii), intermediate goods which are outputs of the non-planned sector. (See Figure XVI–1.) Inputs which come from the stock of resources available

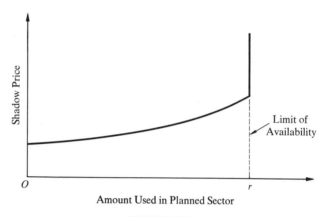

FIGURE XVI-2

at the beginning of the planning period are characterized by the fact that each primary factor (and foreign exchange) has a strict upper limit of availability which is determined by the amount existing in the initial stock. As long as the amount of any primary factor (or of foreign exchange) used as an input into the planned sector is less than the availability limit, then the shadow price of that factor (or of foreign exchange) must equal its marginal revenue productivity (i.e., the opportunity cost of using that input) in the non-planned sector. Once the planned sector is using all of the available stock of a factor, then the shadow price of that factor must be greater than the marginal revenue productivity of the factor in the non-planned sector. The actual shadow price cannot, however, be predetermined in this case, since the final shadow price depends on the marginal revenue productivity within the planned sector; this can only be determined as the plan is formulated. This is demonstrated in Figure XVI–2. The shadow price opportunity cost of a primary input (or of foreign exchange) rises as more is used as an input into the planned sector because marginal revenue productivity increases in the non-planned sector as less of the factor is available for use. Once use in the planned sector reaches the limit of availability, the final shadow price may attain any one of an infinite number of values depending on the final marginal revenue in the planned sector.

2. *Labor*

The shadow price of labor should equal the marginal social utility of leisure. All that this rule says is that the plan should not employ labor where the returns from leisure would be greater than the value to society of the potential output to be produced. The situation in which there is involuntary unemployment will be one in which the planners may well see there to be little marginal social utility of leisure, forming one justification for a very low shadow price for labor inputs in that situation. Sometimes the planning authorities may wish to place a lower estimate on the value of leisure than the private evaluation of the worker.

In practice, the market wage rate will not necessarily equal the private evaluation of the marginal utility of leisure. This is both because there may be an institutional floor under the wage rate, thus making it higher than the private utility of leisure in times if involuntary unemployment; and because of the peculiar character of the labor market in which the worker may not be faced with a marginal choice between work and leisure, but will rather be offered the more brutal choice between working full time or not at all. In the latter case the market wage rate may be below the worker's estimate of the marginal utility of his leisure. The planner is, therefore, likely to have little evidence of the private valuation of leisure. In practice, the opportunity cost of leisure is not likely to be one of the costs with which the planners will be greatly concerned in devising the plan.

3. *Intermediate Good Inputs*

An intermediate good used in the planned sector will be part of the product of the non-planned sector. Its shadow price should be equal to its marginal cost in the non-planned sector. Where there are imperfections at work in the non-planned sector it may be necessary to adjust the marginal cost actually experienced in the sector by some factor allowing for the difference between social and private marginal cost.

I. Conditions for Maximum Social Welfare

If the shadow prices of all outputs and inputs of the planned sector satisfy the above conditions, then social welfare is maximized if each output is produced up to the point where its marginal revenue productivity within the planned sector is equal to its price (all in terms of shadow prices). If the shadow price of an output is too high, over-valuing its marginal contribution to social welfare, too much of that output will be produced by the planned sector. If the price is too low, then too little will be produced. If the shadow price of an input is too low, then too much of that input will be used by the planned sector. Social welfare would be greater if more of that input were released for use in the non-planned sector, as its addition to total revenue is greater there than in the planned sector. Similarly, if the shadow price of an input is too high, too little will be used by the planned sector and more should be withdrawn from the non-planned sector.

J. Financing Investment and Shadow Prices

In calculating the proper shadow prices for planning purposes, care must be taken to consider the effects of market prices on the financial flows within an economy. Although shadow prices alone may indicate that a certain investment project has social benefits which exceed the social costs, the prices actually paid by purchasers of the output will be market prices not shadow prices and the financial costs of the project will be based on market prices of the various inputs not shadow prices. Thus market prices determine the revenues and costs of both private and governmental economic activities.

Government expenditures are limited by the ability of government to obtain finance through taxes or other revenue sources. The expenditures on investment by the private sector are limited by private investors ability to finance their expenditure through retained profits or borrowing in the capital market. If two projects are ranked in terms of social profitability as measured by shadow prices alone but have differential impact with regard to government finance, private profits, or demand and supply conditions in the capital markets, then, in a broader sense, the social profitability of the two projects may be reversed. For example, suppose one can build a dam by one method using labor intensive techniques or by another method using large quantities of heavy earth moving machinery. If there is considerable unemployment, the shadow price of labor may be low—perhaps near zero. This would seem to indicate the use of the labor intensive techniques in constructing the dam. On the other hand, unskilled labor is rarely paid a near zero wage, and in fact, market wage rates may be considerably above any opportunity cost of labor because of political pressures by wage earners and trade unions for minimum wage legislation. Thus, the government may find itself in a situation in which the wage and salary costs of the labor intensive method of dam construction make it several times as expensive in money terms as the method which uses only a few heavy machines. Here the repercussions on government finance may override the strict opportunity cost calculations and the labor intensive construction technique be rejected.

In theory the effects of different projects on government budgets and the financing of investment can be taken into account by formulating properly specified budget constraints (see the next chapter on linear programing). In practice the importance of financial considerations is often neglected by planners and economists who like to concentrate on the "real" opportunity costs of investments. On the other side, finance ministers and bankers tend to emphasize financial limitations on investments and neglect some of the "real" factors. The truth lies somewhere in between.

XVII

A LINEAR PROGRAMING MODEL OF

THE PLANNING PROCESS

This chapter introduces some of the basic principles of linear programing and indicates how the planning process may often be viewed as a problem in linear programing (by making linear approximations to non-linear relationships). Emphasis will be placed on the role of shadow prices in the analysis of linear programing. The first part of the chapter will be devoted to a very simple, hypothetical planning problem which will be formulated in terms of a linear program. The second part of the chapter will indicate the way in which more complex planning processes can be viewed in a similar manner. The final part of the chapter discusses the application of rules of thumb in planning and indicates their relationship to linear programing.

A. A Hypothetical Planning Problem

Suppose there are only two different projects under consideration in the planned sector. The planners have been given upper limits of availability (in volume terms) of four different inputs or resources which can be used in the planned sector. The planning problem, then, becomes one of allocating the available resources between the two projects in such a way as to maximize the return to society from the operation of the planned sector while staying within the imposed limits of availability for the four resources.

Another aspect of the planning problem is to find the shadow prices which satisfy the conditions laid out in the previous chapter for each of the four inputs. The linear programing model of the planning problem enables one to solve for both the optimal (best) allocation of resources between projects in the planned sector and at the same time to determine the shadow prices which provide the test of optimality. The determination of the final shadow prices may be facilitated if the planners make initial estimates of the shadow prices. The initial estimates of the shadow prices of the resources used as inputs in the planned sector may be related to estimates of the opportunity cost of employing those resources in the non-planned sectors in the absence of any planned sector, or they may be based on an estimate of the opportunity cost of using inputs in previous planning periods. In any case there is no reason to assume that the initially estimated shadow prices will turn out to be the final shadow prices which provide a test of optimality of the plan.

The following information is known about the two projects: the first project uses a_{1U} units of unskilled labor, a_{1S} units of skilled labor, a_{1K} units of capital, and a_{1F} units of foreign exchange as inputs, and results in b_{1C} units of consumption goods, b_{1K} units of capital goods, and b_{1E} units of export goods. The second project uses a_{2U}, a_{2S}, a_{2K} and a_{2F} units of unskilled labor, skilled labor, capital, and foreign exchange, respectively, as inputs, and results in b_{2C}, b_{2K} and b_{2E} units of consumption goods, capital goods and export goods, respectively, as outputs. Assume that the initial estimates of the shadow prices (the opportunity costs of employing a unit of unskilled labor, skilled labor, capital, and foreign exchange in the unplanned sector) are constants, o_U, o_S, o_K, and o_F, respectively, and that r_U, r_S, r_K, and r_F are the respective limits of availability of the same inputs. Then the graph of the function relating price to the amount available of capital, for example, looks like that shown in Figure XVII–1 where q_K is the quantity of capital used as an input. When q_K reaches r_K, the limit of availability, the shadow price may rise above the initial shadow price.

The assumption that the opportunity costs or initial shadow prices are constant up to the limit of availability must be recognized as a particularly restrictive one which will be relaxed later. Recalling the discussion of the last chapter, note that it will generally be true that prices of inputs will rise as more are withdrawn from the unplanned sector. The shadow price should be above the opportunity cost in the unplanned sector if the total available supply of the factor is drawn into use in the planned sector.

The initial shadow prices of outputs of consumption and capital goods are estimated to be p_C and p_K respectively. If p_F is estimated as the opportunity cost of using foreign exchange and if p_E^* is the price of export goods in terms of foreign currency, then

$$p_E = p_F p_E^* \tag{17-1}$$

is the expression defining the initial shadow price of export goods in terms of domestic currency.

An extremely important assumption is made about the projects under

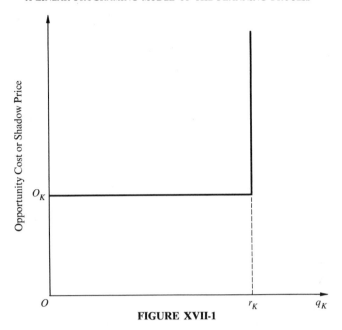

FIGURE XVII-1

consideration. It is assumed that as the scale of the project is changed, the proportions in which each input is used remain constant. As the scale at which the inputs are used is varied, the scale of output varies exactly in proportion. That is, constant proportionality of inputs and constant returns to scale are assumed. Thus, since project 1 uses a_{1U}, a_{1S}, a_{1K}, and a_{1F} units of unskilled labor, skilled labor, capital, and foreign exchange, respectively, to produce b_{1C}, b_{1K}, and b_{1E} units of consumption goods, capital goods, and export goods, respectively, constant returns to scale imply that $2a_{1U}$, $2a_{1S}$, $2a_{1K}$, and $2a_{1F}$ units of the same inputs can produce $2b_{1C}$, $2b_{1K}$, and $2b_{1E}$ units of the same outputs and no more. A similar statement may be made about project 2.

The scale at which project 1 is operated is denoted by x_1 and the scale at which project 2 is operated is denoted by x_2.* That is, the scale determines the number of units of each of the various types of inputs which are used and the number of units of output which are produced. For example, if $x_2 = 1$ (project 2 is operated at the unit scale), this implies that a_{2U}, a_{2S}, a_{2K}, and a_{2F} units of inputs of unskilled labor, skilled labor, capital, and

---

* The scale of a project is sometimes called an "activity level." The project itself is often called an "activity" if there is only one technically efficient way of conducting the project. If there are several alternative ways of conducting a project each using different combinations of inputs of the factors of production, then each technically efficient way of conducting the project is called an "activity."

foreign exchange, respectively, are used to produce b_{2C}, b_{2K}, and b_{2E} units of output of consumption goods, capital goods, and export goods, respectively. If $x_2 = 5/2$, however, $5/2 \cdot a_{2U}$, $5/2 \cdot a_{2K}$, and $5/2 \cdot a_{2F}$ units of the same inputs are used to produce $5/2 \cdot b_{2C}$, $5/2 \cdot b_{2K}$, and $5/2 \cdot b_{2F}$ units of the same outputs.

Now the total value of output or revenue of the first project when operating at a unit scale is the sum of the values of each type of output.

$$Z_1 = p_C b_{1C} + p_K b_{1K} + p_E b_{1E} \qquad (17\text{–}2)$$

Similarly the total value of the output or revenue of the second project when operating at a unit scale is

$$Z_2 = p_C b_{2C} + p_K b_{2K} + p_E b_{1E} \qquad (17\text{–}3)$$

The total opportunity cost of the first project when operating at a level to produce output Z_1 is the sum of the opportunity costs of employing each type of input.

$$O_1 = o_U a_{1U} + o_S a_{1S} + o_K a_{1K} + o_F a_{1F} \qquad (17\text{–}4)$$

Similarly, the opportunity cost involved in operating project 2 at Z_2 level of output is

$$O_2 = o_U a_{2U} + o_S a_{2S} + o_K a_{2K} + o_F a_{2F} \qquad (17\text{–}5)$$

The social product (or net value) resulting from the operation of project 1 at the accepted unit scale is defined as the value of the outputs less the opportunity cost of the inputs.

$$V_1 = Z_1 - O_1 \qquad (17\text{–}6)$$

For project 2 the social product is

$$V_2 = Z_2 - O_2 \qquad (17\text{–}7)$$

Then the total social product resulting from the operation of project 1 at scale x_1 and project 2 at scale x_2 is defined as:

$$SP = V_1 x_1 + V_2 x_2 \qquad (17\text{–}8)$$

This social product function then is the one that the planners attempt to maximize subject to the limits of availability of the inputs. If, in the extreme case all possible projects when operated at unit scale resulted in negative social product, then no projects would be undertaken in the planned sector, and all resources would be used in the non-planned sector. Clearly such a decision could not be arrived at from a consideration of only the output function. (For purposes of this problem it will be assumed that V_1 and V_2 are positive.)

The maximization of SP as given by equation (17–8) implies that the social welfare function is maximized as well. This is only the case if the shadow prices of the outputs are proportional to their social marginal utilities. It also implies that the level at which project 1 is operated does not affect the relative social gains which may be obtained from project 2, i.e., that there is no interaction between the two projects. For example, the social gains to be obtained from putting in a new rail line to a city depends on the projected industrial development in and near that city. This is a case of interaction and either the rail line and the industrial development of the city must be lumped together as one project or methods other than linear programing must be used.

Some authors claim that maximization of SP is not a correct way to maximize social welfare since SP does not take into account the effects of income distribution. Purely in "value-judgment" terms, of course, planners and politicians may have reasons for preferring more equitable income distributions to those which create or perpetuate great disparities between rich and poor. Leaving these judgments aside, it is still true that income distribution may legitimately be held up as a proper concern of planners. This is primarily because of the effect of income distribution on savings.*

For example, consider two projects one of which uses more labor (relatively) and the other of which uses more capital (relatively). These "more" and "less" judgments depend, of course, on the ability to measure the value placed by society on the two outputs. It is generally true that savings will form a very small percentage of incomes received by households (savings will be a very small percentage of wages). It is also typically true that savings will form a significantly greater proportion of the returns paid for the services of capital (gross profit including interest). Thus, the project which uses relatively more labor and has a relatively higher wage bill may produce a considerably lower total of savings than will the other. Such effects will be neglected when SP is considered in isolation.

In maximizing SP, the planner must take into account the restrictions resulting from the limits of availability of the various inputs. Let $q_U, q_S, q_K,$ and q_F be the total amount of the input of unskilled labor, skilled labor, capital, and foreign exchange used up, respectively, by both projects in the plan. The amount of unskilled labor input used up by project 1 is $a_{1U}x_1$ and the amount used up by the second project is $a_{2U}x_2$. The total amount used up is $q_U = a_{1U}x_1 + a_{2U}x_2$. The total amount of unskilled labor used

* See W. Galenson and H. Leibenstein, "Investment Criteria, Productivity and Economic Development," *Quarterly Journal of Economics*, Vol. LXIX (1955), p. 343.

up must be less than r_U, the total amount available. In mathematical form this relationship is expressed by an inequality, $q_U \leq r_U$. There are four such inequalities, one for each of the inputs as follows:

$$q_U = a_{1U}x_1 + a_{2U}x_2 \leq r_U$$
$$q_S = a_{1S}x_1 + a_{2S}x_2 \leq r_S$$
$$q_K = a_{1K}x_1 + a_{2K}x_2 \leq r_K \tag{17-9}$$
$$q_F = a_{1F}x_1 + a_{2F}x_2 \leq r_F$$

In order to be an optimal development plan (one for which SP is maximized within the restrictions adopted) the plan must include the proper scale of operation for each project. The scales of operation x_1 and x_2 must not be negative since it is assumed to be impossible to operate a project in reverse. In addition, x_1 and x_2 must satisfy the inequalities in (17–9). The set of values for x_1 and x_2 which satisfy these inequalities may be shown graphically as in Figure XVII–2. Any set of values for x_1 and x_2 represented by a point in the shaded area of the diagram satisfies all the inequalities, i.e., represents a scale of operation for project 1 and project 2 such that the amount of no input exceeds its limit of availability.

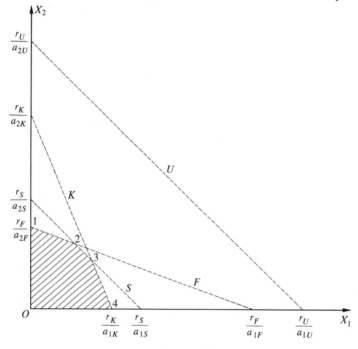

FIGURE XVII-2

All points on the dotted line labelled U in Figure XVII–2 represent combinations of x_1 and x_2 which use up the total available supply of r_U of unskilled labor, i.e., all points which satisfy the equation

$$q_U = a_{1U}x_1 + a_{2U}x_2 = r_U \qquad (17\text{--}10)$$

This is the equation of a straight line with a slope of a_{1U}/a_{2U}, and intercept on the x_2 axis of r_U/a_{2U}, and an intercept on the x_1 axis of r_U/a_{1U}. The intercept on the x_2 axis is the amount of unskilled labor which project 2 can use at the maximum and still not exceed the available supply. The intercept on the x_1 axis is the maximum of unskilled labor which can be used by project 1 and still not exceed the available supply. Any point which lies below the dotted line labelled U represents combinations of x_1 and x_2 which use less than the available supply of unskilled labor. Similarly, the dotted lines labelled S, F, and K represent combinations of x_1 and x_2 which use up the available supplies r_S, r_K, and r_F of skilled labor, capital, and foreign exchange, respectively. Points which lie below and to the left of these dotted lines represent combinations of x_1 and x_2 which use less than the available supply of the various inputs. The shaded area is the set of combinations of x_1 and x_2 which lie below all the dotted lines simultaneously, i.e., which use up no more than the available supply of all inputs.

The slope and positions of the dotted lines drawn in Figure XVII–2 imply that unskilled labor will never be used to the limit of availability by the projects in the planned sectors. Rather the limitations imposed by the availabilities of skilled labor, capital, and foreign exchange are always more serious than those imposed by the availability of unskilled labor. This is what is usually meant by the phrase "development planning with unlimited supplies of labor."* The availability of unskilled labor r_U is not infinitely large but is so much greater than r_K, r_S, and r_F relative to the needs of the projects in the plan, that it may be disregarded.

Linear combinations of x_1 and x_2 giving different values for social product ($SP = V_1 . x_1 + V_2 . x_2$) are represented in Figure XVII–3 by the series of dotted lines. The dotted line labelled SP_3 represents all combinations of x_1 and x_2 which give a value of SP equal to a specific value, SP_3. All dotted lines above and to the right of the one labelled SP_3 give a higher social product and all dotted lines below and to the left of the line SP_3 give a lower social product. The slope of all the dotted lines is the same, and the absolute value of the slope is V_1/V_2 or the ratio of the net values of project 1 and project 2. The maximum possible value of social product

---

* See W. Arthur Lewis, "Economic Development with Unlimited Supplies of Labour," *The Manchester School*, May, 1954, reprinted in A. N. Agarwala and S. P. Singh, editors, *The Economics of Underdevelopment*, New York, Oxford University Press, 1963, p. 400.

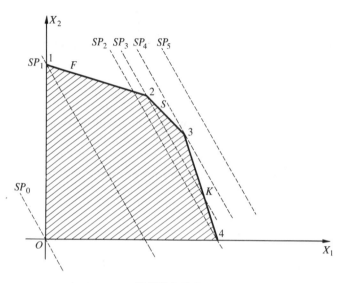

FIGURE XVII-3

in the problem is determined by the dotted line which just touches the shaded area. In Figure XVII–3 the maximum occurs at point 3. From Figure XVII–2 it is seen that this means that skilled labor and capital are used to the limit availability since point 3 lies on the dotted lines labelled K and S, but that the amounts used of foreign exchange and unskilled labor is less than the available limit since point 3 lies below and to the left of the lines labelled U and F.

It is important to realize that the particular shape of the technically feasible area in Figures XVII–2 and XVII–3 depends on the relative sizes of the various a's and r's. Furthermore, the slope of the set of lines SP in Figure XVII–3 will depend on the shadow prices of the inputs and outputs of the planned sector; on the technical characteristics of each project (i.e., on the relationships existing among the various a's and b's for each project), and in particular on the ratio V_1 to V_2.

It is important to understand that the result obtained in the example depends entirely on the implicit assumptions made about the relative values of the a's and b's, and about the ratio of V_1 to V_2, i.e., if the slope of the SP lines were decreased in absolute value, the optimal point could be shifted to point 2, and if V_1 were still lower relative to V_2 the optional point might be point 1. In more intuitive terms, as the net return of project 1, is assumed to fall relative to that of project 2, the tendency will be for project 2 to be increased in size relative to project 1. At the same time, this tendency will cause the factor or factors used most heavily by project

2 to become the scarce factors. The opposite effects will be noticed if V_1 is assumed to rise relative to V_2. These various possibilities are illustrated in Figure XVII–4 and are expressed in a different way in Table XVII–1.

The reader might consider how the results would change as the relative values of a_{1F} and a_{2F}; a_{1K} and a_{2K}; a_{1U} and a_{2U}; and a_{1S} and a_{2S} change.

B. The Final Shadow Prices

The solution for the optimum scales of projects 1 and 2 found above depend on the assumption that the initial shadow prices were, indeed, constants over the whole range of factor usage up to the limit of availability. As has been suggested above, when the use of a factor in the planned sector

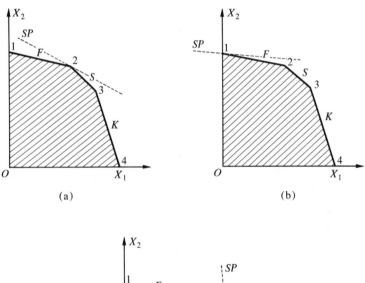

(a)   (b)

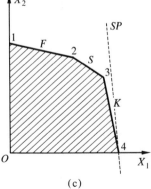

(c)

FIGURE XVII-4

TABLE XVII–1

Alternative Optimum Points

Values of V_1, V_2 and V_1/V_2	Optimum Point	Scarce Factors	Project Mix	Comments
V_1 very low relative to V_2	1	Foreign exchange only	Project 2 only	Project 2 uses foreign exchange relatively heavily.
V_1 somewhat larger relative to V_2	2	Foreign exchange and skilled labor	Project 2 and Project 1	Project 2 uses foreign exchange relatively heavily. Both projects use skilled labor to about the same degree.
V_1 still larger relative to V_2	3	Skilled labor and capital	Project 1 and Project 2	Projects 1 and 2 use skilled labor to about the same degree. Project 1 uses capital relatively heavily.
V_1 very large relative to V_2	4	Capital only	Project 1 only	Project 1 uses capital relatively heavily.

reaches the limit of availability, its price will rise above its opportunity cost in the unplanned sector. The new price set for the factors of production will be known as the final shadow prices. For factors used up to the limit of availability these will be the opportunity costs of shifting the factor within the planned sector from one project to another. For factors not used up to this limit, the final shadow price will equal the initial shadow price.

The final shadow prices must satisfy a number of conditions and these are the subject of this section. The prices themselves would be solved for on the basis of the required conditions. Such problems are, in general, difficult of solution.

1. Condition A.

Every project included as part of the optimal plan must not result in a loss when operated at a positive scale (and every project not included must not result in a profit) when all inputs are valued at final shadow prices.

The following notation will be adopted:

L_K = final shadow price of capital.
L_U = final shadow price of unskilled labor.
L_S = final shadow price of skilled labor.

L_F = final shadow price of foreign exchange.

x_1^* = the optimal scale for operation of project 1.

x_2^* = the optimal scale for operation of project 2.

P_1 = profit (total revenue − total cost) resulting from operation of project 1 at a unit scale ($x_1 = 1$).

P_2 = profit resulting from operation of project 2 at a unit scale ($x_2 = 1$).

Symbolically,

$$P_1 = Z_1 - L_U a_{1U} - L_S a_{1S} - L_K a_{1K} - L_F a_{1F} \qquad (17-11)$$
$$P_2 = Z_2 - L_U a_{2U} - L_S a_{2S} - L_K a_{2K} - L_K a_{2F}$$

where Z_1 and Z_2 are the net revenues of projects 1 and 2, respectively, as given in (17–2) and (17–3). In this notation, the condition becomes:

If $x_1^* > 0$, then $P_1 \geq 0$ (17–12)

If $x_2^* > 0$, then $P_2 \geq 0$

and,

If $x_1^* = 0$, then $P_1 \leq 0$ (17–13)

If $x_2^* = 0$, then $P_2 \leq 0$

2. Condition B.

A project which is included in the plan must result in zero profit and not a positive profit. A positive profit of a project under the assumption of constant returns to scale means that total profit can be increased indefinitely by increasing the scale of that project. This condition allows the modification of (17–12) to

If $x_1^* > 0$, then $P_1 = 0$ (17–12a)

and if $x_2^* > 0$, then $P_2 = 0$

3. Condition C.

The final shadow price of each input must not be less than the opportunity cost of that input in the non-planned sector. Clearly it would pay to shift factors into the non-planned sector if their final shadow prices were less than their opportunity costs in that sector.

Symbolically,

$$L_U \geq o_U$$
$$L_S \geq o_S \qquad (17-14)$$
$$L_K \geq o_K$$
$$L_F \geq o_F$$

4. *Condition D.*

If the final shadow price of an input is greater than its opportunity cost in the non-planned sector, then the planned sector must be using that factor up to the limit of its availability. This new price represents the opportunity cost involved in shifting the input *between* projects in the planned sector. In symbols, we may write Condition D as follows:

If $L_U > o_U$, then $q_U{}^* = r_U$

If $L_S > o_S$, then $q^{S*} = r_S$ $\qquad\qquad$ (17–15)

If $L_K > o_K$, then $q_K{}^* = r_K$

If $L_F > o_F$, then $q_F{}^* = r_F$

where $q_U{}^*$, $q_S{}^*$, $q_K{}^*$, and $q_F{}^*$ are the amounts of the four factors used when projects 1 and 2 are operated at their respective optimal scales $x_1{}^*$ and $x_2{}^*$. For example,

$$q_U{}^* = a_{1U}x_1{}^* + a_{2U}x_2{}^*$$

It is possible to prove that any set of final shadow prices which satisfies the above conditions also minimizes the following function:

$$L = L_U r_U + L_S r_S + L_K r_K + L_F r_F \qquad\qquad (17\text{–}16)$$

This function is simply the total value of the resources.

The task of finding the final shadow prices can be reduced to a linear programing problem, the *dual* linear program to the original linear programing problem of maximizing social product subject to resource constraints. The dual linear program involves maximizing (17–16) subject to a set of constraints which specify that no project can make a profit, namely

$$P_1 \leqq 0 \qquad\qquad (17\text{–}17)$$
$$P_2 \leqq 0$$

C. More Complex Planning Processes

The hypothetical planning problem discussed in the first part of this chapter was extremely simple and involved very rigid assumptions in order that the basic concepts could be made clear. In practice, the planning process and the objectives and constraints in planning may be much more complex. First, the number of constraints may be greater than the four considered in this chapter, the very general limits on the availability of unskilled labor, skilled labor, capital, and foreign exchange. One may have to consider limitations on the availability of several different types of capital rather than the all-inclusive limitation on capital goods in general. There may also be certain types of land which are in limited supply such as land with desirable locations near commercial centers and agricultural land of high fertility and good rainfall. There may be several different categories of skilled labor. In addition, some of the objectives in planning may be stated in terms of output targets for certain sectors of the economy. In principle, targets on the output of certain sectors can be treated similarly to resource constraints (limitations on the availability of certain resources). The output of all projects within a given sector can be subject to the condition that they must sum up to an amount greater than the specified target. This condition can be specified mathematically in terms of an inequality, similar to the mathematical inequalities which represent resource constraints. When targets are specified, then the maximization of social product involves minimizing the social (opportunity) cost of achieving the target rate of output. Mathematically, minimization is no different in principle than maximization (minimizing cost is the same as maximizing the negative of cost). Thus the linear programing format may be used to handle output targets in planning.

A second complication which arises in actual planning problems is a rising opportunity cost as more and more of a resource is used in the planned sector. Throughout the first part of this chapter it was assumed

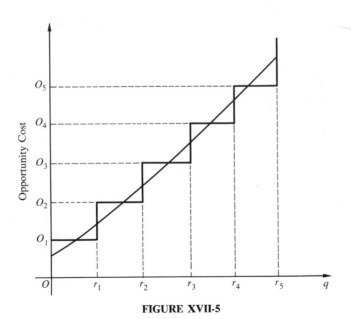

FIGURE XVII-5

that the opportunity cost of using resources in the unplanned sectors was constant up to the absolute limit of availability. It is possible to allow for the effect of increasing opportunity costs, and in practice it will probably be desirable to do so. A rising opportunity cost is approximated by the "step" function shown in Figure XVII–5 where the curved line represents the true rising opportunity cost as the amount q of the resource approaches the limit of availability r. One then assumes that there are as many different types of the resource as there are "steps" in the step function shown in Figure XVII–5. In this case there are five "steps," corresponding to five different levels of opportunity cost, o_1, o_2, o_3, o_4, o_5, and hence one assumes five different types of the resource with upper limits of availability of r_1, r_2-r_1, r_3-r_2, r_4-r_3, and r_5-r_4, respectively. It is assumed that each of these five different types of resources have a constant opportunity cost. For example, the opportunity cost for the third of these five types is shown in Figure XVII–6 as a constant o_3 up to where the amount q_3 of the third type of resource reaches the limit of availability r_3-r_2.

The breakdown of one resource into five types of that resource introduces four additional constraints into the problem (i.e., four additional inequalities like those shown in (17–9)). In addition, there will be a number of new projects involved in the planning decisions. For each project which uses the resource which has been split up into five types must be decomposed into five different projects. The a's and b's of each of these five projects will remain the same as the original project, i.e., the projects when operated at a unit scale use up the same number of units of each of the five types of resources as the original project used of the original single resource, but the opportunity cost of each of the projects will be different, depending on the five different levels of opportunity cost for the original resource.

A third assumption in the hypothetical planning problem discussed in the first part of this chapter is that there are constant returns to scale. It is possible to take into account decreasing returns to scale through approximation and in practice decreasing returns often are prevalent. The method can be illustrated briefly by a discussion of a single project planning problem. Let the single project use up a_1 units of one resource and a_2 units of a second resource to produce y units of output. Suppose that as x, the scale of operation, varies, the average output (output divided by the scale of operation, y/x) falls (decreasing returns) as illustrated by the curved line in Figure XVII–7. As the line flattens out constant returns are achieved for large values of x. The falling average output curve in Figure XVII–7 is approximated by a step function.

The single project may be divided into four conceptually different projects, one corresponding to each of the "steps" in Figure XVII–7. The scales of each of these projects is denoted by x_1, x_2, x_3, and x_4, respectively.

When x is between 0 and c_1 $(0 \leq x \leq c_1)$, the scale x is denoted by x_1 and average output $y/x_1 = b_1$ or $y = b_1 . x_1$. If p_1 is the value of a unit of output, then the net social product of the first project per unit scale of operation $(x_1 = 1)$ is

$$v_1 = p_1 b_1 - a_1 o_1 - a_2 o_2 \qquad (17\text{--}18)$$

where o_1 and o_2 are the opportunity costs of the two resources. Similarly, the net social product per unit scale of operation of the three other conceptually different projects is

$$
\begin{aligned}
v_2 &= p_2 b_2 - a_1 o_1 - a_2 o_2 \\
v_3 &= p_3 b_3 - a_1 o_1 - a_2 o_2 \\
v_4 &= p_4 b_4 - a_1 o_1 - a_2 o_2
\end{aligned}
\qquad (17\text{--}19)
$$

The total social product is

$$SP = v_1 x_1 + v_2 x_2 + v_3 x_3 + v_4 x_4 \qquad (17\text{--}20)$$

The scales x_1 through x_3 only apply over a limited range. For example x_3 only applies where x is between c_2 and c_3. Thus x_3 must be less than the difference, $c_3 - c_2$. The scale x_4 applies over all values greater than c_3; hence there is no absolute limitation on the scale x_4. The limitation on the first three x's may be written symbolically.

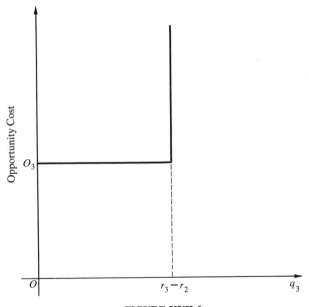

FIGURE XVII-6

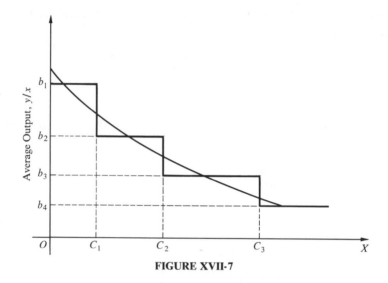

FIGURE XVII-7

$$x_1 \leqq c_1$$
$$x_2 \leqq c_2 - c_1 \qquad (17\text{-}21)$$
$$x_3 \leqq c_3 - c_2$$

In addition the amounts of the two resources used by the planned sectors must not exceed the limits of availability r_1 and r_2

$$a_1 x_1 + a_1 x_2 + a_1 x_3 + a_1 x_4 \leqq r_1$$
$$a_2 x_1 + a_2 x_2 + a_2 x_3 + a_2 x_4 \leqq r_2 \qquad (17\text{-}22)$$

The planner tries to maximize SP as given in (17-20) provided that the x's are not negative and satisfy the inequalities in (17-21) and (17-22).

In taking account of decreasing returns to scale, the planner increases the complexity of his problem. New conceptual projects are added and new constraints such as those in (17-21) are introduced. The increased complexity often makes the use of linear programing techniques a more realistic approach,* but at the same time makes a solution more difficult

---

* The increased complexity makes programing techniques more realistic in another sense. It is a well known theorem that the solution to a linear programing problem never results in more projects being operated at positive scales than there are constraints. If all projects are characterized by constant returns and all resources have constant opportunity costs, then this theorem reduces to the statement that the number of resources places an upper limit on the number of projects which are carried out. This would seem to be an unrealistic limitation in practice. With the introduction of decreasing returns and increasing opportunity costs, the number of projects being operated may be much greater than the number of scarce resources due to the increased number of constraints such as those in (17-21).

to obtain. The planner must always strike a judicious compromise between these two aspects of programing techniques.

While linear programing techniques may be modified to approximate decreasing returns and rising opportunity costs, such techniques must be abandoned when dealing with problems involving increasing returns or falling opportunity costs (due to increasing returns in the unplanned sector). Very little is known about how to attack such problems either conceptually or in practice.

One approach is to use integer programing methods.* Integer programing is similar to linear programing except that certain scales of operation are required to be integers, 0, 1, 2, 3, etc., and are not permitted to attain fractional values. A discussion of these techniques, however, is beyond the scope of this volume.

D. Methods of Solution of Linear Programing Problems

If the planners can specify a social product function such as (17–8) and can indicate the constraints on the use of resources imposed by the limits of availability or the constraints imposed by targets on various outputs in terms of inequalities as in (17–9), then the planning problem has been reduced to a problem in linear programing. A small problem might be solved by hand calculations but for most practical applications of this technique, the number of projects and constraints would be so large that computation by electronic computer would be necessary. Many different numerical computation schemes have been proposed for solving linear programing problems. All of them have one thing in common. A solution is reached by successive approximations to an optimal or best plan. Some of the techniques involve allocating the available resources to different projects or groups of projects, calculating the returns from this allocation, and then reallocating the available resources in a way which increases the total social product. The process is continued until it is no longer possible to reallocate resources so that total social product increases. The rule for reallocation is that where marginal returns to projects or groups of projects are positive, more resources should be allocated. Other techniques work directly on the shadow prices. Shadow prices are estimated and compared with the marginal revenue productivity of the various resources within the planned sector. If the marginal revenue productivity of a resource is greater than its shadow price, the shadow price is raised. An optimal solution is reached when the marginal revenue productivity of each resource used within the planned sector is equal to its shadow price. Finally, still other

* See H. M. Markowitz and A. S. Manne, "On the Solution of Discrete Programming Problems," *Econometrica*, Vol. 25, No. 1.

techniques operate on resource allocation and shadow prices simultaneously to reach a solution.

Economists have pointed out that the principles used in linear programing solution techniques may be applied to the actual planning process in order to arrive at an optimal or at least an approximation to an optimal plan. The way in which this might be done is explained in the last chapter of this book. At the same time actual linear programing solution techniques might be applied to specific planning problems if sufficient data is available and if the objectives and constraints can be meaningfully identified. The field of application for actual linear programing techniques, however, is probably severely limited in most countries and especially in the less-developed countries due to lack of data and the tremendous cost often involved in specifying the objectives and constraints. Linear programing techniques often find more fruitful application in solving very specific and well defined problems within particular sectors of the economy. This may be true, for example, of the transport sector in which costs and benefits may be much more susceptible to this kind of analysis. A study of the principles involved in linear programing, on the other hand, can lead to a better understanding of the entire planning process and the rationale of using the principles of shadow pricing in actual programing of development plans.

E. Rules of Thumb and Linear Programing

It is often the case that linear programing techniques will not be feasible to use in planning because of the difficulties of computation and the very large quantities of information needed. There are, however, certain simple rules which have been suggested as criteria for the choice of projects and for allocating resources to different sectors of the economy. These simple rules are called *rules of thumb*. If a planner uses certain rules of thumb, he is often implicitly assuming that where they are applied, planning problems can be reduced to very simple types of linear programs. In this section we will describe some of the more commonly suggested rules of thumb, possible assumptions implicit in them, and the limitations of rules of thumb in planning.

Some of the simple rules which have been suggested in the literature on investment criteria are set out below:

(1) *Maximize ratio of net output (social product) to capital*: If this rule is used projects will always be chosen or resources allocated to sectors which most economize on capital.

(2) *Maximize ratio of net output (social product) to foreign exchange input*: In this case the projects will be chosen which most economize on foreign exchange.

(3) *Maximize the ratio of net output (social product) to skilled labor input*: Projects and sectors will be chosen as to minimize the use of skilled labor.

(4) *Maximize the ratio of unskilled labor input to capital input*: By this rule the attempt would be made to utilize scarce capital in the best possible way by applying it to the maximum amount of unskilled labor with its very low opportunity cost.

Each of the above rules provides a plan which maximizes social product provided certain assumptions concerning final shadow prices are satisfied and provided the planning problem can be reduced to certain simple types of linear programing problems. Rule (1), for example, is correct if capital is the only scarce resource (capital and only capital gives a marginal revenue productivity in the planned sector greater than its initial opportunity cost in the unplanned sector). If any other input is used in the planned sector, it must not be used up to its limit of availability and its opportunity cost must not have risen from its initial value in the unplanned sector. This implies that the final shadow price of capital is above its initial opportunity cost in the unplanned sector while the final shadow prices of all the other inputs are equal to their initial opportunity costs. Rule (1) is applicable if the planning problem can be reduced to a linear (or non-linear) programing problem in which there is one constraint, namely a limitation on the amount of capital which is available.* Rules (2) and (3) can always be applied correctly if foreign exchange and skilled labor are the *only* scarce factors, respectively.

Rule (4) is sometimes suggested as an alternative to Rule (1). Rule (4) says to choose projects which are more labor intensive, i.e., use more unskilled labor per unit of capital. This rule can be extremely misleading since it does not incorporate a measure of the addition to social product. For example, one project may use both less labor and less capital than another project to obtain the same net addition output, although the other project may have a greater ratio of unskilled labor input to capital input. Clearly the first project may be preferable, although the criterion of rule (4) would lead to the choice of the second project. If capital is the only scarce resource and if for the same addition to net output, project 1 uses less capital than project 2 while using more labor than project 2, then project 1 is preferable to project 2. That is, rule (4) is equivalent to rule (1) under certain circumstances. Since rule (1) is always optimal if capital is the only scarce resource, rule (1) is preferable when it can be applied.

In applying any of the first three rules of thumb it is important to

---

* A non-linear programing problem results whenever there are decreasing returns or rising opportunity costs. Such a non-linear problem can be reduced to a linear programing problem by linear approximations of decreasing returns or rising opportunity costs.

maximize the ratios of net output to the scarce resource. That is, one must take the output valued at the proper shadow prices and subtract out the opportunity cost of intermediate products. The planner must be careful, however, of the way in which he calculates net output. Net output (or social value added as one may call it) may be approached from an output point of view or from a cost point of view. From the cost point of view, net output may be considered as the payments to all factors of production. Estimates of net output based on this approach may be inflated, especially for projects which are not socially profitable. The output point of view is the preferable one to use when estimating net output for the purpose of applying rules of thumb.*

The first three rules of thumb may be applied even though other resources have positive opportunity costs. When applying each rule, however, the proper procedure is to value output net of intermediate product inputs *and* net of the opportunity cost of non-scarce factors. For example, rule (1) may be applied even though the opportunity costs of skilled labor and foreign exchange are not zero. Output (social product) should be measured net of intermediate product costs and net of the opportunity costs of skilled labor, foreign exchange, and any other resources used. If social product is not measured in this manner, it is possible to produce an example of a planning problem in which social product is not maximized upon application of rule (1) even though capital is the only scarce factor. When social product is measured net of intermediate input costs but not net of the opportunity cost of other resources, rule (1) is generally applicable only if the opportunity cost of other resources, rule (1) is generally applicable only if the opportunity cost of other resources is zero.

Any of the first three rules may be applied even though the opportunity cost of the scarce input rises as more and more of that resource is used. As opportunity cost in the unplanned sector rises, it becomes less and less profitable to extend the size of the planned sector. The planned sector reaches its optimal size whenever enough projects have been chosen so that the addition to net output per unit of the scarce input used is equal to the opportunity cost of the scarce input.

The first three rules of thumb may also be used even though there are decreasing returns. When decreasing returns prevail for some projects, it is important to interpret the rules of thumb in terms of *marginal* net output. As the return to a project decreases with increasing scale, other projects may become more desirable. A project should be increased in scale only up to the point where the ratio of marginal net output to capital is no longer greater than the ratios for other projects not included in the plan.

So far, emphasis has been placed on specifying the conditions under

* Cf. the discussion in Chapter XI.

which each of the suggested rules of thumb is applicable, i.e., always provides an optimal plan. The conditions under which any of the suggested rules of thumb is applicable are quite restrictive. In general, one would expect more than one scarce resource. The rules may retain some validity, however, if it can be shown that they provide good guide-lines for the allocation of scarce resources even though they do not necessarily provide optimal plans. For example, if capital is a scarce resource (but not the only scarce resource), then rule (1) ought to provide a better guide to allocation than some rule involving a non-scarce factor. Unfortunately, it can be shown that in some cases it would be better to maximize the ratio of net output to unskilled labor, even though unskilled labor is not scarce, than it would be to maximize the ratio of net output to a scarce factor such as capital. That is, a plan resulting in greater social product is obtainable by using the former criterion rather than the latter.

One way in which the rules of thumb may be modified to account for more than one scarce factor is to maximize a weighted average of ratios involving the scarce factors. For example, if capital, foreign exchange, and skilled labor are all scarce factors, one might choose projects which maximize:

$$w_1 R_1 + w_2 R_2 + w_3 R_3 \qquad\qquad (17\text{--}23)$$

Where w_1, w_2, and w_3 are weights and R_1, R_2, and R_3 are ratios of net output to capital, foreign exchange, and skilled labor. The major difficulty in this approach is the choice of proper weights. It is possible to demonstrate that ratios between the proper weights are equal to the ratios between the final shadow prices for the scarce resources. Thus the choice of proper weights is equivalent to the choice of final shadow prices. The modified rule of thumb is really no more simple to use than linear programing techniques.

F. Conclusion

The discussion of linear programing and rules of thumb in this chapter completes our introduction to most of the quantitative techniques which may be used in planning. Business accounting, inter-industry accounting, and national accounts were discussed in the first three sections of this book. The way in which all of these techniques may be used in the planning process will be summarized in the next and final chapter which systematically outlines the three stages in the planning process.

XVIII

STAGES IN THE PLANNING PROCESS

The process of drawing up a development plan usefully can be divided into three stages:

(i) The *aggregate stage* involves setting a target rate of growth for gross domestic product and determining the amount of investment (capital formation) and government activity which are necessary to achieve this goal.

(ii) The *sectoral stage* requires targets to be set for each individual sector of the economy. Capital is allocated to each sector to achieve these targets.

(iii) The *project stage* entails the choice of specific projects to be included in sectoral investment programs.

Planning at all three stages may proceed simultaneously in time. Information revealed at one stage of the planning process will very often be useful and necessary for other stages. Planning must be viewed both as a forward process and as a backward or feedback process. An initial set of plans may first be drawn up for the first (aggregate) stage and then for the second (sectoral) and third (project) stages. Planning is a feedback process in the sense that once the second stage plans have been formulated, the result may be incompatible with the first stage plans as originally conceived. In this case, the first stage plans will then have to be revised in light of the information revealed in second stage planning. Ideally, this process should repeat itself continually until a mutually compatible, consistent, efficient, and optimal set of plans for all stages has been worked out. In practice, the process is repeated one or two times at best.

At each stage in the planning process, the three planning criteria discussed in the previous chapter ought to be checked. The checking of plans for consistency, efficiency, and optimality often involves the use of the techniques outlined in the previous chapters of this volume. At the aggregate stage, social or aggregate accounting techniques will prove most useful. At the second or sectoral stage, input-output techniques may help in checking consistency and may also be utilized in conjunction with the related techniques of linear programing and rules of thumb to check for optimality. At the third (project) stage, business accounting techniques should prove invaluable. Here again linear programing and rules of thumb may play their part, perhaps even more so than in the second stage.

A. The Aggregate Stage

The first stage in the planning process involves choosing a target rate of growth for the whole economy. In order to enable that choice to be consistent, efficient, and optimal, the planners and policy makers must take into account the relationship between the rate of growth of the economy and the amount of capital formation (investment), the amount of private savings, government current expenditure and taxation, foreign investment, the balance of payments, the rate of growth in trained manpower, and the rate of population growth. All of these factors are inter-related in various ways and the relationships must be accounted for in any reasonably comprehensive plan.

1. *Capital Formation and Growth*

The rate of growth of the economy depends to a large extent on the rate of capital formation—the proportion of gross domestic product which goes into investment. In general, the greater the rate of capital formation, the greater is the rate of growth of the economy. The relationship between rates of growth and rates of capital formation is usually formulated, as a first approximation, in terms of the marginal capital-output ratio, sometimes called the incremental capital-output ratio (ICOR). As pointed out in Chapter XV, the marginal capital-output ratio indicates the amount of capital formation necessary to produce a unit increase in gross domestic product. For example, if the marginal capital-output ratio is 3 (sometimes stated 3 to 1), then an increase in gross domestic product of $1,000 requires an investment of $3,000. In using the capital-output ratio, the planner should, of course, be aware of its limitations. There is no reason to believe that every $1,000 increase in GDP requires an investment of $3,000. Some investment projects may have a very high capital-output ratio (a hydroelectric project for example) while other projects may have very low ratios (e.g., a handicrafts project). Some sectors of the economy are characterized by high capital-output ratios (public utilities) and others by low ratios (peasant agriculture). The capital-output ratio is particularly sensitive to the life of the capital, i.e., the length of time during which the capital investment can be expected to yield returns. Investments with long lives tend to have high capital-output ratios because output is usually measured in terms of annual contribution to GDP. Thus the incremental capital-output ratio is highly dependent on the project mix in each sector and the relative sectoral development patterns. Capital-output ratios, however, have shown remarkable stability over time for many countries, indicating that at least as a first approximation the capital-output ratio may be inferred from past behavior. The use of such ratios, however, must be accompanied by close attention to possible changes in relative sectoral development. Such changes will become more obvious in the second (sectoral) stage of planning and, if significant may require a reformulation of the first stage analysis.

The rate of growth of gross domestic product as determined by the capital-output ratio and the rate of investment can be expressed in terms of the following formula:

$$dY = \frac{I}{a}, \qquad\qquad (18\text{--}1)$$

where Y is gross domestic product, I is investment, and a is the incremental capital-output ratio. dY represents an increase in GDP. For example, if the marginal capital-output ratio is 3 and investment is $6,000, then the increase in GDP will be $6000/3 = $2000. If we divide both sides of (18–1) by Y, the result is a formula which gives the *rate* of increase of GDP, i.e., the absolute increase in GDP divided by the total amount of GDP, as a function of the capital-output ratio and the *rate* of investment.

$$\frac{dY}{Y} = \frac{1}{a} \cdot \frac{I}{Y} \qquad\qquad (18\text{--}2)$$

The relationship for some specific capital-output ratios, and investment rates is illustrated below:

If a equals,	and I/Y equals,	then dY/Y equals
2	.10	.050
3	.10	.033
4	.10	.025
2	.20	.100
3	.20	.067
4	.20	.050

This table illustrates two facts. First, obviously the higher the rate of investment, the higher the rate of growth with a given capital-output ratio. For example, if the capital-output ratio is 4, and the rate of investment is 10 per cent of GDP, the rate of growth is 2.5 per cent. If the rate of investment is increased to 20 per cent of GDP with the same capital-output ratio, the rate of growth increases to 5 per cent. Secondly, the higher the capital-output ratio, the slower the rate of growth of GDP given the rate of investment. While a 10 per cent rate of growth of GDP may be achieved with a capital-output ratio of 2 and 20 per cent of GDP going to investment, the rate of growth is only 5 per cent if the capital-output ratio is 4 and the rate of investment the same.

2. *Domestic Saving, Foreign Investment, and Growth*

The rate of growth of the economy depends on the capital-output ratio and the rate of investment. The rate of investment, in turn, depends on private domestic saving, government saving (government revenue for development purposes or total tax revenue less recurrent government expenditure) and the amount of foreign investment. The following formula expresses this relationship:

$$I = S_p + S_g + F \qquad (18\text{--}3)$$

We may substitute this expression into (18–1).

$$\frac{dY}{Y} = \frac{1}{a} \cdot \frac{(S_p + S_g + F)}{Y} \qquad (18\text{--}4)$$

This result shows that the rate of growth of the economy can only be increased by increasing the ratio of private or government saving, or foreign investment to gross domestic product.

3. *The Balance of Payments and Growth*

Another consideration which must be taken into account at the aggregate stage of planning is the relationship between the balance of payments and the rate of growth of GDP. There are three basic sources of foreign exchange to finance the total import bill of a developing economy, foreign exchange obtained in return for exports, from foreign loans, and by running down foreign exchange reserves. Thus

$$M = E + F + R \qquad (18\text{--}5)$$

where M is the total import bill, E is exports, F is foreign investment, and R is the reduction in foreign exchange reserves. From this equation, it is obvious that the only way to *increase* imports is by increasing exports, foreign investment, or the running down of foreign exchange reserves, i.e.,

$$dM = dE + dF + dR. \qquad (18\text{--}6)$$

If b_m is the marginal propensity to import out of GDP, then an increase of income, dY, will be accompanied by an increase of imports given by the following equation:

$$dM = b_m dY \tag{18-7}$$

Now substitute (18–7) into (18–6)

$$b_m dY = dE + dF + dR, \text{ or} \tag{18-8}$$

$$\frac{dY}{Y} = \frac{1}{b_m} \cdot \frac{(dE + dF + dR)}{Y} \tag{18-9}$$

That is, the rate of growth of GDP is dependent on the ratio of the increase in exports, in foreign investment, and in running down of reserves to gross domestic product and on the marginal propensity to import out of GDP. A lowering of b_m, the marginal propensity to import, increases the possible rate of growth of GDP. If b_m cannot be decreased, the only way to increase growth is to increase the rate of running down of foreign exchange reserves. This policy cannot be continued indefinitely, and eventually the rate of growth will have to fall off when a balance of payments crisis is reached, i.e., when reserves are in danger of being exhausted.

4. Skilled Manpower and Growth

A third relationship which must be taken into account at the aggregate planning stage is that between the rate of growth of income and that of skilled manpower. An increased supply of skilled manpower is dependent on the output of skilled personnel from the educational system (including students educated abroad) and the net importation of skilled expatriate manpower.

$$dW = O_e + M_w \tag{18-10}$$

where dW is the increase in skilled manpower, O_e is the output of the educational system, and M_w is the net importation of skilled expatriate manpower. The demand for increased high level manpower is dependent on the rate of growth of GDP.

$$dW = b_w dY \tag{18-11}$$

where b_w is the increase in skilled manpower needed per unit increase in GDP. Combining (18–10) and (18–11), we get

$$\frac{dY}{Y} = \frac{(O_e + M_w)}{b_w Y} \tag{18-12}$$

The rate of growth of GDP is dependent on the amount of increased manpower needed per unit increase in GDP, and on the ratios of the output of skilled manpower from the educational system and the influx of expatriate manpower to gross domestic product.

5. *Population Growth and Per Capita Income*

One further consideration at the aggregate planning stage is the relationship between population growth and growth in *per capita* incomes. An increase in total income may not give rise to increased *per capita* income if population is growing quickly. In general, one may approximate the growth in *per capita* incomes by the following formula:

$$\frac{dY}{Y} = \frac{dZ}{Z} + \frac{dP}{P} \qquad (18\text{--}13)$$

where Z is *per capita* income, Y is total income and P is population. That is, the rate of growth in *per capita* incomes is equal to the rate of growth of total income less the rate of growth of population. If total incomes are growing at a rate of five per cent and population is growing at three per cent, then *per capita* incomes will grow approximately at a rate of two per cent. If the planners hope to achieve a given target rate of growth in *per capita* incomes, they must be aware of and allow for population growth. The development planners must also be aware that certain of their policies may have an effect on the rate of growth of population. For example, the provision of drains and sewage disposal in urban areas is likely to lower the death rate. Anti-malarial campaigns can result in a very significant reduction in the death rate. Thus past population trends must be combined with a knowledge of possible changes in the death rate and birth rate which might occur during the forthcoming planning period.

6. *Checking for Consistency*

The planners, having specified precisely all of the relationships between the rate of growth of the economy on the one hand, and the amount of investment, private and government savings, foreign investment, the balance of payments, the rate of growth in skilled manpower, and the rate of population growth, are in a better position to check for the consistency of plans at the aggregate stage. For example, equation (18–1) can be used to check whether the target rate of growth of the economy is consistent with the planned rate of investment. In order to use this equation, however, it is necessary to compute the incremental capital-output ratio. The incremental capital-output ratio is usually calculated from past data on gross domestic product and capital formation. A fairly long time series for these data are essential to eliminate atypical values due to minor fluctuations in the series arising from statistical errors and omissions, and, more importantly, to take into account investments such as railroads, main roads, and hydro-electric projects which often take a long time before they begin to give results. If a consistent series for gross domestic product and capital formation is available for a period of eight to ten years, then the total capital formation for that period can be divided by the increment in gross domestic product between the beginning and the end of the period to get a rough estimate of the incremental capital-output ratio.

The planners must also check to see whether the proper amount of domestic private savings, government savings, and foreign investment will be available to achieve the target rate of growth in output. Here equation (18–4) becomes useful. From the right hand side of (18–4) it is clear that the following ratios must be determined: S_p/Y, S_g/Y, and F/Y. The ratio of private domestic savings to gross domestic product S_p/Y may be determined from past data on savings and gross domestic product. Care must be taken, however, in projecting past ratios of private domestic saving to gross domestic product to future years of the plan, since the marginal propensity to save out of increased income is likely to differ from the average ratio of savings to income. Various statistical techniques are available for estimating the marginal propensity to save. These methods cannot be discussed at length in this volume. Suffice it to say that if consistent time series covering a long enough period of time are available, rough estimates can be made. It is often better to separate the analysis into two parts by estimating the marginal propensity to save by households and the marginal propensity of businesses to save out of profits separately. Since these two marginal propensities are likely to be quite different, the total private domestic savings available depends on the ratio of profits to other types of incomes. Total private domestic savings is the sum of savings from households and savings by businesses. The following equations will be useful in estimating the separate components of savings:

$$S_h = S_h^o + b_h^o dY \qquad (18\text{–}14)$$
$$S_b = S_h^o + b_b dY$$

where S_h and S_b are projected household and business savings, respectively; S_h^o and S_b^o are the initial levels of household and business savings, respectively, at the beginning of the planning period; b_h and b_b are the marginal propensities to save out of household and business incomes, respectively; and dY is the increase in income projected by the plan.

The ratio of government saving to gross domestic product S_g/Y may be estimated by projecting government tax revenue and government recurrent expenditure. Recurrent expenditure is determined by government budget considerations and can be adjusted fairly easily by conscious government policy decisions. Tax revenues, however, are not entirely under government control. Government can set the rates. The actual revenue depends on how incomes are distributed, the rate of growth of various components of income, wages, profits, etc., the rate of growth of imports on which there are customs duties, the rate of growth of exports on which there are export taxes, the rate of growth of sales of exciseable commodities, and many other miscellaneous considerations. Various statistical techniques are available for estimating the marginal increase in tax revenue per unit increase in incomes given the structure of tax rates. The following formula can be used in estimating total tax revenue:

$$T = T_0 + b_t dY \qquad\qquad (18\text{--}15)$$

where T is total tax revenue, T_0 is the initial level of tax revenue at the beginning of the planning period, and b_t is the marginal increase in tax revenue per unit increase incomes.

The last term on the right hand side of (18–4) is the ratio of foreign investment to gross domestic product, F/Y. For many developing countries, this will be composed largely of foreign aid grants which are usually determined by inter-governmental negotiations. The amount of private foreign investment which can be expected is very difficult to determine and this is often the most volatile element of investment.

The equation (18–9) can be used to check the consistency of the target rate of growth in terms of its balance of payments implications. This is a most difficult formula to apply as the rates of growth of exports and foreign investment are not easy to determine. The running down of foreign exchange reserves is a conscious policy decision provided government control over reserves is sufficient, but the government is constrained by many factors in running down foreign exchange reserves too low.

Similarly, the equation (18–12) can be used to check for consistency between the target rate of growth and manpower planning policy as revealed by educational plans and planned efforts to recruit trained manpower from abroad. The target rate of growth of total incomes can be checked against the target rate of growth of *per capita* incomes and population projections by equation (18–13).

What can be done if the target rate of growth does not turn out to be consistent with planned investment, domestic savings and foreign investment, the balance of payments, growth in skilled manpower, and population growth? Either the target rate of growth must be adjusted, upwards or downwards, whatever the case may be, or government policy must be altered. For example, if the target rate of growth is not consistent with the planned rate of investment, then investment may have to be raised which implies that the necessary savings or foreign investment will have to be raised also. Government can increase its savings and investment by reducing recurrent expenditure or by raising taxes or both. Private investment, both domestic and foreign, can be encouraged in numerous ways. Income taxes can be designed to promote growth by provision of increased depreciation allowances or by reducing tax rates for fast growing firms or industries. Capital gains can be taxed lightly. Tariff protection and tax holidays can be afforded or subsidies paid to new industry. Easy repatriation of profits for foreign investors may be offered. Savings can also be promoted by government pressure to hold wages down, by imposing high taxes on consumption goods, by government propaganda campaigns to save more through investing in development bonds, through government sponsored lotteries, and in various other ways.

If the target rate of growth is inconsistent with the constraint imposed by the balance of payments, three general policy lines are available. First, there is the possibility for increased appeals for foreign aid. These appeals may not be successful. The only alternatives are either a policy of export promotion or import substitution. Promotion of exports as a policy is very often limited by poor demand prospects, especially for primary product exports. Import substitution can be promoted chiefly by high tariff protection. This affects consumers by making it more expensive to buy imported goods, encouraging them to switch to local products. Producers are affected because it becomes more profitable to manufacture the protected products, encouraging them to invest in increased production of those products. If a policy of import substitution is successful, the result will be to lower the marginal propensity to import, b_m on the left hand side of equation (18–9), making an increased rate of growth possible as far as the balance of payments is concerned.

If the target rates of growth in *per capita* and total incomes are inconsistent with the rate of population growth, then attempts may be made to alter the rate of population growth. It is nearly always easier, however, to *increase* the rate of population growth through a reduction in the death rate than to *decrease* population growth by lowering the birth rate. Death rates can be reduced through conscious government policy concerning medicine, health, and sanitation, while birth rates are so dependent on traditional social and cultural factors, that government propaganda campaigns to reduce the birth rate are rarely successful, at least in the short run. In addition, traditional religious attitudes may make it politically difficult for government to pursue a conscious policy of population control. Thus, in the short run, the only feasible alternative is to alter the target rate of growth of income or *per capita* income if these are incompatible with the rate of population growth.

7. *Choosing the "Right" Target Rate of Growth*

The decision of a target rate of growth and a rate of capital formation with its implications for foreign aid, taxes, and domestic savings is usually considered to be a high priority decision, made at the cabinet level with the consultation of planning experts. The experts can be particularly helpful in pointing out to the policy makers the relationship between target rates of growth and rates of capital formation and the wage policy, government current expenditure policy, tax policy, etc., implied by these rates of capital formation.

The planning experts may also point out that a decision to attempt to achieve a given target rate of growth may conflict with other social goals when the policy implications of that rate of growth are considered. For example, the promotion of a sufficient amount of investment might require a substantially regressive tax policy. This may conflict with a social goal of equity in income distribution. A sufficient rate of growth in highly trained manpower may be achieved by reducing the expenditure on primary education. Thus the goal of universal primary education may have to suffer. A sufficient level of investment may be achieved by a heavy reliance on foreign investment. This might conflict with a social goal of economic self-sufficiency.

Most important, a high target rate of growth implies a high rate of capital formation. A high rate of capital formation means, initially at least, that consumption will not grow as fast as it would with a low rate of capital formation. There is a limit imposed by political considerations on the amount of goods which the consumer is willing to give up. It must be kept in mind, however, that although initially the rate of growth of consumption might be lower with a high rate of capital formation, the mechanics of growth indicate that in a relatively short period of time, the level of consumption may soon surpass the level which could be expected from a lower rate of capital formation. The economic policy makers, in choosing the target rate of growth, must account for all of the diverse social goals which a society may have and the underlying political difficulties which might be encountered in pursuing their policies.

B. The Sectoral Stage

The second stage of the planning process is the translation of an overall growth objective into a set of target rates of growth for the individual sectors of the economy or to allocate the overall investment target to the individual sectors. This analysis need not involve any attempt to study the likely project composition of the plan. Differences in the expected rates of growth of the sectors might be derived from assumptions regarding the desired structural change or from the high levels of aggregate investment resulting from the overall growth goal. At this stage of analysis it is probably necessary that the balance between major sectors be set more with reference to an *a priori* view of the strategy of development than by an empirical analysis of costs and returns.

An input-output table which specifies the relationships between sectors might be especially useful in making sectoral projections. Projections cannot be made using the input-output table alone. Assumptions about future growth of consumer demand and judgments about the composition and level of investment, among others, will be necessary. If an input-output table is not available, projections may be based on a set of simpler assumptions concerning intersectoral relationships, but the basic method of projection is often similar even if a full scale input-output table is not used.

Rules of thumb may also be useful in making rough sectoral allocations. For example, if the planners believe that capital is the only relevant scarce factor, not much may be allocated to the residential housing sector because this sector usually has a very high capital-output ratio. If foreign exchange is also scarce, however, the housing sector may become an attractive sector in which to invest large sums, since residential housing, if properly designed, can have very little import content. Rules of thumb, however, ought to be used most carefully at this stage, since the capital-output, foreign exchange-output, and skilled labor-output ratios of various sectors may be highly dependent on the project composition of the investment program in each sector. The project composition will not be revealed except in the third or project stage of planning.

The sectoral allocation at the second stage of planning may have important repercussions regarding the assumptions which were made at the first stage of planning. If investment is not allocated wisely among sectors, the target rate of growth of the economy may not be achieved. This may require a reallocation of investment to sectors or a reappraisal of the originally envisaged target rate of growth.

C. The Project Stage

The third stage of the planning process is the allocation of investment among the different projects in each sector. This stage in the planning process differs from the earlier stages, in two important aspects. First, the problem of co-ordination of different parts of the plan becomes more crucial. For example, the bill for total transport investment is likely to be consistent with a range of different manufacturing programs; however, when a particular manufacturing plant is created, then some part of the overall transport bill must be allocated to quite specific transport facilities complementary to the particular industrial project. Secondly, at this stage in the planning process, a much wider range of administrators must be included than at the earlier stages, which were mainly the concern of the highest political authority and the central planning staff. This stage, therefore, involves the most administrative difficulties as it probably includes many advisers who are not familiar with the rationale of planning but are included because of their special expertise within their own field. The third stage is crucial because it translates the overall objectives into the actual projects which give reality to the grand design.

The task of the central planner at this stage is one of co-ordination and communication. There are two tactics which the central planning staff may adopt. First, they may explain as fully as possible to the sectoral planning groups the overall strategy of the plan and place the planning of their own sector in perspective. Secondly, detailed guidelines for project evaluation and choice of projects should be provided to the sectoral planning groups.

1. *Communication with the Sectoral Planning Groups*

There is a range of possibilities for enhancing the amount of communication both between the central planners and the sectoral planning groups and between the sectoral planning groups themselves. Each sector group may contain a member of the central planning staff who is responsible for maintaining a two-way communication. Secondly, the central planning staff can issue documentary material both in the form of specific terms of reference and in the form of general information regarding progress and design of the plan. Sectoral planning groups whose investment projects are particularly interdependent may want to have joint meetings from time to time to ensure that their plans are not widely divergent and to minimize the amount of effort needed later in reconciling any divergencies which may arise. Finally, all those participating in the planning process could be called together from time to time to a general meeting for an exchange of ideas and to receive, from the highest level, some sense of common purpose and feeling of what the plan is to achieve as a whole. For this purpose as much of the picture of what is going to happen to the economy, implicit in the second stage of the plan, should be transmitted to all individuals participating in the planning process as is consistent with the desires of the planning authority to avoid premature public commitment to specific targets. This involves an interpretation in non-technical terms of the planning documents produced at the second stage of the plan.

2. *Guidelines for Sectoral Groups*

At the third stage of the planning process problems of consistency become most acute and at this stage more specific attempts can be made to achieve efficiency. In addition to communicating the overall strategy decisions concerning the plans to those on the sectoral working parties at the very outset, the planners or planning committees should also be given some detailed guidelines or criteria for choosing among the various investment projects. If no criteria are given, then there is the danger that sectoral planners will trot out their pet projects and schemes. The various sector plans are likely to be uneven in quality and based on a variety of, and perhaps conflicting, criteria. An initial set of plans for each sector, once submitted, tends to acquire the ardent support of those who formulated it. Vested interests are created which tend to make it administratively difficult to change the initial set of plans. Hence much importance should be attached to ensuring that the original plans are formulated along reasonable lines.

The guidelines given to the sectoral planners should specify that both monetary and non-monetary returns to various projects should be considered. Government policy toward different types of non-monetary returns should be specified. An appeal to non-monetary returns should not be used to justify any project but the different types of non-monetary returns should be stated fairly specifically.

Secondly, the guidelines should emphasize that certain resources are relatively scarce and need to be economized. The resources which are to be economized probably include foreign exchange, skilled labor, and capital. In general it is probably safe to say that local costs—both recurrent and capital—are relatively less scarce in a real sense than foreign costs. A no less real problem may arise, however, if both the public and private sectors find it difficult to finance local costs. In the case of countries which lack a central bank, financing of local costs can be a serious problem. It is imperative in such cases that some aspects of the plan deal with the problem of obtaining the necessary local finance.

In providing the guidelines for the sectoral planning groups, it is extremely important that the central planners specify two things. First, a *standardized* format for evaluating projects should be provided. Second, some rules should be provided for choosing among projects.

3. *Standardized Format for Project Evaluation*

In making their project evaluations, the sectoral groups ought to standardize their method of calculating costs and returns. As much as possible, costs should be divided into several distinct categories. First of all the distinction between capital costs and recurrent costs must be made clear. This may involve many problems of measurement. For example, the distinction between maintenance, a recurrent cost, and various capital costs is not always clear. Is the repair of washed out road culverts to be regarded as maintenance or as a capital investment? Business accountants have worked out various criteria for classifying costs as capital and recurrent, and while the planner may have some quarrels with these criteria, the accountants' classification is often useful. Government accountants, on the other hand, have a much more difficult time in separating government recurrent expenditure from capital or development costs. Much government expenditure is not designed to produce immediate productive results but goes to provide general services which only indirectly enable greater productivity activity. Because of this, very often government budget figures have to be reclassified in order to be useful to the planner and the economic policy maker. Secondly, local costs (involving purchases of local goods), both capital and recurrent, should be kept distinct from foreign costs (involving purchases of imported goods). The distinction between local and foreign costs is not usually made by government and business accountants. The economist or planner must use supplementary sources to determine this breakdown. The annual trade reports, if available, may be particularly useful for this purpose. Sometimes industrial censuses are designed to provide this sort of information. Thirdly, the distinction should be made between costs of intermediate products, labor costs, and other types of costs. Finally, it is often useful to list wages and salaries paid to high-level managerial and technical manpower separately.

The calculation of returns involves fewer distinctions than those involved in the determination of costs, but special problems are introduced by the estimation of non-monetary returns. In addition costs, which often depend on rather well-defined technical considerations, can often be estimated more accurately than returns both monetary and non-monetary. Returns are dependent on the demand for the product or service being provided by an investment project. This demand may be well defined, such as the electricity demand of a nitrogenous fertilizer plant. On the other hand, it may depend on fluctuating business fortunes, personal incomes, and tastes, and on a multitude of private investment decisions, such as the traffic demand for use of a new rail line. Statistical demand analysis may aid in estimating demand, but the margin of error, especially in developing countries with limited data, may be quite large. Non-monetary returns are quite difficult to evaluate and may have to be listed separately by the sectoral planners and described in a qualitative way.

Since different projects have varying lives, both costs and returns of all projects must be reduced to a common basis for comparison. Two alternative methods of reduction to a common basis are available: (1) the present value method, and (2) the typical or "normal" year method. The present value method is often the more desirable from a theoretical point of view in that it takes into account variations in the time path of returns from a capital investment. The typical year method, however, is often easier to apply.

4. *The Present Value Method*

In the present value method, both costs and returns over the whole life of the investment are reduced to a single figure, the present day value. The way in which future returns and costs are reduced to present day values is based on the assumption that capital is productive. That is, if extra resources are devoted to turning out capital goods, the total product in the future will be greater, i.e., there will be a positive rate of return on capital. Therefore, the prospect of receiving returns in the future is less attractive than immediate returns, and the prospect of paying costs in the future less onerous than costs paid immediately. An immediate return, invested in capital resources, can result in a greater future product, and a cost to be paid in the future can be covered by investing a smaller sum today. The rate at which future costs and future returns are discounted to the present is called the rate of discount or the rate of interest. The rate of interest used for this purpose is not necessarily the rate of interest obtainable at the local commercial banks, in the London money market, or from local money lenders, but is a shadow price which indicates the marginal rate of return on capital, i.e., the opportunity cost of capital.

A cost incurred in a future year or a return to be received in the future is discounted by the following formula:

$$X = \frac{Z_n}{(1+r)^n} \tag{18-16}$$

where X is the present value of a return or cost Z_n, n years in the future, and r is the rate of discount. The principle behind this formula is that if an amount X is invested at a compound rate of return r, it will be worth Z_n, n years hence. For example, an amount X invested at a rate of return r is worth

$$Z_1 = X + rX = (1+r)X \tag{18-17}$$

after one year. The present value of X is given by

$$X = \frac{Z_1}{(1+r)^1} \tag{18-18}$$

After two years, an amount X will be worth

$$Z_2 = Z_1 + rZ_1 \tag{18-19}$$

Substituting (18–17) into (18–19), we obtain

$$Z_2 = (1+r)X + r(1+r)X \tag{18-20}$$

We may factor out the common divisor $(1+r)X$ of both terms on the right hand side of (18–20)

$$Z_2 = (1+r)X(1+r) \qquad (18\text{–}21)$$
$$= (1+r)^2 X$$

The present value of X is given by

$$X = \frac{Z_2}{(1+r)^2} \qquad (18\text{–}22)$$

From examination of (18–18) and (18–22), it is easy to see that the formula given by (18–16) is a generalization of the present value formula for any value of n.

Given an investment which has an initial capital cost C_0 and involves recurrent costs $C_1, C_2, \ldots\ldots, C_n$ in the n years of the life of the investment, the present day cost of the investment is

$$C = C_0 + \frac{C_1}{(1+r)^1} + \frac{C_2}{(1+r)^2} + \ldots\ldots + \frac{C_n}{(1+r)^n} \qquad (18\text{–}23)$$

Similarly, if returns are $R_1, R_2, \ldots R_n$ for each of the n years of the life of an investment, the present day value of such returns is given by the formula:

$$R = \frac{R_1}{(1+r)^1} + \frac{R_2}{(1+r)^2} + \ldots\ldots + \frac{R_n}{(1+r)^n} \qquad (18\text{–}24)$$

In using these formulae for present day values, one should be aware that there has been a certain amount of controversy over the use of a positive rate of discount to determine present day values. Objections to the use of the rate of discount often involve the contention that while individuals may discount future earnings, society need not place this same discounted value on future returns. Society as a whole has responsibility for the unborn children of a future generation while individuals need not necessarily take future generations into consideration. Another objection to the use of a rate of discount is that individuals tend to be over-obsessed with immediate gain and cannot view the prospect of future gain with any degree of rationality. These arguments, however, if accepted, do not obviate the need for rates of discount in planning. They may be used to argue against adopting the rate of interest prevailing in the market place, whatever that might be. They may also be used to argue that the rate of investment in a private economy is less than the socially desirable rate of investment. On the contrary, one can argue the necessity of a rate of discount in planning even assuming that a given amount of product *per capita* ten years hence is no less preferred from society's point of view than the same amount of product *per capita* today. The rate of interest is used in planning as an accounting device to separate out more productive investments from others. As long as capital is productive at all, and as long as the amount of capital is limited, the rate of discount is positive.

5. *The Typical Year Method*

The second method of reducing costs and returns to a common basis for all projects involves choosing for every project some future year which can be expected to be typical or "normal" with regard to the output or returns from that project and with regard to the recurrent costs. The returns in that year are matched against all costs, including the capital costs. The returns from a project and the recurrent costs can easily be stated in annual terms. Capital costs, on the other hand, all occur at the beginning of the project and therefore must be reduced to an annual basis. The annual capital cost of a project is composed of two elements, amortization (depreciation) and interest. Two of the most common ways of treating these two elements are:

(i) Amortization is composed of equal instalments over the life time of the investment. Annual interest calculated as the annual interest on the unamortized balance of the investment. In this case amortization plus interest is a declining sum throughout the life of the investment since interest on the unamortized balance becomes smaller and smaller as the unamortized balance becomes smaller.

(ii) Amortization and interest on the unamortized balance are calculated so that their sum each year is equal during the life of the investment. In this method of calculating annual capital costs, the capital cost in earlier years is composed mostly of interest. In the later years of the life of the investment, amortization comprises a larger part.

Neither of these two methods is ideal from the economist's point of view. A better case can be made for calculating amortization as the reduction in the present value of future returns less the reduction in present value of future costs. A calculation of depreciation in this manner, however, is much more difficult and therefore either of the above two methods is often regarded as an adequate approximation.

The annual capital cost using either of the above two methods can be determined readily by consulting appropriate interest and amortization tables. The average annual capital charge over the life of the investment can be approximated, however, by the following procedure: Divide the cost of the investment by n, the life of the investment, and add to this one half of the interest charges on the full amount of the investment. For example, suppose that an investment of $1000 has a life of five years and that the rate of interest is 10 per cent. Then the average amortization charge is

$$\frac{\$1000}{5} = \$200.$$

The approximate average interest charge is

$$\frac{.10}{2}(\$1000) = \$50.$$

The approximate average total capital charge then is

$$\$200 + \$50 = \$250.$$

The typical year method is more applicable when an investment involves capital assets which are likely to run at full capacity soon after the investment is completed. For then the output resulting from that investment is likely to be constant year after year. Some investments, such as railroads, roads, power projects, irrigation schemes, and other social overhead types of investment are likely to exhibit growing returns over a very long period of time until the limit of capacity is reached. In such cases, the present value method makes more sense, since it is the rate of growth of returns which is important and not the returns from a hypothetical typical year.

The above discussion of calculation of present values and annual capital costs is much simplified and idealized. First of all, there may be many difficulties in actually calculating costs and returns, especially for the present value method where the future time path of returns and costs is important. The planner would also want to inject considerations of non-monetary returns into the analysis. Ideally, one would like to place a monetary value on such benefits, but it is not always possible to do so in any meaningful way. In some cases, moral objections are raised against putting a monetary value on non-monetary benefits. For example, how does one evaluate the reduction in number of lives lost and in number of injuries by investing in road safety devices? Difficulties also occur with complicated investments which involve several years of building and construction, building in stages, or phasing over time with other investment projects. For such complex projects, more complicated formulae are involved in calculating present day values although the principles remain the same. Finally, when the time path of returns follows an unusual or erratic patterns, the interpretation of present day values is not necessarily straightforward. Despite these difficulties, the techniques described above are powerful tools which the practical planner has at his disposal.

6. *The Choice Among Projects*

After costs and returns of various projects have been calculated, then the sectoral planning groups are in a reasonable position to pick and choose among projects in order to arrive at an investment program for their sector. What criteria should be used in drawing up this investment program? One of three commonly suggested techniques, among others, may be used:

(i) Each sector planning group may be given a target in terms of value added by that sector to be achieved by the end of the planning period. The sectoral planning group is told that it should minimize the cost (either on an annual basis or in terms of present day values) of achieving that target rate of value added.

(ii) Each sectoral planning group is allocated a specified amount of capital. The planning group is told to maximize total net returns (returns less costs, either on an annual basis or on a present day value basis) on their allotted amount of capital.

(iii) Each sector may be allocated both a given amount of capital and a given amount of foreign exchange. The sectoral planning group is told to maximize total net returns staying within both their allotted capital and their allotted foreign exchange.

The first of these methods has the advantage of forcing the sectoral groups to formulate a project program which will ensure at minimum cost that the target rates of output for each sector which were formulated at the first stage of planning will be achieved. The major drawback is that there is no assurance that the capital allocation to each sector will be enough to achieve that target rate of output. In addition, for some sectors it is extremely difficult to formulate meaningful output or value added targets. This applies especially in the case of many government activities and in the provision of social overhead services. Where output targets are difficult to formulate, the second or third technique outlined above becomes more appropriate. For example, in the transport sector it is extremely difficult to assess the results of any project in terms of vehicle-miles or ton-miles, especially for road or rail projects in which the main benefit is the lowering of costs of transport which stimulates productive activity in other sectors of the economy. It is often better to allocate the transport sector a given amount of capital or given amounts of capital and foreign exchange and ask the transport planners to maximize net returns.

If the second method is used, an important quantity to calculate for each project is the net benefit-capital cost ratio. This is the ratio of net return to capital cost for each project. The sectoral planning group can then maximize net returns on its allocated capital by choosing projects which have high net benefit-capital cost ratios. When a project is subject to decreasing returns as the project is operated on a larger scale, the important consideration is the *marginal* net benefit-capital cost ratio.

Several very important points should be made in spelling out the guidelines to the sectoral planning groups. First, the distinctions, discussed above, between capital and recurrent, foreign and local, labor, intermediate product, and other costs should be made by the planning groups in their project evaluations. Secondly, shadow prices rather than actual market prices should be used in calculating both costs and returns. In practice, this will probably involve making initial calculations in terms of market prices and then adjusting later for differences between market prices and shadow prices. The distinctions between different types of costs are useful for this purpose since the shadow price relating to capital costs is likely to be different from the shadow price relating to recurrent costs. The shadow price of foreign exchange is likely to be higher than the current exchange rate which would necessitate an adjustment of foreign costs upwards. Thirdly, in comparing projects within any sector, a common basis of project evaluation should be used. That is, either the present value method or the typical year method should be used, but not both, for evaluating projects within the same sector. Ideally, the same method of project evaluation should be used by all sectors to enable the central planners to make a comparison of projects among sectors. The practical difficulties of doing so may be so great, however, that different methods will have to be used in different sectors.

7. *Re-evaluation of Projects*

Once an initial set of project plans have been drawn up, the planning process is not complete. Checks for overall consistency should be carried out by the central planning bureau. First of all, the central planners will want to check to see that inconsistencies among projects have not crept into the plans. For example, the plans for setting up industries in an urban area may not be consistent with the railways plans for industrial sidings, plans of the public utilities companies to provide power and water to that area, and so on. The sectoral planning groups may be advised of these inconsistencies and asked to alter their plans accordingly. Secondly, overall sectoral targets may be inconsistent. Service sectors such as distribution, transport, and utilities may have target rates of growth which will not satisfy the demands of other growing sectors. Although this type of consistency is checked at the second (sectoral) stage, the initial project analysis may reveal that certain assumptions regarding intersectoral relationships used in earlier analysis were mistaken as a result of the specific project composition of the plan. If this type of inconsistency arises, sectoral targets will have to be adjusted accordingly. Finally, the project plans can be combined for each sector to see whether they imply a greater amount of capital formation and a greater amount of foreign exchange and skilled manpower than originally envisioned at the first stage of analysis. Two approaches to correct this imbalance are possible. Target rates of growth for various sectors can be lowered to bring about balance, or the shadow prices of those resources which are relatively scarce can be readjusted upward and those which are relatively abundant can have their shadow prices adjusted downward. In either case, the sectoral planning committees will be required to re-evaluate their project plans in the light of new directives from the central planning authority. With higher shadow prices on the scarce resources, the sectoral planners will be encouraged to economize on the use of the scarce resources. That is, the new set of project plans will probably include more projects which use less of the scarce resources and more of the abundant resources.

Ideally, the process of project planning followed by re-evaluation and the issuing of new guidelines to sectoral planning groups should continue, until a mutually consistent and optimal set of project plans has emerged. In practice, this sort of re-evaluation at best will take place only one or two times. A better set of plans will be formulated, however, if at least one re-evaluation takes place.

D. Some Practical Points

In the discussion of accounting for planning decisions the emphasis has been on the formal framework. Even this framework has been no more than introduced. To some readers it may seem that the elaborateness of the planning system implied is in advance of likely practice. However, the techniques of mathematical programing may bear fruit if applied in some sectors even if general application is not feasible. This may be true, for example, of the transport sector, in which the costs and benefits may be much more susceptible to this kind of analysis than in the social service field. Even in areas where formal maximization models are not applicable great savings can be made if the economic planner is willing to be constantly aware of a few very basic principles. Such principles may be viewed as common-sense translations of economic theory.

In analyzing the monetary costs of projects the planner should keep three things in mind. The first is to examine a range of alternatives. Is this the only way of fulfilling a need? Might it be done by a different sort of project, or might the project in question be done with different standards and methods? The professional expert designing the project might be asserting perfectionist professional standards when a adequate job could be done at much lower cost through a lowering of standards. The designer of the individual project may not always realize that high costs on his project may mean the postponement of some other very desirable project. Also, it will be difficult for the individual specialist to believe that too much could be spent on his project, that the accommodation of a college could be too luxurious, or a hospital too elaborate. The project organizers must therefore be forced into offering a range of alternatives. It is the planner who sees the whole picture and is budgeting against an overall constraint; he may see that to provide more comfort in a student hostel may well mean one less rural dispensary or 10 less students.

When the policy decisions are finally made regarding the choice of projects, the desirability of the choice will not only depend on the wisdom of the selection from among projects suggested but, perhaps more important, will also depend on the preliminary organization of a suitably wide range of alternatives. Particularly in considering very large projects, the impact of which will be decidedly non-marginal, the possibility can arise that the ultimate end may be achieved by an alternative project which at first appears to be not at all similar in purpose. For example, major transport expansion might be avoided by changing the location of production facilities.

This first common-sense principle of project accounting could be called *accounting for alternatives*.

The second general principle which may be applied is that the project must be costed not only in terms of its immediate capital costs but also in terms of its recurrent costs. There must be an attempt to estimate the burden that a project will place on future budgets through its operations. It may well be that this will be a more decisive factor than the level of initial capital costs. It is important to note, however, that high recurrent costs are not necessarily undesirable. If one of the objectives of the plan is to create employment, then a project with high recurrent costs may also provide considerable opportunities for expanding future government employment in desirable directions.

This second precept could therefore be called *concern for future costs*. The planner must be concerned with future budgets as well as the current one.

The third general principle that should be a guide for the planner is that *monetary costs are not always the relevant costs*. As has already been suggested at length, there may be other constraints on the plan which are more serious than the monetary. Even where the precise programing techniques discussed above are not available this problem must be at the forefront of the planners mind. Typically, financial experts and political leaders will think exclusively, in monetary terms and it will be the planners' responsibility to guide their attention to the nature of the real constraints. This precept, identifying real constraints is the first step toward the more formal planning procedures discussed above.

Another practical point is that quite extraordinary savings can be made by the routine checking of the cost of facilities proposed against the costs operating in similar environments. If, for example, it is evident that hospital costs were much higher in Tanzania than Uganda, then there would be a *prima facie* case for further examination of budgets (by both countries—for the country with the lower estimates might be unrealistic and be formulating plans which in practice will not be realizable or may be sacrificing standards to an undesirable degree).

The very basic notions of introductory economics are also of considerable use in clarifying the nature of policy decisions. In particular the relationship between average, marginal, and total concepts are frequently confused in the thinking of policy makers. For example, a conflict of interest and opinion over the question of standards often involves a confusion between the average and total. Sometimes it is argued by educationalists that the correct procedure is to maintain the "highest possible standards of education," this being taken to mean that the highest possible average standard be achieved. It is evident that the educational system would achieve the highest average standard if it only educated the most intelligent student in the society! Similarly it is incorrect for a business to aim for the maximum profit per unit of output. Total profit will be maximized when the profit from a unit of additional output falls to zero. The difficulty arises, however, that it is often easier to estimate average quantities than marginal—the average cost and the average revenue are likely to be easier for the businessmen to identify than the similar marginal quantities. Estimates of marginal quantities can often be deduced, however, from knowledge of the average relationships. If it is believed that an average is in a range within which it is rising then it may be presumed that the marginal quantity is above the average; if the average is falling, then the marginal is below the average. For example, if it is known that the average cost of educating a student in a college falls as the number of students increases then it may be deduced that the marginal cost is below the average cost.

This final principle may be viewed as that of *identifying the correct total to be maximized*. The planner must clarify the social objectives which it is intended the project should fulfill and relate the maximization criteria within the individual project to those overall objectives.

FURTHER READING FOR PART FOUR

1. I. Adelman and E. Thorbecke, editors, *The Theory and Design of Development*, Johns Hopkins Press, Baltimore, 1966.
2. W. J. Baumol, *Economic Theory and Operations Analysis*, 2nd edition, Englewood Cliffs, Prentice-Hall, 1965.
3. S. Bowles, "The Efficient Allocation of Resources in Education," *The Quarterly Journal of Economics*, May, 1967.
4. S. Chakravarty, *The Logic of Investment Planning*, Amsterdam, North-Holland, 1959.
5. H. B. Chenery, "The Application of Investment Criteria," *Quarterly Journal of Economics*, Vol. LXVII, No. 1 (February, 1953), p. 76.
6. H. B. Chenery, "Development Policies and Programmes," *Economic Bulletin for Latin America*, Vol. 3, No. 1 (March, 1958), p. 51.
7. H. B. Chenery and M. Bruno, "Development Alternatives in an Open Economy: The Case of Israel," *Economic Journal*, Vol. LXXII, No. 285 (March, 1962), p. 79.
8. H. B. Chenery and P. G. Clark, *Inter-industry Economics*, New York, McGraw-Hill, 1959.
9. H. B. Chenery and K. Kretschmer, "Resource Allocation for Economic Development," *Econometrica*, Vol. 24, No. 4 (October, 1956), p. 365.
10. H. B. Chenery and A. Strout, 'Foreign Assistance and Economic Development," *American Economic Review*, Vol. LVI, No. 4 (September, 1966), pp. 679–733.
11. E. Domar, *Essays on the Theory of Economic Growth*, New York, Oxford University Press, 1957.
12. R. Dorfman, P. Samuelson and R. Solow, *Linear Programming and Economic Analysis*, New York, McGraw-Hill, 1958.
13. O. Eckstein, "Investment Criteria for Economic Development and the Theory of Intertemporal Welfare Comparisons," *Quarterly Journal of Economics*, Vol. LXXI No. 1 (February, 1957), p. 56.
14. O. Eckstein, "A Survey of the Theory of Public Expenditure Criteria," in Universities National Bureau Committee for Economic Research, *Public Finances: Needs, Sources and Utilization*, pp. 439–504.
15. J. C. H. Fei and D. S. Paauw, "Foreign Assistance and Self-Help: A Reappraisal for Development Finance," *Review of Economics and Statistics*, August, 1965.
16. W. Galenson and H. Leibenstein, "Investment Criteria, Productivity, and Economic Development," *Quarterly Journal of Economics*, Vol. LXIX, No. 3 (August, 1955), p. 343.
17. A. E. Kahn, "Investment Criteria in Development Programmes," *Quarterly Journal of Economics*, Vol. LXV, No. 1 (February, 1951), p. 38.
18. N. Kaldor, "A Model of Economic Growth," *Economic Journal*, Vol. LXVII, No. 268 (December, 1957), p. 591.

19. W. A. Lewis, *Development Planning*, New York, Harper and Row, 1966, *passim*.

20. Ronald MacKinnon, "Foreign Exchange Constraints in Economic Development," *Economic Journal*, June, 1964.

21. Edward Mason, *Economic Planning in Underdeveloped Areas*, Fordham University Press, New York, 1958.

22. R. Mukherjee, "Scientific Approach in Planning," in C. R. Rao, editor, *Essays on Econometrics and Planning*, New York, Pergammon Press, 1966.

23. Organization for Economic Cooperation and Development, *Quantitative Models as an Aid to Development Assistance Policy*, Report by the Expert Group on the Uses of Analytical Techniques, Paris, 1967.

24. A. R. Prest and Ralph Turvey, "Cost-Benefit Analysis: A Survey," *Economic Journal* (December, 1965), pp. 683–718.

25. G. Ranis and J. H. Fei, "A Theory of Economic Development", *American Economic Review*, Vol. LI, No. 5 (September, 1961), p. 533.

26. A. K. Sen, "Some Notes on the Choice of Capital Intensity in Development Planning," *Quarterly Journal of Economics*, Vol. LXXI, No. 3 (November, 1957), p. 561.

27. A. K. Sen, *Choice of Techniques*, London, Oxford University Press, 1960.

28. Jan Tinbergen, *The Design of Development*, Baltimore, The Johns Hopkins Press, 1958.

29. J. Tinbergen and H. C. Bos, *Mathematical Models of Economic Growth*, New York, McGraw-Hill, 1962.

30. J. Tinbergen and H. Bos, "A Planning Model for the Educational Requirements of Economic Development," in O.E.C.D., *The Residual Factor and Economic Growth*, Paris, 1964, pp. 147–200.

31. United Nations Economic Commission for Asia and the Far East, *Programming Techniques for Economic Development*, Development Programming Technique Series, No. 1, Bangkok, 1960.

32. United Nations Economic Commission for Asia and the Far East, *Formulating Industrial Development Programmes*, Development Programming Technique Series, No. 2, Bangkok, 1961.

33. J. Vanck, *Estimating Foreign Resource Needs for Economic Development*, New York, McGraw-Hill, 1967

34. A. Waterston, *Development Planning: Lessons of Experience*, Baltimore, The Johns Hopkins Press, 1965.

NOTES ON FURTHER READING FOR PART FOUR

An excellent work of general planning principles and policies is W. Arthur Lewis (19). Three other sources in this area are the two United Nations Economic Commission for Asia and the Far East publications, (31) and (32), and Tinbergen's classic work (28). Mason (21) and Waterston (34) place less emphasis on statistics and quantitative techniques. The work by Chakravarty (4) is advanced, but recommended reading for the mathematically inclined.

Linear programing is explained in a way which appeals to the intuition of the economist in Dorfman, Samuelson, and Solow (12), and in Baumol (2). These two books also give clear expositions of the simplest techniques for solving linear programs. Chenery (6) explicitly shows the relationship between linear programing and shadow prices used in planning.

Mathematical models of economic growth which can be applied to the aggregate stage of the planning process are presented in Tinbergen and Bos (29), Domar (11), Ranis and Fei (25), Mukherjee (22), and Kaldor (18). Chenery and Strout (10), Fei and Paauw (15), MacKinnon (20), and Vanek (33) discuss the use of simple growth models in estimating foreign exchange requirements. Chenery and Bruno (7) apply a linear programing model to planning at the aggregate stage for Israel. Tinbergen and Bos (30) and Bowles (3) use programing models for planning of manpower and education while Chenery and Clark (8) and Chenery and Kretschmer (9) apply linear programing to determine sectoral allocations in the case of southern Italy. The O.E.C.D. volume (23) contains a general discussion of the use of growth models and programing models for planning purposes. Adelman and Thorbecke (1) is a collection of articles on theories of economic development and applications of programing and input-output models to development planning.

Kahn (17) and Chenery (5) attack the use of rules of thumb in evaluating investment projects and propose a social marginal profitability (SMP) criterion. Galenson and Leibenstein (16) and Sen (26) and (27) attack the SMP criterion and place the emphasis on the flow of income resulting from a project and its effect on reinvestment. Eckstein (13) synthesizes the views of the SMP and reinvestment theorists.

Prest and Turvey (24) and Eckstein (14) are classic surveys of the theory of cost-benefit analysis.

INDEX

DATE DUE